Four-Wheeler's Bible
2nd Edition

Four-Wheeler's Bible
2nd Edition

Jim Allen

Dedication

As always, to Linda.

First published in 2009 by Motorbooks, an imprint of MBI Publishing Company, 400 First Avenue North, Suite 300, Minneapolis, MN 55401 USA

Motorbooks titles are also available at discounts in bulk quantity for industrial or sales-promotional use. For details write to Special Sales Manager at MBI Publishing Company, 400 First Avenue North, Suite 300, Minneapolis, MN 55401 USA.

To find out more about our books, join us online at www.motorbooks.com.

Library of Congress Cataloging-in-Publication Data

Allen, Jim.
Four-wheelers bible / Jim Allen. -- 2nd ed.
p. cm.
Includes bibliographical references and index.
ISBN 978-0-7603-3530-7 (sb : alk. paper)
1. Four-wheel driving. 2. Four-wheel drive vehicles.
I. Title.
GV1021.A55 2009
629.28'3042--dc22

2009005065

About the author:
Jim Allen's zest for machinery started with things that floated. He became a soldier-seaman in the closing years of the Vietnam War, training to operate and repair U.S. Army watercraft. An ASE Certified Master Technician for most of the next 20 years, he followed that up by a few years as an Off-Highway Driving Instructor, working seasonally for Land Rover. He filled in the off time as a freelance automotive journalist and has been doing that full-time since. You can add part-time farmer to that resume for the past six years. He lives on a small farm in Ohio these days, continues to write for 4x4, truck, and automobile magazines, and still loves four-wheeling.

Editor: Chris Endres
Designer: Laura Rades, LK Design

Printed in Singapore

contents

PREFACE

Welcome to the second edition of *Four-Wheeler's Bible.* I hope you'll enjoy this armchair trip as a companion to the real thing. More to the point, I hope what you read and see here will enhance your enjoyment of the world of four-wheeling. You won't be rinsing any grit out of your hair after taking this paper journey, but if it inspires you to more and better real trips, I will be content.

In addition to being a four-wheeler of more than 30 years experience, I had the opportunity to teach the four-wheeling arts for one of the world's great four-wheel-drive manufacturers, Land Rover. That company has a stunning program for teaching these skills, both to vehicle owners and to their own employees. In the course of a bit more than three years, I taught thousands of people in assorted situations and venues. It was a rewarding experience personally, but it also offered an opportunity to see the areas where many people have problems. Combining that experience with the years of four-wheeling and observing people on the trail, I ended up with some ideas on how and what to teach.

Much of the motivation for this book came from seeing some of my favorite four-wheeling spots closed. With the ranks of the four-wheeling public swollen to highest-ever numbers, our impact must be measured and minimized. Some people say the only way to do this is by locking us out. Many others say that by adopting land-friendly techniques and responsible behavior, four-wheelers can accomplish the same thing. While there is a destructive element in our midst determined to ignore common sense, the majority of us are willing to work to keep what we have. Newcomers can benefit from learning the right way to do things, and the rest of us can always use a refresher course. My hope is that this book serves both purposes.

The 2009 edition encompasses more learning and some updates in perspective and technology to bring it up to current standards.

Jim Allen

Northwest Ohio, Fall 2008

Acknowledgments

A great many people helped in the writing of this book. Some didn't even know they were doing it! Over a 30-plus-year period, that's a lot of people. To every four-wheeler that aced an obstacle with exceptional skill and made me nod my head in respect, I say thanks. To every person who walked up with an idea on how to tackle the problem that was overwhelming my Right Guard and my patience, a humble thank you. To the people who stripped their rig of parts to get mine going again, I say thanks. To every student driver who came up with a brilliant line over an obstacle I thought was figured out, thank you for the lesson in humility. To the gearheads who teach by fine example, many thanks. Thanks to all the 'wheelers who drove in front of my hungry camera, only to be gobbled up by the celluloid, later a CompactFlash card, for all time—especially those of you who were having a bad day at that moment.

There are also a number of people who were directly involved in this book. I'll start with some of my four-wheeling role models. Thanks to Tom Collins, one of the best 'wheelers on the planet and a great team leader. And the same to the rest of the gang from those storied days at Land Rover—Bob Burns, Don Floyd, Tim Hensley, Mike Hopwood, Lea Magee, Mark McDonald, Fred Monsees, J. P. Slavin, Jim Swett, and Jim West. They were good times!

Thanks Bill Burke, instructor extraordinaire, for the help under very tough circumstances. Thanks Don Haines and Chris Overacker for helping to set up and endure the seemingly endless photo sessions. Ken Brubaker came through with some photos at the right time; thanks Ken! Ditto to the legendary Jimmy Nylund, who came through with perfect timing. Randy Lyman, the "Diffgod" himself, enhanced my understanding of axles at a critical time. Steve Watson was always a willing ear and an agile brain to bounce deep technical concepts against and see where they landed. Thanks to John Radloff for educating me on the ham radio world. I may yet take that test! Jun Yoshioka, thanks for setting me straight on the math. Tom Telford, thanks for the first insights into engineering practice. Tom Wood, thanks for making sure I was properly versed in the world of driveshafts. Thanks to Mark Filonowitch, who endured photo sessions for the second edition. Thanks to the staff at the Iron Range OHV Park for a wonderful place to shoot photos. Thanks to Toni Keller at "The Wilds" for permission to shoot in that wonderful southeastern Ohio wild animal preserve. To everyone else whose names have been left off to save precious paper, or have slipped from my feeble memory's grasp, a final word of thanks.

Introduction

Four-wheeling has become a wildly popular pastime. Despite astronomical fuel prices and economic turmoil, it remains so. Four-wheeling combines an enjoyment of the outdoors with what has become an American obsession, the motor vehicle. To some, the four-wheel-drive vehicle is the means to an end. It delivers them to the spots they want to enjoy on foot, bike, snowmobile, ATV, skis, or horseback. To others, it's the end itself. The challenge of mastering terrain and vehicle is the motivation. Either way, the better a driver masters the skills needed to surmount the obstacles, the safer and more enjoyable the trip.

Four-wheeling encompasses elements beyond driving skill. Vehicle preparation and modifications play a big part as well. The choices in these areas can be mind-boggling. My technical experience and deep involvement in four-wheeling may offer you some useful insight and perspective. I have included enough technical details and straightforward advice from manufacturers and experts to get you started, at least. Because of the wide-angle scope of this book, I've had to assume a little technical knowledge on your part. You may be above or below the arbitrary mark I set, but other books and a number of great magazines can help fill you in on the technical part of 4×4 buildups in much greater detail. I would also refer you to three of my other books—*Jeep 4×4 Performance Handbook, 2nd Edition*, *Differentials*, and *Chevy and GMC Truck Performance Handbook*—for more information on this topic. In some ways, they are very universal, so they may be worth a look even if you don't drive a rig wearing one of those nameplates.

Four-wheel-drive vehicles can also go beyond the grit-in-their-teeth crowd. This technology is used to enhance traction and safety on the highway, particularly in areas of severe winter weather. Comparing the all-wheel-drive cars and SUVs designed for street use to off-highway-capable four-wheel-drive rigs is like comparing apples and oranges. Each type has its place and use, and each has advantages and disadvantages. The problem is that you can't substitute oranges in an apple pie, and you can't put apples in an Orange Crush soft drink. This book will keep the apples in the pie and the oranges in the Crush, but bear in mind that it's slanted toward off-highway driving and the vehicles capable of that. We won't be dealing much with all-wheel-drive cars or crossover SUVs and their use on the highway.

This book is a clearinghouse of information and techniques that will be most useful to novice and middle-level four-wheelers. By the time you get into the advanced category, you will have figured things out on your own, or through the school of hard knocks. Knowing that even the most grizzled gear grinder is always looking for a new edge, however, I imagine they might find something of use here, too.

Finally, I hope that you can integrate all the do's and don'ts into a mental program that runs in the background and doesn't take away from your deep enjoyment of experiencing the outdoors in your 4×4. Happy trails!

CHAPTER 1
Attitude and Emergencies: Zen and the Art of Four-Wheeling

Where does it go? Seeing what's over the next ridge or around the next bend is part of what draws us into the outback. A 4×4 can be either the means to an end or the end itself. Some of us use our rigs to carry us to the truly remote areas where we can enjoy the outdoors outside the vehicle. For others, the vehicle is a vital part of the enjoyment. Either way, knowing the ins and outs will carry you up this trail in safety and enable you to enjoy the experience fully.

To be a successful four-wheeler, you'll need to acquire the necessary tools and equipment. At the top of that list are good judgment and common sense. Everything else stems from these attributes, including the fun part of the hobby. We'll call the combination of these things "attitude." Most of us would agree that it's more fun to be a successful, thinking driver than it is to be a disaster on wheels. It's also cheaper!

Imagine yourself as the captain of that little four-wheel-drive land-ship. Just like any commander, your choices dictate the fate of the ship and the people aboard. Ask yourself if you'd rather be the skipper of the Titanic, haunted forever by one major error in judgment, or a captain who finishes an exciting career without the notoriety of a major disaster.

Inevitably, all of us have moments when our best judgment fails us. Overall, these times are mercifully few, and we hope they occur when we are strapped into a recliner, not the driver's seat. Other than sheer fate and human error, there are two influences beyond abject carelessness that can cause lapses of judgment out there on the trail. One is universal, and the other limited to the male of the species.

Adrenaline Poisoning

The excitement and healthy fear of a new or tricky situation may induce a shot of adrenaline. Without the physical exertions of fight or flight, a shot of adrenaline in a relatively inactive human body is like racing a car engine at 5,000 rpm in the garage! Beyond lapses of judgment, other notable symptoms can occur, including deterioration of motor skills, freezing up, tunnel vision, and an odd perception that the world has slowed down. This last symptom is very common and results in drivers that tend to drive too fast. Adrenaline poisoning temporarily takes the fine edge off our capabilities when we can least afford to lose that edge. Time, oxygen, and exercise tend to cancel out the bad effects of adrenaline. Often a few deep breaths and a moment of pause are enough to regain equilibrium. A short rest or some walking may also help to slow you down.

PAVEMENT ENDS

ADRENALINE POISONING:
Nature intended adrenaline (a.k.a. epinephrine) to be our bodies' supercharger in times of danger. It gives us the strength to fight harder or to run faster. Unfortunately, it also seems to shut down a good deal of our higher brain functions.

Testosterone Poisoning

This is a little tongue-in-cheek, but it's my way of describing the sometimes inexplicable actions in groups of men facing a challenge. In the effort to outdo the other guy, we are vulnerable to taking unnecessary chances with

Is it adrenaline or testosterone inducing this gent to risk damage and rollover at the dreaded Double Whammy near Moab, Utah? Perhaps it's a cocktail with elements of both! The double ledge is a risky challenge for short-wheelbase vehicles, and with a crowd watching and "honor" at stake, it's easy to let the moment overcome good judgment. It takes a high level of skill and finesse to get a Wrangler up the "Whammy." When facing a challenge like this for the first time, watch and analyze others before making your attempts. Give it three or four shots, and if unsuccessful, back off to let your adrenaline disperse. You can always try it again later, whether that's in 15 minutes or next year.

our equipment and our safety. I suppose it's an offshoot of our animal instinct to attract mates by showing our manly prowess. Unfortunately, we do it even when there are no females around. Wherever it comes from, men, resist!

CONTROL YOURSELF:
If adrenaline affects the way you feel at the wheel, take whatever time you need to regain total control before you tackle something that requires your best judgment and motor skills.

The Camel Credo

From 1980 to 1998, an annual international four-wheel-drive adventure/competition created a new definition for the phrase "tough four-wheeling." It was known as the Camel Trophy. The locations varied, but the common elements were the extreme four-wheeling and endurance challenges contestants faced over a 1,000-mile (or more) excursion across almost trackless terrain in some very remote parts of the world. Sometimes the daily mileage was counted in single digits . . . and that could be for a full 24-hour day of work!

The teams trained in their own countries with coordinators who were past participants or acknowledged experts. Land Rover supplied the identically prepared competition and support vehicles for all but the first and last events, and their experienced instructors aided in developing the driver-training program. In the long years of practice, someone in that organization distilled four-wheeling into one sentence. If you remember one thing from this book, remember this:

As slowly as possible, as fast as necessary.

This is the essence of four-wheeling. Recreational four-wheeling is not a race, and the single most common mistake is to drive too fast. Part of that is the result of the "speeded-up" effect of adrenaline poisoning we talked about earlier. The second part of the Camel Credo, "as fast as necessary," recognizes that there are times when a more aggressive driving style is needed.

TESTOSTERONE POISONING:
Don't let testosterone poisoning take you in the wrong direction. Use your testosterone wisely!

The Camel Trophy was an international adventure/competition held annually from 1980 to 1998 in many out-of-the-way corners of the world. The goal of the event was getting essentially stock vehicles through thousands of miles of barely navigable terrain. Vehicles like this Land Rover Discovery endured a lifetime of hardship on just one event that often measured daily mileage in single digits. The keys to getting through at all were good driving, judgment, and, as in this obvious predicament, recovery skills. Participants like Fred Hoess, shown here in the 1996 Kalimantan event, were often challenged as athletes. Training and experience got them through areas where even the stout Land Rovers were overwhelmed.

The Learning Curve

Don't overlook the value of formal training. Because even advanced techniques are but an extension of the basics, learning those fundamental moves provides a solid foundation for the rest of your 'wheeling "career." A look through the appendix will yield a number of possibilities; a Google search on your PC will yield a more current and comprehensive list.

The national and international four-wheel-drive associations, such as United Four Wheel Drive Associations, have training days, often held in each of their regional chapters. Some vehicle manufacturers, or their dealers, will hold classes for owners of their particular brand. Hummer, Jeep, Land Rover, Porsche, and Toyota are notable in offering training programs for owners of their vehicles.

Individual off-highway driving instructors can be found all over the country; a few of them are listed in the appendix. A common instruction format is a group training day, where small or large groups of people are brought together for instruction. Often, that takes the form of a guided trail run, where the instructors bring the group to a 'wheeling hot spot, lead the group safely through, and offer "on-the-job training" along the way as needed.

Instructors are usually available for individual coaching as well, though that can be pricey. Groups of friends or clubs can make cost-effective use of them by splitting the cost of hiring them for a day or more, or to lead a trip. In this way, they can ask for a focus on certain techniques or on mastering a specific vehicle.

Picking an off-highway driving instructor requires a bit more than a coin toss. Obviously you want a competent, experienced person with good teaching skills. Recommendations and word of mouth can go a long way, but some objective means of evaluation are also valuable. The big four-wheel-drive associations usually have their own training and certification courses, as do some of the vehicle manufacturers. One group, the International 4-Wheel Drive Trainer's Association (IAWDTA), aims to provide a more universal and readily available source of certification for instructors. This organization was just getting off the ground as this book was being written, so the list of I4WDTA trained and certified instructors is short. The idea to provide universal certification is a good one, however.

LEARNING CURVES:
Be kind to yourself as you learn. It's important to take lessons in humility to heart and mind, but not obsessively so.

COURAGE AND JUDGMENT:
Turning back may not be easy in the face of needling from companions, but if your best judgment dictates it, the truly courageous act is to hang a "ueey."

SKILL AND EQUIPMENT:
You may reach a point where your skill level exceeds your equipment's capabilities. In that case, modifications or a more capable vehicle are needed to progress further.

Whether you are a beginner or going up from one level of difficulty to another, you will be faced with failures and mistakes that seem outrageously stupid in retrospect. The trail will soon become a familiar and comfortable environment, and your skill level will increase with practice.

As you learn, choosing trails becomes an important way to further your skills and to keep within your current skill level. How can you determine the degree of difficulty of a given trail relative to your skills? Often you can't. If you start up a trail that exceeds your limits, simply turn back when the trip gets too hairy. The learning curve includes gradually increasing the level of difficulty as your skill and comfort levels increase. You will naturally develop to a level where you wish to stop.

ORV Parks

Off-road-vehicle (ORV) parks, also known as OHV (off-highway-vehicle) or "Pay-to-Play" parks, are a growing phenomenon as more and more public land is being closed to vehicle access. Some parks are privately owned, and others are run by local, state, or federal authorities. The best ones have some local club involvement. When that working relationship is cultivated, it results in more and better trails being built. More than a few offer driver training courses as well.

This is what happens when drivers bypass a wet spot on the trail. First, the trail gets wider, visible to the right of the Bum-V. Eventually, a whole new road is created (far right). Instead of a 10- or 12-foot swath through this mountain meadow, you now have 40 feet, and with wet weather ahead, it will probably grow even wider. This is what helps get trails closed.

Tread Lightly

The upswing of 4×4 popularity has drastically increased the numbers of vehicles on public and private lands. This can have a very negative impact on these areas if we don't all do our part. Unfortunately, there is a small but very destructive element in our midst that not only doesn't do its part, but goes out of the way to tear things up. Each of these destructive acts supplies ammunition to environmental groups with dedicated lawyers and lobbyists gunning to close more areas on our ever-shrinking list of four-wheeling sites. The rules for treading lightly are simple common sense, and they will not hinder your ability to have fun.

TREADING LIGHTLY BEGINS AT HOME: If you enjoy four-wheeling and want to keep doing it, the first step is to make sure your own behavior is beyond reproach. Next, make sure those in your group are playing the game right.

VEHICULAR HEMORRHAGES: Never leave pools of coolant. Its sweet odor attracts animals to drink, and the coolant will kill them.

Stay On the Established Trail. Never go cross-country, and avoid obviously unauthorized bypasses or spur trails. Bypasses happen when people veer off the trail to avoid an obstacle. Before long, that bypass is avoided by another bypass, and soon you have a 50-foot swath of torn-up ground. Most four-wheelers like a challenge! When a tough obstacle comes, take your lumps. Unauthorized trails happen in a similar way, when someone blazes a trail and later travelers encounter it and want to see where it goes. Given enough time, it can become a fairly established-looking trail. Avoid spurs that are obviously not authorized routes. If in doubt, avoid it altogether. Maps are not always a help. Authorized routes sometimes mysteriously "disappear" from maps. Conspiracy theorists in the four-wheeling groups accuse government agencies of deliberately doing this as a precursor to closing a trail.

Haul Out Your Trash. While you're at it, take the time to haul out a little of someone else's litter. Always leave your campsite or lunch stop area better than you found it. Many four-wheelers stop to pick up trash they observe on or near the trail. In fact, some groups compete to see who hauls out the most. The logic is simple: reduce the mess and reduce the reasons why other people want to keep four-wheelers out.

Be Kind to the Trail. An unpaved road is susceptible to damage. Avoid actions that chew it up unnecessarily, such as tire spinning and rooster tails in wet conditions. Certain unpaved roads are best not driven on when exceedingly wet. If you do tear up a section of trail in

The days when we could go cross-country are long gone. Even when I snapped this photo 25-plus years ago, this was considered poor practice. Though cross-country jaunts weren't strictly illegal everywhere back then, those of us with a long history in four-wheeling probably have some actions in our past to regret. Back then, it didn't seem like a big deal. There were plenty of places to four-wheel. Today, with our available four-wheeling areas reduced to half (my educated guess), we are fighting for the right to continue using motor vehicles in remote areas, and we can't afford even one incident of straying off the trail.

the normal course of travel, a little shovel work could save it from future erosion.

Vehicular Hemorrhages. It's not uncommon in the harder-core four-wheeling realms to have a vehicle problem that involves fluid leakage. Collect what you can in any sort of container or soak it up with rags. After repairs, it's your duty to clean up as much as you can. Oil-soaked dirt can be bagged and taken home, and oily rocks can be wiped up with rags or soaked up with dirt that can be hauled off. Brake fluid and coolant can be rinsed with water and diluted. By taking even the most moderate measures, you can prevent the contamination of streams and the ground, and the poisoning of wild critters.

Hikers, Bikers, and Critters Get the Right-of-Way. Give hikers and mountain bikers the right of way. Your exhaust and dust can lessen their enjoyment of the outdoors. Remember that they don't have a window to roll up! Responsible four-wheelers will stop, perhaps even shut off their engines, and let people and people-powered machines pass. Ditto for people on horseback. If the area is remote and the climate is warm, I may also ask hikers and bikers if they have enough water and maybe offer them a cold drink if I have some to

GATE ETIQUETTE:
Many remote areas are used for livestock grazing, and you may run across gates. The rule of thumb is that, unless there is a sign that says otherwise, leave the gate as you found it, either open or closed.

RIDE 'EM COWBOY:
Horses are flight animals, and some are easily frightened by loud machinery. Give riders a wide berth so their horses don't rear or bolt.

spare. Finally, let wild critters and livestock pass with a minimum of disruption.

Respect Private Property. Don't drive past "private property" or "no trespassing" signs. Access to private property is at the pleasure of the owner, so don't abuse the privilege if you have it. When you are crossing private property on a public right-of-way, don't assume that the property on either side of the road is free to access. Often, owners will allow you to recreate on their land if you ask permission.

Respect History and Natural Wonders. If every visitor to a historical or natural wonder picked up a souvenir, there'd be nothing left for anyone to look at. Don't be a vulture. Look, pick up, and examine if you must, but leave it there. In the case of a significant find of some sort, mark the area, get GPS coordinates, and report it to the most likely interested authority.

Trail Etiquette

Beyond treating our land with respect, a certain four-wheeling trail etiquette has evolved in the 50 or so years of the sport. Learning these informal but common sense courtesies will allow you to fit in with any group of four-wheelers.

Bring a Vehicle in Good Condition. Nothing will get you on the fecal list faster than ruining a group's trip with an avoidable breakdown. Your companions are obligated by common decency to offer aid and not leave you stranded alone in the wilderness. Most four-wheelers will strip their own rig of parts to get you going again. But if it's obvious that your breakdown was easily avoidable by maintenance or some pre-trip repairs, you can look forward to some unpleasant looks, rather edgy jibes, and a reputation you'll have to work hard to overcome. Bring the food, fuel, and sundries you need for the trip. Don't be known as the mooch.

Towing Points and Gear. Life gets tough for everyone when you get stuck or disabled and don't have proper recovery points. We'll get into this in some depth later, but trail etiquette dictates at least one solidly mounted recovery point front and rear. Even better, have a good tow/recovery strap and a couple of shackles in your kit.

Animals. Dogs and other animals can make great four-wheeling companions and are commonly seen on the trail. Always remember that your animal reflects on you. A friendly, good-mannered pooch can make you a lot of friends. A dog that has to mark every tire on the run and sniff every crotch can have the opposite effect. Overly protective animals that may lunge at or bite people walking close to their owners' rigs will not earn you high marks either. You may see other domesticated critters on the trail as well. I've seen cats, ferrets, parrots, cockatiels, and one huge iguana riding gleefully in their owners' 4×4s.

Trail Improvements. Every vehicle is different, so it stands to reason that some owners might need to

Whether your nonhuman traveling companion is reptile or canine, it's your responsibility to keep it under control. This good-natured critter was particularly well behaved (and stylish), earning mondo popularity points for its owners. I won't show you pics of the pooch that bit the sunshade off my camera or the other that urinated on my camera bag.

KIDS AND FOUR-WHEELING:
Sharing four-wheeling with your kids can be rewarding for all, but you need to be extra vigilant. Beyond avoidance of dangers that can get them hurt or lost, make sure they behave.

RECOVERY POINTS:
Improper recovery points can be dangerous to people and equipment, and some four-wheelers will not render aid to an improperly prepared vehicle.

TOTAL CONTROL:
On the trail, mistakes that occur are likely to be your own. That fact gives you a great deal of control over your environment.

pile a few rocks here or there to create clearance for their rig while others may not. The people with better-equipped rigs find it annoying to encounter a path that's been made too easy. It's customary that if you have to make more than just a few modifications to an obstacle, undo the roadbuilding for the next person or group. Exceptions to this may be if the area looks like most, if not all, the vehicles passing through will need the trail mods. In that case, you are doing the next person a favor.

When All Else Fails, Read the Manual

The manual for your 4×4 truck or SUV is chock full of good information on the operation of controls, vehicle specifications, and, often, some pretty good driving tips. Take the time to familiarize yourself with this little book. The main points of interest are the operation of the controls and vital specifications like fording depth; approach, departure, and ramp breakover angles; tire pressures; and service specifications. It will be the most specific information available for your rig.

Safety

Four-wheeling is very safe overall. Certainly your odds are better on the trail than they are in rush hour. Unlike the daily commute, what happens on the trail mostly comes down to the driver, and most of that is within his or her control. Drive well and safely, and nothing bad happens.

One safety consideration many new 4×4 owners fail to grasp before purchasing an SUV or pickup is how differently these vehicles handle from an ordinary car. That's not to say that a properly driven four-wheel-drive vehicle is inherently unsafe, despite what you may have seen on the "gotcha"-style TV news shows. The very attributes that make them perform on the trail, however, detract from their highway prowess. Driving a 4×4, especially a built-up one, as an everyday transporter should be an informed choice. You need to drive any 4×4 with more respect and with a finer touch. They are not sports cars!

Another cardinal rule is to avoid traveling alone in remote areas. The dangers of this are obvious. Out there, a breakdown, illness, or injury is more difficult to deal with and potentially more dangerous. It's safer and more fun to go in groups of two or more.

Vehicle maintenance is a safety issue. Breaking down in a remote area is a potentially fatal problem. A rig that has been regularly serviced and checked usually does not break down because problems are caught early. That's not to say that problems will

Make it easy for folks to help. Having a safe recovery point at each end of your rig, whether it is bone stock or highly modified, is both common sense and a trail etiquette must.

It's much more fun and safer to travel in a group, though a group this large can test your patience. You always travel as slowly as the slowest member of the group . . . but then the whole idea is to enjoy your time in the slow lane.

TRAVELING SOLO:
If you must travel solo in a remote area, have a topnotch 4×4, be well-prepared with emergency supplies, file a trip plan with a responsible party, and have long-range communications capability to mitigate danger.

never happen to a well-maintained 4×4; the odds are just reduced to a more acceptable level.

As mentioned before, vehicle damage is a possibility that gets more probable as the degree of terrain difficulty increases. OK, so once you've got your rig intact enough to limp back, you're home free. Right? Wrong-o! Temporary repairs involving tires, suspension, steering, certain parts of the drivetrain, and the fuel system should be dealt with in a permanent manner before you take the highway home. Until that happens, you crawl along at a safe pace. More than a few four-wheelers have made corncob repairs on the

On-the-spot trail repairs and roadbuilding are often necessary, especially for less extreme 4×4s. It can take any form, from the simple chucking of a rock under a tire to an elaborate stack of material that rivals the Roman ramp up to Masada. It's considered good manners to chip in when the work is being done to get an entire group through. The other aspect to roadbuilding is considering the harder-core types coming along later who might like a challenge. Owners of stock rigs that need lots of roadbuilding help should consider undoing their work before proceeding, unless it's clear that all vehicles will need the help.

The ultimate limp! With a broken rear axle shaft (a C-clip type) and no spare, the owner of this Wrangler was faced with a grim dilemma. Leave the rig out in the boondocks for the better part of a day, possibly to be picked clean before he could get back; spend the night with the rig until help and parts returned; or nurse it back to a spot where it could be hauled onto a trailer. With the help of enterprising friends, he was able to nurse the rig along on three wheels after some special preparation. The vehicle was driven about 10 miles over tough terrain this way. A truck and a trailer waited on an easier section of trail to bring him to civilization for proper repairs. This is not an advisable solution in every case, but it shows that ingenuity and persistence can solve almost any problem.

trail and blithely headed home, only to "crash and burn" on the highway.

Emergency Gear. I regard emergency items as insurance. Paying out the money and investing the time is often a sort of cosmic "get-out-of-jail-free" card. On the other hand, it only takes one potentially dangerous incident for which you were totally prepared, and that equipment earns "paid in full" status. I have found my own emergency equipment more an aid to others than myself. That's how things sometimes seem to work, but I don't tempt fate and invite the universe to bite me in the butt.

Fire Extinguishers. Since the day after I had to beat out an engine fire with a neighbor's doormat, I have had a fire extinguisher in all my vehicles. From that day in 1975, I have never had another fire, though I have

BREAKDOWNS:

Even brand-new vehicles can have a breakdown, so a sensible array of spare parts and tools geared to your particular flavor of four-wheeling and vehicle is a must for any outback traveler.

EMERGENCY REPAIRS:

If you jury-rigged a trail repair that could possibly affect safe steering, handling, braking, or control, fix it properly before you hit the road home.

emptied my extinguisher three times to save other rigs. Fire's destructive and life-threatening potential is obvious, making a fire extinguisher mandatory gear. By the way, good manners dictate that if someone empties an extinguisher on your behalf, you offer to pay for the refill.

There are many types of fire extinguishers, some of which are not practical for vehicle use. The most common and inexpensive extinguisher is the dry chemical type. These are divided into two general categories: the standard "department store," or stored-pressure, variety; and cartridge-operated designs.

In the first type, the dry chemical is stored in a pressurized container. The chief advantages of this type are low cost and compact size. Disadvantages are the relatively vulnerable container and the possibility of the unit losing pressure over time.

In the cartridge-operated extinguisher, the chemical is stored in one container and a small, separate, nitrogen-charged container provides the pressure when actuated. These extinguishers are very efficient but bulky and expensive to buy and maintain. They are more effective than a stored-pressure extinguisher and more durable in harsh environments.

Fire extinguishers are rated A, B, C, and D, for different types of fires. Class A fires are of combustible materials like wood and paper that can be extinguished with water and with certain (but not all) dry chemicals. Class B fires involve flammable liquids or vapors, and Class C fires are electrical in nature. Both B and C classes require smothering by a substance that will not spread the fire or conduct electricity (using water on high-voltage electrical fires can get you electrocuted). Class D fires occur with materials like magnesium, titanium, sodium, and zirconium. Putting out these difficult fires requires very specialized equipment that is beyond the scope of our discussion.

Looking at the classifications, Classes B and C come to mind for vehicles, but consider that you may need fire suppression for other things, such as a campfire that gets out of control or a brush fire started by a catalytic converter. In this overall situation, an ABC extinguisher has you covered for everything. The difference is in the chemicals used. The B- and C-rated units use plain old sodium bicarbonate (baking soda), which is white in color. The ABC units use monoammonium phosphate, which is a good smother agent and is yellow in color.

Mount your extinguisher in a place that is easily accessible and readily visible. Fires demand immediate attention, and the person who needs to find and retrieve your extinguisher won't necessarily be you.

The Iron Range OHV Park, in northern Minnesota, is one of the best such parks in the country. In fact, it won BFG's coveted Outstanding Trails Award for 2008. This park, one of many in the country, stands out because it has such good club involvement and is run by volunteers. Part of your entry fees pays for well-marked trails like this one. The park is also expanding, with new trails cut every year. The park was built in an old iron mining area.

Check the gauges regularly and service them every couple of years. Not only can the pressurized charge leak slowly, but the powder inside can get compacted, and you may not get a full charge when you need it.

You can go to a discount store and buy a cheap, non-serviceable, one-shot extinguisher. These units are better than throwing dirt, but since some of their vital parts are made of plastic, they may not hold up well in a rough-and-tumble four-wheeler. For a few more dollars, you can get an extinguisher with metal parts. These can be serviced over and over and are essentially lifetime units, as long as the containers don't get dented.

First Aid. A first-aid kit may be most important to a four-wheeler who is farther away from medical help, but people have died beside the freeway for the lack of a simple first-aid kit and the knowledge needed to use it. A first-aid kit of some type is a must for any well-equipped 4×4. How elaborate you get depends a lot on your planned destinations. Obviously, crossing the Sahara will require more preparation than a highway day trip, but some basics should be in every first-aid kit.

CARGO TIE DOWNS:
Don't let a piece of flying equipment ruin your fun. Before you head into the rough stuff, tie your gear down securely.

A FIRST-AID KIT

Here is a common-sense kit that includes most of what a person may need off road. It does not cover every eventuality, but it is usable within the realm of most people's first-aid knowledge. If you have any medical training, add to the list as your experience dictates. I strongly suggest that all frequent four-wheelers take a Red Cross CPR and First Aid class.

Pain
Aspirin
Ibuprofen

Stomach
antidiarrheals (Imodium, Pepto Bismol, etc.)
antacids
ipecac (for inducing vomiting)

Antiseptic
antiseptic towelettes
alcohol (liquid, in plastic bottle)
hydrogen peroxide
iodine

Bandages
selection of Band-Aids
sterile pads, nonstick (Telfa), assorted sizes
burn pads
tape
sterile gauze roll
sterislips (for closing wounds)
large sterile dressings
elastic wrap (e.g., Ace) bandage

Tools
compact first-aid manual
flashlight + extra batteries
blanket
fine tweezers
scissors
splint
cervical collar
cold pack (for sprains and burns)
CPR mask (for rescue breathing)
tourniquet
sterile latex gloves
sterile eyewash
plastic bags
sturdy case for first-aid kit

Skin
sunblock
calamine lotion
hand sanitizer
Oak & Ivy Armor (for appropriate areas)
hydrocortisone cream
antibacterial ointment
antihistamine (Benadryl, etc., for stings)
burn gel

Good stewardship knows no age boundaries. Members of the 4 Wheels To Freedom 4-Wheel Drive Club of Central Indiana clean up trails at the Redbird State Riding Area. Overall, visitors have been kind to the park, but there are always a few who won't carry out their trash. Here, from left to right, Randy Ball, Jeff Ritter, young Duncan Rowda, and his dad, Brian, scrounge to fill a bag.

The first items would fall under the heading of prescription drugs. If anyone in your party has special needs in that area, it's appropriate to ensure that that person has sufficient medication for the time away from home, plus a little extra in case of a delay. An obvious example is insulin for diabetics, but the rule applies to any necessary medication.

Most medical situations are minor. A headache, diarrhea, indigestion, or altitude sickness can take the fun out of a trip, so it makes sense to have some remedies around for these minor ailments. Too much fun can also result in minor cuts and abrasions, so antiseptic and small bandages are in order. Sprains are not unusual in outdoor frolicking, so elastic-wrap bandages can be handy. Skin lotions, sunblock, bug repellent, and a poison oak or ivy protectant (in the areas where it abounds) are all common-sense items.

When you get into more major injuries or illnesses, the focus shifts to your knowledge of first aid. Even if you're not trained in this area, there may be someone around who is, and having the right stuff on hand could mean life or death for an injured person. You have the option of taking first-aid courses as well. The Red Cross, for one, offers both basic first-aid and CPR classes in most larger towns.

You can buy first-aid kits in any form, from a few Band-Aids in a box to something that beats many Third World hospitals. You need not go to elaborate extremes if you are an occasional day-tripper. But if you like really offbeat locales, think about a high-end kit. Look at the suggested first-aid kit contents in the nearby sidebar for some ideas on what to carry.

Cargo Tie Downs. Have you ever been beaned in the back of the head on a steep downhill by some small bit of cargo that came adrift? Perhaps you can't remember because of the resulting brain injury? Imagine your overloaded toolbox hitting you in the head. It might be the last thing you imagine! You can buy nifty, flush-mounted tie downs for the cargo area. You can also head down to the wrecking yard or surplus store and find something that works. The main goal is to get your heavy gear secured.

Rollover Protection. An open-topped rig should have at least a minimal roll bar. Since the 1970s, open-topped rigs have come so equipped from the factory. Harder-core 'wheelers often make improvements to the basic setup for increased protection. Hardtopped rigs sometimes will have internal protection built in. Modern hardtops come with some built-in protection that is adequate in most situations. Older hardtops may actually be more at risk, despite their reputations of being built tougher in the "good ol' days."

My recommendation for all open-topped rigs is to have at least one bar. If the rig is used in upper-medium to difficult terrain, I recommend a full cage setup. Hardtops are pretty safe overall, so the addition of a bar or cage is not generally necessary. The few hardtopped rigs that operate in the hard-core realms often have cages built into them.

Survival. Most of us don't go so far into the boondocks that dying of thirst or hunger is a significant danger, yet a few people die in just these circumstances every year. The root cause is usually going out alone and unprepared. Weather is often a primary issue as well. Heading alone into the mountains with a snowstorm imminent, for example, is asking for trouble. In a similar vein, people have headed to remote desert spots alone, gotten stuck or broken down, and died. Extreme conditions of hot or cold cause people to suffer the most and die the quickest. In most other areas, you can live for more than two days without food, shelter, or water.

There are many survival books on the market devoted totally to the subject. These typically advise you to stay with the vehicle in adverse weather, unless there are compelling reasons to do otherwise. The vehicle will provide at least some measure of shelter and comfort, and depending on its color and that of the surroundings, it may be easier for rescuers to spot than a person alone. Weigh those considerations against the distance to help, a *known* route to help, the weather conditions, how well you are prepared (health, clothing, shoes, supplies, and so on), and the potential of help finding you in short order. Compelling reasons to take more risks would be if you are in a vulnerable position somehow or you have an injured person that needs aid. (You shouldn't leave an injured person alone in most cases.)

The first line of defense is not to put yourself into these dire situations. Travel in a group. The second defense is knowledge. People have died of exposure because they didn't know how to replace a fuse or perform the most rudimentary recovery operation. People have been stranded by what they forgot. I once ran across a family stuck for the better part of a day with a well-equipped rig because they had left the winch control at home. Finally, a common-sense array of survival gear can give you the basics to last until help arrives. You can find a list of such gear in the appendix.

What do you get when you hire an off-highway vehicle instructor? In Bill Burke's case, you get at least a couple of decades of four-wheeling experience and 15 years of experience in training people how to do it, not to mention certification out the wazoo. An instructor should have a good resume of experience . . . not just in four-wheeling itself, but on the training side.

A small bag or pack with a few survival items appropriate to the area can be a lifesaver. In winter, appropriate clothing, including a warm hat, gloves, and winter boots, a sleeping bag, high-energy food, and water are all it takes to keep you from doing a Popsicle imitation. In the desert, water and more water is what you need, as well as shade (a tarp or sun shade is better than the vehicle, which soaks up heat) and a flashlight for signaling and working at night. Remember that you have two or three signal mirrors on the vehicle. There's more to know, of course, but these are the basics. Carry more if you deem it necessary, but at least *think* about potential survival situations every time you hit the dirt and make a few simple preparations.

CHAPTER 2
Traction 101: Get a Grip!

Traction at work! The grip those four tires have on *terra firma*, however firma the terra, is what makes the trail a go or no-go situation.

Half the battle in learning to four-wheel well is understanding the dynamics of your vehicle and translating that knowledge into effective driving technique. It's a complex equation, but when you boil it down, there are only two elements your 4×4 needs to perform in the dirt: traction and clearance. How much or how little of these two elements a vehicle possesses will dictate its trail performance.

What is Four-Wheel Drive?

Four-wheel drive doubles the amount of traction available to an ordinary two-wheel-drive rig by providing a second driving axle. What is traction? It can be defined a few different ways. For the purposes of our Traction 101 discussion, let's call it the transformation of engine torque into vehicular motion. Most of that transformation occurs where the tires meet the ground. Therefore, the tire's grip on the ground surface plays a big part in the traction equation, as does the number of gripping tires that have power applied.

The basic and perennial four-wheel-drive system consists of three components. First is the transfer case, which splits the power from the engine to drive the other two components, the front and rear axles. The transfer case may also contain a selectable gearing-down mechanism called low range, which drops the overall gear ratio. This gearing step-down, over and above the gearing steps in the transmission, is used to provide increased engine torque multiplication or engine braking capabilities needed for descending in steep terrain.

Part-Time Four-Wheel Drive. For most of four-wheel drive's history, part-time systems have been the norm. Until recently, the means to shift from two-wheel to four-wheel drive was a mechanical lever. These days, that has been replaced in many vehicles by a pushbutton or selector switch setup that actuates an electric servo-motor that does the actual shifting.

PART-TIME 4×4:
A part-time four-wheel-drive system is one that drives only the rear axle until a gear selector is engaged to drive the front wheels also.

PART-TIME ADVANTAGES:
The main advantage of a part-time system is that the vehicle drives like a "normal" 4x2 until the extra traction capability is needed for rough terrain. Driving only two wheels burns less fuel and reduces tire and mechanical wear and tear, especially on dry pavement.

Before Arthur Warn made freewheeling hubs popular in the late 1940s, the front axles of four-wheel-drive vehicles would spin along with the tires, causing extra drag and wear and reducing fuel economy. Warn's invention uncoupled the axles from the hubs, allowing the wheels to spin separately from the axle shafts. When needed, the axles could be recoupled manually. This simple manual device has been refined over the years to include automatic units that lock when four-wheel drive is engaged. In the past, a part-time four-wheel-drive vehicle gained 2–3 miles per gallon by the addition of freewheeling hubs.

Into the 1980s, 4×4s with part-time systems came from the factory with freewheeling hubs of some type, either standard or optional. At that time the Center

A basic four-wheel-drive system consists of three main components: the transfer case and the front and rear axles, between which it splits the torque. Most true four-wheel-drive systems also have a gearing step-down—a low range for when extra torque multiplication is needed.

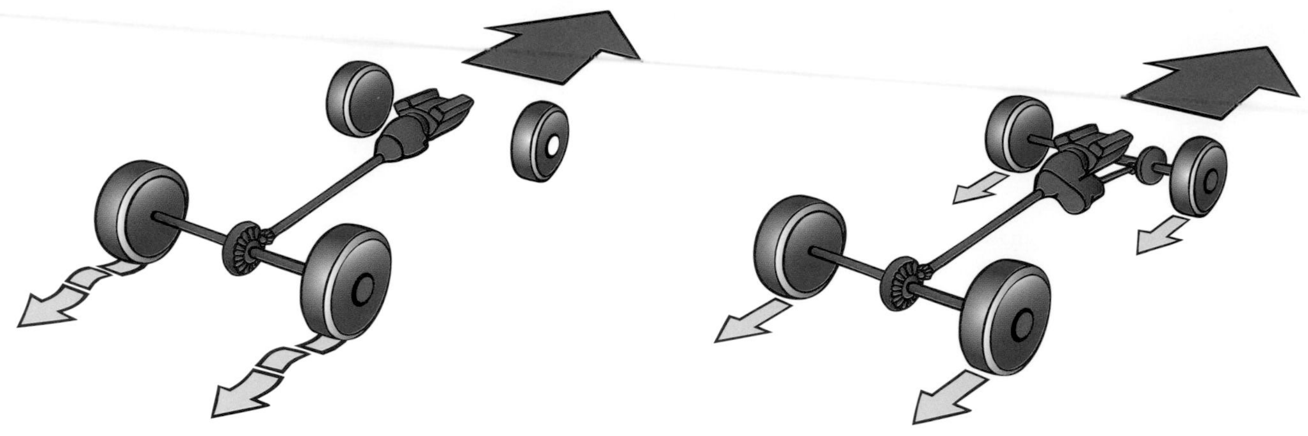

Four-wheel drive provides twice the grip, or at least the *potential* for twice the grip. True four-wheel drive requires locking differentials in both axles, but a highly tractive surface underneath all four wheels does almost as well.

Axle Disconnect (CAD) was introduced. In the Dana-style CAD, the axle shaft on one side is split into two sections with a sleeved coupling between them. An actuator with a forked lever operates the sleeve. Typically that actuator is powered by vacuum. The GM/American Axle IFS-style unit does essentially the same thing but does it close to the differential and is actuated by a thermal piston device or a servo-motor. The 1997 and up IFS Ford system is similar.

The commonality among CAD is that by disconnecting one axle, the ring gear no longer rotates (nor the pinion and front driveshaft), but the remaining connected axle is still driving the side and spider gears. With no load applied, wear (and drag) is minimal.

More recently, it has been found in today's smaller, lighter diffs, particularly IFS units and those with sealed, unit-bearing hubs, that a CAD or hubs are unnecessary complications. The difference in drag is considered minor and doesn't have much effect on fuel economy. The recent larger pickup truck axles often still have CADs because the drag on a bigger, solid axle is more significant.

Full-Time Four-Wheel Drive. Full-time four-wheel drive was actually the norm until the development of the part-time transfer case by Timken for a production Dodge military truck in 1934. The modern era of full-time systems began in 1973, when AMC Jeep introduced the Borg-Warner 1339 transfer case in the Wagoneer and J-Series trucks and called it Quadra-Trac. From there, full-time systems have developed into a very common element in the 4×4 arena, especially for SUVs.

YOU CAD:
A Center Axle Disconnect (CAD) is an internal axle device that eliminates the need for locking hubs by disconnecting one axle from the differential via a sleeve. This prevents the ring gear and pinion from being driven, which reduces drag, but it does still allow the other axle to spin the side and spider gears of the differential.

MANUALLY LOCKED CENTER DIFFS:
If the center differential is not locked, power will take the path of least resistance and go to the one tire with the least traction. (Read more in the "Open Differentials: The Path of Least Resistance" section.)

Full-time systems continuously supply torque to the front and rear axles, but because front and rear wheel speeds differ in turns, a differential device is needed in the transfer case to allow the front and rear driveshafts to turn at different speeds. In most 4×4s, this center differential can be locked when a true 50/50 torque split is needed in rough terrain. Some full-time systems use a manual lock, and others use an automatic lock or limited-slip. Automatic locking has been accomplished in various ways, from the crude clutch packs of the first-generation Quadra-Trac system, to the silky smooth viscous couplings of the recent past, to electronic clutches of today.

ALL-WHEEL DRIVE:
Many all-wheel-drive systems work quite well, providing seamless traction in a variety of low-grip driving situations, but they often lack the robust qualities needed for serious trail work.

Even slicker are the "smart" systems that use the wheel speed sensors from the ABS brake system to constantly monitor wheel speed and engage and disengage center-diff locks, and sometimes even axle-diff locks, to maintain traction at all four wheels. These systems are generally not up to hard-core use, but with sufficient motivation by manufacturers, they easily could be.

The advantages of full-time systems are user-friendliness and improved traction on the highway, especially in inclement weather. A full-time system with a center diff is significantly better in snow than an engaged part-time setup. A part-time system engaged on the highway must break tires loose in a turn because there is no center differential. In icy conditions, the momentary loss of traction from even a single tire could send the vehicle on an unscheduled tour of the roadside ditch. A full-time system allows a speed differential between the two axles so the tires maintain a more constant grip.

The disadvantages of a full-time system can include a loss of fuel economy from barely noticeable to significant, increased tire wear (low to moderate), some quirky road feel issues and vibration, and increased maintenance and repair costs. The most modern systems, especially those controlled by computer, are nearly seamless in operation and minimize the negatives.

A few recent vehicles use a transfer case with both full- and part-time modes. Part-time can be used to maximize fuel economy day to day. Full-time can be used in inclement weather, and the center diff can be locked for true four-wheeling situations.

Automatic Four-Wheel Drive. Some of the newer SUVs and trucks have automatic four-wheel-drive systems that operate in two-wheel-drive, part-time mode until slippage is sensed at the rear axle (via the same wheel speed sensors used for the anti-lock brakes). They then shift into a four-wheel-drive mode automatically until the need has passed. These units can usually be locked

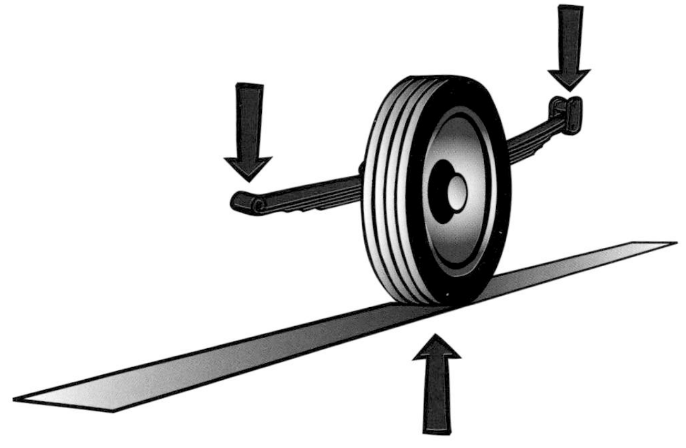

Weight plus tire footprint plus ground surface equals grip. Part of what creates traction, or grip, is ground pressure. Ground pressure is a combination of weight and the tire footprint. More weight or a smaller footprint equals more ground pressure and vice versa. High ground pressure works *for* you on hard ground by increasing grip, but it works *against* you on soft ground by letting you sink into the surface.

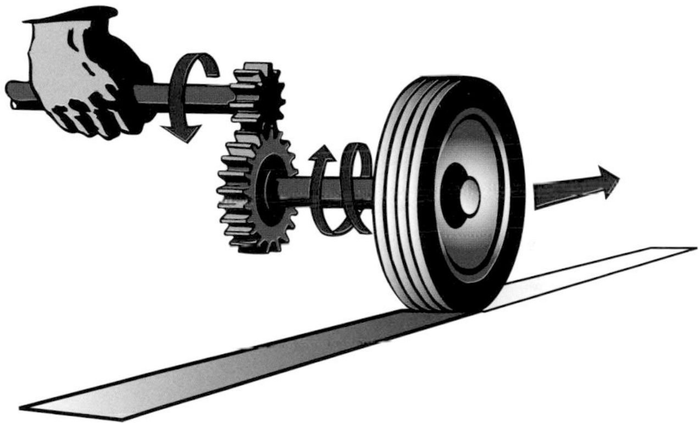

Torque plus grip equals traction. Torque multiplication takes what the engine produces; multiplies it by the transmission gear ratios, the transfer case gear ratios, and the axle ratios; and turns it into motion. How much grip the tire can generate determines how much of that torque can be turned into forward motion. When a tire cannot generate the required grip, one cure is to reduce the torque load to the tire by decreasing the throttle application or reducing the torque multiplication by shifting up a gear.

AUTOMATIC 4×4:
Automatic four-wheel drive combines attributes of part-time and full-time four-wheel drive. When traction is good, the system functions in two-wheel mode. When it detects wheel slip, the system switches to four-wheel mode on its own.

into a two-wheel-drive or four-wheel-drive mode, but the "auto" feature makes it a no-brainer when conditions change rapidly. These systems are designed mostly for inclement weather in highway situations.

All-Wheel Drive Versus Four-Wheel Drive

The term *all-wheel drive* goes way back but has lately been applied to vehicles that use a four-wheel-drive system designed more for improved road holding and inclement weather traction rather than for off-highway pursuits. AWD systems are fitted to cars and minivans as much as trucks and SUVs, but what's the difference between AWD and four-wheel drive?

The first major difference between all-wheel- and four-wheel-drive systems is that all-wheel-drives do not have a low range in the transfer case. Many AWD vehicles are front-wheel-drive–based and do not even have a transfer case in the traditional sense of the word. A simplified description of this setup would be that they have a power take-off from the transaxle that drives the rear axle and they use a viscous coupling or an electronically controlled center-differential-like coupling. Also, many of them do not have a means of locking the transfer case (if they have one in the traditional sense) to supply a 50/50 torque split front

Is this America's first 4×4 SUV? This one is not quite the first but certainly the earliest successful one and the first production 4×4 in America with a steerable front axle. The Badger Four-Wheel-Drive Auto Company's *Battleship* was built originally in 1908 with a steam engine but modified in 1909 with a new body and a gasoline engine. Badger became known as the Four Wheel Drive Auto Company in 1910 and produced a small number of similar four-wheel-drive touring cars until 1911. The *Battleship* was used as a sales tool, traveling around the Midwest to fairs and motoring events with a $1,000 reward for any car and driver that could follow it for 15 minutes on a cross-country course. Nobody collected in two years' worth of events. The *Battleship* is in original, running, and unrestored condition at FWD's Pioneer Park Museum in Clintonville, Wisconsin.

and rear. They usually rely on sophisticated torque- or wheel-speed-sensing devices that can determine which tire has grip and direct power there.

Certain newer SUVs, like the Honda CR-V, Ford Escape, Toyota RAV4, Geo Sidekick/Vitara, Kia Sportage, GMC Yukon Denali, Subaru Forester, Hyundai Santa-Fe, Jeep Compass, and a few others, fit between the street-oriented all-wheel-drive rigs, commonly known as "crossover" SUVs, and the true off-highway machines. While they lack a low range, they partially make up for it by being more robust and having a bit more clearance. Some are able to lock into a true 50/50 torque split at the transfer case and are generally capable of dealing with true off-highway terrain from the easy stuff into the lower area of moderate terrain.

Where Did Four-Wheel Drive Come From?

Four-wheel drive has existed in various forms since 1824, when the Burstall and Hill steam-powered four-wheel-drive coach was built in England during the early days of steam power. Largely forgotten by history, it was a small part of the entrepreneurial development process that led to the steam locomotive.

More four-wheel-drive ideas followed as the motorized era gained momentum at the end of the nineteenth and beginning of the twentieth centuries. Some of these early four-wheel-drive systems were successful, but most were not. The idea persisted because the automobile predated a system of paved roads. Early inventors recognized that driving all four wheels would improve traction on the primitive roads of the time, but the technology for doing so proved elusive. Developing a front axle that could steer the vehicle effectively while delivering torque to the wheels was a difficult part of the problem. Splitting the torque front and rear, via a transfer case, was relatively easy in comparison.

FOUR-BY FIRST:
In 1908, Otto Zachow and William Besserdich were the first in America to produce a four-wheel-drive vehicle with a steerable, driving front axle and a four-wheel-drive system of the general design we still use today.

FOUR-BY HISTORY:
Four-wheel drive was uncommon in the early days because of its cost. Adding four-wheel drive to a design virtually doubled the cost of any vehicle.

Wisconsin machinist and inventor Otto Zachow summed up the logic for four-wheel drive in 1907, exclaiming, "Who ever heard of a mule who walked on two legs?!" After laboriously recovering his 1906 two-wheel-drive Reo from an accidental "tour" of a ravine, Zachow was sufficiently annoyed to design, patent, and produce a four-wheel-drive system with his friend and partner, William Besserdich.

Their labor provided the building blocks for the big truck four-wheel-drive dynasty that remains in business to this day, the FWD Corporation. FWD owned the design patents for what is now the standard four-wheel-drive layout until World War I, when they surrendered them to the U.S. government to aid the war effort. FWD was not the first with the idea, however.

The very first application of a four-wheel-drive system similar to what we use today appeared in the Dutch-built Spyker race car of 1903. It was a one-off, but a few similar cars were built later. The system was built primarily for roadholding on the dirt roads of early Europe. We Americans like to think that four-wheel drive begins and ends here, but various European and Asian nations have pursued the technology with at least as much vigor over the past hundred years.

Early four-wheel-drive systems were most common in commercial or military use, where the extra cost could be justified. This slowed development of the technology on the civilian side and left most of the major breakthroughs to military designers. Fortunately, most of those breakthroughs trickled down to the civilian markets eventually.

Speaking of the military, you'll see the terms "4×4" and "4×2" bandied about here and elsewhere. They began as military nomenclature to describe the wheel and drive configurations of military vehicles. The first number signifies the number of wheels on the vehicle and the second the number of those that are powered. You could have a 4×4 (four wheels, all powered), 4×2 (four wheels, two powered), 6×4 (six wheels, four powered), 6×6 (six wheels, all driven), and so on, in any number of combinations.

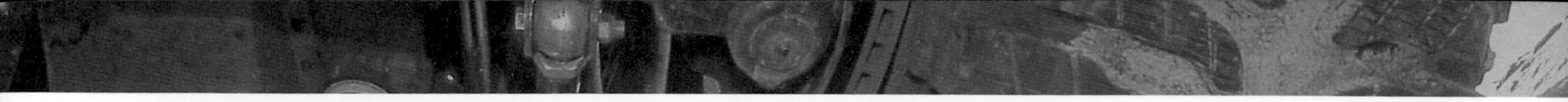

The physics of four-wheeling at work! Sometimes a small patch of rubber is all you have. Learning to use it is what four-wheeling is all about.

The Battle for Traction

Traction is the battle between engine torque, via the drivetrain, and the grip of the tire onto the ground. It's a complex equation that is infinitely variable when looked at under a microscope, but it's largely predictable with a broader view. Many factors contribute to traction or detract from it.

Ground Conditions. The first major traction-controlling factor is the ground surface. Two primary attributes determine the traction the ground can provide: surface strength and shear strength. Surface strength supports, or fails to support, the weight of the vehicle. In the latter situation, the tire sinks into the soft ground. Snow, sand, and mud are three well-known ground conditions that offer low surface strength.

FRICTION COEFFICIENT:
The friction coefficient describes available traction based on the tire's grip and the ground condition, with 1.0 being perfect traction. In practice, the figure is an average and will always be less than 1—often much less in four-wheeling environments.

TIRE TREAD DESIGN:
A good tread design for rocks will be able to move and conform to irregularities. This is made possible by small blocks of tread with many void areas.

TIRE FLOTATION:
If the tires allow the vehicle to sink to the point where the axles and chassis are touching the ground, the resulting drag is usually way past the traction available to overcome it.

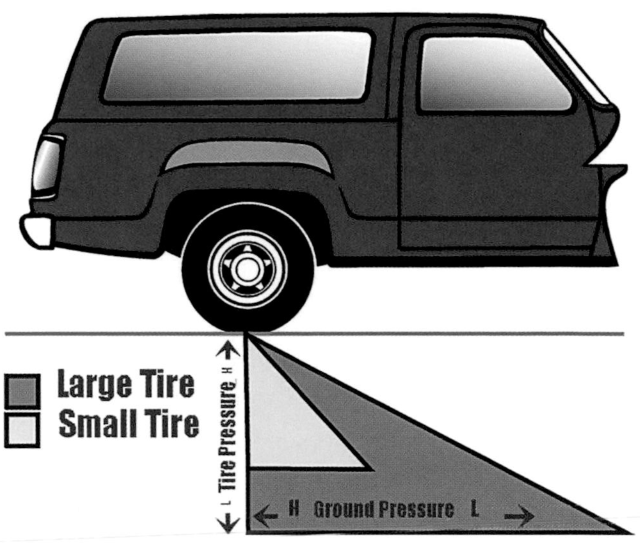

The forces acting on the ground are infinitely variable according to ground conditions and tire footprint. Airing down the tire (you'll learn about this precisely in a later chapter) increases the footprint and therefore flotation, and usually traction increases as well. This illustration shows the difference between a small tire and a big tire, aired up and aired down. Lower pressure decreases vertical thrust (lower ground pressure), and higher pressure increases it (higher ground pressure).

The second attribute affecting traction is the shear strength of the ground surface. Shear strength controls how much grip is available to the tires. If shear strength is low, the surface tears away and the tire slips. Pavement, concrete, solid rock, and other similar surfaces have a high shear strength, while sand, dirt, gravel, mud, and so on have low shear strength.

The available traction of any ground surface is expressed as a coefficient that combines the grip of the tire and the ground condition. Perfect traction is expressed as 1.0. Pavement runs from 0.60–0.80 for "normal" tires of a type used for most 4×4s and 0.90-plus for high-performance street tires. The coefficient for ice is about 0.15–0.20, depending on the tire. Mud ranges from 0.20–0.40, and dirt has a high of about 0.50. The traction coefficient is infinitely variable depending on the combination of tire and ground condition. You may see it expressed as an absolute, but such numbers are really an average that combines an "average" tire with "average" mud.

Tires. Of all the vehicular elements involved in the traction equation, tires are the biggest controlling factor. Tire grip varies according to the ground condition and the design of the tires. Tread pattern and the composition of the rubber are the primary variables in tire design. On hard surfaces, the rubber compound plays the bigger part. On hard, dry surfaces, the rubber compound provides 75 to 80 percent of the grip. The softer the rubber, the better the grip.

Rubber compounds vary in softness according to design. Softer compounds grip better on hard surfaces but wear faster. Finding the right combination is the tire manufacturer's eternal battle. Performance tires, either for street cars or 4×4s, are often biased toward the softer, more grippy compounds, but a good tread design can give harder, longer-lasting tire compounds a chance to compete with softer rubber.

Grip on a hard surface comes down to the weight on the tire and the shear strength of the ground. Within a certain range, more weight equals more traction, but more weight also *requires* more traction, so the equations spiral upward in that case. Mud tires do well in rocks, too, because they have many voids that increase the ground pressure on each of the little blocks of tread. Many a rig has been pulled up an otherwise impossible climb by one knob of tread that has glued itself to a rock by a concentration of weight.

On soft surfaces, tread design plays the major part in creating the overall traction capability of the tire—as much as 75 percent—with the cleated edges of the tread working much like paddles in water to provide traction. In the soft ground environment, flotation comes into play. The tire's ability to stay *above* the ground is vital. To start with, the deeper the tire sinks, the greater the drag; more traction is needed to overcome it.

Flotation is a product of tire size, or more precisely the size of the tire's footprint on the ground in relation to the vehicle weight. With a larger footprint, vehicle weight is spread out over a larger section of ground. Ground pressure is measured in pounds per square inch (psi, or the metric equivalent), and a lower number means better flotation.

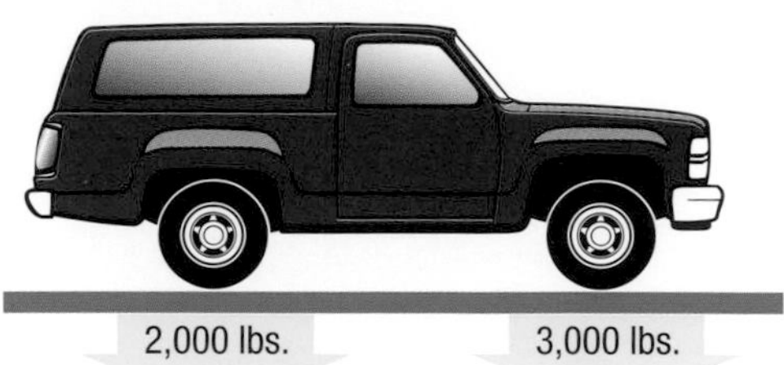

Here is a typical distribution of weight on a full-sized SUV on level ground. The front tires almost always carry more weight unless the vehicle is carrying a load in the cargo area. We're assuming a 5,000 pound total weight for this SUV.

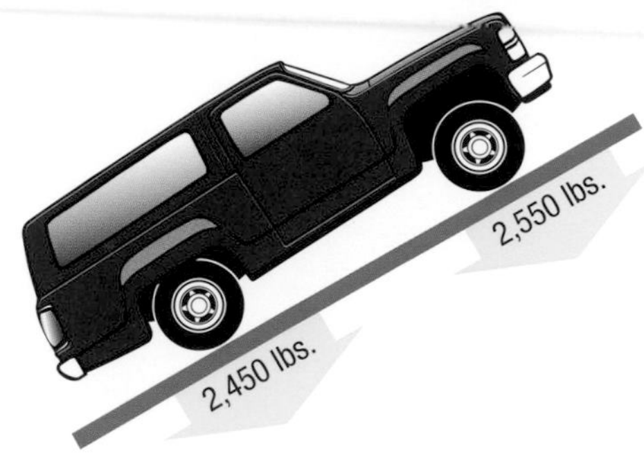

Climbing throws some of the front weight to the rear. How much depends on the steepness of the climb. Longer-wheelbase rigs transfer less weight at any given angle than short-wheelbase rigs.

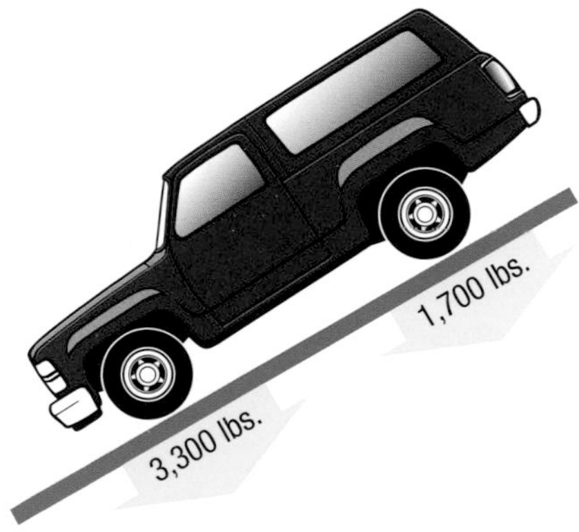

Descents can be spookier with vehicles that are very nose-heavy because even more weight will transfer from the already light rear and can severely reduce traction there.

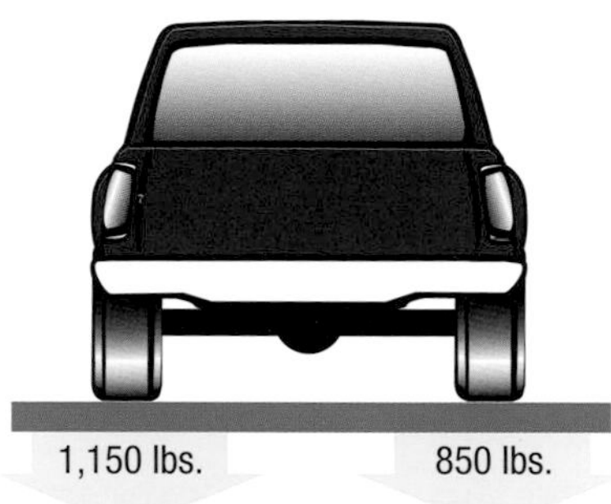

Side-to-side weight can also vary, even at one end or the other. The driver's side is almost always heavier.

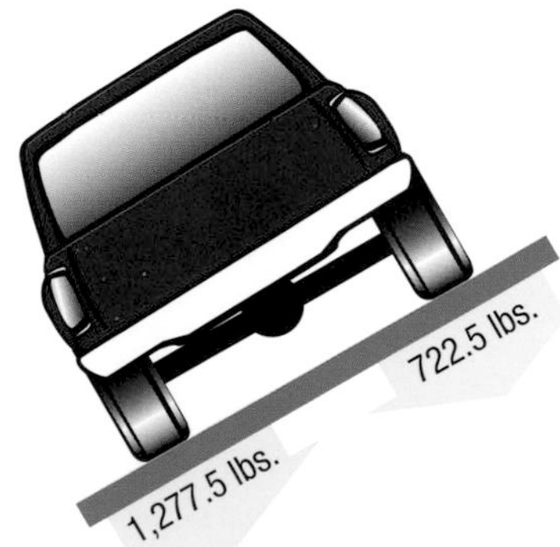

Figure on having more weight on the driver's side when it's at the low end of a sidehill.

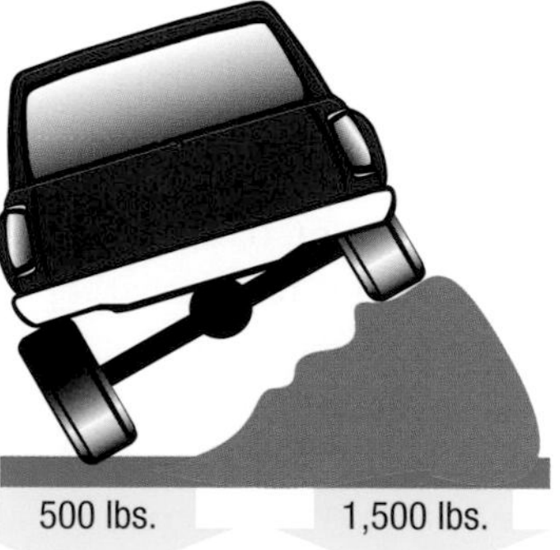

When the axle is articulated, the compressed side will be carrying most of the weight, which could allow the low side tire to slip due to lack of ground pressure.

The traction equation at work. Grip equals tire footprint times weight. This aired-down tire has fully conformed to the rock and is being pushed into the rock. Yeah, it's got grip to spare, but does that grip exceed the strength of some drivetrain part?

Take a set of 235/75R-15 tires on a vehicle that weighs 4,500 pounds. At 35 psi, these tires have a footprint of approximately 6.5×6 inches, or about 39 square inches per tire, multiplied by four tires. Assuming a 50/50 weight distribution (not likely in any front-engine vehicle), that's a ground pressure of 28.8 pounds per square inch (4500÷(39×4) = 28.846). If you lower the tire pressure of those 235s, the footprint increases to 61.2 square inches per tire, and ground pressure decreases to 18.4 psi. If you upgrade to 33×12.50-15 tires, their 35 psi-inflation footprint, 20.4 psi, offers almost the same ground pressure as the aired-down 235/75R-15. When aired down to 15 psi, the upgraded tires have a ground pressure of 13.7 psi, less than half that of the fully inflated smaller tire. These changes in ground pressure numbers from tire pressure or size may mean the difference between being *on* or *in* terra firma!

Finally, bear in mind that the above calculations do not take into account the tire voids. A mud tire, for example, may only put 70 percent of its footprint directly onto the ground. The rest is open voids in the tread. An all-terrain tire might put 85 percent of its tread in direct contact with the ground. But once the mud tire sinks into the ground a little, the voids fill and the flotation increases.

Vehicle Weight. The heavier the vehicle, the more tire grip is required to maintain traction. It will also need more engine torque and suitable gearing. It's relatively easy to find and fit the big tires that can supply enough grip to make a light or moderate-weight vehicle perform well, but as weight increases it gets tougher. Really big tires are available, but the modifications needed to fit them can be complicated.

Weight Transfer. Traction also changes according to weight transfer. When you climb, weight is transferred from the front to the rear. The opposite is true when you descend. Similarly, on side slopes, weight will transfer from the uphill to the downhill side. When the suspension is articulated, i.e., when one tire is at the upper end of suspension travel and the other tire is at the lower end of suspension travel, the upper tire is bearing most of the weight.

The actual amount of weight transfer is dependent on many factors, including the angle of the slope and the center of gravity of the vehicle. In general, a longer-wheelbase rig will transfer a bit less weight than a short-wheelbase rig. At about 25 degrees of slope (a fairly mild climb), upslope to downslope weight transfer will be 5 to 10 percent.

Tire grip on a hard surface is partially dependent upon weight or, more precisely, ground pressure. More weight, or ground pressure, will result in increased grip, but it's not proportional to the weight change. Adding 25 percent more weight will not necessarily result in 25 percent more grip. In many cases, overall grip will be reduced because the extra weight may exceed the tires' ultimate grip. Similarly, reducing the weight on a tire will decrease traction but not in proportion to the weight loss. Each tire has a weight range, at a given tire pressure, when the grip will remain relatively constant. Above or below that range, grip will be reduced. Unfortunately, that range is difficult to plot because of the many variances in tire design and construction. It becomes a "seat-o-the-pants" determination that each driver learns by feel. There are things you can predict:

1) A smaller tire footprint will lose grip sooner than a larger one.
2) Your rear tires may slip on a climb due to overloading, and the fronts may slip due to underloading.
3) Vice versa on a descent.
4) An articulated axle will usually slip first on the low, least-loaded tire.
5) If you are cross-axled (axles articulated opposite each other), both or either of the low tires will be the first to slip.

Torque Multiplication Versus Grip. The grip offered by any tire or any ground surface can be overcome by torque. Even the best tire or tractive surface can be overcome by enough torque. Torque from your engine is multiplied by the drivetrain before it's delivered to the tire. If the engine makes 100 lbs-ft. at a given rpm and has a 4:1 first-gear ratio, a 2:1 transfer case low range, and a 4:1 axle ratio, the torque delivered to the wheels will be 3,200 lbs-ft (100×4×2×4 = 3,200). That torque is pitted against the four tires' ability to grip, as well as the ground's resistance to shear. The moral here is that in some conditions you must reduce the torque delivery to the tires to maintain traction. This can mean using less throttle, using a higher gear to reduce multiplication, or substituting vehicle momentum, which will allow use of a higher gear and reduce the need for grip.

Arthur Warn's 1940s freewheeling hub invention helped transition the 4×4 into the mainstream of American society.

What's the Diff?

The differential is the heart of the axle and of many full-time four-wheel-drive transfer cases. It's a relatively simple device that has a complicated job to perform. The simple part is that it has to deliver torque to the wheels to provide motive power. It gets complicated when the vehicle turns. Then, the inner and outer wheels will rotate at different speeds, with the inner wheel slowing down and the outer wheel speeding up because the outer wheel has more distance to travel around the turn. This difference in speeds also occurs between the front and rear axles in a full-time four-wheel-drive system. Something has to give, and a system without a differential will lose traction on one tire during the turn, causing excessive tire wear, handling problems, increased steering effort, and stress on the drivetrain components.

Open Differentials—The Path of Least Resistance. The so-called "open" differential is the standard type that's been used in motor vehicles since the dawn of the motorized era. The open diff works best when there is roughly equal traction available to both tires. As the difference in traction increases, the torque through the open diff tries to take the path of least resistance, transferring to the tire with the least amount of traction. It boils down to this: if you have one wheel on pavement and the other wheel in goo, torque will go to the one in the goo. That's not going to help you when you attempt to put power to the ground and move forward.

Full-time four-wheel-drive systems with center differentials face the same problem times three. With the center diff unlocked, you can put three tires on pavement and one in goo, and the torque will go to the one in the goo, regardless of where that one tire is located. That's why full-time rigs intended for trail work have a lockable center differential.

DIFFERENTIAL THEORY:
The differential allows the wheels to rotate at different speeds for turns. The wheels' speeds will remain directly proportional to each other; i.e., one will speed up as much as the other slows down.

The pinion gear (in red) takes the torque from the driveshaft and delivers it to the ring gear (in yellow), and two things happen. First, it turns that torque 90 degrees and delivers it to the tires through the differential and axles. The differential seen in the other pictures nearby lives in the center of the ring gear. Second, the ring and pinion combine to create the axle gear ratio. The number of teeth on the ring gear divided by the number of teeth on the pinion equals the gear ratio. If there are 37 ring gear teeth and 9 pinion teeth, the ratio is 4.11:1. This means the pinion gear rotates four times for each revolution of the axle. This multiplies the torque by the high number of the gear ratio but reduces the output speed by the same amount.

The other open differential rule is this: The average speed of both axles is always equal to the speed of the ring gear. Going straight down the road, the axles and ring gear are at the same speed. Turning, the outside axle speeds up and the inside axle slows down, but the average speed of the shafts is still equal to the ring gear. With one tire in goo and the other on pavement, the pavement axle may be stopped, but the goo axle is spinning at twice ring gear speed. When averaged, it still equals ring gear speed.

The Limited-Slip Differential. The limited-slip (LS) differential operates more or less like an open diff in everyday use. But in low-traction situations, it may

DIFFERENTIAL THEORY:
With an open-diff 4×4, if one front tire and one rear tire are in traction-free goo, you are stopped, spinning one tire up front and one in back.

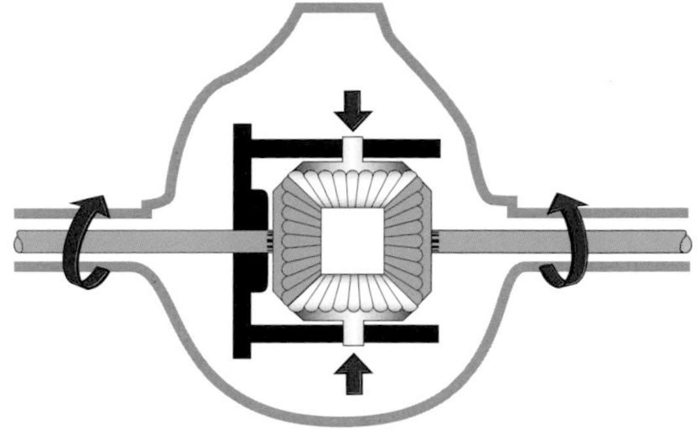

The open differential delivers torque equally to both axles (green) when the traction is equal on both sides and the vehicle is going straight. In this situation, the diff carrier (black) is turning at the same speed as the ring gear, as are the side gears (green) and the spider gears (white).

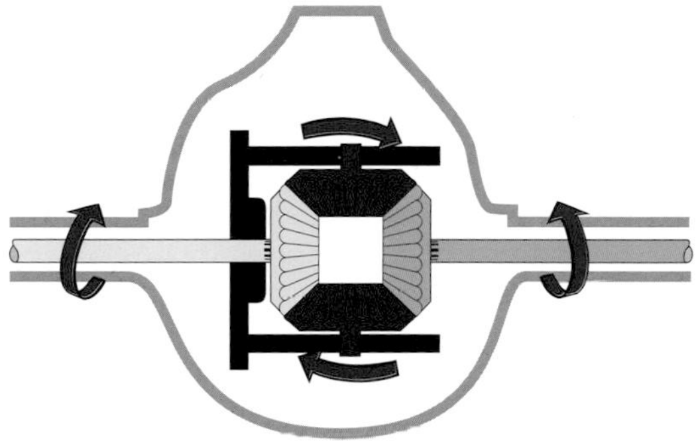

In a turning situation, one axle speeds up (green) and the other slows down (yellow). The speed changes are proportional to each other, according to the number of teeth in the side and spider gears. The carrier (black) is turning at the speed of the ring gear, and the side and spider gears are turning independently within it.

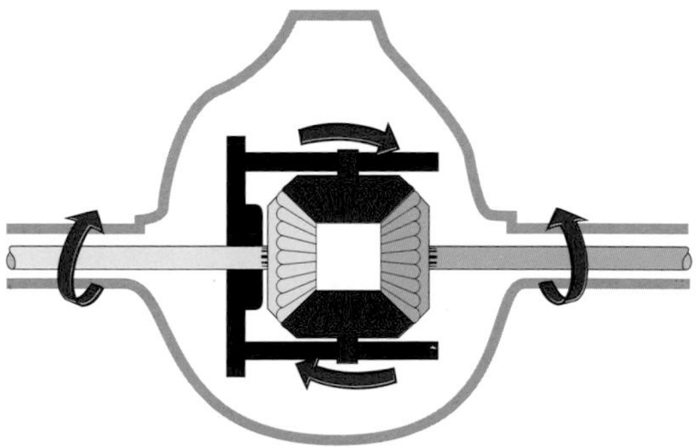

In a low-traction situation, the torque will take the path of least resistance. In this case, the green axle is in soft stuff and the yellow is on more solid ground. The yellow axle and side gear are stationary, and the carrier (black) is rotating around it. Because the spider gears are locked to the carrier, they are turning around the stationary yellow side gear and forcing the green gear to rotate and spin the loose tire at twice ring gear speed.

transfer some torque to the wheel with the most traction. The two most common types of LS are clutch-type and gear-type.

Clutch-Type Limited-Slips. The most common clutch-type LS diffs have a set of normal differential gears but with clutches at each axle. In effect, they provide a "brake" to discourage the torque from taking the path of least resistance. Call it "artificial traction!" Gear separation forces of the side and spider gears provide some clutch actuation, but in most clutch-type units, springs apply a certain amount of preload to the clutch packs. The more preload, the more braking action is applied to the axle. But what happens in a turn?

In order for the side and spider gears in the differential to work, those clutches must slip. In other words, they must overcome the built-in preload by "breaking away." If the torque required to break away is high, the clutch may not release smoothly, and the result is a chatter. If breakaway torque is very high, a tire may actually lose traction *before* the clutches release, and you get barking tires. Applying power through a turn adds to the breakaway torque by increasing gear separation forces.

There are a couple of ways to express the amount of torque that a limited-slip can transfer to a single wheel. It can be expressed as a locking factor (in percent) or as a bias ratio (x:1). A totally locked differential has a 100 percent locking factor because all the available torque can be applied to the low-traction tire. An open differential has a 0 percent locking factor because the high-traction side can receive only as much torque as the low-traction side can hold. Actually, because of the friction of the mechanical parts in the diff, not even open diffs are quite as low as 0, but they can get pretty close. Seldom do you see limited-slips with locking factors near or above 80 percent because they are so close to complete lockup that they are nearly intractable on the street.

LIMITED-SLIP THEORY:
The locking factor indicates, with a percentage, how much of the input torque can be applied to only one axle.

Bias ratio is how most manufacturers describe the performance characteristics of their limited-slip differentials. A 4:1 bias ratio (60 percent locking factor) would allow four times more torque to be supplied to the high-traction side than the low-traction side. If the low-traction tire can support 100 lbs-ft, then the

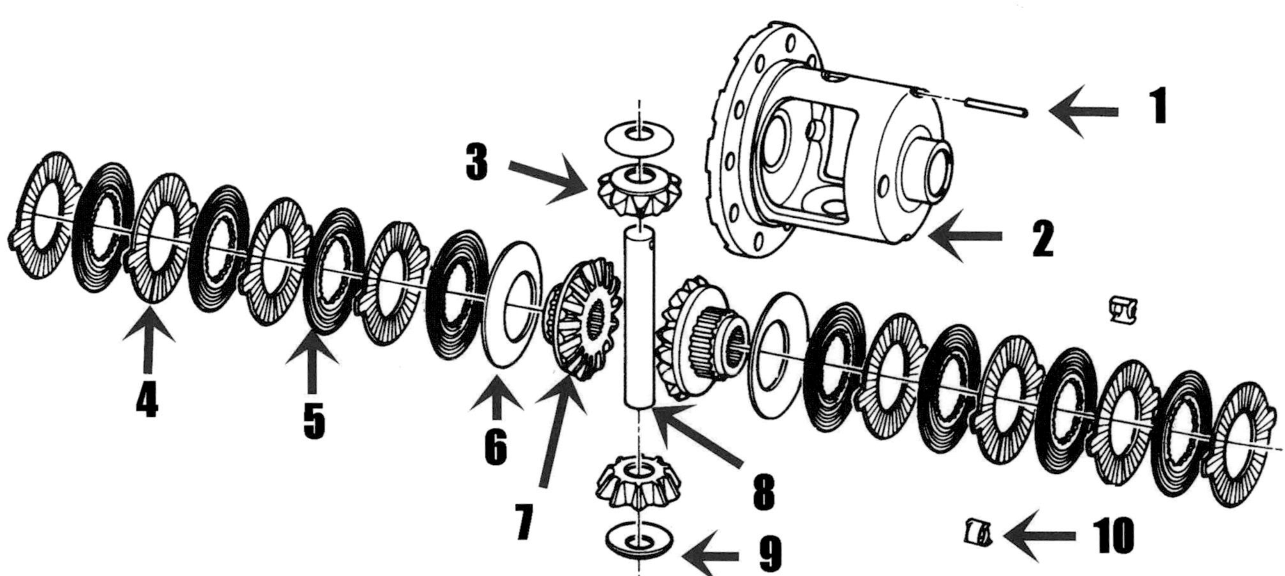

A typical clutch-type limited slip, in this case a Dana Trac-Lok, which is found in many OE 4×4 axles. **1-** Pinion shaft lock pin **2-** Differential case **3-** Spider (differential pinion) gear. **4-** Tabbed clutch plate (tabbed to case) **5-** Splined disc (splined to axle shaft) **6-** Preload spring (Belleville type) **7-** Side gear (splined to axle shaft) **8-** Pinion shaft (a.k.a. cross-shaft) **9-** Pinion thrust washer **10-** Clutch retainer clips. *Courtesy the Spicer Axle Division of the Dana Corporation*

BIAS RATIO:
The bias ratio indicates how much torque the differential can transfer to the high-traction wheel relative to the amount of torque the low-traction side can support.

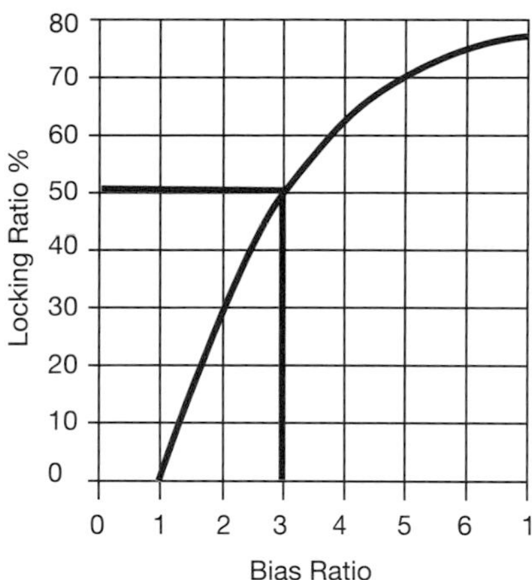

This chart shows the correlation between locking factor and bias ratio. If you understand one concept of expressing how a limited slip works, use this chart to help yourself convert from one to the other.

differential can deliver up to 400 lbs-ft to the opposite side. The amount of torque the low-traction side can absorb includes the preload or braking action built into the LS. The graph at right illustrates how locking factor and bias ratios correlate.

Clutch-type limited-slips can be set "loose" or "tight," referring to the difference in the preloaded locking factor that is built in. These range from about 25 percent on up, with the lower ratios being the milder units. Standard equipment limited-slips are built deliberately loose (25 to 50 percent) to make sure they will reach breakaway torque easily and smoothly in a turn. The smoother they do that the better, in the opinion of the OE manufacturers, even if it costs some trail performance. Their downfall is that they can be easily overcome in trail situations where a great difference in traction exists between the two tires. This can occur when a tire lifts in extreme terrain, for example, or when there is a great deal of weight on one tire and little on the other. A tight clutch-type unit will operate better when the differences in traction are greater side to side, but it may exhibit some adverse characteristics on the street, just like a true locker, inducing harsh breakaway (or none at all) in turns.

Clutch-type limited-slips usually use plate-type clutches or cone clutches. Because the cones have a metal-to-metal contact with the case halves, the cone units can be more expensive to overhaul. The plate-types are very sensitive to lubricants and need special limited-slip additives to work smoothly. In fact, if your limited-slip chatters, it could be due to the lack of that special additive. Eventually, it will destroy itself without the additive. Cone clutches are not as sensitive to lubricants, but they also can chatter. Just like any product with a friction material (brakes, clutches, etc.), the LS clutches wear and gradually get looser with time. The harder they are worked, the faster this happens.

Gear-Type Limited-Slips. Gear-type limited slip units do essentially the same thing as the clutch units, but they work quite differently. They do not have differential gears or clutches but a case full of small gears. These gears provide resistance just like the clutches. In one type, the Eaton-Detroit Truetrac, small worm-type pinion gears provide resistance via the pressure angle of the gears on the pinion, which forces them against the case and increases resistance (see the nearby illustration for more info). This provides a "brake," and the unit begins to transfer some torque to the other side. Locking factors can be changed according to the number of pinions in the unit and by varying the pressure angles (how the gears mesh) on the teeth of the worm gears. The Truetrac models use bias ratios between 2:1 and 3.5:1 (36 to 55 percent locking factor), depending on the application.

The Torsen unit (short for Torque-Sensing) is similar in concept to the Truetrac in that it uses gears and friction to provide the braking action needed to create a favorable torque bias. There are several versions of the unit, including the original Type 1 and a later Type 2, plus a few variations built for specialty markets. The Type 1 is offered in bias ratios of between 2.5:1 and 5.0:1, while the milder Type 2 is available in ratios from 1.4:1 to 3:1.

LIMITED-SLIP WORKING LIFE:
By the time a rig hits 100,000 miles, the average clutch-type limited-slip has turned into an open diff. An exception might be Eaton's relatively new carbon disc LS units that use a space-age textured Pyrolytic carbon material that is essentially a forever product.

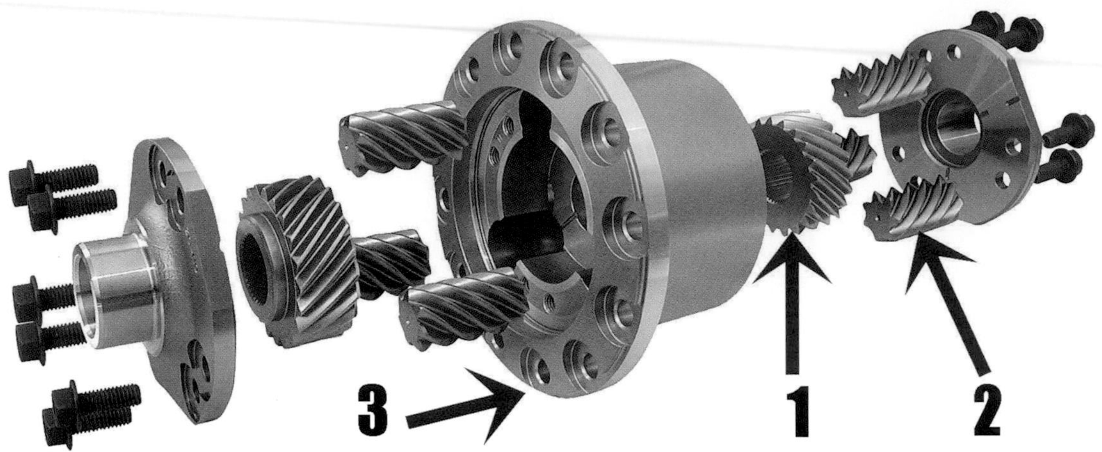

A gear-type limited slip, such as this Detroit Truetrac, uses gear friction to provide braking action. The best analogy to use is the worm gear principle. A worm gear operates freely in one direction but not the other. In the Truetrac, the element gears (2) are the "worm" and the side gears (1) are the drive gear. Locked into their pockets in the case (3), as power comes from the ring gear, it drives the case, which also pushes the element gears. Because they are being pushed in the "hard" direction, they force the side gears to turn also, which drive the axles. In turns, one axle (the outer) covers more distance than the inner, so it is essentially spinning faster. That's the "easy" direction. Because the element gears on both sides are in mesh, wheel speeds side to side are relative to each other according to the tooth ratios of the side and element gears. *Courtesy Eaton Detroit Locker*

Both the Torsen and the Truetrac require a small application of the brake pedal to be totally effective when there is a large difference in traction side to side. While the gear-type units are generally more seamless on the street than the clutch-types, even given higher bias ratios, they are more expensive and less positive in their operation without some brake pedal manipulation by the driver. For the most part, the gear-type LS units are life-of-the-vehicle products, and their purchase price reflects this.

Using Limited-Slips. Limited-slip driving techniques vary somewhat depending on whether you have a tight or loose unit, or a gear or clutch unit. On the street, the loose unit will be nearly, if not completely, transparent. Driving with the tighter clutch units, with a locking factor much above 60 percent (4:1 bias ratio), you may experience some barking of tires or unusual handling. These tendencies will increase with the locking factor.

On the trail, you can finesse a limited-slip into locking up tighter by applying a little brake. This is true of both gear- and clutch-type limited-slips. The idea is to supply a little extra braking to the unloaded tire and transfer a little more torque to the other one. You can use either the foot brake or the parking brake. In a situation where you've lost traction all around, the foot brake will help, whether your front axle is open or equipped with an LS. If it's primarily the rear slipping, using the parking brake is the best method (assuming it actuates the rear brakes) because it doesn't add braking resistance to the front tires and thereby increase the vehicle's overall traction needs. A partial application of the parking brake for the duration of the difficult situation may be all you need. If it doesn't work with the parking brake applied halfway, odds are good that giving it more parking brake won't work either.

LIMITED-SLIP FINESSE:
Unlike an automatic locker, you can't finesse a tight limited-slip into letting loose and behaving. Most people think that a gear-type limited-slip is smoother than a clutch-type with the same locking factor.

Locking Differentials. All sorts of traction-aiding differentials have been tossed under the heading of "locker." This usage not totally accurate, as you will learn. The "true" lockers are best looked at individually.

Automatic Lockers. Automatic lockers will deliver 100 percent torque to either wheel, and under light loads and equal traction, they will mimic an open diff. They may exhibit some handling quirks on the street, and this

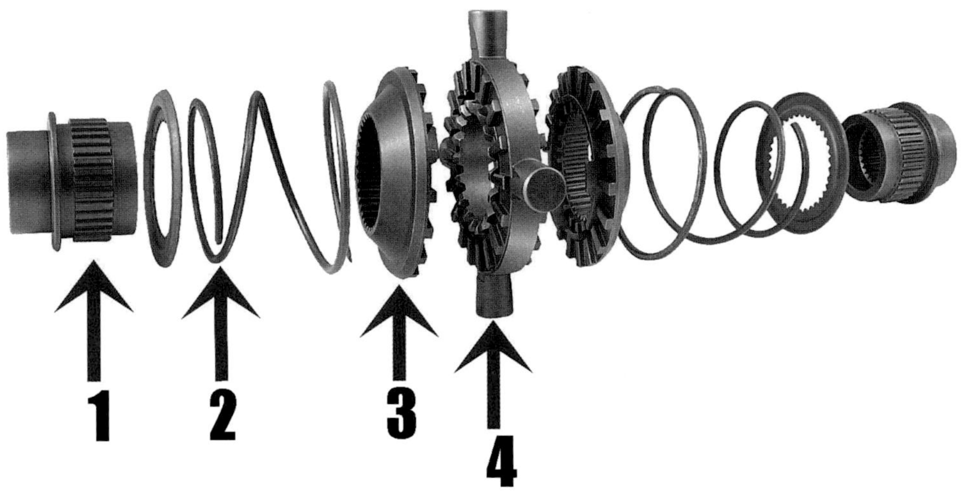

The Detroit Locker is one of the strongest, most positive lockers on the market. The basic design dates back to before World War II. The torque comes in via the central driver (4, a.k.a. the spider). The teeth on the spider mesh with the driven clutch (3). The clutches engage with the side gears (1), which are splined to the axle shaft. The clutch is splined to the side gear and can slide in and outboard a small amount. The spring (2) holds the clutches engaged with the driver, but the design of the teeth is what primarily engages the clutches and driver, and the drive torque holds them that way. When the vehicle needs to turn, center cam slots in the clutch center allows the faster wheel to "ratchet" forward against spring pressure. Too much drive torque in turns (power through a turn) may hold the unit engaged. *Courtesy Eaton Detroit Locker*

will vary from one type to another. Most use a clutch arrangement that engages when it senses a difference in wheel speed while torque is being applied.

Many people use an automatic locker in front-axle applications, but these drivers must sometimes unlock a hub or disengage the front axle to make a tight turn. An automatic locker is generally not much more expensive than a limited-slip (in some cases they are less expensive), but they are preferred by the hardercore crowd of drivers who are willing to sacrifice some on-road user-friendliness for better traction.

TRUE LOCKERS:
A true locking differential has a 100 percent locking factor—in other words, it will supply all the torque to either wheel.

ON-DEMAND LOCKERS:
An on-demand locker is ideal for front or rear axles and is safe for full-time systems. Because they are manually operated, pilot error becomes an issue, but then again, many pilots feel they can "out-think" an automatic locker.

Automatic lockers can be divided into those that replace the carrier and the "plug-in" units that use the OE carrier but replace the spider and side gears. The latter setup has the advantage of being easy to install and inexpensive. On the downside, it relies on the OE carrier for its basic strength. A good carrier combined with the plug-in locker ends up being a stout unit, but a weak carrier can make it a weak unit overall. The lockers with replacement carriers are stronger overall but are more expensive and more difficult to install.

The Lock Right and the No-Slip are plug-in lockers from PowerTrax, and the E-Z Locker and Gearless Locker are plug-ins from Eaton Detroit. The Aussie Locker operates in a similar fashion but is reputed to be a little stronger. The Detroit (or No-Spin) Locker from Eaton Detroit is an integrated carrier automatic locker for most applications.

On-Demand Lockers. On-demand lockers achieve 100 percent lockup by various means, but they are all driver-controlled. They can be operated hydraulically, by a cable, via air, by vacuum, or even electrically. The beauty is that until they are actuated, they operate as a normal open diff. This gives you 100 percent traction when you need it, with no side effects. This makes them ideal for full-time four-wheel-drive rigs, or in front-axle applications. They are the most expensive and the most complicated type of locker.

The four brands you will see in North America are the ARB Air Locker, the electric Eaton E-Locker, the electric Auburn ECTED, and the Ox cable locker. A couple of others have come and gone. Between these four, you can find applications for most popular axles and 4×4s.

Variable-Bias Lockers. Back in the 1980s, Eaton, most famous for building the GM "Posi-Traction" limited-slips, built an automatic locker that has been often called the "Gov-Lok," though Eaton does not advocate that term. It came as an option on a variety of GM trucks and SUVs. A new version, the Command Traxx, is similar in operation and is available on recent GM trucks as an option. Equipped with clutch packs, it has a very loose limited-slip capability, but it also uses a complex flyweight governor device that senses differences in wheel speed. With a 100- to 150-rpm difference in wheel speed, the flyweight setup ratchets against the clutch packs to apply increased clamping pressure, effectively locking them up solid. When wheel speed equalizes, the unit releases the clutches and unlocks itself. The flyweight releases the locker at around 25 miles per hour to prevent handling problems.

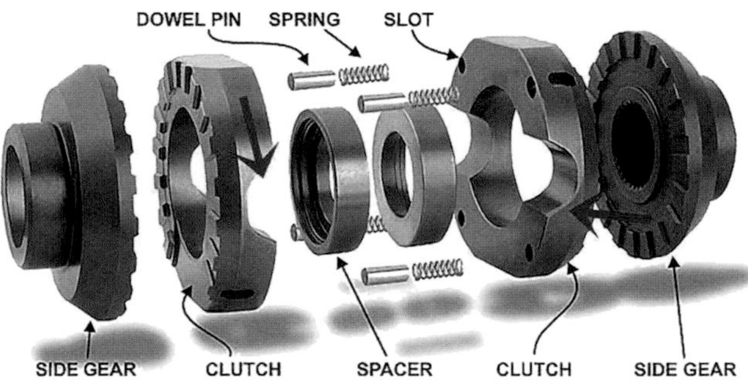

The Detroit E-Z Locker operates in a manner similar to the PowerTrax Lock-Right Locker and the Aussie Locker. Torque comes from the original carrier via the original (or a high-strength replacement) pinion shaft (not shown). It comes down between the two clutch halves in the slot marked with red arrows. The slots are very carefully designed to be sized larger than the pin. Torque pushes the pin up onto the ramped outer edges of the slots, forcing them outboard into the side gears, which are splined to the axle shaft and fit where the original side gears are mounted in the carrier. The teeth on the clutches mesh with the teeth on the side gears. More torque forces them into tighter mesh. In turns, the faster side can overrun and ratchet ahead because it releases the torque on that side, allowing the clutch to ramp down on the pinion shaft. The pins and springs keep the clutches mildly preloaded outboard and aligned. The spacers keep the clutches centered on the axle shafts. *Courtesy Eaton Detroit Locker*

Using Automatic Lockers. The on-demand lockers operate as an open diff when disengaged, so they do not offer any adverse symptoms on the street. With most of the automatics, you will need to adopt a new style of driving to avoid the worst of the clicking and clacking, barking tires, and unusual handling characteristics. This information should forearm you and not steer you away from any type of locker. I've used a Detroit Locker in the rear of my own rig (more for trail than street) and think the compromises made in driving style are more than worth the utility and awesome strength of the unit on the trail. As I've mentioned before, informed choices are the best ones.

Because the automatic lockers (Detroit Locker, E-Z Locker, Lock-Right) operate via differences in wheel speed, every time you make a turn, they may make a ratcheting noise as the wheel on the faster side releases. This is because the teeth of the clutches are snapping past the teeth of the driver according to the differing speed of the wheels. Don't worry, the noise is not harmful, though it sounds like it is. In fact, I once heard a locker manufacturer's representative call this noise "free advertising." The PowerTrax No-Slip is reputedly an exception to the "ratcheting rule" because it contains a synchronizer system. The "SofLocker" version of the Detroit Locker is also considerably quieter than its earlier iteration.

Lockers will go from ratcheting to lockup as soon as more than a tiny bit of power is applied. If it locks, that's when our second adverse characteristic starts. The tires bark because they are locked together at the same speed. The locker doesn't allow one to speed up and one to slow down, as is normal for an open diff in a turn. Something's gotta give, so the tires let out a few barks as they slip. At that moment, you have lost some traction.

Suddenly applying throttle while going around a long, sweeping turn at speed can result in momentary locking. The same thing can happen when you suddenly lift off the throttle in a turn—you can get a momentary wiggle of the tail. Fortunately, the lockers usually release quickly on deceleration. If you continue to use power in a turn at higher speeds, you can get into trouble in slippery conditions.

So what's the answer to tricky lockers on the street? The installation or owner's manual for the particular unit will outline the cautions specific to that locker, but here are some general tips. One primary key is not to apply power, or much power, in a turn. Try to coast around the corner or use only very light throttle. Obviously, making a turn from a dead stop cannot be done without use of the throttle, but you can minimize the bad effects by going light on the accelerator. If the unit locks up at an inopportune moment, a partial lifting of the throttle (reducing the torque load) is usually enough to "finesse" it into releasing. The adverse effects are variable according to the particular combination of vehicle characteristics. Long-wheelbase, heavy vehicles seem less affected than shorter, lighter rigs.

On the trail, the automatic locker becomes your best buddy. It provides instant traction when you need it. Since traction here is almost always less than on pavement, the unit will feel quiet and docile. Some of the aforementioned handling quirks may occasionally be an issue in low-traction situations, such as on a snowy dirt road. There are very few other issues with an automatic locker on the trail. Occasionally, it may lock up and make tight maneuvering difficult.

If you have an automatic locker up front, your first trip probably taught you what to do. If the unit engages, it's nearly impossible to maneuver, and it's very hard on the front axle shaft universal joints when you have the wheels cranked over hard. Sometimes releasing the bind on the drivetrain by going to neutral or backing up will get you through the turn. Most often, you can simply unlock one hub to make the turn. If your vehicle is equipped with a twin-stick transfer case (either OE or aftermarket), you can disengage the front axle momentarily to make the turn.

Using On-Demand Lockers. As previously mentioned, on-demand lockers are virtually transparent on the street. A general caution: make sure they don't get accidentally engaged on the pavement in day-to-day use. Locate the controls so they cannot be accidentally activated by a curious kid pulling a "What does this do, Daddy" while you are cruising down the highway.

With the ARB Air Locker, I further recommend that you install a master isolating switch between the ignition power source wire and the main relay. A switch like this effectively kills the system when it's switched off. This will make sense when you see the ARB harness or wiring diagram. The switch is an easy retrofit if yours was not wired this way originally. Just about any type of locker can be protected from accidental application with some ingenuity. I would recommend the effort if you have kids or a vehicle that is driven by a number of people, some of whom may not be familiar with all the controls.

LOCKER FINESSE:
When your automatic locker locks up, you can finesse release by unloading the drivetrain. Do this by gently reversing or going into neutral briefly and letting the vehicle roll a few feet.

The ideal method is to engage the locker just before you need it. Read the terrain and hit the button or work the lever just prior to assaulting the obstacle. If you misread the terrain and find the locker isn't needed, you may disengage it at any time. The bigger problems come if you misread the other way and find the locker is needed partway through an obstacle. It's OK to engage the locker in the middle of the obstacle, but don't do it while wildly spinning the tires or with the drivetrain under a severe load. In either situation, the locker may refuse to engage fully, or it may break due to shock loading. Bear in mind that the unit may not immediately engage or disengage if the axle is under a torque load. The on-demand locker can be useful on the street in snow and ice, mostly to get you moving. Once the vehicle is in motion, however, be sure to disengage it, or the severe handling changes a fully locked rear axle imparts may send you into the nearest snow bank.

You won't need a front on-demand locker often, but it can mean the difference between making it or not on some very hard obstacles. A locker up front will induce many odd handling characteristics, so it's not something you'll need on the street. Trying to turn with the unit locked is very hard on front axles, particularly front-axle U-joints or CV joints. For these reasons, you will find that the on-demand front locker is generally used only for brief periods. Bear in mind

FRONT LOCKER FINESSE:
The most obvious vehicle quirk with the front locker engaged is an unwillingness to turn. The vehicle will want to travel in a straight line.

The Power Path

- Blue: Potential Path,
- Red: Absolute Path,
- Gray: Low-Traction Surface,
- Green: High-Traction Surface.

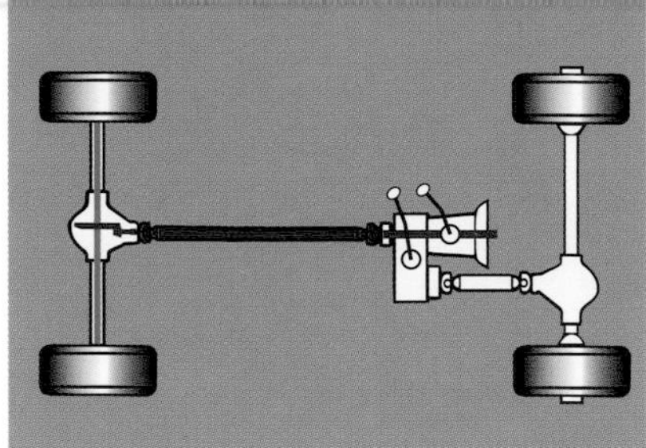

Part-time four-wheel drive in two-wheel drive. Power is delivered through the trans and the T-case to the ring gear. On this high-traction surface, the power can use both axles.

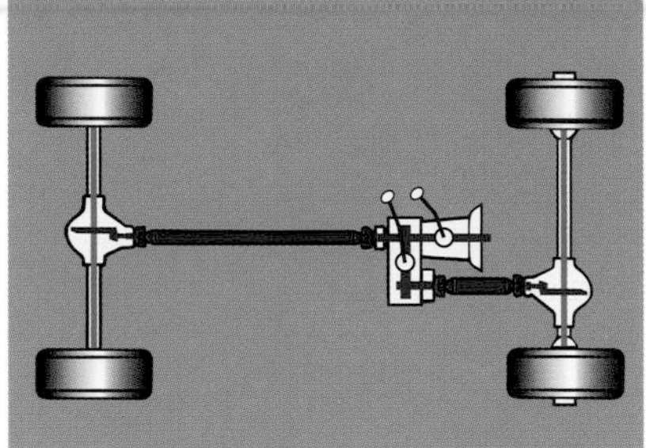

Part-time four-wheel drive in four-wheel drive. On this high-tractive surface, both the front and rear diffs are delivering power equally to all four wheels.

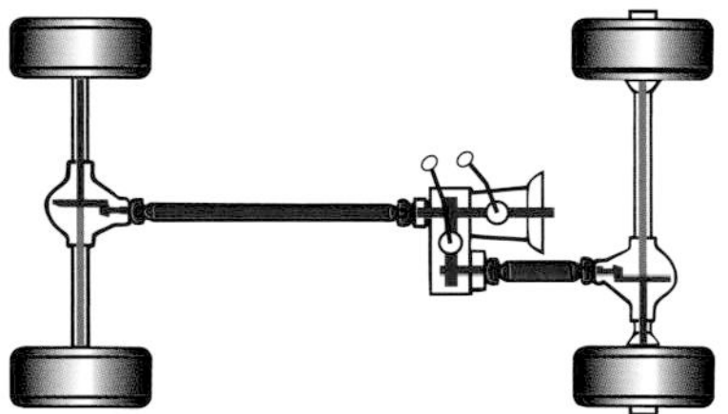

Part-time four-wheel drive on a low-tractive surface. You can see that the power has taken the path of least resistance and gone to one tire on each axle. Which side it will take depends on which tire has the best traction. It could be opposite, like this, or both on one side or the other.

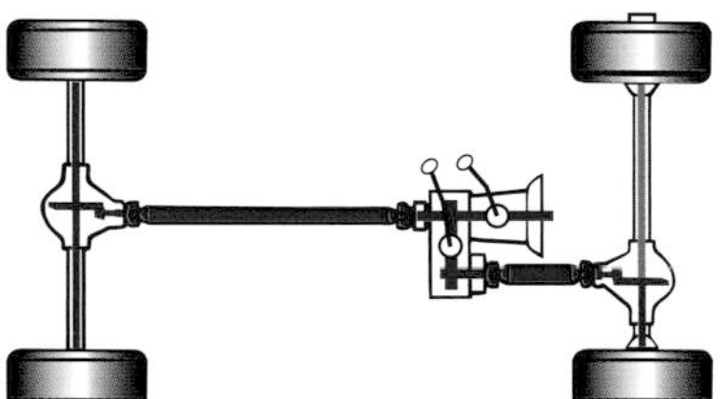

Here's a part-time system on a low-traction surface in four-wheel drive with a rear locker. In this configuration, you've got three tires pulling.

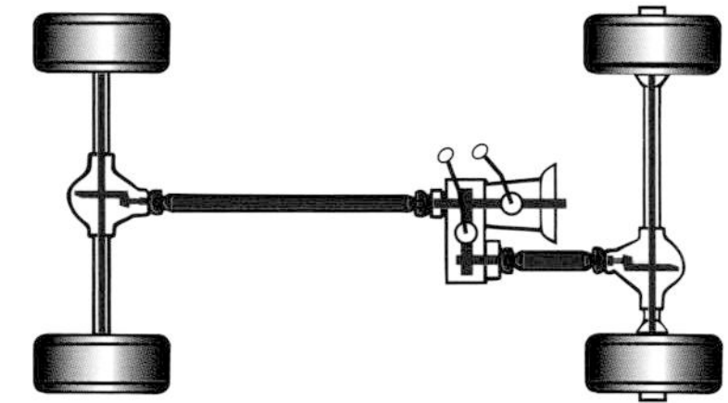

A part-time system with *true* four-wheel drive, meaning lockers in both axles. All four tires are pulling in this configuration.

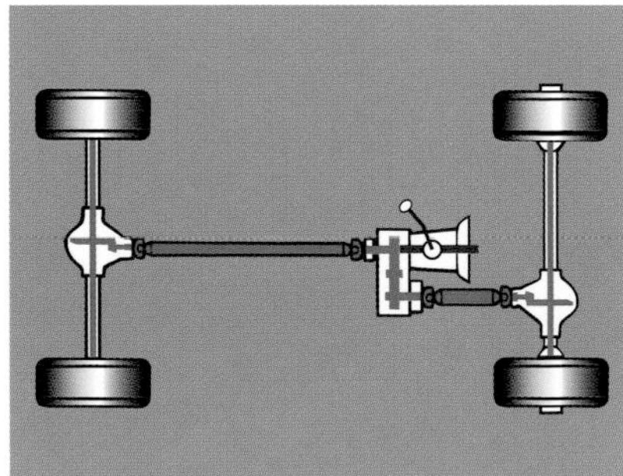

This a full-time system with the center diff unlocked. On hard pavement, it can deliver power to the front or rear and allows some difference of speed front to rear. With open diffs, the same thing happens at the axles.

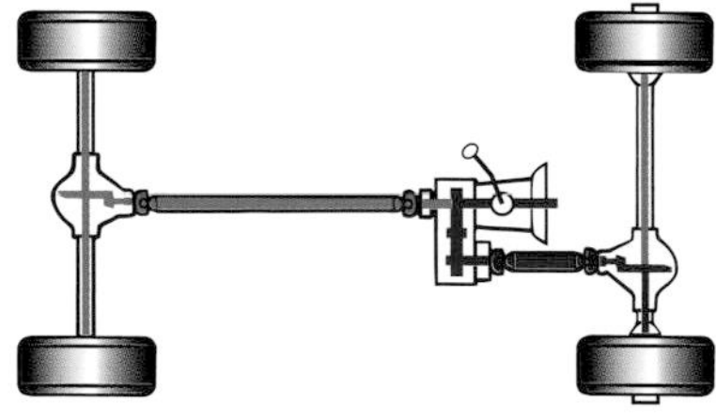

This is what happens when a low-traction situation is encountered with the center diff unlocked. Power will take the path of least resistance . . . to one tire! Could be any of the four.

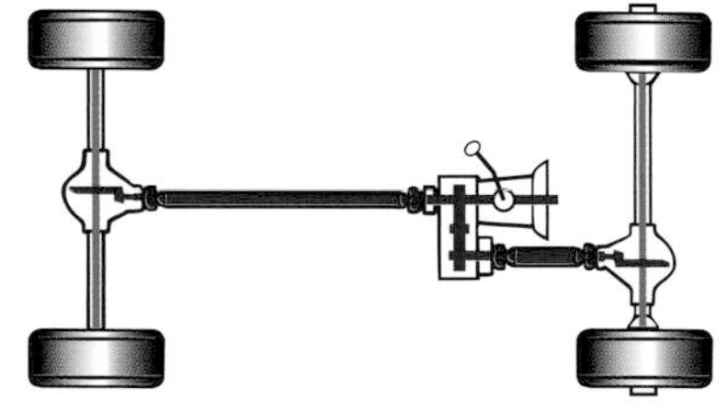

With the center diff locked, the full-time unit becomes just like a part-time rig in four-wheel drive.

The ARB Air Locker is an on-demand locker that is actuated by air. It works as a standard differential, albeit with four spider gears rather than two (which makes the unit stronger), until the operator applies air pressure. Here is the example of how the first-generation Air Locker works: The air pressure pushes the U-ring (1) and piston (2), which actuates the clutch gear (4) to lock it against the splined side gear (3), which is splined to the case. This effectively locks the two axles to the case and provides a 100 percent lockup. *Courtesy ARB*

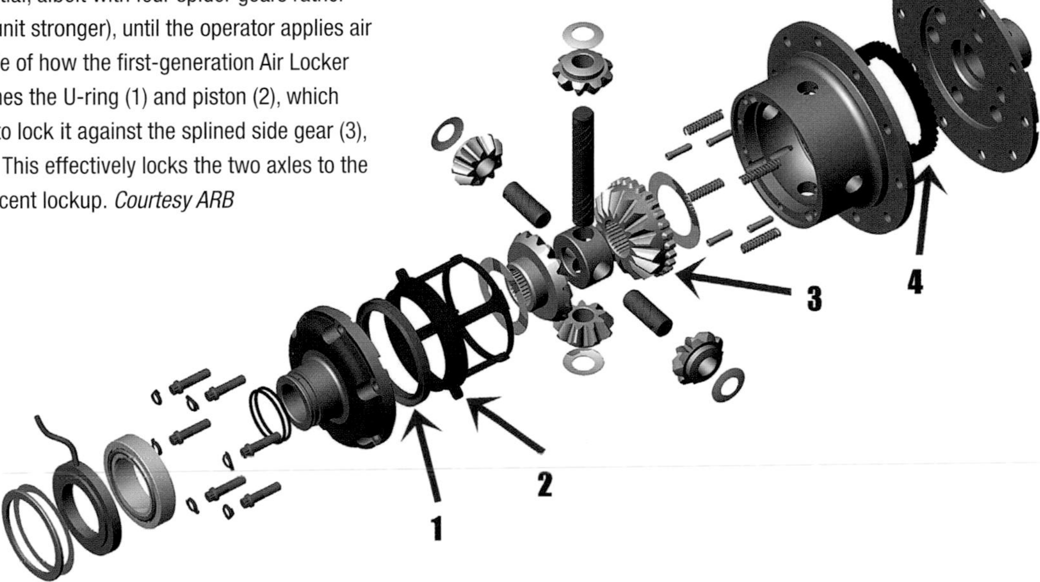

again that if you have the drivetrain in a bind or with a torque load on the front axle, the locker may not immediately disengage, so you may be forced to back up or roll in neutral to coax disengagement.

Traction-Control Systems. Electronic traction control (ETC) appears on some newer SUVs. ETC is a slick adaptation of the ABS system that, with a little extra programming, uses the same equipment to do a completely different job. When the wheel speed sensors read a large differential in wheel speed on one axle, the ETC system will partially engage the brake on the faster wheel, assuming it is the low-traction side. As discussed in the open diff section, this will force the differential to transfer torque to the opposite wheel, which is presumed to have more traction. The system works reasonably well, but in my experience, it is usually a little slow to engage. You may have to induce a little more wheelspin than you think is prudent before it fully engages. Each system is different, and you will need to experiment to determine the best techniques for each one.

TRACTION-CONTROL FINESSE: Some traction-control systems will shut down after certain periods in operation to keep the brakes cool. Others have brake overheat warnings.

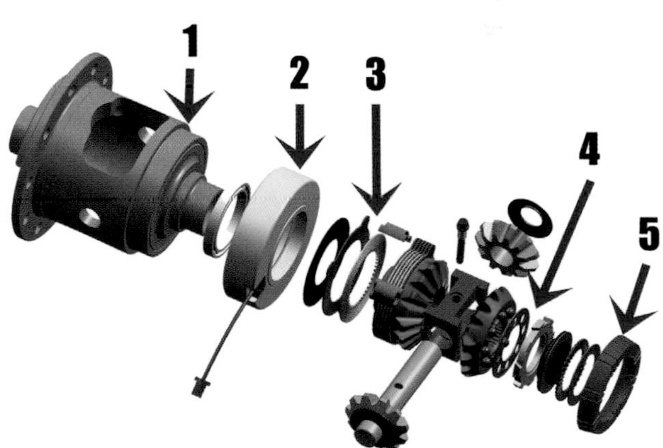

The Auburn ECTED is one of a new generation of electrically actuated lockers. They all use an electromagnet but work somewhat differently in detail. The ECTED (for Electronically Controlled Traction Enhancing Differential) has a mild limited-slip feature, which uses gear separation forces to apply a small amount of pressure on the clutch pack (3). With power applied to the electromagnet (2), the pilot cone is pulled hard into its slot in the case (1), and that extra friction allows the bearing balls to ride up on their ramps. That pushes the side gears hard against the clutch packs, which locks the unit. *Courtesy Auburn Gear*

CHAPTER 3
4×4 Ratings: 1960–2008 4×4s

For the few years it was available in the U.S. (1994–1997), the Land Rover Defender 90 earned high marks. The North American version is one of the best stock performers on the planet. It came with relatively big tires, a stout aluminum V-8, a five-speed manual or four-speed auto (on '97s only), a flexible coil-spring suspension, and four-wheel disc brakes. It's very durable and modification-friendly. Buildup parts are not overflowing, but there are more than enough to build the D90 to a high level. On the downside, you can buy two used Jeep Wranglers for the price of one used D90, and the buildup parts are similarly priced.

What follows are some clues to picking a 4×4 suitable for four-wheeling. I didn't deal with 4×4s prior to 1960 (unless there was a model that straddled the cutoff year) because they are either too primitive to be of much use on today's highways or they would require a tremendous amount of upgrading to become so. To qualify for inclusion, they had to be a "true" 4×4, i.e., have a transfer case with a low range. They also had to be domestically manufactured or imported to the United States. Sorry, Canadians. I can't promise to include some of the unusual import models you got that we didn't, but you will find most of yours are here. In some cases I have grouped years of particular vehicles together—even if there were significant changes in the model within that time period—if they were all similar in performance. Here are explanations of the different categories used for the ratings.

On-Road Performance: This is the vehicle's suitability as a daily driver in stock form. The criteria I used were those qualities that make a vehicle suitable in today's driving environment for what I perceive to be an "average" driver. You will find that most older vehicles are rated with lower numbers and vice versa. Factors taken into account are economy, ride quality, handling, braking, noise, and comfort features. Because I have not driven each and every vehicle listed, in some cases I relied on period tests, third-party test information, and specifications to make my rating. I did not break these ratings down according to the bazillion trim levels offered but instead, again, give an "average" rating. In looking at particular vehicles, common sense would tell you that a "bare-bones" rig would be less comfortable than an optioned-out version.

Off-Highway Performance: The vehicle's trail prowess in stock form. The criterion here is being able to get into off-roading of lower-middle-level difficulty. If a vehicle can do that, it gets a "3."

Modification Potential: I assigned a rating that describes how suitable the vehicle is for the common,

ALL-WHEEL DRIVES:
For day-to-day use and inclement weather only, all-wheel-drive cars and SUVs are a better choice. With a lower center of gravity and superior handling, they will always outperform the off-highway-capable rigs on the highway, in good or poor weather. If you plan to venture off the paved roads, then the advantage turns to the four-wheel-drives built for that purpose.

Off-highway legend Ned Bacon's buggy sorta looks like a Jeep, but it's not. It's a hand-built rig with components selected for maximum trail performance. It's missing even the most elementary comfort items. While there are only a few rigs that could follow this rig in tough terrain, if Ned had to drive it on the highway, he wouldn't get around as much as he does.

At the other side of the Great Divide is this stock S-Series Jimmy four-door SUV that's stymied by one of the milder trail challenges. On the other hand, this owner wouldn't hesitate to drive this rig on a 3,000-mile jaunt to Florida. The S-series trucks and SUVs in general have a good basic platform, limited mainly by a weak front axle. A good solid-axle conversion is the "hallelujah" element for these trucks that turns them into super 'wheelers. Unfortunately, such kits have come and gone several times over the years. At this writing, the only option is a custom conversion. That could change.

basic mods necessary to increase trail performance. The yardstick I used was a dual-purpose rig capable of traversing a difficult trail but also of being driven on the street—not an extreme rig, trailered to and from the trail. This does not indicate how much coverage the vehicle has in the aftermarket, just its suitability, so a vehicle could get a high score here and a low score for aftermarket coverage. The vehicle must be somewhat suitable for a basic lift to incorporate a larger tire, have a reasonably stout drivetrain for the tire upgrade, and have reasonably good clearances, approach, departure, and breakover angles, and suitable dimensions for moderately difficult trail work. If a vehicle meets these criteria, it will get a "3."

Aftermarket Coverage: How well is the vehicle served by the aftermarket? I looked to see if the buildup basics like lifts, wheels, basic recovery gear, basic performance equipment, gearing changes, and traction enhancements are available in bolt-on form. If a vehicle is able to get into the moderate 'wheeling level with said mods, and there are at least a couple of choices in each area, it gets a minimum of "3." Bear in mind that products come and go, so my aftermarket evaluations could be rendered moot by changes in product availability over time.

Here's the 4×4 that started the recreational 'wheeling craze. The Jeep flatfender is eternal and a cornerstone of the hobby. Though getting fewer in numbers, it's still a part of the four-wheeling scene. Lots of buildup material is still available, though unaltered older CJs are in the collector category. The flatfender is not an easy buildup in many ways. The stock suspension (short springs) has many limitations, and beyond a very basic level it needs to have a completely new suspension system installed with longer springs. Also, there isn't much room under the hood for an engine bigger than a smallish V-6. Converting to V-8 power leads to many compromises and a very nose-heavy unit.

The 1986–1995 Samurai is one of the formerly unsung heroes of the SWB crowd. It came into great favor in the 1990s and still has a good aftermarket following. Its size enables it to fit just about anywhere, and because it's a basic, straightforward design, it lends itself to modifications. Comfort isn't a strong suit, but it's no worse than many other SWB utility rigs. The key buildup caution is to keep it light. The stock engines don't have a lot of power. An engine swap to a bigger four is a big help.

4×4 SAFETY:
A four-wheel-drive vehicle, whether it be SUV or truck, is not a sports car, and even the safest car is not idiot-proof. Four-bys are not inherently unsafe, but they are much less forgiving of driver error than the ordinary car.

Key: 1 = Very Low, 2 = Low, 3 = Average, 4 = High, 5 = Very High	**On-Road Performance**	**Off-Highway Performance**	**Modification Potential**	**Aftermarket Support**
Acura				
1996–1999 SLX	4	3+	2	1
AM General				
1993–1994 H-1	3	5	5	3
1995–2006 H-1	3+	5	5	3
Austin				
1958–1968 Gipsy	2	3	2	1
Cadillac				
1999–2008 Escalade	5	3	3	2
Chevrolet				
1960–1966 Pickup	2	3	4	2
1960–1966 Suburban	2+	3	4	2
1967–1972 Pickup	3	3	4	3
1967–1972 Suburban	3	3	4	3
1969–1972 Blazer	3	3	4	3
1973–1986 Pickup	3	3	4	4
1973–1991 Suburban	3	3	4	4
1973–1991 Blazer K	3	3	4	4
1979–1982 Pickup LUV	3	3	3	1
1983–1993 Pickup S	3	3-	3	3
1983–1994 Blazer S	3	3-	3	3
1987–2000 Pickup K	3	3	3	4
1992–1994 Blazer K	3+	3	3	4
1992–1999 Suburban	3+	3	3	4
1994–2003 Pickup S	3	3	3	3
1994–2003 PU ZR2 S	3	3+	3	3
1995–2005 Blazer S	3+	3	3	3
1995–2008 Tahoe	4	3	3	4
1996–2005 Blazer ZR2 S	3+	3+	3	3
1999–2004 Tracker	3	3	3	3
2001–2008 Pickup K	3+	3	3	4+
2000–2008 Suburban	4	3	3	3+
2002–2008 TrailBlazer	4	3-	2	2
2002–2008 Avalanche	4	3	3	3
2004–2008 Pickup Colorado	3+	3	3	3

Key: 1 = Very Low, 2 = Low, 3 = Average, 4 = High, 5 = Very High	**On-Road Performance**	**Off-Highway Performance**	**Modification Potential**	**Aftermarket Support**
Dodge				
1946–1968 WM Power Wagon	2-	3+	4	2
1950–1968 M-37	1	3+	4	2
1960–1971 W-Series Pickup	2	3	4	2
1960–1966 Town Wag/Panel	2+	3	4	2
1972–1993 W-Series Pickup	3	3	4	3+
1974–1993 Ramcharger	3	3	4	3
1982–1993 Ram 50	3	3	3	2
1987–1996 Dakota	3	3	3	2
1997–2004 Dakota	3+	3	3	3
1905–2008 Dakota	3+	3	3	3
1987–1989 Raider	3	3	3	1
1994–2008 Ram Pickup	4	3	4	5
1998–2008 Durango	4	3	3	3
Ford				
1960–1966 F-Series Pickup	2	3	4	2
1966–1977 Bronco	3	3+	4	5
1967–1979 F-Series Pickup	2	3	4	2
1978–1979 Bronco	3	3+	4	4
1980–1996 F-Series Pickups	3	3	4	4
1980–1996 Bronco	4	3+	4	4
1983–1997 Ranger Pickup	3	3	4	4
1984–1990 Bronco II	3	3	4	3+
1990–1997 Explorer	3+	3	4	4
1997–2007 F Series	3+	3	4	5
1997–2002 Expedition	4	3	4	3
1997–2006 Excursion	4	3	4	4
1998–2008 Explorer	4	3	3+	3+
1998–2008 Ranger	3	3	3	3+
2003–2008 Expedition	4	3	3	3
Geo				
1989–1997 Tracker	3+	3	3	3

TRAIL MONSTERS:
If your vehicle begins to creep further and further into that "trail monster" category as you add to it, consider relegating it to "trail use only" status and use a more suitable vehicle for day-to-day transportation or hauling your precious family around town. You may even wisely consider trailering it to and from the trail.

One of your best bets in a SWB is the 1987–1995 Wrangler YJ. This is a solid platform for a buildup at any level. They can be made into relatively comfortable daily drivers and still retain a high level of trail prowess. At the other end of the spectrum, they can be turned into radical trail machines with few peers. There isn't much you can't do with a YJ, from V-8 power on down. The leaf-spring suspension isn't as trendy as the newer coilers, but it's pretty easy to get it dialed in for maximum performance.

The ubiquitous 1973–1991 solid-axle Suburban does surprisingly well on the trail with a few modifications. Because it starts out as a very truck-like machine, the mods don't become a major detriment. The '73–'91 K-series GM trucks and Blazers/Jimmys are all very buildable, and performance products abound. They also have great swapability among the GM range, allowing things like sliding a three-quarter-ton drivetrain under a half-ton. This older Sub made quite a reputation for itself around Moab 10 years ago. There's room in this rig for everyone and everything. If there is a downside, it would be a lack of day-to-day comfort (compared to a newer truck) and poor fuel economy.

The short full-sized SUVs of past years like the Blazer, Bronco, and Ramcharger offer a decent compromise between size and capacity. Using truck chassis and drivetrains, they have a good deal of buildup potential without major sacrifices in day-to-day drivability. You also have the option of upgrading the drivetrain with three-quarter-ton axles (bolt-in for the most part) to mount big tires safely.

One of the best, most comfortable, and most affordable bridges over the Great Divide is the 1993–1998 Jeep Grand Cherokee ZJ. A mild lift, a tire upgrade, and lockers turn it into a force to be reckoned with, but it retains the "Grand" part of its personality. Its upper-level buildup potential is somewhat limited by its rather vulnerable body, but there are fixes. The basic platform shares many common features with the popular Jeep Cherokee XJ and even the Jeep Wrangler.

HALF-TON 4×4S:
The compact, midsized, or short-bed full-sized half-ton pickups are better choices than three-quarter or one-ton trucks for combined street/trail work, if their more limited cargo and towing capacities fit your needs.

The 1984–2001 Jeep Cherokee XJ is a bargain machine with lots of potential in stock or built-up forms. They are a little short of fenderwell space, requiring more lift for bigger tires, but they are very well-addressed by the aftermarket suppliers, so mild to wild buildups are possible. They have good trail dimensions, and the unitized body is stout enough in stock form for most types of four-wheeling. The structure of the four-door bodies is reputed to be a bit stronger than the two-doors because of the extra door pillar.

This older Range Rover is tackling one of the hardest trails in western Colorado, the notorious 21 Road. Note the armor up front, the rocker protection, and the rear quarter-panel guards. These make the expensive aluminum bodywork safe from all but the worst encounters. This protection is the key element in any SUV's successful trail forays into the harder-core realms. More vulnerable than a more utilitarian rig, they are also expensive to repair when they are damaged. The 1988–1995 "classic" four-door Range Rover is the most common type in the United States. You won't find them on every street corner, but they are not outrageously priced, and buildup parts are available.

The Chevy Avalanche (2004 shown) raised some eyebrows with its 2002 introduction, but it has proven to be a useful SUV . . . or should I say SUT (Sport Utility Truck). It's essentially a half- or three-quarter-ton Chevy Suburban (they are available in both ratings) with a small pickup bed. Most aftermarket products that are available for the same-year Chevy pickup/Suburban are applicable to the Avalanche. The wonderful GM swapability is still present after all these years, so the buildups can go beyond the aftermarket. As with many GM IFS trucks, the weak links are the front axle and suspension, especially the 8.25-inch front diff on half-tons. Beyond solid front-axle swaps (which are available for many late GM trucks), tire size moderation (no more than 35s) and avoiding front lockers are the best ways to keep the IFS GMs in one piece. *Courtesy Chevrolet*

Key: 1 = Very Low, 2 = Low, 3 = Average, 4 = High, 5 = Very High	**On-Road Performance**	**Off-Highway Performance**	**Modification Potential**	**Aftermarket Support**
GMC				
1960–1966 Pickup K	2	3	4	2
1960–1966 Suburban	2+	3	4	2
1967–1972 Pickup K	3	3	4	3
1967–1972 Suburban	3+	3	4	3
1970–1972 Jimmy	3+	3	4	3
1973–1986 Pickup	3	3	4	4
1973–1991 Suburban	3	3	4	4
1973–1991 Jimmy K	3	3	4	4
1983–1993 Pickup S	4	3-	3	3
1983–1994 Jimmy S	4	3-	3	3
1987–2000 Pickup K	4	3	3	4
1992–1999 Suburban	4	3	3	4
1994–2003 Pickup S	4	3	3+	3
1994–2003 PU ZR2 S	4	3+	3+	3
1995–2001 Jimmy S	4	3	3+	3
1992–2008 Yukon	4	3	3	4
2000–2008 Yukon XL	4	3	3	3
2001–2008 Pickup K	4	3	3+	4+
2002–2008 Envoy	4	3-	2	2
2004–2008 Pickup Canyon	4	3	3	3
Honda				
1994–2002 Passport	4	3	3	3
2006–2008 Ridgeline	4	3	3	2
Hummer				
2003–2008 H2	4	4	4	4
2006–2008 H3	4	4	3	3
Infiniti				
1997–2003 QX4	5	3	3	2
2004–2008 QX56	5	3	3	2
International Harvester				
1961–1965 Scout	2	3+	4	2
1966–1971 Scout	3	3+	4	2
1961–1968 Pickup C	2	3	4	2
1961–1968 Travelall	3-	3	4	2
1969–1975 Pickup D	3	3	4	2
1969–1975 Travelall	3	3	4	2
1972–1980 Scout II	3	3	4	4-

Key: 1 = Very Low, 2 = Low, 3 = Average, 4 = High, 5 = Very High	**On-Road Performance**	**Off-Highway Performance**	**Modification Potential**	**Aftermarket Support**
Isuzu				
1981–1987 PUP Pickup	3	3	3	1
1984–1991 Trooper II	3	3	3	2
1989–1995 Pickup	3	3	3	2
1991–1997 Rodeo	3+	3	3	3
1992–2002 Trooper	4	3	3	2
1990–1994 Amigo	3	3	3	2
1996–2000 Hombre Pickup	3	3	3	3
1998–2004 Rodeo	4	3	3	3
1998–2000 Amigo	3+	3	3	2
1999–2001 VehiCROSS	3+	4	3	2
2003–2008 Ascender	4	3-	2	2
2006–2008 i350	4	3	3	2

Even ultralong pickups can do some trail work. This one is bone stock and is traversing a moderately difficult trail. The key element is maneuvering room. The serious detriments to long-wheelbase trucks are ramp breakover angles and the turning circle. They need really big tires and lifts to get clearance under their vulnerable midsections, and this can create other problems and costs. Not much can be done from the turning circle perspective.

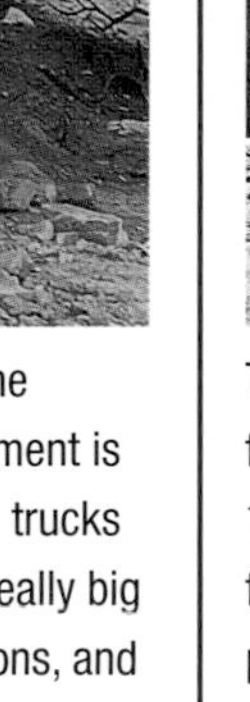

The Toyota 4Runner is an SUV with legions of buyers and a fanatical following. It comes in four generations from 1984 to 2009 (1984–1989, 1990–1996, 1997–2002, and 2003–2009). Its popularity comes from a combination of innate performance and high quality at a good price. The SUV has also proven to be a good buildup platform over its nearly 25 years of production, with the first- through third-generation models being the best bets in that regard.

GEARING:
Regardless of transmission type, axle gearing is the most easily alterable factory element in the drivetrain.

When GM took over the Hummer name in 1999, they started the process of designing a "Little Brother" for the venerable H1. The H2 debuted for the 2003 model year, and it somewhat upstaged its burly big brother. While not quite as capable off-highway as the H1, it comes with big 35-inch tires, 4.10 gears, and a rear locker. It is no slouch. The platform is GM truck–based and assembled from a variety of heavy-duty parts from the GM stable, including the burly 6.0-liter V-8. Where the H2 really shines, especially compared to the H1, is in the comfort and daily-driver departments. Popularity brought good aftermarket support, and that great GM swapability is also a plus.

IFS VERSUS SOLID AXLE:
Independent front suspension, or IFS, uses half-shafts and a chassis-mounted differential instead of a solid axle. Each wheel can travel independently. IFS provides for nice handling on the street, and it saves weight. On the downside, as generally built, it's more fragile than a solid axle, with many more parts to fail or break.

Compact pickups represent a good compromise between size and utility. This first-generation Ranger (1983–1992) has gone a lot farther into the trail realm by being modified with a Dana 44 front axle swap and a 302-cid V-8. This truck is awesome in capability but remains relatively streetable, and could be even more streetable had the owner opted to do so. The Ranger pickups are an adaptable platform with a solid foundation. Ditto for their progeny, the Bronco II and Explorer. What works for one generally works for the others.

When it debuted in 1993, the AM General Hummer, later to be called the H1, was the tough guy on the American 4×4 block. That didn't change when GM began distributing them, and it didn't stop when the civilian version was discontinued in 2006. For years, it was the most capable factory-spec trail rig offered in the United States. That title was taken away by the Jeep Rubicon, of which you could buy three or four for what an H1 cost. Nonetheless, the H1 is an icon and no *poseur* if you can swing the high price. The heart-stopping prices for vehicles and buildup parts ($16,000 for one brand of lift kit) are the only major detriment, though their size and configuration offer a steep learning curve for a new driver.

ON WEIGHT:
A two-door SUV is generally lighter than a four-door. A half-ton pickup is lighter than a three-quarter or one-ton. Power windows, seats, etc., will add several hundred pounds. More fuel equals more weight, so the larger-capacity fuel tank may be a liability unless you need the extra range.

The Toyota Land Cruiser FJ-40 is a legend in trail circles. It was imported in relatively small numbers from 1958 to 1983 and is now getting to be uncommon and fast entering classic status. It is an extremely stout basis for a buildup, however, and has a following that makes up for its small numbers by rabid fanaticism. Comfort-wise, it's in the same category as contemporary rigs, meaning downright Spartan by today's standards. In general, the newer FJs, mid-1970 and up, are the best if they will be used stock or in lightly modified form. Rust is a serious problem for these rigs.

The Hummer H3 debuted in 2006 on what amounted to the compact Colorado/Canyon truck platform, and it used the smaller four- and five-cylinder powerplants (except the Alpha model, which has a 5.3-liter V-8). This made it a more economical alternative to the two bigger Hummers. It could be had with 31- or 33-inch metric equivalent tires, 4.56:1 gears, and an optional rear locker. *Courtesy Hummer*

Key: 1 = Very Low, 2 = Low, 3 = Average, 4 = High, 5 = Very High	On-Road Performance	Off-Highway Performance	Modification Potential	Aftermarket Support
Jeep				
1947–1965 Willys Pickup	2	3	4	3-
1949–1965 Willys Wagon	2+	3	4	3-
1953–1968 CJ-3B	1+	3+	4	3+
1955–1971 CJ-5, CJ-6	2-	3+	4	3+
1956–1965 FC-150/170	2	2+	3	2+
1963–1970 Wagoneer	3+	3	4	3
1963–1970 J-Series Pickup	3	3	4	3
1967–1973 Jeepster Commando	3	3	3	2
1971–1991 Grand Wagoneer	4	3	3	3
1971–1987 J-Series Pickup	3	3	4	3
1972–1986 CJ-5, CJ-6,	2+	3+	5	4+
1974–1983 Cherokee SJ	3+	3	3	3
1976–1986 CJ-7	3-	3+	5	4+
1981–1985 CJ-8	3-	3	5	4+
1984–2001 Cherokee XJ	3+	3+	4-	5
1984–1990 Wagoneer XJ	4	3+	4-	5
1986–1992 Comanche Pickup MJ	3	3	4-	4
1987–1996 Wrangler YJ	3-	3+	5	5
1993–1998 Grand Cherokee ZJ	4+	3+	3+	4
1997–2006 Wrangler TJ	3	3+	5	5
1999–2004 Grand Cherokee WJ	4+	3+	3+	4
2002–2007 Liberty KJ	4	3	3+	3
2003–2006 Wrangler Rubicon TJ	3	5	5	5
2004–2006 Wrangler Unlimited	3	3+	5	5
2005–2008 Unlimited Rubicon	3	5	5	5
2005–2008 Grand Cherokee WK	4+	3	3	3
2006–2008 Commander XK	4+	3	3	3
2007–2008 Wrangler JK	3	3+	5	5
2007–2008 Wrangler Unlimited JKL	3	3	5	5
2007–2008 JK Rubicon	3	5	5	5
2007–2008 Patriot w/Freedom II	4	3	2	2
2008 and up Liberty KK	4	3	3	3
Kia				
2003–2008 Sorento	4	3	2	1

Key: 1 = Very Low, 2 = Low, 3 = Average, 4 = High, 5 = Very High	On-Road Performance	Off-Highway Performance	Modification Potential	Aftermarket Support
Land Rover				
1960–1974 88, 109	2	3	4	3
1987–1989 Range Rover	4	3	3	2+
1990–1995 Range Rover & LWB	4+	3	3	2-
1993 Defender 110	3	3	4	4
1994–1997 Defender 90	3	4	4	4
1994–1998 Discovery	4	4	4	4
1996–2002 Range Rover	5	3	3	1+
1999–2004 Discovery II	4	3	4	1
2003–2008 Range Rover	5	3+	2	1
2005–2008 LR3	5	3+	2	1
Lamborghini				
1982–1990 Cheetah LM002	4	4	4	1
Lexus				
1996–1997 LX-450	4	3	3	3
1998–2007 LX-470	5	3	3	2
2004–2008 GX-470	5	3	3	2
Lincoln				
1998–2008 Navigator	5	3	2	3
2006–2008 Mark LT	5	3	2	2
Mazda				
1987–1993 B2600 Pickup	3	3	3	1
1991–1994 Navajo	4	3	4	4
1994–1997 B-Series	3	3	4	4
1998–2008 B-Series	3	3	3	3+
Mercedes				
1998–2005 M-Class	4	4	3	3
2002–2006 G-Class	3	4	4	2
Mitsubishi				
1982–1995 Mighty Max Pickup	3	3	3	1
1984–1991 Montero	3	3	3	1
1992–2000 Montero	4	3	3	1
1997–2004 Montero Sport	4	3	3	1
2001–2006 Montero	4	3	2	1
2006–2008 Raider	3+	3	3	3

Approach and departure angles are part of the clearance equation. A vehicle with steep angles will perform better because it can approach a steeper climb without touching. Departure angles are important for climbing as well as the transition part of a descent. Lift and taller tires both increase these angles.

Ramp breakover angle is also important. The transition from a flat to a descent and the transition from a climb to flat ground are common hanging-up points for rigs with a poor ramp breakover angle. Having a flat, skid-plate-protected belly is an advantage for all 4×4s.

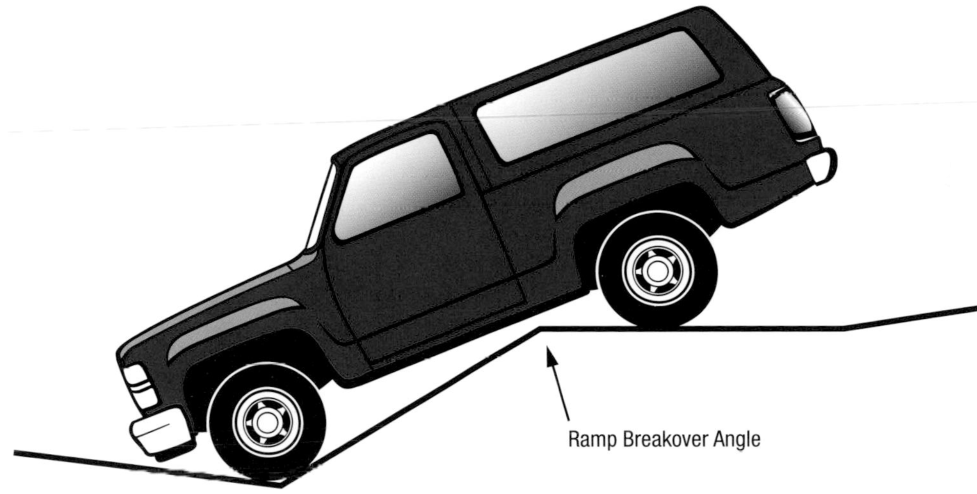

It's harder to get fording depth info these days, and when it's given, it's usually about like it is shown here, the level of the hubs.

THE IFS/SOLID AXLE COMBINATION:
Many trucks and SUVs combine IFS with a solid rear axle. This leads to some inherent instability in certain types of terrain due to the disparity of the way these systems operate. Typically, the front does not articulate or have much travel. If the rear articulates too much it results in more severe roll angles when the front and rear suspensions are on opposite terrain angles.

ENGINE SIZE:
All you need is enough engine to get the job done, plus a little reserve. In the four-wheel arena, torque is the most important engine performance specification, and the amount of torque available is usually relative to engine displacement.

When the Wrangler Rubicon debuted in 2002, it took the crown as the most capable stock 4×4 you could buy in North America, and maybe the world. Combine compact dimensions with factory front and rear lockers, 4.10:1 gears in Dana 44 axles, sticky Goodyear MTR tires, four-wheel disc brakes, a Rock-Trac transfer case with a 4:1 low range, and a supple suspension and you have one gnarly 4×4. In stock condition, it's not torture to drive every day. In addition, a plethora of aftermarket parts is available. With any coil-sprung Jeep, the most important element is the suspension. If a lift over 3 inches is needed, it should be a "long arm"–style lift to reduce the angularity of the axle links.

The 2007 and up Wrangler JK was a ground up redo of the "traditional" Jeep. Many feared the new Jeep would be an emasculated shadow of itself, but to the 4×4 community's glee, it's even better than ever. A Rubicon version is also offered in the line, and in many ways, it's an even better iteration of a "King-o'-the-Hill" trail package. *Courtesy Jeep*

When Jeepers clamored for more room, they were offered the Unlimited model in 2004. Call it a modern version of the CJ-8 Scrambler. It was stretched out to a 103.4-inch wheelbase. It offered double the interior cubic feet without detracting much from trail prowess. It was also every bit as buildable as the standard Wrangler TJ. *Courtesy Jeep*

Key: 1 = Very Low, 2 = Low, 3 = Average, 4 = High, 5 = Very High	On-Road Performance	Off-Highway Performance	Modification Potential	Aftermarket Support
Nissan/Datsun				
1962–1969 Patrol	2+	4	5	2
1980–1986 720 Pickup	2+	3	3	2
1987–1995 Pathfinder WD21	3	3	3	3
1986–1997 Hardbody D21 Pickup	3	3	3	3
1996–2000 Pathfinder	4	3	3	3
1998–2004 Frontier D22	3	3	3	3
2000–2004 Xterra WD22	3	3	3	2
2001–2004 Pathfinder	4	3	3	2
2004–2008 Titan	3+	4	3	2
2005–2008 Pathfinder	5	3	2	2
2004–2008 Armada	5	3	3	2
2005–2008 Frontier Pickup	4	3+	3	3
2005–2008 Xterra	4	3+	3	3
Plymouth				
1974–1980 Trail Duster	3	3	4	3
Porsche				
2002–2008 Cayenne	5	5	3	1
Suzuki				
1986–1995 Samurai	2+	3+	4	4
1990–1998 Sidekick	3	3	4	4
1996–1998 X-90	3-	3	3	3
1999–2005 Vitara	3+	3	3	3
2001–2006 XL-7	3+	3	3	3
2006–2008 Grand Vitara	3+	3	3	3

The 2000 and up Nissan Xterra comes in two generations, the 2000–2004 (shown) and the 2005 and up. The 2005 and up shares many underpinnings with the Frontier pickup. These are sporty, economical, and compact SUVs with buildup potential. The aftermarket for them isn't huge, but all the basics are there. *Courtesy Nissan*

ELECTRONIC TRACTION CONTROL: Electronic traction control comes in various forms, and while it's certainly better than nothing, don't depend on it as the end-all-be-all, despite the advertising hyperbole you may see and hear.

Key: 1 = Very Low, 2 = Low, 3 = Average, 4 = High, 5 = Very High	**On-Road Performance**	**Off-Highway Performance**	**Modification Potential**	**Aftermarket Support**
Toyota				
1960–1983 Land Cruiser FJ-40	2+	3+	5	4
1963–1967 FJ-45 L & S Pickup	2+	3	4	2+
19'63–1967 FJ-45 Wagon	2+	3	3+	2+
1968–1979 Land Cruiser FJ-55	3	3	3+	3
1979–1985 Pickup	3	3+	5	4+
1980–1990 Land Cruiser FJ-60/62	3	3	3	3
1983–1985 4Runner	3	4	5	5
1986–1994 Pickup	3	3	4	4+
1986–1996 4Runner	3+	3	3+	4
1991–1997 Land Cruiser FJ-80	3+	4	4	3+
1993–1998 T-100	3	3	4	3
1995–2005 Tacoma	3+	4	4	4+
1996–2002 4Runner	4	3	3	3
1998–2008 Land Cruiser UZJ-100	4+	4	3	3
2000–2008 Tundra	4	3+	3	3
2001–2008 Sequoia	4+	3	3	3
2003–2008 4Runner	4	3	3	3
2007–2008 FJ Cruiser	3+	4	4	4
Volkswagen				
2003–2008 Touareg	5	4+	3	1

The Toyota FJ Cruiser was an instant hit upon its intro in 2006 as a 2007 model. Not only did it hark back to the glory days of the FJ-series Cruisers, it had some serious "go" along with the "show." With 31-inch metric-equivalent tires, 4:1 axle gears, and an optional locker, it was a solid, capable trail performer with few vices on the street. With its popularity came an abundance of aftermarket buildup products.

In the truck realm, the 2005 and up Dodge Power Wagon rules as the trail workhorse alpha-wolf. Equipped with metric-equivalent 32-inch tires, 4.56 gears, front and rear lockers in heavy-duty AAM axles, along with an optional factory winch, the Power Wagon has everything you need to hit the trail and hit it hard. Annual production is limited. The only issue with this truck is that the electronic locker will not engage in high range. A little creative rewiring cures that, however. *Courtesy Chrysler*

The 2004 and up Nissan Titan was that company's first foray into the full-sized realm. The full-size Armada SUV appeared on a similar platform. It was immediately popular, and the aftermarket rapidly added products to accommodate new owners. These trucks can be built to a moderately high level with bolt-on parts. *Courtesy Nissan*

TIRE UPGRADES:
Along with fender well clearance, drivetrain strength and the suspension's suitability to being lifted (which is almost always a part of a serious tire upgrade) must be considered as well.

The 2003 Porsche Cayenne does a pretty good sports car imitation while being a very capable stock off-highway machine. It's no die-hard rockcrawler, but with a low range, low gearing, a decent amount of clearance, and lockers at both ends, it can get down and dirty ahead of most other stock 4×4s. The VW Touareg is built on the same platform but differs in technical detail. Ultimate buildups may be limited by a design that's not easy to alter and a dearth of buildup parts. *Courtesy Porsche*

The mighty 2000–2005 Ford Excursion is essentially an F-250 fitted out as an SUV. It is capable of monumental towing feats, and unlike its same-class competitor, the GM Suburban, it can be had with a diesel powerplant. Essentially, all the buildup stuff available for the line of Super Duty Ford trucks will work with the Excursion. Like any big pickup, size limits its trail ability, but with the right mods, it's very capable in all the places it will fit. *Courtesy Ford*

Though not really "crossovers," the Suzuki Vitara/XL-7 (2004 Vitara shown) and re-badged Chevy and Geo models are often tossed into that class. They are small and fuel efficient but remarkably stout SUVs. Best of all, they have a true low range, and there are enough buildup parts to make a significant trail performance improvement. *Courtesy Suzuki*

CHAPTER 4
Controls and Communications: What Does That Lever Do?

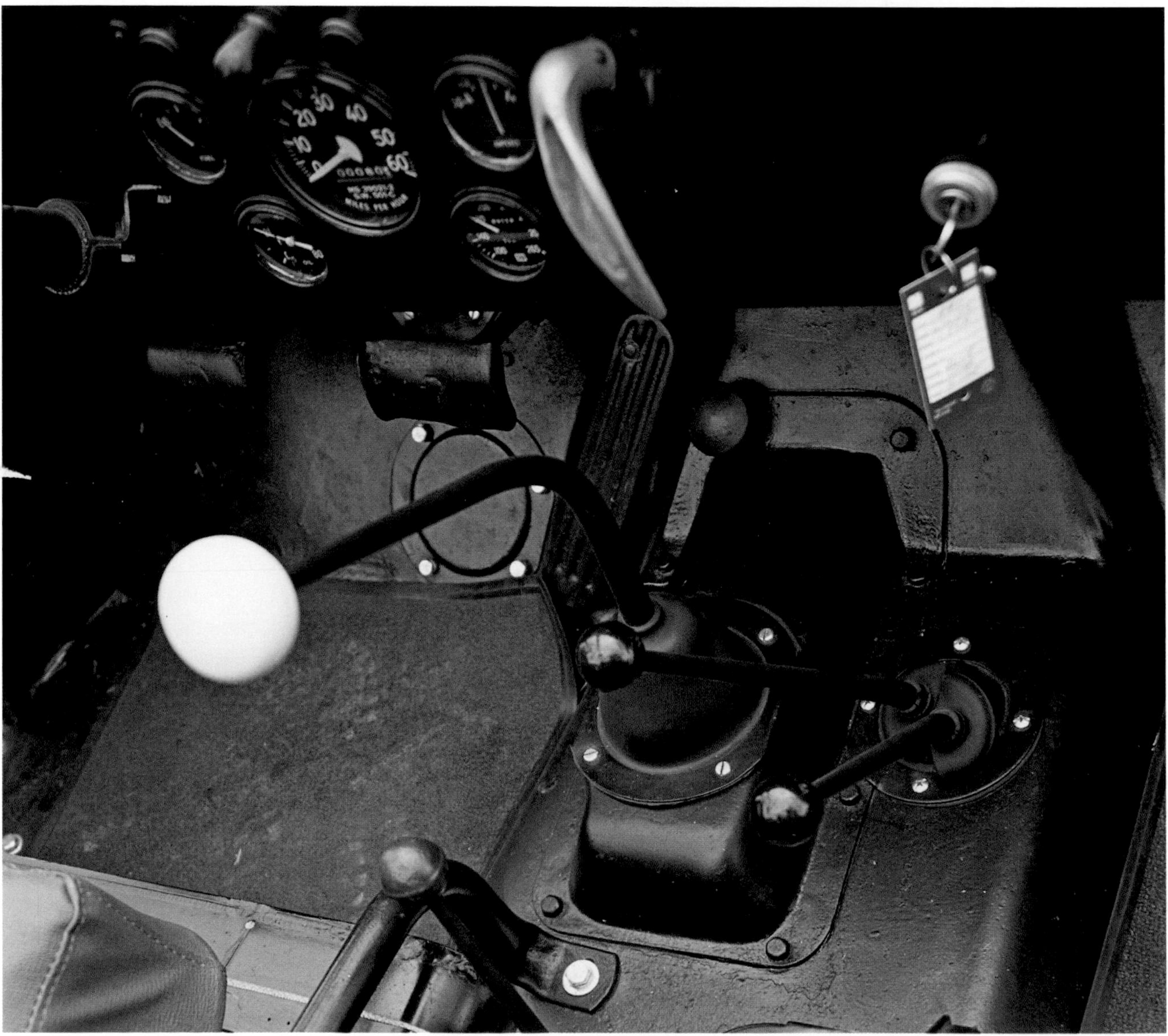

There are enough sticks here to inspire lever envy, or perhaps lever aversion. This 1947 CJ-2A Jeep features not only the floor shift for the main three-speed transmission but the twin sticks of the old Model 18 Spicer transfer case. The left lever engages the front output to power the front axle. Forward is disengaged and back is engaged. The right lever engages the range box, with forward being low, center neutral, and back high. This operation is typical of many vintage rigs. As if three levers aren't enough, the fourth lever between the seats operates a power take-off unit to run farm machinery. Optionally, this vintage rig could also have had a fifth lever for an overdrive unit. All these controls offer great flexibility, but you need to know the wherefores and the whys to make full use of the capabilities they offer.

You can't do much with a tool unless you know how to use it. A 4×4 is a tool that is often taken for granted because, in essence, it operates pretty much like an ordinary car. The familiar controls are all in the right places, but there are a few extra ones that can really throw you a curve when you hit the trail. A whole new set of rules apply, and things don't work quite the same as they do on the street. This section covers the items you will find on virtually every standard four-wheel drive, though not every item covered here will be on every vehicle, and not every feature of every vehicle is discussed.

Communications on the trail is both a convenience and a potential lifesaver. From the convenience side, a simple, inexpensive CB radio allows you to converse with trail buddies, warn of impending problems, and summon help. Ditto for the little FRS (family radio system) handhelds. You can move up into the single sideband (SSB) radios or even mobile ham radios (VHF/UHF/HF), if you need longer-range commo. Don't forget the ubiquitous cell phone, either. All of these options add a measure of fun and safety.

ROUGH ROAD

CASUAL DRIVING:
The one-hand-casually-draped-on-the-steering-wheel driving style doesn't cut it on the trail. The irregular surfaces and bumps can easily yank the wheel out of a casual grip.

WHITE-KNUCKLE STEERING:
A white-knuckle, tensed-muscle grip contributes to fatigue and imprecise use of the steering wheel. Stay relaxed but aware, ready to apply firm force when you need it.

The Steering Wheel

I can hear some of you already! "Get serious! The steering wheel needs special instruction? Gimme a break!" The short answer is, yes.

Ten and Two or Nine and Three? For most of driving history, the best positions for your hands on the steering wheel were at the typical 10 o'clock and 2 o'clock positions. Now, especially with the advent of steering wheel–mounted airbags, many experts advocate a nine and three position. Why? It's said that with the hands at ten and two, airbag deployment may knock your hands off the steering wheel.

Either position gives you plenty of leverage and control. When actually steering, use the "push-and-slide" method rather than the cross-arm method you see race drivers use. Push-and-slide keeps your hands more or less in the right position, and you grip with one hand, and slide the other for a new purchase, alternating hands.

Thumbs 'n' Things. The other steering wheel caveat is to keep your thumbs outside the inner rim of the steering wheel. Regardless of power steering, in certain situations the steering wheel can suddenly kick back, and if your thumb happens to be in the way of a steering wheel spoke, a serious ouch will result. It

Hands at 9 and 3. Keep those thumbs outside the rim of the steering wheel. Power steering and steering dampers have all but ended the days when steering kickback would yank the wheel out of your hand, but it still happens. If one of the wildly spinning spokes happened to catch your thumb, ouch! That's one part of the "good old days" I don't miss!

happens infrequently these days, with the advent of power steering and steering dampers, but one incident is usually a cure for ever inserting your thumbs inside the rim again, street or trail. In the old days, before power steering, broken thumbs were not uncommon.

Death Grip. After reading the above, it might seem appropriate to have a death grip on the wheel the next time you hit the trail! Just the opposite is true. Loosen up and lighten up, but be ready to exert the force needed, when it's needed.

You Drive. Severe articulation may cause the suspension to exert a certain amount of force on the steering wheel. For example, on some rigs, when the left wheel droops to its bottom position, it tends to pull the steering wheel right. When faced with that experience the first time, many people just let it happen, some to the point of letting the wheel spin wildly like the wheel of the S.S. *Minnow* on *Gilligan's Island*. Hold that steering wheel in the position you want it.

The Brake Pedal

The brake pedal has been anointed by long-time street drivers as the magic cure for all problems. Even on the street that's not really true, but on the trail it's even less so. The brake pedal can actually get you into trouble. In many ways, braking traction is the same as driving traction. You either have tire grip or your don't. If you are trying to climb a steep, slippery slope and don't have the traction, you just say, "Oh, well," and back down. If you are coming down that hill, apply too much brake, and lose traction, your words will be much stronger as you slide out of control.

Light Foot. A light and sensitive foot is best. Two braking methods are known to work well. The first is simply to be attuned to tire grip. Apply a little brake until you hear or feel tires starting to slide on the ground surface (it almost always will be the unloaded rear tires first on a downhill). You either reduce pressure on the brake pedal or remove your foot altogether. The other method is cadence braking, which is a gentle, continuous on-off, on-off application of the brakes, never applying enough pressure to lock the tires.

Left Foot. Left-foot braking is a useful tool for the trail, especially with automatics. If you're not used to using that foot, it can take some practice to train it for the job, but the benefits are a much smoother technique and better performance overall. In certain situations, such as rockcrawling, you might even use the throttle and brake simultaneously. Hold just a bit of throttle and vary brake pressure to keep your speed controlled going up and down the sides of the rocks.

The Throttle. Also known as the gas pedal, the accelerator pedal, the foot feed, the go pedal, the hammer, and other terms, the throttle is a vital control to master. The most common mistakes involve too much throttle, though timidity is also common. Analogous to the three bears story, there's too much, too little, and just right. The problem with just right is that it changes constantly according to the obstacle. In most cases, just a little is just right, but sometimes you need the opposite approach. The trick is to know when and where to put the hammer down.

Use of the accelerator pedal is so variable that I can give only a few generalities. First, work the level of throttle up gradually. Start off with small amounts

Left-foot braking is the accepted technique for automatics and even low-geared manuals. It may take some time to train that "atrophied" left foot, but it will save lots of hassles and right-foot-tap-dancing on the pedals.

LEFT-FOOT BRAKING:
Left-foot braking is a great trail tool, especially with automatics. It offers fine and simultaneous control of throttle and brake, with no lag while you move your foot between pedals. You can even apply throttle and brake at the same time. How much throttle to use varies somewhat. Use as little as possible, keeping in mind that it takes about 1,000–1,500 rpm on most rigs with automatics to get the torque converter pulling. Rigs with manuals and very low gears may offer the chance to left-foot brake as well.

GEAR SELECTION:
Remember these two mnemonics: *Go up, shift up. Go down, shift down.* The general rules are that when you climb, you use the *highest possible* gear and when you descend, you use the *lowest possible* gear.

and work your way up as needed. Second, it matters where on the pedal you place your foot. With a foot suspended over the pedal with no side support, your tiring ankle and calf may be subject to uncontrolled applications of throttle due to bumps or bouncing. A foot wedged against the transmission tunnel will be much more stable and controlled, and less subject to fatigue.

Many newer vehicles have an electronic throttle, meaning there is no direct connection from the pedal to the engine. They tend to be more sensitive than a linkage or cable throttle. In some cases, the pedal slope calibration (how the engine responds to the throttle) is altered by the engine's management system when the vehicle is in low range.

The Transmission and Transfer Case

Gear selection is one of the most important parts of four-wheeling. Gear selection is especially important if you drive a manual-transmission vehicle because you often have to select the gear without a chance to change your mind partway through.

To maximize grip on a climb, you want as little torque multiplication as possible. This is critical on low-traction climbs. That means as little throttle as possible and as high a gear as possible without lugging the engine. Choose a gearing and throttle combo that keeps the engine in a useful torque range, the speed of the vehicle as slow as possible (while still utilizing some momentum), and the torque multiplication under control. The combination of those elements will vary greatly across the many vehicles out there.

Going down is the opposite. Use the lowest possible gear to let engine braking slow the descent. Let the hill be your guide. Second low may be OK for a mild slope or if you have very deep gears. On descents with low traction, you may find a situation analogous to excessive braking; the tires will slip, especially the rear. In this case, you can shift up, or increase the speed of the vehicle with the throttle. More on that in the next chapter.

The typical three-speed automatic shifter. A four-speed auto might differ in having a "3" position below "D." In the case of this three-speed, most of your wheeling would be done in "D." A four-speed auto would use "3." At very slow speeds, it would be acceptable to use "2," especially if you were doing a lot of shifting down to "1."

The Automatic Transmission. Though ages old, there are still strong debates in the four-wheeling world over the automatic's place on the trail. But frankly it's all moot. Drive what you like, though in most cases, for most people, the automatic is superior.

Gear selection with the automatic is easy: let the transmission do it! With three-speed autos, keep the unit in "D" or "3," and for four-speed autos, use "3," which will lock it out of overdrive. Ditto for five-speed autos. The trans will select the correct gear for the terrain or obstacle. This rule is flexible according

AUTOMATIC VERSUS MANUAL:
Overall, the automatic has the performance advantage in most terrain. It takes a very skilled stick shifter with low gearing to match the smoothness of an automatic on rough ground. Without the worry of stalling, the average automatic can creep safely over terrain that a similarly geared manual will lurch, stall, and bounce over.

Starting in gear is a useful tactic in many venues, but it's not always possible in modern rigs because the clutch must be depressed before the starter circuit will operate. Toyota is one manufacturer that offers a momentary bypass switch so you can start the vehicle in gear when needed. This is a feature that you can wire in yourself on nearly any rig.

to conditions. There's nothing wrong with using "2" if speeds are slow enough and you are doing a lot of shifting down to "1." If you want or need to avoid an automatic upshift or downshift, such as on a hill where you need a fair bit of throttle and you don't want the unit to suddenly downshift, you can select a particular gear. Some rigs have a lockout button that will hold the vehicle in the preselected gear. Avoid using that overdrive gear—usually "D" on four- or five-speed autos—on the trail while in low range. It's not the strongest set of gears in your transmission.

The biggest performance difference between the automatic and the manual is in engine braking on descents. With a mechanical lockup, the manual has the advantage in slowing the vehicle more on descents. Low gears or a low-rpm stall torque converter will help the automatic, but that fluid coupling simply does not allow a 100 percent lockup. The manual trans may

TRAIL GEARING:
If you find yourself having to slip the clutch constantly to avoid stalling in tough terrain, you probably need lower gearing.

MANUAL TRANSMISSION TIPS:
It's not safe or advisable to shift a manual transmission partway up a steep climb. You also have to be smooth. A herky-jerky driving style transmits severe shock loads to the drivetrain, breaking parts much more often on manual transmission 4×4s than automatics.

not require use of the foot brake on a steep downhill, but the auto almost always needs a judicious foot on the brake pedal.

With an autobox, you can get away with somewhat taller gearing because, in effect, the torque converter is a variable-ratio first gear. The mechanical first-gear ratios of most automatics, 2.4–3:1, don't sound impressive until you multiply it by the torque converter ratio, typically 2.0–2.5:1. This ratio, combined with the mechanical ratios, gives you the effect of a lower ratio. That "ratio" changes with engine speed. You might have a 2.5:1 converter ratio (times the mechanical ratio) at 850 rpm but by 1,000 rpm, it's down to about 1.5:1 and by 1,500, the converter is producing nearly 1:1.

The Manual Transmission and Clutch. Driving a manual-transmission rig requires you to be decisive. Often, you have to pick the right gear for the job without an opportunity for a second chance. If you drive a manual, get in the habit of gently letting the drivetrain wind up its slack before putting the hammer down. Above all, don't ride the clutch any more than you must. Except for the actual moment of the shift, keep your left foot flat on the floor—if it's not on the brake. There are some screaming emergency situations where you might slip the clutch, like when your sputtering engine is ready to die in the middle of a fast-moving stream taking you to Newark. If your rig is high-geared, you may be more or less forced to slip the clutch at times. This is not ideal and will severely shorten the life of the clutch if taken to extremes. If you find yourself having to do this regularly, a change of axle ratios is probably the answer.

On hills, being uncoupled from the engine means that you are one step closer to being out of control. Exceptions are those dead slow conditions where you have to creep off a rock. Most rigs aren't geared low enough to do that, and the driver has to rely 100 percent on the brakes.

Single-stick transfer cases were the big improvement in four-wheel drive of the 1950s, and they remain common today. The shift pattern is usually in a line front to back. Note the position of neutral. This unit is in a mid-1980s Ford pickup but is typical of many other single-stick T-cases.

The best of the electrically shifted transfer cases offer a neutral position. This GM truck also has an Auto setting that can be used when traction problems are imminent. When rear-wheel slippage is sensed (via the ABS wheel speed sensors), four-wheel drive is engaged.

Starting in Gear. It's often difficult or impossible to start a stalled engine on a slope and start moving again in the same manner as you would on level ground. You need three feet to do it right (see the "Parking Brake" section further on for more tips). It can also be a little hairy because declutching the engine from the drivetrain deprives you of the most efficient means of descent control. Backing down a hill tends to unload the front (steering) wheels due to weight transfer. Application of the brakes in this situation tends to make the front tires lock up, and you immediately lose some, or all, steering control.

It's often safer and more practical to leave the clutch out and simply turn the key to restart the engine. Whether your engine will, in fact, restart going uphill depends on the steepness of the hill, how well the engine runs, overall gearing, and the strength of your starter and battery. Is it inherently hard on the starter to do this? Yes, but not overly so, unless it's a very regular occurrence. If it's clear that your vehicle will not restart in this manner, don't beat the poor horse to death; instead, perform a failed climb procedure as outlined in the next chapter.

Bypassing the Clutch Pedal Starter Lock-Out. All of the newer manual transmission–equipped 4×4s have a switch on the clutch pedal that prevents the vehicle from starting unless the pedal is depressed. The idea is to prevent you from accidentally starting the vehicle in gear and taking out the back wall of your garage. Since it's sometimes advisable to start the vehicle in gear on the trail with the clutch out and the switch prevents this, some owners will bypass it by connecting the two wires on the switch together. This is a choice you have to make and a responsibility you will assume if you think this modification is needed for your style of four-wheeling. The most serious danger is that you will forget, or another driver may not realize, what you have done and accidentally start the vehicle in gear. At least one manufacturer, Toyota, has the needs of four-wheelers in mind and offers a dash-mounted momentary bypass switch so the vehicle can be started

MANUAL CENTER DIFF LOCK OPERATION: Engaging the manual center differential lock with wildly spinning tires can cause breakage of epic proportions.

T-CASE OPERATION: Your owner's manual will detail the best method for your particular unit, but generally the transfer case is most easily engaged with the automatic transmission in neutral, or the clutch disengaged with a stick-shift transmission.

in gear. This is an optional modification anyone could make. By wiring in a momentary switch (meaning that the switch is spring loaded and you have to hold it in), you could have the bypass when you need it without the worry of accidentally starting in gear on the street.

The Transfer Case Controls

Engage four-wheel high as soon as you get to the point where you wouldn't drive the family car and use low range on uneven terrain or if the going gets tough. Simple! If the transit speeds will be low over the easier areas, some drivers prefer using low range from the start because they are more ready for the unexpected and have better engine braking.

If you drive a vehicle with full-time four-wheel drive and a manually locked center differential, lock that center diff when the going gets tough or if you are

T-CASE OPERATION:
When engaging or disengaging low range, it typically works best to have the drivetrain unloaded, i.e., foot off the brakes.

STUCK IN PARK:
If your transmission gets jammed in Park, another vehicle pulling you slightly uphill will take the weight off the pawl and should allow you to shift.

STICKS AND BUTTONS: TRANSFER CASE CONTROLS

Transfer case controls have evolved substantially from the days when drivers had one or two sticks coming up through the floor. Most T-cases are electronically shifted these days. The driver activates a simple switch or button, and a servo motor does the shifting at the transfer case. This is both good and bad from a four-wheeling perspective.

The good part is user friendliness. There is no need to reach down and jerk on a recalcitrant stick with both hands. These modern designs are often shift-on-the-fly systems that can be operated at substantial road speeds. There are also "smart" systems with automatic features that will shift into four-wheel drive when sensors detect slippage at the rear wheel. This does not include the almost seamless full-time systems now available.

The concerns with the push-button systems are mainly related to reliability in tough environments. With a lever, the stick has a direct, or nearly direct, connection with the gears in the transfer case. When you pull it into four-low, you know it's in four-low. That isn't always true of the servo types, where electrical circuits and motors can fail due to dirt or water intrusion or simply from normal wear. These failures correspond to how the vehicle is used, and they will fail more often in harsh environments. Some manufacturers offer an emergency method of shifting the T-case, usually in the form of a large Allen wrench. Your owner's manual will detail this.

Some manufacturers still offer a choice of manually or electrically shifted transfer cases, but these choices are few and far between. If you plan on being a regular on the trail, my advice is to go with a manually shifted T-case, the simple and reliable choice. Beyond that rare choice, look for units that offer a neutral position. Many systems do not have a neutral button, so if the time comes to tow your rig, you will be restricted to short distances or risk transmission or transfer case damage. A true neutral position allows much more leeway in towing without having to undergo the onerous process of removing driveshafts.

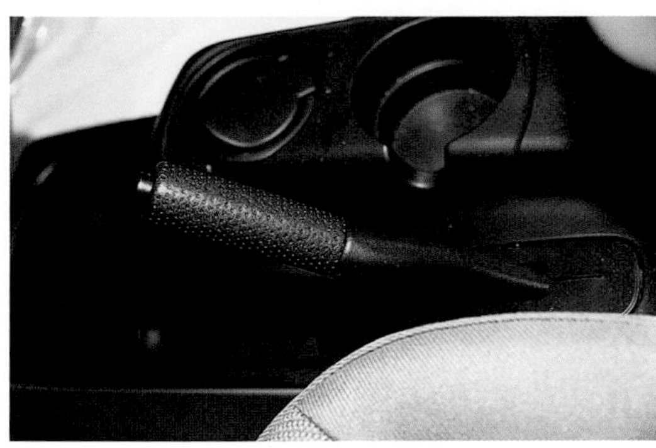

The parking brake is an important control for secure parking at any angle, but it is especially important for manual transmission–equipped rigs. A hand-operated brake makes starting on a grade easier. The best setups are the Euro-style brakes (above). The type that pulls out of the dash (right) can also be used effectively. The most important consideration is that they can be used with one hand and used without locking. The foot-operated brake is useless. If you had the third foot, you wouldn't need the parking brake at all!

using low range. Engage the center diff-lock only when the vehicle is nearly stationary or when the drivetrain is not under a big load.

Many full-time transfer cases have viscous couplings or other devices that automatically engage when a major traction differential is sensed between the front and rear tires. Bear in mind that they also unlock automatically and can do so at inopportune times. You just need to be sensitive and give the unit time to adjust to varying conditions.

"Shift on the fly" is an overused term that implies that you can shift the transfer case at any speed. This is not completely true. You can shift into or out of four-wheel high at nearly any speed, but not into low range. Shifting into low is best done with the vehicle stopped or just barely rolling.

I always double-check once I've shifted the transfer case by backing off on the throttle and giving the shift lever another shove. If your rig has a T-case shifted by a servo, the unit will continue to try to fully engage the gears, so merely backing off for a second may allow it to finish the job if the gears didn't completely engage. If your rig pops out of gear, which all rigs may do occasionally, go back into neutral and drop the T-case back into gear. If this becomes a continual problem, you may have an internal transfer case problem or a linkage problem.

On occasion, the transfer case may pop out of gear, or you may miss the shift. You may find that, even with the trans in neutral, you get grinding when trying

PARKING BRAKE OPERATION:
Parking brakes can freeze up in cold climates, or from repeated exposure to water and mud without proper cleanup afterward.

TRAIL PARKING:
Leave a manual transmission vehicle in first gear on an uphill lie and reverse gear if the vehicle is aimed downhill.

to re-engage the T-case. If you're driving an automatic, you may get some clunks trying to then put the trans in Park. The simple cure is to shut the engine off. That stops all shafts from rotating and allows you to make all the shifts without any grinding.

TRAIL BRAKING:
There are times when you want locked-wheel braking on the trail, and ABS prevents this.

The Parking Brake

Also commonly called the "emergency" brake, the parking brake has many uses on the trail, not the least of which is parking. Unlike the street, where "Park" on the automatic trans or leaving the manual trans in gear is often considered sufficient to keep the vehicle from rolling away, the more acute grades on the trail make parking brake use mandatory.

The automatic trans has a "parking pawl" that locks it in place when you put the gear selection lever in Park. If you park on a grade and let the pawl hold the entire weight of the vehicle, you might find it impossible to get out of park. To avoid this dilemma, apply the parking brake first, then put the shift lever into Park. That way the parking brake takes the load, and the transmission pawl becomes the backup device.

With manual transmissions, a vehicle held in place only by the gearbox and engine will still move if the hill is steep enough; the engine will simply turn over. Locking the wheels with the parking brake will prevent this.

The parking brake can be used to great advantage with manual-trans rigs, especially if it's the Euro-style, lever-type unit that mounts between the seats. Starting on a hill is the ages-old predicament for stick shifters. Some people start in gear, though this is not possible for all rigs all the time. Others master a heel-and-toe approach that would make Mr. Bojangles proud. But the easiest method is to use the parking brake.

You won't find this control on many factory rigs. A rear-diff lock is a real asset and makes any OE rig capable of greater trail prowess. This feature comes on many Toyota trucks when the TRD option is ordered.

Here's how:

1. While holding the vehicle with the foot brake, shift the vehicle into the appropriate gear;
2. With the right hand, pull the parking brake up hard, keeping the button pressed in so the lever doesn't lock. Assuming the hill is not super steep and your parking brake is properly adjusted, it should hold the vehicle;
3. Release the foot brake and use that foot on the accelerator pedal;
4. As you engage the clutch and apply throttle, the clutch will begin taking the weight of the vehicle, and you can gradually release the parking brake.

As you have probably figured, this trick will not work with rigs that have foot-actuated parking brakes. If you had the extra foot, you wouldn't need the parking brake.

Some four-wheelers with open differentials will use the parking brake as a poor-man's traction control. In situations where all the torque is going to a slipping or unloaded rear tire, applying some parking brake can help stop or slow that spinning tire and force the diff to transfer some torque to the wheel with traction. This applies only to vehicles that have parking brakes that actuate on the rear wheels. Rigs like older Jeeps, Toyotas, and Land Rovers with transfer case–mounted parking brakes will gain nothing.

As with almost everything in the four-wheeling world, there are a few caveats to parking brake use. Dedicated snow bashers will sometimes avoid using the parking brake because as the vehicle rapidly cools to ambient temperature, the melted snow on or in the brakes can freeze solid and lock the mechanism. I remember seeing one hapless four-wheeler urinating on his brakes after a snow trip lunch break to free them up so he could continue. Similar problems can happen in mud and water, though it's usually a case of repeated dunkings and neglect afterward. People who run in water and mud with regularity will need to clean their brakes often to ensure proper operation.

Freewheeling Hubs

Many 4×4s these days are full-time systems, which have no freewheeling hubs at all. Some part-time systems use a Center Axle Disconnect, or CAD, also eliminating hubs from the equation. Many others use automatic-locking hubs that engage when four-wheel drive is selected. If you have manual hubs, lock them in when you hit the dirt. Pretty simple.

Traction Control

As mentioned in the previous chapter, some 4×4s use an electronic traction control (ETC) system that utilizes the anti-lock brakes to slow the spinning tire and transfer some torque to the tire with the most traction. They operate automatically but sometimes are slow to engage. Sometimes they need more wheelspin than you might think necessary. You'll soon get a feel for the conditions and situations that fool your ETC. These systems work well in mild to moderate situations, but some of them have a built-in timer that temporarily shuts the system down to prevent the brakes from being overheated. Fate usually decrees this to happen at the moment you need it most. Traction control also may interfere with certain types of aftermarket lockers.

Anti-Lock Brakes

Anti-lock brakes are great on the highway. For most drivers, they shorten stopping distances and improve control. Double ditto on slippery pavement, but sometimes they can complicate four-wheeling. Anti-lock brake systems (ABS) come in two-channel (with anti-lock capability on only two wheels, usually the rear) or four-channel (operating on all four wheels) design. The system operates via wheel speed sensors, an electronic control unit, and a complicated set of electric valves in the hydraulic part of the brake system. The ABS's goal is to keep wheel speed equal and keep the wheels rolling. (Remember, on pavement, a skidding tire delivers little traction.) It prevents wheel lockup by momentarily releasing hydraulic brake pressure at the wheel. By constantly monitoring wheel speeds, the control unit can regulate wheel speed and lockup at each wheel individually using these electronically controlled valves, and do it well enough to compensate for all sorts of road surface conditions. The response time is measured in milliseconds, and the ABS usually offers arrow-true stopping.

Some anti-lock brake systems are disengaged when the vehicle is put into low range. Others may have an on-off switch. Every system has a threshold speed below which the ABS is inoperative. This speed varies according to the vehicle type, but it ranges from about 3 to 6 miles per hour. I have not done a survey of every four-channel ABS system available on 4×4s, but I know that some systems may be able to distinguish between road or trail situations and adjust that threshold speed somewhat.

The problems come in the more difficult realms of the four-wheeling world, where a whole different set of forces are at work. Here are some situations where ABS may cause problems.

Weight Transfer Situations. One primary example is a failed climb. Because brake bias is to the front when backing down on a failed climb, the front tires tend to lock up first due to weight transfer. You may be carefully modulating the brake pedal to avoid lockup, but if you accidentally let a wheel lock momentarily, or even if the front wheels slow down significantly compared to the rear, the ABS system may sense the difference in wheel speed front to rear and start releasing the rear brakes. Since this is your primary set of brakes for the duration of the failed climb, the vehicle speeds up. You instinctively mash harder on the pedal, to no avail. About all you can do at that point is try to maintain control. Going down frontways can cause a similar problem. The key here is to keep the speed below the ABS's threshold speed, which may or may not be possible.

Lifted Tires. Lifted tires can cause the ABS to read differences in wheel speed and engage. Say you are coming off a rock and fully articulated. If you have an open diff on the wheel that's lifted, the ABS may sense a different wheel speed one side to another and kick in while you are easing off a rock. Again, staying below the threshold speed is the key.

AUTOMATIC HUBS:
There are a few caveats to certain automatic hubs. Some will disconnect on steep descents under the right circumstances. When they get old and gummy, sometimes they won't engage at all. Manual hubs are generally better and stronger for a frequent four-wheeler.

Ground Conditions. A locked-up wheel will sometimes stop you faster than a continuously rolling one. For example, a locked-up wheel will create a plowing effect in gravel, loose shale, or sand as it piles up material in front of the tires. You could call it a "dynamic wheel block," and it works well. To avoid having the ABS prevent this phenomenon, you need to stay below the speed threshold.

Read the Manual. Since the ABS is built-in, and few, if any, have an "off" switch, it behooves you to read the section of your owner's manual that details how the system works. Knowing what it's designed to do will allow you to adjust your driving style to account for it. Unfortunately, you may find a lack of detail in some manuals. A call to the dealer or the vehicle manufacturer with specific questions may be necessary. Lacking any other information, eventually observation will show you how the system works on your vehicle.

Hill Descent Control

Some of the newer SUVs also have hill descent control (HDC). It's another clever adaptation of the ABS. Essentially, it does what you do with your foot; it controls the speed of the descent by engaging the brakes and keeping the wheels turning at equal speeds. It is engaged in various ways and is usually canceled by application of the brake pedal or the accelerator. In some cases the speed is preset, and in others the descent speed can be adjusted by the cruise control. HDC is pretty slick and a useful feature for AWD rigs with less-experienced drivers. Many skilled drivers would rather take a beating than use it.

CB RADIOS:
CB radios allow 'wheelers to warn members of their group about upcoming obstacles or to offer instructions or directions. They also carry a lot of fun banter. If you 'wheel in a group without a CB, you are definitely missing out on a lot of fun.

Communications

There are basically four levels of communications available. They start with CB (citizens band) then jump to SSB (single sideband) and UHF/VHF (ultra-high frequency/very high frequency) and finally HF (high frequency). There are some divisions within these groups, but they are listed in order of the buy-in costs and knowledge required. Another option would be the cell phone, which has become a useful device, even in some very remote areas.

A Word on FCC Licensing and Legalities. The Federal Communications Commission (FCC) licenses access to transmit over radio waves. The only exempt bands are the citizens band, a narrow range of frequencies on the AM band, the FRS (family radio system) broadcasting on low-power FM, and certain bands of the SSB. Beyond these, an amateur radio ("ham") license is required, and they have different levels for different types and complexities of radio, tests reflecting the amount of knowledge required.

You don't need an FCC license to buy an FCC-regulated radio, or to turn it on and listen, but a license is required to press that mike button and talk. If you

These very compact VHF and UHF units can reach stations across the nation as long as they are within line-of-sight and range of a repeater. Repeaters are common in many parts of the country, even in more remote areas, but terrain or natural obstacles can block transmissions. An FCC license is required for these units. The sophisticated equipment in the background is a sure sign of a dedicated ham operator.

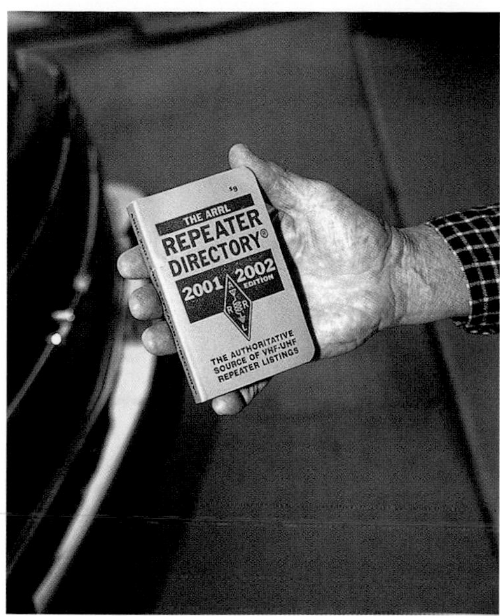

This repeater directory gives licensed operators the codes for repeaters all over the United States. It's necessary when you go traveling. It will give you the locations for the repeaters so that you can determine what your communications capability will be wherever you go.

used a regulated radio in a life-or-death emergency without being licensed, it's likely you'd get a pass, both from the government and from the ham radio community. Otherwise, watch out!

Amateur radio licenses come in several basic categories, the *technician class*, *general class*, and *extra class*. There are a couple of other divisions in there and some old categories for which no new licenses are being issued. The technician class test consists of 35 questions, and you must get 26 questions right to pass.

CB ETIQUETTE:
It's always mannerly to announce a clear channel at the completion of your conversation. That might sound like, "Seldom Seen, clear (or out)."

The equipment limitations for the technician class have recently been relaxed to offer the opportunity for newbies to use more powerful equipment. To get a general class license, you must also pass the 35-question test, as well as a Morse code test. If you want the amateur extra class license, you have to pass an additional 50-question test. The basic level entitles the operator to use equipment in a certain frequency range, with access to more frequencies and more power as you move up the license levels.

CB Radios. CB radios can be anything from a cheap handheld to a fancy dash-mounted unit with lots of bells and whistles. CBs use an FCC-allotted band of AM (amplitude modulation) frequencies, sometimes called "double sideband." No license is required for a CB operator. By law, CBs of any type are limited to a 4-watt output. This provides a useful communications range of about 2 to 5 miles, basically within the unit's natural ground wave effect (a radius around the antenna) with a good antenna and perfect conditions. On a really good day, with an outstanding setup, 25-mile two-way conversations are possible. The CB's AM radio waves can "skip" off the atmosphere, and in very rare circumstances, when the right atmospheric conditions exist, you can actually have a conversation

THE CB RADIO 10-CODE

10-1 Signal Weak
10-2 Signal Strong
10-3 Stop Transmitting
10-4 OK
10-5 Relay To
10-6 Busy
10-7 Out of Service
10-8 In Service
10-9 Say Again
10-10 Negative
10-11 On Duty
10-12 Stand By
10-13 Existing Conditions
10-14 Have Message
10-15 Message Delivered
10-16 Reply to Message
10-17 En Route
10-18 Urgent
10-19 In Contact
10-20 Location
10-21 Call by Phone
10-22 Disregard
10-23 Arrived at Scene
10-24 Assignment Complete
10-25 Meet
10-26 ETA
10-27 License Information
10-28 Ownership Information
10-29 Records Check
10-30 Danger
10-31 Pick Up
10-32 Units Needed
10-33 Need Help Fast
10-34 Time
10-100 Potty Break

Having UHF/VHF and high-wattage HF capability in your vehicle does not require a cockpit that looks like a Boeing 747 jumbo jet. The control heads of longtime ham John Radloff's mobile setup are compact, with UHF/VHF on the left and HF in the center. The actual units are housed in a box in the cargo compartment. This compartment is ventilated with small 12-volt fans, since the units can generate heat. Antenna needs are modest as well, with one of the two in view through the windshield.

with someone very far away. Technically, it's illegal to have a conversation with someone more than 150 miles away on the CB.

The limited range of CBs may make them impractical for use in all emergency situations, especially for a lone vehicle in a remote area. In some cases, there may be enough people within range to form a communications chain and relay an emergency message to the right authority. Often, the solution in an emergency situation might be to summon a person that's only a short distance away, from your own traveling group perhaps. Another option is to dispatch a member of your group to a point where they can summon help, or at least pass a message.

The main use of a CB in the four-wheeling realm is for fun and information. The running CB commentary heard in a group of four-wheelers on a trail run is better than any TV show.

Using the CB. Many CBers have a "handle," or radio nickname. Pick whatever you like, or use your actual name if you prefer. The handle is better because there may be lots of Janes, Bills, Bobs, Wendys, and so on. Odds are that you can come up with a handle that suits your personality and is less common than your name. Handles are unofficial, so you're not stuck with your first pick.

CB OPERATION:
Channel 11 is used mostly as a "hailing" channel. From there you would agree with your party on another channel and switch there for conversation.

CB etiquette calls for not hogging the channel, using brevity in your messages, and avoiding bad language. The airwaves are first come, first serve. That means a person using the channel in your range gets to finish before you get your chance. In an emergency, feel free to break right in and demand a clear channel.

When you want to contact someone, you follow a standard form about like this: "Buffalo Hunter, this is Seldom Seen." Wait a moment, and if there is no reply, try again a few times. If you don't make contact, get on one last time and say, "Negative contact Buffalo Hunter, Seldom Seen clear (or out)." The reason for this is that there may be others waiting to use the channel and by clearing, you are opening the channel.

If you need to use a channel that has some traffic, normal etiquette is to allow the speakers some time to complete their conversation. If they are overly windy, wait for a lull and jump in with, "Break One-One" ("Break" and whatever channel you are on). This is a hint that you need to use the channel and could they please give you a "break" and wrap up the talk. Most often, one of them will reply, "Go, breaker," and you will be allowed to conduct your business. They may ask for a moment to complete their conversation and then give a postponed, "Go breaker," or announce a clear channel.

CB EMERGENCY:
Channel 9 is the emergency channel. CB operators use this channel only for emergencies. It is often monitored by rescue organizations.

CB OPERATION:
Channel 19 is the semiofficial trucker's channel. Many groups or four-wheel clubs will adopt a particular channel.

Some ex-military people have a certain radio procedure ingrained, which includes the phonetic alphabet (Alpha, Bravo, Charlie, Delta, Echo, etc., or the older Able, Baker, Charlie, Dog, Easy, etc.), saying "over" after each completed sentence and using "Roger" and "Wilco" (will comply) as affirmatives. That's OK but not necessary. The "10-Code" (see page 71 sidebar,) is a police code that has long been a part of CB use. This is not necessary either, but it's cool, and many four-wheelers use the codes that apply. It wouldn't hurt to know the common 10-codes so you understand what you're hearing.

Use of CB Controls. Every CB unit is different, but there is much commonality in the controls. Some of what follows is universal, and some is optional and appears only on the higher-line units.

Microphone: The "mike" is simple, with a "grille" area into which you speak and a transmit button (a.k.a. the PTT or push to talk switch). Hold the mike about 2 inches from your mouth, press the transmit button, and speak normally. Release the button when you finish speaking. There is usually an LED indicator on the face of the radio that goes red when transmitting. The unit cannot transmit and receive at the same time, so you need to release the mike button to listen.

Channel Selector: Modern CBs use 40 channels; older units had 23.

Squelch: This control tunes out noise. Generally, you will turn the squelch down (counter-clockwise) until you hear hissing and then slowly turn back until the noise just disappears. More squelch (quieter) tends to limit the range of incoming transmissions. If someone is at extreme range, you may have to live with the squelch way down and try to hear over the static.

S/RF Meter: This is a small meter that indicates the strength of both the incoming and outgoing signals, usually on a scale of 1 through 9. The higher number indicates the more powerful signal. Many radios have this feature.

Local/DX: This switch controls receiver sensitivity. On local, the unit will hear only the stronger nearby stations but hear them more clearly and without as much background noise. On DX, the radio will hear all stations, weak or strong, to the accompaniment of more background noise.

ANL: This is a noise limiter that helps to tune out extraneous external noise, such as the crackling from ignition systems or whines from alternators. It does tend to reduce the clarity of reception, so it's usually off until needed. If your CB is troubled by noise from the vehicle in which it's mounted, there are various filters that can be installed to insulate the radio from them.

RF Gain: This is a manual control for reception sensitivity. Set at maximum, it will pick up very weak signals but will also be subject to bleedover interference from other channels on either side of the one selected.

CB Radio Choices. The beginning range of choices is the handheld unit. Though all CBs will have a 4-watt output, the handheld's short antenna and low and short-term battery power put them at a disadvantage. With these units, a 12-volt power adapter/charger becomes an important accessory. They can be very handy on a slow trail for helping guide vehicles though tough obstacles or where people are walking around. The higher-priced units are better performers.

A mounted transceiver is the best overall choice. There are many out there, from under $100 to nearly $1,000. It all comes down to the quality of the components and the features. Some units will allow your CB to be used as a mini PA system. You can also make microphone upgrades to clarify or amplify your voice. A few CBs incorporate an SSB transceiver. Among options, the weather channel is the most useful. This channel gives you the opportunity to monitor weather changes that could be inconvenient or even deadly.

Antenna Choices. With your output limited to 4 watts, your antenna choice becomes of paramount importance to good range. Handhelds are at the bottom of the food chain in this area and are usually limited to a mile or so with their tiny antennas. Many can be temporarily converted to work on an outside vehicle antenna. This equipment makes a worthwhile supplemental purchase.

Bear in mind that the radio and antenna must be matched, or tuned, to the vehicle via an SWR (standing wave ratio) meter. Each vehicle is slightly different, so adjustments made after installation are akin to a performance tune-up on your engine. It's a relatively simple process, and SWR meters are not expensive, so it can be a do-it-yourself task or one you reserve for a

This may not seem to be the ideal spot for a CB antenna, but the SWR meter liked it. The body of the vehicle is fiberglass, so the ground plane effect is somewhat limited. This was helped by the addition of a big stainless-steel toolbox in the bed nearby.

pro. The primary adjustment is tuning the length of the antenna. This can be done by physically shortening or lengthening the antenna or, in the case of a loaded-coil antenna, making an adjustment via a tuning screw on the antenna, or by "bobbing" the antenna to the right length. Sometimes the length of the coaxial cable connecting the radio to the antenna is important. On a new installation, making the adjustments is vital to performance; a severely out-of-tune radio can suffer component damage.

Antennas work best when they have a sizable ground plane, which is a "capture" or "mirror" area below the antenna. The ideal size is 18 by 18 feet, but in a vehicle, the best you will find is a few square feet of metal roof. That's the best place to mount a CB antenna. If you have a ragtop, do the best you can. The person who tunes your radio might be able to find the next best spot. It varies from vehicle to vehicle. One specialist I spoke with told me that two identical vehicles can be completely different in this regard. Magnetic mounts on roofs are popular, as are clamp-on mounts on the side-view mirrors, bumper mounts, and windshield frame mounts. Some folks don't even mind putting a hole in the side of the body and mounting a bracket there.

There are many types of antennas, from 108-inch whips to short, loaded antennas. Obviously the loaded units are easiest to deal with, but a taller antenna reaches out farther. A tall antenna offers a better ground wave effect and therefore a longer effective range. A loaded antenna contains extra coils of wire inside that simulate a longer antenna. Fiberglass or carbon-fiber antenna bodies are used, with the wire inside. Some are metal.

The antenna is connected to the radio via coax cable. There is definitely a quality difference between department-store cable and professional-quality stuff. This material can mean the difference between really good range and being able to shout farther than your CB can transmit. In conclusion, the taller antenna has greater range, but physical limitations may dictate a short, loaded antenna.

External Speakers. In a loud or open-topped vehicle, hearing your CB may be difficult. Almost all units have a small, built in speaker, but often an external speaker is necessary to hear over the whine of tires. These are specially designed to make the human voice sound louder and clearer. Almost all CBs have a jack for this speaker. Many also have a jack for a low-power PA-type speaker. This can be very useful for the trail, but take care using it in street traffic because they are illegal in some locales.

Single Sideband. SSB radios are a variation of the AM technology used with CBs. I've avoided radio theory up to now, and I won't get into the technical differences here. SSB opens up more channels and offers quite a bit more range—the right setups can reach hundreds of miles. Some SSB frequencies require an FCC license, but some do not. Radios that combine CB and SSB are available, and these units have the "legal" SSB frequencies that do not require a license. SSB transmits at 12 watts and is also more efficient (some sources say 16 times more efficient), resulting in a much longer range. SSB is the logical choice for four-wheelers wanting to reach out farther in case of an emergency. According to some amateur radio people, the available channels may not be well monitored in some areas.

Ham: VHF/UHF. UHF and VHF are part of the FM (frequency modulation) band used for TV and high-quality radio, but a certain batch of frequencies are allotted to amateur radio. These are the most popular of the amateur radio frequencies. They have some limitations because FM is line-of-sight. That means when a mountain or other obstacle is in the way, the signal stops. Your experiences with TV reception prior to cable may be the best example of line-of-sight radio wave problems.

What's happened over the years with amateur radio is that tens of thousands of repeaters have been set up all over the country. All but the most remote areas now have repeaters. A repeater is a radio that takes your transmission and rebroadcasts it to another repeater, and another. The repeaters are individually coded, requiring a special code to be entered on the radio to trigger it. Each one has a special code, and you need to know the code for the repeater nearest you to make it work. The repeater codes are available for sale in booklets, and the proceeds go to maintain the repeaters. Repeater maintenance and setup is most often done on a volunteer basis by the legions of hams and ham associations around the country.

If a repeater is available, you can speak to someone almost anywhere. In fact you can even get a phone line if your set (and the repeater) have what's called a "patch." You can dial up and make a phone call, just like a cell phone. That includes a 911 call or just a call to let the spouse know you'll be late and to hold dinner. If no repeater is available, then your transmission is limited to line-of-sight. UHF/VHF is very well monitored, and help is available 24 hours a day. Some VHF/UHF units are handhelds, but if a repeater is within its more limited range, you can still speak to someone on the other side of the country.

Ham: HF. The HF bands, also commonly known as short wave, are part of the AM band and can reach all over the world. Power output is very high, in the thousands of watts, though most mobile stations are in the hundreds of watts or less. An upper-end FCC license is required for this type of unit. They do not need repeaters, and you will find this realm well monitored. Many hams with upper-end licenses often have equipment that has SSB, FM, and HF combined.

Family Radio Systems. FRS radios have become popular and useful family tools, enabling members to stay in contact at crowded events, on hikes, or wherever they are separated but in the same general vicinity. Their low power output, 0.5 watt, limits range to under 2 miles in the best conditions. Unlike CBs, which operate on AM frequencies, the FRS units use FM. Voice clarity is better, but they are strictly line-of-sight. Many have a feature that transmits a sub-audible tone that only another FRS unit tuned to the same tone can read. This offers "private channel" communications, even when others are using FRS units on the same frequency. FRS radios could be used by four-wheeling families to stay in touch when some of them are out of the vehicle on a slow-moving trail. No license is required for FRS units.

Cell Phones. It's surprising how many remote places have cell phone service and equally surprising how many less remote places don't. There's no guarantee that your cell will work in the boonies, but bring it anyway. Also bring an extra charged battery or a 12-volt adapter/charger. In a serious situation, you don't want the battery dying before all the important words are spoken. Among the lessons of September 11 was the value of a cell phone.

CB ANTENNAS:

How tall an antenna you can deal with depends on where you travel. If it's mostly open country, the tall whip is ideal. For driving among the trees a short, loaded unit is the best choice.

CHAPTER 5
Essential Skills—Outlook and Basic Technique: Solid Foundations

High mountain shelf roads, like this one in central Colorado, are within the realm of almost any stock 4×4 and even many all-wheel-drive rigs. Some drivers find them intimidating at first. In this case, the trail is a fairly smooth dirt and gravel road that would be a "no worries" jaunt if it weren't for the 3,000-foot drop on one side. With plenty of room to negotiate this section, only abject stupidity by the driver or an act of God comparable to the great flood would pose a danger.

Some years back, a four-wheeling friend from Britain came for a visit, and, no big surprise, we went 'wheeling in some of the toughest nearby terrain. Andy had a good deal of experience, but between having to drive on the "wrong" side of the vehicle and the fact that my full-size Blazer was bigger than anything he had ever four-wheeled, it took some time for him to get oriented. As he situated himself behind the wheel and looked over the vast expanse of the Blazer's hood (or should I say bonnet?), he exclaimed, "It's like looking out over the flight deck of the bloody Nimitz!" Andy's example illustrates the need for all of us to fine-tune our four-wheeling "whiskers" to get a feel for the vehicle.

Whiskers? Have you ever wondered about those long whiskers on a cat's face? These are the feline equivalent of sensors. With them, he can determine how big a gap he can crawl through. The four-wheeling equivalent is when the driver has a feel or sense of his rig in tight quarters. This comes from practice, but rather than practicing by peeling the sheet metal off the passenger side of your shiny 4×4, take some time for a walk around. The goals are to commit the layout of the vehicle to memory and develop a feel for where the less directly visible parts of the vehicle are at all times. With practice, a driver can develop this into an almost instinctive sense.

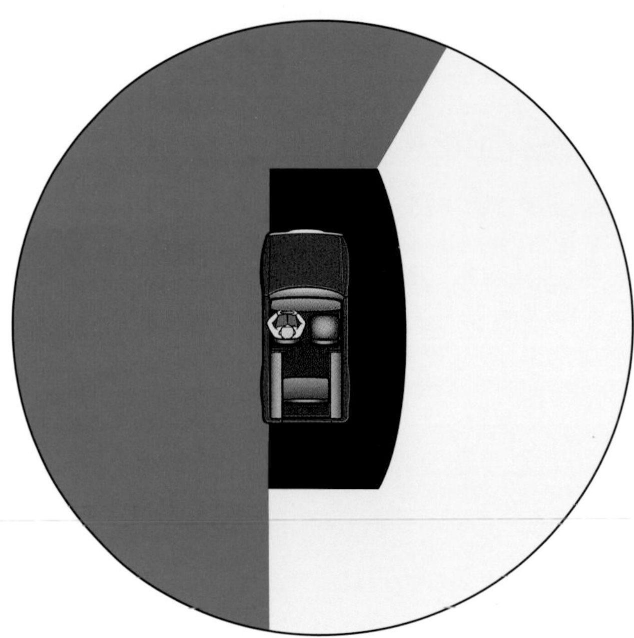

The driver's point of view has many areas where vision is restricted or outright blocked. This graphic represents the driver point of view of a typical SUV. A compact, doorless, open-topped rig like a Jeep utility would offer better visibility. The green areas show the areas with the best visibility. The yellow areas show the restricted places, and the black areas are where the driver's view is completely blocked or shadowed. Because the driver can hang his head out the window, the entire driver's side of the vehicle is in the green area.

Common Sense

Many people lament the apparent death of common sense. It's not dead, but it sometimes hides behind people unwilling to admit stupid mistakes. I'm relying on you to apply common sense to any formula you read here. Properly securing the vehicle every time you step out to evaluate the terrain, for example. Common sense comes from paying attention. Don't get so lost in the yuks of 'wheeling that you forget to realize that a vehicle will roll away if not secured by the parking brake or "Park." (See the previous chapter for more on using the parking brake.) That's why I'm not going to burden either of us by constantly mentioning the basic common-sense items in my descriptions of techniques.

TECHNIQUE:
If what you are doing isn't working, try something different!

Driver POV: Reading Terrain

The driver's point of view (POV) is obstructed in many ways. The long hood means you cannot see the ground 10 feet or more in front of your vehicle. Vision to the rear is even more obstructed. You can see well enough on the driver's side (and toward the front) by hanging your head out the window, but vision is obstructed on the passenger's side.

The illustration above shows the driver's point of view, where vision is best, restricted, or completely blocked. In effect, you are blind to certain areas, not the least of which is right in front of you. The defense is to memorize the terrain as you approach. Many novice drivers stretch their necks like E.T. trying to look over the hood and see the ground directly in front of the vehicle. The end result is that their POV is restricted to a very narrow arc and they are merely reacting to changing terrain as it appears inside that narrow arc, rather than preparing well in advance.

The better approach is a scanning technique, where you observe the general terrain features as far up the trail as you can see and then scan back to 20 or 30 feet ahead of the vehicle and memorize the terrain features. You then have plenty of time to react and get set up to tackle obstacles. It's a continual scan that increases in intensity with the terrain's difficulty or complexity.

Driver POV: Picking Lines

A "line" is an approach and path over or through an obstacle that allows the vehicle to surmount the obstacle without damage. One hopes the line picked is the "best" line, but to paraphrase an old pilot's adage, any line that gets you up and over without damage or injury is a good line. Picking lines comes very naturally to some people and with more difficulty to others. Rest assured, even those with the least amount of innate ability can learn to do it well enough. The trouble is that it's a very difficult skill to teach in a book.

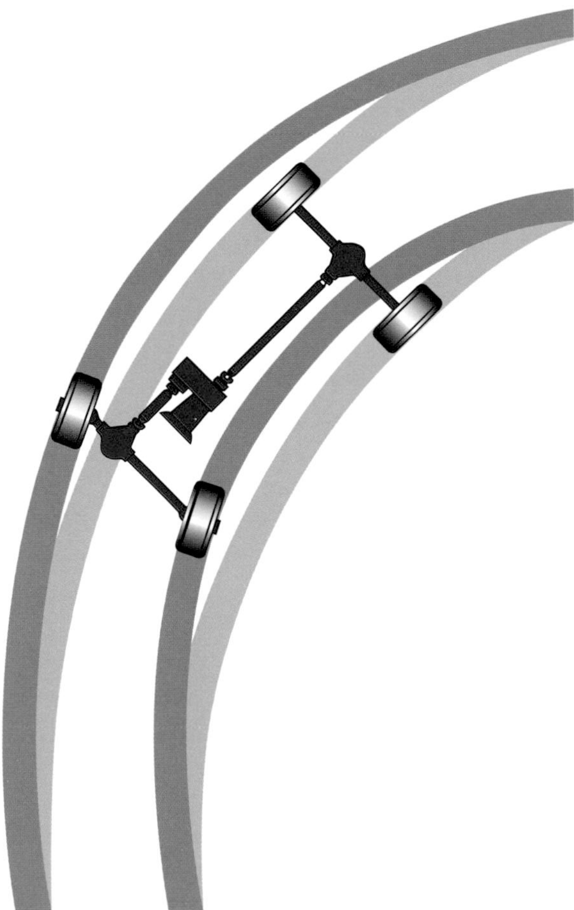

One critical element that all drivers must, and will, learn quickly is that the front and rear tires do not follow the same path. It's easy for newbies to steer the front end clear and forget about the rear. This could put your rear tire into something you're trying to avoid. The trick is to wait until the rear axle is nearly even with the offending item and then steer hard to pivot that tire around it. Maneuvering on the trail is often done with large amounts of steering input.

Watching an experienced driver is a great way to learn the art of picking lines. Comparing his line, and the end results of that line, with the one you charted in your head can be a useful exercise.

A well-known British off-highway driving instructor, who spent at least 40 years teaching people the fine art of four-wheeling, has a colorful saying when it comes to lines. "Pick the high ground," Don Green is fond of saying, "just like John Wayne." This alludes to one of the absolutes in picking lines, which is to pick a path for your tires that keeps the undercarriage clear and unobstructed. You will also seek to keep the vehicle as level as possible. As you learned in Chapter 2, an unloaded tire resulting from a vehicle at a severe angle, or a tire in the air, is not providing traction. Drivers must also look for the spots with the best surface for maximum traction. You may only be able to place one axle at a time on good ground, but often one axle is enough to move the few feet needed.

TIGHT FITS:
In tight spots, keep toward the side you can see well and judge more precisely. Assuming you have overall clearance, cut the driver's side close and be sure you clear the side you can't see as well.

ON LINES:
One fact you will learn quickly is that there are often many more lines over an obstacle than even the most experienced driver can see. Vehicle dynamics play a big part, and a good line for one rig may be a bad line for another.

OPEN-DIFF TRACTION TRICKS:
If you have an open diff, try to keep traction equal side to side to avoid spinning the wheel with the least traction. You will learn to pick the places that do not present traction obstacles at all four wheels simultaneously.

Spotters

Nobody rides for free. The person sitting in the passenger's seat should assist the driver in keeping an eye out for hazards, particularly on that side of the vehicle. It doesn't take much skill to notice a fender is in danger of being torn off, so virtually anyone can be of some use. Should the person riding "shotgun" be skilled and knowledgeable in the four-wheeling arts, so much the better.

There comes a time when a view from outside the cockpit is needed, and a clued-in spotter can be walking disaster prevention. Using a spotter comes with a price; the driver has to relinquish some control. The only way it works well is if the driver gives the spotter control of the situation and does no more and no less than ordered by the spotter. The driver, and we'll assume he's the owner of the vehicle, retains overall veto power and the option to "fire" the spotter, but a spotter is worthless if the driver doesn't follow instructions. The spotter then takes responsibility for what happens, assuming the driver follows instructions. Friendships, and closer relationships, have gone awry in situations where mistakes were made and damage resulted. It pays to keep an adult perspective on these things, a little *que será, será* (whatever will be, will be) perhaps, and also to delegate spotting duties to people who are qualified. If you get help on the trail from relative strangers, it's a little more problematic. Another *que será, será* time, I suppose.

Basic Spotting Rules. There are some basic rules that both spotters and drivers should understand. Some clubs have adopted spotting rules like these for use at events. You can invent your own. The main thing is that both the spotter and driver are reading from the same page of rules. Even spectators can be a help by understanding what's going on and letting the spotter and driver do their work without interference. That doesn't prevent you-the-spectator from helping; just do it in a way that doesn't disrupt the process.

General

1. At least 99 percent of spotting should be nonverbal. Use hand signals. This avoids words being misunderstood or drowned out by engine noises or spectators. Verbal conferences should be face to face with the vehicle stopped and secured.
2. There's only one official spotter: The person the driver has chosen. The spotter should ignore the more vocal armchair quarterbacks on the sidelines. If spectators get to be a problem, make an appeal for silence. If you are not the spotter and you see a better or safer way, make a quiet comment to the spotter.

With capable spotting, even stock rigs can be taken into extraordinary terrain. With 100 percent visibility, the spotter can direct the vehicle over the best lines and safely past the bad stuff. It's a team effort, with the spotter making clear, decisive hand signals and the driver following those instructions to the letter, no more or less than directed.

This spotter is standing far enough away to have a clear view of the terrain and is in clear view of the driver. The spotter should also be far enough ahead to be safe from an accidentally applied stab of the throttle of a foot slipping off the clutch or brake pedal. Moving around for vantage points is dangerous for spotters. It's easy to get caught up in the job and not pay as much attention to footing as you should. As the vehicle pulls closer, the spotter should stop the vehicle and devote 100 percent attention to his own safety before moving back to another strategic location.

3. The spotter directs other helpers, such as in piling rocks, pushing, and so on.

Driver Tips

1. You have the right to refuse a spotter, or fire him, but you also take the responsibility for what happens.
2. You are handing over 50 percent of the control and 50 percent of the responsibility to your spotter.

3. Keep your eyes on the spotter. If you can't see the spotter, stop and get his attention. It's worse than uncool to run over your spotter.
4. Do no more and no less than your spotter directs. Continue with the last instruction until your spotter tells you to stop, or changes the instruction. If it becomes clear that your spotter isn't paying attention, stop and get his attention.
5. If you disagree with your spotter, don't just ignore him. Stop and have a conference. His perspective is a little different from yours, so it's good to know why he's made a particular decision.

Spotter Tips

1. Take the time you need to get a clear picture of the problem and a good solution before giving directions. The odds are good that you are dealing with someone's pride and joy. Take as much care as if it were your own.
2. Stay in view of the driver.
3. Make clear, bold hand signals that can't be misunderstood.
4. Don't stand too close to the line of travel. A foot slipping off a clutch pedal or an accidentally applied throttle could take you out. In some cases standing 10 or 15 feet away gives you the advantage of being able to see the whole picture.

SPOTTER'S HAND SIGNALS

Stop immediately! Fists can be shaken for emphasis.

Come ahead at a slow pace. Can be used one-handed in conjunction with other hand signals, such as come ahead, steer right.

Steer left and come ahead. Driver to hold this steering input until directed to make a change.

Steer right and come ahead. Driver to hold this steering input until directed to make a change.

Slow down!

Go back.

A little bit. The little bit signal can be added to any other, such as come ahead a little bit.

5. You are responsible to keep any extra help clear of the vehicle when it moves. Rock pilers have a bad habit of getting run over if the spotter isn't paying attention.
6. Watch your step. Spotters spend a fair bit of time walking backward or moving around on instinct while watching their vehicle. While not always possible, it's better to stop your vehicle and find a spot to stand than to split your focus between walking uncertain ground and providing guidance. Seek the best way to protect yourself and the driver throughout the run.

Momentum: The Two-Edged Sword

One dictionary describes momentum as "the impetus of movement" and a "complex mixture of mass and velocity." Inertia is another word that fits. For our purposes, the definition of inertia, "a body in motion tends to stay in motion," is the most useful. The weight of your vehicle carries it along until friction, air resistance, and other factors slow it down. That inertia/momentum is a useful tool for four-wheeling, but it must be used wisely.

It takes a certain amount of traction to put your vehicle in motion. When circumstances don't make that traction available, a *little* momentum can carry you through. Sometimes that just means a steady speed over a problem area, and other times it means gaining a little speed on good ground before you encounter the obstacle. Emphasis is on the "little," at least at first.

Momentum just right! The correct amount of momentum isn't always discernable in a still photo, but this Defender 90 is using it correctly. Though on highly tractive slickrock, this climb is steep enough to overcome the available traction of a vehicle without lockers. A steady pace, faster than a creep but at a slow walking pace, is enough.

Always try going easy the first time and increase the level of intensity gradually until you reach the no-go point and abort the attempt.

Momentum in Mud, Sand, and Snow. All three of these ground conditions are similar in that they combine low surface strength and low shear strength. Not only do you sink, but you have no traction. Momentum

Not enough momentum. This is what happens when there isn't enough momentum or traction. In the case of this unlocked Land Rover, this left front tire and the opposite rear tire have broken loose and are spinning on the rocks. Beyond approaching at too low a speed, this driver was making a couple of other mistakes. The first obvious mistake was the application of too much throttle for the available traction. The second was that he didn't air down significantly. Correction of either of these two errors might have resulted in a successful "one-shot" climb, even with a paucity of momentum.

Too much momentum. Faced with a steep climb on a rock slab made slick by rain and mud, this driver chose to hit it hard. The results were spectacular! He did make the climb but was risking severe damage in the process. He was betting on the strength of the upgrades made to the Jeep. Other drivers proved, however, that a less radical approach could also make the climb.

Momentum in mud, sand, and snow. Keeping up momentum on soft surfaces will keep you *on* the surface rather than *in* it. When making a turn in the sand, the tires will begin to dig in and slow the vehicle down. There won't be enough traction to overcome the extra drag, so momentum will carry you through.

can launch you completely across some soft areas or provide you with just enough help to claw your way across with the minimal traction available. With enough speed you can actually hydroplane across a soft surface, but control is just about impossible. Using momentum across soft ground requires that you evaluate the surroundings along with the obstacle. Are you going to end up sideways or lose it completely and slam into a tree or a rock?

Momentum on Hillclimbs. There are many hills on which you could not start from a dead stop, but if you have a little motion, you can keep going. That means a steady speed on a hill. You may encounter spots of lesser traction, or a steeper slope, and momentum may be enough to carry you past it. If not, you must be ready to respond instantly before you come to a stop.

ON MOMENTUM:
With practice, you can gauge the need for momentum, or the amount of momentum needed, for assorted obstacles pretty accurately. Momentum can be used in nearly any off-highway situation, from crossing mud to climbing hills.

Sometimes that means a little more throttle; other times it means backing off for torque control.

Momentum can also be used at the start of a low-traction climb to help you up. The momentum is built up on flat ground. On a short hill without enough traction to climb slowly, this may take you up without spinning a tire. On a long hill, safe and sane levels of momentum may just carry you halfway and leave you perched with spinning tires and a failed-climb maneuver to perform. The approach to a hill also may limit your momentum options with a sharp transition from horizontal to vertical. In other cases, you may be able to build up quite a head of steam but, just as with soft ground, you can have control problems with too much speed.

Momentum for Rockcrawling. Momentum is as useful in rocks as anywhere else, but because rocks are unyielding by nature, contact usually results in the vehicle getting the short straw. As often as not, momentum for rocky

NO BANZAI:
In general, if crossing a soft area will require a high-speed banzai charge, look for another way across or a way around.

terrain comes into play when weight transfer unloads one axle and overloads the other. This can happen on a straight climb, usually a very steep one if a highly tractive rock face is involved, or on ledges. On a straight climb on rock faces, such as slickrock, play the game much like you would elsewhere: maintain a steady speed and react appropriately if needed. On a boulder-strewn landscape, your speed potential will be severely limited, but even the momentum imparted from speeds as low as ¼ mile per hour can be useful. Again, try to maintain whatever movement you can rather than starting and stopping. Climbing in loose rocks may require momentum, just as with soft ground, but too much speed can result in bouncing, slamming, cut tires, or a loss of control.

The ledge scenario involves the use of a "bump." Usually the front axle is up, though unloaded by weight transfer, and it's the rear axle that can't make the climb. The bump combines momentum with a judicious stab of throttle at just the right time. As illustrated in pictures nearby, if the driver applies a stab of throttle just as the rear tires hit the ledge, the momentum has the effect of momentarily "gluing" the tires to the rock by increasing ground pressure. This can make the rig hop up that ledge like a jackrabbit. As you can imagine, the forces acting on the tire, suspension, and drivetrain are great, so the amount of momentum used, the amount of throttle, and the duration of the throttle application must be carefully chosen. On a typical ledge, a "roll" of just a couple of feet is enough momentum for the bump.

Momentum on a hillclimb. Momentum is necessary even on rough-surface climbs like this. It requires thoughtful line picking and commitment. You pick the line, select a reasonable amount of momentum, and go for it. The mistake many novice drivers make in this situation is backing off too soon. Stay with it until it's clear that you are stopped. The second most common mistake is inducing wheelspin from too much throttle. The biggest danger on terrain like this comes from wheel hop and tire spinning, and the end result can be broken drivetrain parts. In fact, one of the next vehicles on this Moab, Utah, trail destroyed a driveshaft U-joint and a front axle universal simultaneously.

Momentum in rockcrawling. This lightly modified Wrangler is negotiating a particularly difficult climb consisting of large boulders and ledges, all covered by a dusting of sand. Few vehicles can crawl this section, so a careful application of momentum is in order after selecting a line and committing to it. Despite how it looks (low shutter speed accentuates the visual wheel speed), this driver had the right amount of "mo." This situation was a bit on the hairy side, requiring good judgment and calm application of basic principles.

It's steep, but there's a good bit of traction on the rocky surface, degraded only by a powdering of sand. This Range Rover is not low-geared enough to no-brake this slope, so the driver will control wheel lockup with careful application of the brakes.

Mud and a steep descent is the devil's brew. In this case, the mud has partially dried to a more tractive consistency, well out of the greasy consistency but not quite back to regular dirt. There is enough traction for a controlled descent, but there could be patches of more slippery stuff to catch you unaware. In this situation, you should be ready for steering correction and perhaps a stab of throttle to keep you going straight downhill.

Easy Dirt Roads: More Dangerous Than You Think!

One of my jobs here is to warn you, or remind you, about situations where complacency leads to trouble. One of those areas is the dirt or gravel road. It can come at the beginning or the end of the more difficult four-wheeling. Many people regard the end as the most dangerous part for many reasons. You're tired by then and not paying as much attention. Perhaps you are in a hurry to get home, so you are combining tired with fast, and that's the devil's brew. Perhaps your vehicle has suffered some unseen damage. Just like on the highway, a failure combined with greater speed increases the chance for a very bad result. As it often happens, the dirt road is a transition area from the more difficult parts of a trail to the highway. Because it is not highway-smooth, many drivers delay airing up their tires until they reach the edge of the pavement to maintain better ride quality. That's fine as long as the driver understands how handling is adversely affected.

Lock It Down

"Locking it down" is a trail term for parking, but unlike the street, there are many angles on the trail that make your vehicle prone to rolling away if it's not properly secured. You read about the park pawl and the parking brake in the Controls section of Chapter 4. Always take care to lock your rig down on the trail by applying the parking brake (bearing in mind the caveats discussed in Chapter 4)

BRAKING ON DESCENTS:
Engine braking alone may not provide the safe, slow descent you need. This is especially true with automatics. In that case, you'll need to apply the brakes gently. The key is to keep the wheels rolling. Keeping the window(s) down helps you hear a tire that's beginning to slip.

CATS IN THE GRASS:
Catalytic converters get very hot. If you park a vehicle with a hot cat in tall grass, you may start a fire, with your pride and joy as the first victim. This situation has been the cause of a few significant range or forest fires.

A descent may be combined with irregular terrain. In the case of this stock Nissan, it resulted in moderate rear tire lift. This is also very characteristic of a rig with a combination of IFS and a stiffly sprung live rear axle. No worries at this level, but the factors to keep in mind are the reduced traction and the weight transfer. Remember that you need traction as much for a controlled descent as for a climb. Traction is reduced by one tire in this case. Weight transfer would be a concern if the terrain increased in angle. In this case, the driver used his brakes for a very slow, controlled descent.

and using Park with an automatic or putting the manual trans in gear. On steeper terrain many prudent drivers will also throw a rock behind a tire or park in such a spot that the ground provides natural wheel chocks. Someday, you will have to park in steep terrain, and the precarious nature of the spot will no doubt encourage you to lock 'er down good!

Descending a Slope

Gravity can be a friend or an enemy. Gravity will "help" you down the hill, but like some of your most "helpful" friends, it may be more help than you want at the moment. People often forget that traction is needed going down as well as going up. The difference is that if you lose traction going down, you will continue going down . . . just in a less controlled manner.

A descent starts with a look at the hill. Many times you can see your path from the driver's seat, but if you can't, step out and have a look. Evaluate the surface for traction and contours. Evaluate the steepness and where it ends up at the bottom. Just like going up, you can handle some very steep angles if there is enough traction, but a very steep descent on a loose surface could be the "yeehaw" toboggan ride of your life.

The general rule is to select the lowest possible gearing combination. That means the lowest transmission gear and low range in the transfer case. That rule is variable, of course, according to the conditions and your vehicle's gearing. On a mild descent with good traction, second gear might be OK. Try to let the engine and drivetrain be the primary means of slowing your vehicle. In compound low, especially with a manual trans, it's amazing how much holdback you can get from the engine alone. The nice part about engine compression braking is that it's evenly applied to all four wheels, though weight transfer may influence traction.

The less speed you have at the top of a descent, the less you'll have at the bottom. In cases where you can see well enough to drive over the edge without getting out to survey, you may be tempted not even to stop before doing so. On a mild hill this can be OK, but on a steeper hill, it can induce extra speed that you will have to deal with. In these cases, creeping over with the least possible momentum is the better choice.

On very loose surfaces, too low a gear may cause the tires to slide, especially the unloaded rear tires. If you choose a higher gear to maintain traction, you may go down the hill a bit faster than is comfortable or safe. Gauge the potential problems of that situation against the limited traction and decide if this is a hill you really need to go down. If there are no major undulations and a clear rollout at the bottom, a little speed shouldn't be much of a problem.

If you are caught on the hill in too low a gear, it's usually best not to shift up—especially with a manual trans. The moment you push that clutch pedal in, the vehicle will take off as if a JATO (jet-assisted take-off)

One: Complications to a descent could include a situation like "The Slide" on Red Cone Pass. It's a long, steep descent on a face covered with scree and rock powder. It's doable by most stock vehicles. The run is complicated by relatively deep holes that must be crossed at a low speed to avoid going airborne. Even at a low speed, they cause articulation and weight transfer. The steepness and loose surface guarantees locked-up tires with more than a tiny bit of brake application, so step one is to go over the edge at a very slow speed to reduce momentum at the start. In this case, there was a hole immediately after the top, and as the front tires entered, it was possible to increase brake pressure momentarily and slow the vehicle significantly.

Two: The front wheels come out of the hole and it's time to reduce brake pressure to avoid lockup. The Range Rover is beginning to build up some speed at this point, but the driver is resisting the urge to mash hard on the brakes.

Three: Dipping into another hole provides an opportunity to slow down a bit more by increasing brake pressure.

Four: More holes provide opportunities to slow down.

Five: The holes that severely articulate the suspension can be tricky. In this shot, the front and rear are articulated opposite each other, thus unloading one front and one rear wheel. These wheels tended to lock up with more than a tiny amount of brake pressure, but the ABS braking system aided the driver at that point, and there was no adverse effect. With a non-ABS rig, momentary lockup at a very low speed would not be significant. From this hole on, it was a flat-surface run-out to the bottom, and engine braking was enough to maintain control.

rocket were strapped to the roof. The correct response is to increase speed with the throttle until the tires reacquire grip. You may be going faster, but at least you'll be in control, and you can always back off on the throttle when traction is reacquired.

Because a good deal of weight will transfer from the rear to the front tires on a steep descent, be prepared for the rear end to try to swing around on you. This is an extremely dangerous situation because a rollover is usually imminent. If you are on the brakes at the time, as is most often the case, you have either locked the tires or are exceeding the available traction. Either get off the brakes entirely or ease up as needed and steer slightly in the direction the rear end is going (just like a skid). That alone may or may not get you straight, but the next step is to get on the throttle. It may not take a lot of throttle. The adrenaline rush may cause you to mash on the accelerator a little more than is prudent, so beware of the JATO effect. In reality, most situations as outlined above are pretty easy to control. The first time will offer the highest fear factor.

Ascending a Slope

Going up is easier than going down in many ways because gravity or lack of traction may stop you before things get hairy. It becomes a go/no-go situation at the outset. As mentioned before, traction is the limiting factor. Evaluate the trail surface for traction potential and gauge the climb against your approach, departure, and ramp breakover angles. Don't forget the transition to horizontal at the top.

The goal is to use the highest *possible* gear to avoid wheelspin. This is variable according to vehicle, with gearing and transmission type being the controlling factors. An SUV with 3.23:1 axle ratios and a manual trans with a 3:1 first gear will obviously need first gear, but a pickup with 4.10:1 axle ratios and a 6.4:1 first gear may be able to use second. With automatics, the trans is allowed to make the selection, though there may be times when you should manually select the correct gear to prevent an inopportune upshift or a downshift because of having to use a little throttle on the climb.

The applied use of momentum described above is a useful tool. There are times when you need a little speed going up but you don't want to fly over the top like those jeeps in the old *Rat Patrol* TV show. This is controllable by backing off the throttle by the right amount at the right time. Back out too much and you may not clear because momentum will disappear quickly.

FAILED CLIMBS:
Above all, don't hit the brakes hard in a backward descent. The front wheels will probably lock up and cause the tires to slide, or slide more, leaving no traction for steering and initiating a rapidly worsening situation. Very cautious use of the brakes with a light front end is vital.

Climbs are straightforward stuff from a technical standpoint. Find the smoothest path to the top, choose the correct gear, and apply the required amount of momentum. At this steep angle (near 50 degrees), a short-wheelbase rig like this CJ-7 has transferred a good deal of weight from the front to the rear. A rig with less rubber on the ground might lose traction in the back because of overloading. Bear in mind that only on a very tractive surface, in this case Utah slickrock, can grades this steep be climbed successfully.

Failed Climbs. The sad truth is that you won't make every climb. Learning the failed climb technique makes the sting much easier to bear. Imagine that you get to some point on a climb and you stop . . . not by choice. The first decision becomes whether you are safe enough to spend a few moments deciding what to do next.

If the vehicle is sliding downhill with locked brakes, get into reverse ASAP, get off the brakes, and steer it straight down the hill. If you have a manual trans, make sure you have let out the clutch. It's highly likely with a manual trans that the engine has stalled. For engine braking purposes, it doesn't matter if the engine is running or not, but it's nice to have power steering and brakes from a running engine. Most likely, the engine will restart on its own with the clutch out. If you have fuel injection, watch for a surge as it restarts. The idle speed controller may overcompensate for a moment when the engine restarts in this situation.

If you are safely held on the hillside by your brakes, you might evaluate whether you can make a try at continuing. Perhaps you started in too high a gear and what you need is to downshift. If your basic technique was good but there was insufficient traction to get you past the spot where you stopped, it's unlikely you can start from a hillside. It doesn't hurt to try, depending on the overall circumstances, but it's usually better to back down and try again. The next try should introduce a new element into the equation, perhaps in the form of a little more momentum or a better line.

There are some potentially hairy situations to be prepared for with a failed climb. First, the steering can be unpredictable and hypersensitive backing down, so it's easy to overcorrect. Weight transfer unloads the front tires, so your ability to steer on low-traction surfaces may be somewhat reduced. How responsive the steering is depends on the ground surface. The front end may try to swing downhill and put you sideways. As with a regular skid, you can steer into it, but with steering effectiveness reduced by weight transfer, you may find it has little effect. You may have to apply a little throttle to make the rear axle pull the vehicle straight.

Even sidehills as mild as this one become "driver conditioning" the first few times out. The human body seems to accept quickly the up and down angles, but side angles take longer. This easy sideslope would only be a danger if it were muddy instead of rocky. No worries here!

Sidehills

Sidehills are a part of the four-wheeling game that many people like to avoid. In extreme situations, they are very hazardous, but in the "normal" realm, they are nothing to generate adrenaline over. What's normal? Anything under 10 degrees is a cakewalk on a tractive surface. Many four-wheelers will do 20 degrees without batting an eyelid, but almost everyone gets sweaty armpits over 20 degrees. Most vehicles are safe to somewhat over 30 degrees (not counting the dynamics of the vehicle in motion), and many have advertised being stable past 40 degrees. I've been at 40-plus degrees and freely admit to a dry mouth and a tightly clenched sphincter muscle. At 30 degrees it feels like the door handles are scraping the ground. At 40, you're waiting for the crunch of metal and the crash of breaking glass.

The first rule on sidehills is to avoid the really steep ones if you can find a safe, treading-lightly way around. On slippery surfaces, even a mild sidehill becomes potentially dangerous, depending on what's at the bottom of that slippery slope. Don't forget that a vehicle in motion has some dynamics that may work against you. If one downhill tire lurches into a hole, the sudden weight transfer and suspension movement may momentarily lean you over father than you expect, perhaps far enough to be trouble.

ON SIDEHILLS:
When evaluating a piece of ground to traverse, the overall angle is the first consideration, followed by the tractive surface. From there, look at the contours. If the angle seems OK, think about what's going to happen when your downhill wheel falls into that hole or your uphill wheel climbs that rock.

SIDEHILLS:
If you think you're about to roll, turn downhill quickly, with a quick application of throttle if that feels necessary. This move both reduces the side angle and applies some centrifugal force to keep those uphill wheels on the ground. Steering uphill uses the same physics in reverse, and to your detriment.

When the bottom of the upslope tire is even with the top of the downslope tire, you are at the upper limit (or beyond) of sideslope ability for most rigs. The Land Rover Defender is more capable than most in this area, but most would wonder why the driver chose this anxiety-fraught route over the easier one below. For practice, I suppose. Anyway, he made it without a hitch.

The second rule is to stay straight and square in the seat. The natural human inclination is to lean into the slope, as if the minor weight transfer of your body shifted a few degrees will stop your behemoth from rolling over! If you stay square in the seat, you will stay in touch with the vehicle's true angle. By most accounts, the driver's POV is also improved by seeming less "wacky." You are only looking at one tilted angle (your vehicle versus the terrain) instead of two (you versus your vehicle versus the terrain).

The sidehill escape maneuver, to be used when rollover is imminent, is to steer downhill. Sometimes a quick application of throttle is also needed. Many an imminent rollover has been forestalled by quick application of this trick. In my years as an instructor, it seems this is 180 degrees from some natural human instinct to steer uphill. That maneuver is likely to put you on the roof.

Crossing Gullies

This is one of the more common four-wheeling scenarios. Assuming the gully is not too deep to be crossed, you have two choices, the right-angle or straight-through approach, or the diagonal approach. Which you choose depends on the gully and your vehicle's basic dimensions and clearances.

Stock vehicles with limited clearance will almost always use a diagonal approach in crossing gullies. That means one tire at a time will dip into the gully. The angle at which you cross should be chosen carefully. Ideally, that is as close to a right angle from the gully as clearance will allow. This driver chose a fairly obtuse angle, and you can see the result; his suspension is articulated to the maximum level. The danger of that in an unlocked rig is that traction may be lost on each of the low tires, in this case left front and right rear, because of unloading.

Gullies that are along the line of travel can be straddled if they can't be avoided. This Steyer-Puch Pinzgauer barely has the width to straddle this particular rocky crag, but it was preferable to riding on an angle with two tires in the gully and two tires up on the side. Careful piloting is important to make sure that one set of tires doesn't suddenly slip into the hole.

This is your ordinary mudhole with a few inches of water on top. Step one is always to evaluate. There are tracks in and out, so the odds are good that it's navigable. Local knowledge also indicates that bottomless slime pits are unknown in this area. If in doubt, probe for depth or deep holes with a stick or shovel. Pick a line that takes you straight across, or as straight across as possible. Enter the mudhole with a bit of momentum, just enough to make a little splash with the tires, and maintain that momentum using light throttle and avoiding wheelspin. Emerge safely on the other side and test your brakes when clear. Note the many bypasses around this small obstacle. This driver is taking what appears to be the main route, thus avoiding further terrain damage.

Some drivers think that they are better off keeping two tires up on solid ground when crossing a mudhole. Not so if you have open diffs. Creating a situation where one tire is on solid ground and the other is in goo creates the classic open-differential stuck scenario outlined in the earlier "Traction 101" chapter. Better that you have even traction on all wheels. You can get away with this if you have a locker or a very tight limited-slip, but who wants to be tilted at 25 degrees in a mudhole? The weight transfer is putting more weight on the low tires, which could cause them to sink enough to hang the axles up on the edge of the hole.

Too fast for the situation. This is a mild mudhole, so making a big splash will just increase your time at the carwash, or, in the case of this rather wet mudhole, drown the ignition. There are times when an aggressive approach is needed. This isn't it.

The straight-through method offers the best traction but requires more clearance and better approach, departure, and ramp breakover angles. The technique is to ease both front wheels into the ditch simultaneously and across the ditch to climb out the other side. Depending on the size of the gully, your rear wheels may be in the ditch at this point also. The key elements are to take it slow and to make sure you have all the angles and clearance you need.

When clearance or approach and departure angles are a problem, the diagonal approach reduces the need for clearance. Rather than dropping one end of the vehicle in at a time, you will dip one corner at a time. This has the effect of reducing the angle, though it will require more traction because both your axles will be articulated. As discussed earlier, the downhill tire is unloaded and may lose traction. The diagonal approach works better for long-wheelbase rigs because one axle will be farther out of the bad angle, less articulated, and more able to apply some good traction.

Soft Ground: Mud

Mud, sand, and snow all fit into a similar category, and the driving techniques are roughly similar. They share the trait of having low shear strength and low surface strength. That means little traction and a tendency to sink into *terra firma*.

Traction supplies movement across the mud, and flotation keeps you on top of it. Mud can create a great deal of drag, even if only the tires are in it, and the deeper your tires or undercarriage go into the mud, the more drag is created. If the drag exceeds traction, you stop moving. The idea in most types of mud is to keep the undercarriage out of the goo. That's where the flotation of a big tire footprint comes in.

As for traction, tread design will either get you across or leave you stranded. Aggressive mud tires act more or less like a paddle. The danger in some mud is that it will stick to the tires, fill the treads, and turn it into a "mud donut." When this happens, it prevents the cleats from applying traction. Spinning the tires a little or a lot may cause centrifugal force to sling the mud off and allow the cleats to grab.

Types of Mud. There are many types of mud, and each needs a slightly different technique to get through. Here are the basic types and subtypes, with some explanations and methods for dealing with them. The names and descriptions are mine, so don't go looking in the index of any other texts for information on "Chocolate Ice Cream Mud."

Greasy Mud is usually not very deep but, because it contains lots of clay, it's as slick as oiled spaghetti. Greasy mud can be found almost anywhere but is often seen in the Southeast, the Midwest, and the Northwest. It often has good flotation but poor traction. Because it will really gum up your tires, you need a good self-cleaning tire tread. You are more likely to need the spinning-tire technique in greasy mud to clean your tires and get traction. Tire chains are a useful tool here. You are also more likely to need momentum to get across, but not too much. It's easy to lose control and prang a tree or rock when your ability to steer is reduced.

Gumbo Mud is much like greasy mud but a lot deeper. It can be found almost anywhere but is often seen in the Southeast. It still contains very slick stuff, but it's more watery. Well-traveled greasy mud holes often turn into gumbo. Gumbo is tough because it offers neither flotation nor traction. Apply the same techniques as with greasy, but have your winches and tow straps ready.

Chocolate Ice Cream Mud has the consistency of freshly scooped ice cream with grit in it. It's usually found in mountainous areas. Traction is often better than flotation.

Malodorous Mud is usually found in or around swamps and bogs. It's usually a form of chocolate ice cream mud but often more watery and with a stench. It can have, well, *stuff*, in it . . . usually decaying vegetable matter. Sometimes it also has leeches and other critters you don't want to know about. Treat it like chocolate ice cream but adjust for the more watery consistency.

Nitty-Gritty Mud usually contains heavy grit and small pebbles and is most often found in mountain areas. Flotation is usually good. This stuff isn't much of a worry most times, but it can chew up pretty wheels.

Rocky Road Mud is any basic type of mud with larger rocks in it, from fist size on up. The hazards here are undercarriage damage or cut tires. If combined with a slope, as is common at popular four-wheeling spots around Arkansas and Oklahoma, you can have one of the most difficult situations around. While there is not often much danger of sinking, the slicked-down rocks prevent your tires from getting traction. Airing down too much gets you cut tires. Too much air and the tires won't conform to the irregular surface to give you traction. Traction may be on and off, so if you are spinning, you may suddenly acquire massive amounts of traction and, snap, there goes a drivetrain part.

LUGGING:
"Lugging" speed is the lowest rpm your engine can maintain without stalling and while still providing the grunt to accelerate if needed.

Rocky Road Mud. Slipping from one greasy, diff-denting rock to the next can be lots of fun. The key is to keep the speed low and pick a good line through. Try to pick rocks to drive over that provide a surface that won't cause you to slip. Slipping off a rock and high-centering on another is the biggest danger. You can also get high-centered on one large rock with four tires in goo.

Gumbo Mud in its milder form. The only thing keeping this Pinzgauer from sinking deeper is that it's resting on its belly. Yep, he's stuck, as most rigs would be without huge, aggressive tires and lots of tire-spinning power. You might use lots of momentum to cross a patch of gumbo in a mild rig, but it'd be risky. With no other choice of route, you could try to get as far across as possible and then winch out. In this case, not only did this driver have a steep descent into the mud, but a steep climb out. Momentum was in short supply.

Chop Suey Mud. This is an old Colorado mining road that was once paved with logs (they called them corduroy roads) that have deteriorated. This creates a mix of goo and sticks that can puncture tires, tear off brake lines, and cause body damage. If you need to get through, about all you can do is to pull out the chunks you can see and go for it.

Greasy Mud, and rather badly rutted at that. You have no choice but to ride the ruts in mud like this. The clay is just too slippery to climb out. This is where the extra clearance of a lift and larger tires would come in handy. This Range Rover pilot is mogating by spinning up the tires and using the wiggle method. In this case, the wiggling is allowing the cleated edges of the tires to bite on the edges of the ruts and add traction.

Chocolate Ice Cream Mud, but a bit on the greasy side. With all-season-type tires that are badly loaded up, this Discovery driver is having to spin the tires a bit to maintain forward motion. It's also deep enough to allow the diffs to slide in the goo, thus increasing drag and the need for traction.

U-Boat Mud can be of any basic type, but it hides under the water. It can be found in streams, rivers, or ponds, as well as puddles. Sometimes it's silt, sediment, or even sand. In standing water, the bottom is often rocky road, greasy, or gumbo. Rocks and clay hold water best.

Chop Suey Mud can be mud of nearly any type, but it contains sticks, wood, logs, pieces of 4×4s that went before, and anything else. Chop suey mud can often get you cut tires, torn off exhaust systems, and broken brake lines.

Gear Choices. Choosing the right gear for a mud crossing is important. Because gearing multiplies torque to the wheels, too low a gear can cause a loss of traction. In the case of needing to deliberately spin the tires (read below), a higher gear will make your tires spin faster. In general, you will be crossing mud at a moderate pace, in a higher gear, and at a comfortable "lugging" speed for your engine. With manuals, you will generally use second gear low range. With automatics, use "D" for three-speeds or "3" for overdrive types and let the automatic choose the gear it likes.

Tire Spinning and Throttle Control. This is a two-edged sword if ever there was one. There are two ways to spin tires, the major, mud-slinging, tractor-pull way and the more conservative style. Each has its time and place.

You've seen competitive mud rigs wound up to 5,500 rpm, throwing 20-foot rooster tails and crossing bogs that could swallow a Kenworth. Pro mud runners do it, so it stands to reason everyone should, right? Not necessarily. Try this technique in the average 4×4, and you'll usually sink even deeper. Or break something. It works for dedicated rigs built for mud because they use the "hydroplaning" effect of huge, spinning tires to keep them from sinking to China, while the aggressive paddle treads pull them across. The drivetrains are extra stout, the tires extra wide, and the engines built for high rpm.

> PAVEMENT ENDS
>
> **THE WIGGLE:**
> The "wiggle" technique of turning the steering wheel rapidly back and forth about a quarter- to a half-turn works especially well with nonaggressive, all-terrain-type tires that are overwhelmed by mud. In these cases, the edges of the tread are the most aggressive feature.

Whether you should try the "wild and crazy" method depends on your equipment and the opposing mud stretch. If your rig has the qualities mentioned above, you might get by. But this technique is necessary only a fraction of the time. Charging across a mudhole that's only a foot deep and 20 feet across, tires spinning up rooster tails, will make you look a little dumb. Especially when the next guy idles across!

The more conservative approach is best when traction is marginal but flotation is good. In these cases use a higher gear and get the tires spinning a little. You will find that by adjusting the throttle up or down, you may be able to maintain forward motion. As the vehicle speeds up, you can usually back off a little on the throttle.

Wiggle, Wiggle. Here's a scenario. You're crossing greasy mud that requires some wheel spinning. You're moving nicely for a while, but you begin to slow down. Increasing or decreasing throttle has no effect. Here's another tool we'll call the "wiggle" method. Try turning the steering wheel rapidly from side to side a quarter- or half-turn as your tires spin. You may find that, suddenly, you start to move again. What's happening is that the cleated edges of the tires are given a better chance to grab.

The wiggle! When traction is fading fast and your tires are turning into mud donuts, try rotating the steering wheel a quarter- to a half-turn to either side rapidly. This will sometimes give the cleated edges of otherwise overloaded front tires the bite they need to keep you going. It seems to work best in greasy mud and is a very useful tool or rigs with nonaggressive tires. I've seen rigs perched, tires spinning, in greasy mud, and the wiggle would get them moving again.

Snow is a lot like mud. It can be deep, and it's usually slippery. It's fun when only 4 inches deep like this, but you can come around the bend and be faced with a 4-foot-deep drift. Traction can also be marginal and changeable from one stretch to the next. Maintaining steady momentum is the key. This Discovery is actually going uphill and is maintaining about 5 miles per hour without wheelspin. Should he stop, it's very likely that he could not get going again.

Depth is the ultimate controlling factor on how far you go in snow. Snow may provide barely enough traction to move your vehicle under good circumstances, but using the diffs and undercarriage to plow snow will stop you very quickly. You could muscle your way through short stretches this deep, but unless you enjoy punishment, turn back when you encounter long stretches of snow this deep. This Wrangler is shod with 35-inch tires, so the snow is at least 18 inches deep here.

This is about as deep as it's practical to go. This classic Range Rover is in snow about a foot deep and though the axles are plowing some, the soft powder and solid bottom are allowing the vehicle to continue. Were the trail headed uphill or a bit deeper, he might miss his ski appointment. *Courtesy Land Rover*

Soft Ground: Snow

Winter can take your favorite two-wheel-drive, one-finger-on-the-steering-wheel trail and turn it into a Grade-A challenge. How well you do depends on two basic factors: snow depth and consistency. In general, there are two types of snow: powder or frozen, crusty snow. Many more exist if you want to count mixtures or gradations of the two. Often you can find powder under crust or vice versa.

Snow depth is the major controlling factor in whether you can "mogate" (old Army slang for moving under power) or not. Once your rig has sunk down to the point where the diffs are plowing snow, you are generally stopped. At some point, there simply won't be enough traction to push all that snow. Some types of dry, light powder will let you plow more than a heavier, wetter snow.

Snow will either support the weight of your vehicle or compress or compact enough to keep your undercarriage mostly clear of the snow. Many times, there is only a fragile crust between you and being stuck. It might support your rig only when you are exceedingly smooth on the throttle and avoid tire spinning.

Whatever types or depth of snow you encounter, you will experience a loss of traction. This can make even mild grades tricky. Snow generally offers the traction of greasy mud. Most of the time you will do better with a light foot on the throttle, but you will find times when the pedal must see the metal. Be ready for anything because the winter landscape can change radically from one 20-foot stretch to another. Instant good judgment as the situation changes is the key.

Trail running in snow can introduce some complexities. Angles, for example. This Wrangler encounters an off-camber section that would pose no problem on dry dirt. With the icy snow and a drive-straight-through approach, the rig is sucked sideways to the bank and into some deep snow. Forward progress is stopped, but he can back out. The driver then chooses a different line and first swings hard to his left and then steers right uphill. The Jeep's rear will not quite follow the front and slides downhill so the vehicle is actually moving through the slot in a diagonal "crab-walk." Eventually, the driver steers into it, and the vehicle begins to go straight as the ground levels out. A similar scenario could occur on greasy mud.

Avoid tire spinning where possible. It often just digs you deeper into the snow. Conversely, once you've broken through and found bottom, judicious tire spinning may provide traction, just as in mud. Sometimes you will go right down to dirt and find traction there. Sometimes all you find at the bottom of the snow is ice or frozen dirt.

Momentum plays a big part. Once you are running well on top of snow, back off on the throttle, get into a higher gear, and keep the revs low to avoid the torque multiplication that will break traction. You may find slippery areas that cause you to slip and slide. If you are going too fast, you may slip and slide into an obstacle, or slide off the trail. For this reason, speeds over a few miles per hour, or any speed beyond which you can maintain total control, should be avoided.

The vehicle up front has the hardest time because it's breaking a trail through the snow. It's best to rotate the trail-breaking duties to avoid punishing one vehicle too much. It also shares the fun! The vehicles behind are often best off running in the ruts. Many times you have no choice.

DRIVING ON DEEP SNOW:
In cases where you are riding an icy crust over deep snow, the crust may not support following vehicles, so it's better to drive over a different section of crust if you can.

Soft Ground: Sand

Sand is a good deal like snow, except that there's often no bottom to it. Sand comes in many consistencies, from a gravel-like material to something so fine it's like talcum powder. Sand is generally found on beaches and in deserts, but pockets of it can be found just about anywhere. Driving sand successfully is all about flotation, momentum, throttle control, and gentle turns.

How you drive on sand is first determined by the sand itself. Flotation is the main concern, so you need enough rubber for a big footprint. Everybody will air down in sand, but if you have smallish tires and the sand is the fine stuff, you're probably better off aborting. That doesn't mean that you can't traverse short stretches of the talcum-like stuff, but if miles of it lie ahead, you're asking for agony if you proceed.

Many experts will advise using an all-terrain tire on sand, and that's not bad advice. In fact, some beach areas run by government agencies will not allow aggressive tires onto the sand at all. Still, if you are running a radial mudder, you don't necessarily need to fear sand. My own recent experience with modern radial mudders on sand shows that they do quite well. Of course, my opinion will not get you past the park ranger's shack on Cape Cod!

DRIVING ON SAND:
The old rule of thumb for sand is that if you walk in it and leave discernible footprints, it's probably safe to drive over. If your feet leave indistinct depressions that fill almost immediately, you're probably best off avoiding it unless you are very well prepared for it by having huge, paddle-tread tires and experience.

Beach sand is often pretty stable stuff, especially near the water, generally at the high tide mark. It's usually coarse, and when damp, it's pretty solid. Many times it's good near the water too, but you can run into quicksand-like stuff there, and if the tide happens to be coming in, your rig is in for a destructive salt-water bath unless you can do a very quick recovery. Beaches near lowlands, salt marches, and tidal pools are often treacherous because of water flow under the surface. It doesn't hurt to know the beach's layout before you go too far. Playing in the surf, as all of us have been tempted to do, can be great fun, but it's risky and not

Starting on sand can be a chore. Note how the F-250 has sunk into the sand, despite the wide tires. It isn't stuck, but the national park ranger will have to use throttle finesse to get moving again; no wheelspin, but enough throttle to overcome the resistance of the partly buried tires. Bringing the front wheels straight ahead will also help by reducing rolling resistance. Low-powered vehicles may find it more of a struggle in a case like this. No worries here, the park rangers on the Cape Cod beaches are pretty good at sand driving; that was true even 21 years ago when this shot was taken.

so hot for the vehicle. It's easy to get stuck, and the salt spray is very corrosive.

Blow sand, the type you see on coastal or desert dunes, is much finer and more treacherous. Beyond established routes, playing on blow sand needs a lot of rubber for flotation or a lot of speed and skill. For the average four-wheeler, blow sand will be encountered in short stretches in the deserts, and momentum can usually carry you from one patch of solid ground to another. The coarser sand usually found in desert washes and streambeds is firmer stuff and is easier to traverse, even at relatively high tire pressures.

Silt is another form of ground sometimes present near water and in desert dry lakebeds. Since it's most like sand, we'll include it here. Silt was once ocean or lake bottom, and it's a fine talcum-like substance that can be found in a concreted form or as a dry powder. Given a little water, the seemingly solid stuff turns absolutely bottomless. The silty stuff makes blow sand seem like child's play. These silty areas are sometimes called alkali flats, or when wet, alkali mudflats. The wet stuff is corrosive.

You will find that sand tends to make your rig grunt a little. That's because the tires are pushing a small wave of sand. It's like they are continually trying to climb a slope. As a result, most rigs will need low range and first gear to get started (unless they are low-geared or high-powered), but once the vehicle has some momentum, you will want to run in the highest comfortable gear. That means not grunting along but moving in an rpm range where the engine has enough torque to respond to throttle input. The vehicle may momentarily bog down, and the engine has to have enough oomph left to respond without needing an aggressive downshift that could start the tires spinning.

Turning hard can also result in an unscheduled appointment with the shovel. Too sharp a turn will cause the tires to dig into the sand. Going deeper into the sand increases rolling resistance (you're plowing up even more sand with the tires), which will probably leave you short of traction and slow you down. If you run out of momentum before you stop turning you may come to a stop. Don't forget that aired-down tires also limit your handling abilities. It's just as possible to roll a tire off the rim in sand as it is anywhere else.

SONS OF BEACHES:
Overall, you can consider beaches, at least the few that still allow vehicles, as pretty safe places for a stock or near-stock 4×4, assuming you have a safe and sane attitude about it.

DRIVING ON SAND:
On sand, starts and stops need to be gentle. Starting too aggressively results in tire spin and a vehicle that goes down instead of forward. The same thing happens when you stop. The tires can lock on the low-traction surface, and as you come to a stop, you will do so in four nicely dug holes.

Dune-type blow sand is treacherous for the stocker, but the use of copious amounts of momentum can get just about any rig through. Notice how deep the Jeep Liberty's tires have sunk into the sand and are plowing up four little waves. The 3.7-liter engine feels like it's making a perpetual climb. Note also how much sand the driver's side tire is tossing up. That's a sign of sinking even deeper. As long as he doesn't run out of momentum before the turn is completed, this rig should stay on top of the sand. *Courtesy Ken Brubaker*

Water Crossings

Water is not a natural environment for 4×4s, but it's an obstacle four-wheelers have to deal with relatively often. This can get complicated for some of us. Most modern 4×4s are ill-equipped to deal with water of any serious depth, but older units are much less vulnerable. In the end, the vehicle will determine whether you cross that creek or not.

Whatever rig you drive, job one is to determine its fording limits. This specification can be found in the owner's manual, if the manufacturer has established one. Fording depth limits used to always be included in four-wheel-drive vehicle specifications but these days they're harder to find. In some cases, all you get is a vague "below the level of the hubs," which works out to be a meager 8 inches or less.

You wouldn't dive into murky water of unknown depth, so why should you drive into the same situation? In most cases, the crossing will be part of a well-established trail, but don't take it for granted that the bottom conditions or depth haven't changed since the last rig went through. Also, just because a truck with 38-inch tires and an 8-inch lift got safely across, doesn't mean your unlifted rig with 31×10.50s will do the same.

Sometimes you can probe a bit from the banks with a stick to determine the water depth and bottom condition. You may have also observed a vehicle not too different in capability from yours cross safely, and this is as good as a green light most of the time. If it's a large ford, you may have to resort to a bit of wading to determine if you can safely cross with your vehicle. By wading across, you can determine depth and bottom conditions firsthand. Obviously common sense must prevail in this. You won't want to wade into any potentially dangerous situation, such as fast-running water.

ON WATER CROSSINGS:
Before taking the plunge, evaluate the water depth, the bottom condition, and the exit on the far side. It's quite common to forget about the exit and then find that the vehicle cannot climb out.

Bottom conditions are as important as depth. In general, moving water is the safest because deep silt is not usually present. Many streams have a rocky bottom, which is good in the sense that you won't sink but bad in offering more danger of cut tires or large, diff-denting rocks. Larger rocks can hide under the water and cause damage or get you hung up. Stagnant or slow-moving water often hides deep silt, or the U-boat mud mentioned earlier. Make your evaluations carefully. Water recoveries are just about the worst in terms of cold, nasty work.

Don't drive where you won't dive! If you have to get out and check water depth the old fashioned way, so be it. Just make sure it's safe for you to do so. Take note of water depth, bottom conditions, the entrance and exits from the water, and the current.

When you enter the water, do it sedately. Dipping in at an angle will momentarily place the engine compartment in a low position, and a slow entrance will reduce the "tidal wave" effect in the engine compartment if the water is deep.

Use low range and a lower gear. Even though your pace will be slow and steady, it's best to keep the engine revved up a little; perhaps as high as 1,500 rpm. This gives you a little leeway to keep the engine running if water splashes on the ignition system and causes misfiring. In fast-moving water, it's best to cross diagonal to the current. Being broadside to a torrent of water may be enough to sweep your vehicle downstream. Remember that fast-moving water can wash the sand or gravel out from under your tires, so it's best to keep moving.

Enter the water slowly. As you nose in at an angle, the vehicle is most vulnerable to scooping water into the engine compartment and creating problems. Once fully in the water, proceed at a steady pace. Too fast and you are pushing water into places it shouldn't go. Ultimately, your speed through the water is somewhat variable according to bottom conditions. A soft bottom might require more momentum to avoid getting stuck. A rocky bottom needs a slower speed to avoid tire or undercarriage damage.

Be ready to react quickly to changing conditions. These could include holes, soft bottoms, or rocks. In mud or silt some extra throttle might be needed quickly, or even "the wiggle" mentioned in the mud section earlier. If you fall into a hole, and hopefully it's a small one, momentum may carry you through. If it's a big one, you may have time to stop and back out. If it looks like you'll go deep enough for your engine to ingest water via the intake, shutting the engine off before that happens may prevent serious damage. If you hit a rock, get off the throttle quickly, back clear, and steer around or over it.

Once clear of the water, take the time to put your rig back into dry-land form. If you hit a rock, make a quick damage inspection. When you get under way, make a few stops to test and dry the brakes. Wet brakes are considerably less efficient, and a couple of hard stops will generate the heat needed to accelerate the drying process. Drum brakes dry more slowly than discs because they're enclosed and do not have a constant-contact, self-cleaning design.

In deep water or extended soakings, it's very possible that the axles, axle universals or CV joints, or driveshaft U-joints have ingested some water. If you were deep enough, even the trans and transfer case can take on water (though this is less likely unless you drown the rig completely). Remember, oil seals are designed to keep what's inside, inside, not what's outside from getting in. Better drivetrain designs use double-lip seals that prevent outside contamination. Even then, worn seals can allow small amounts of water in but won't let oil leak out.

Unless you have good reason to suspect there's serious water contamination, you can wait until you are home for a thorough underside inspection. At that time, I always recommend a couple of squirts of grease into all the lube fittings (suspension and driveline) to

Once in the water, maintain a reasonable momentum, just enough to generate a modest bow wave. The bow wave is mostly an indicator of correct speed. Too fast, and you are pushing water into areas you don't want it. In some vehicles, the bumper pushing water creates a depression under the engine compartment, keeping the water level lower than it might otherwise be.

When current is present, a diagonal approach is best. In areas of very fast water, a vehicle broadside presents a greater surface area for water to push against. This force can overcome what little grip your tires have on the bottom and push you downstream. This Range Rover is in to the tops of the tires and is somewhat past its maximum rated fording depth.

If, for whatever reason, your engine stops in the water, the exhaust may fill up with water. In and of itself, this is of little consequence, as long as it isn't deep enough to work itself up into the engine through the back door. When the engine starts, it will quickly and spectacularly push that water out. The more worrisome aspect is why the engine quit, and you can read more about that in the "In Case of Vehicular Drowning" section in chapter 9.

In many parts of the country, water crossings will be accompanied by rocks. If you are lucky, the rocks are visible. If not, you may slam and bam your way across, rolling over the hidden rocks, assuming you don't get stuck on one. For that reason, a rocky ford is best taken slowly to avoid damage. In extreme cases, it's advisable to have a spotter to point out the offensive rocks.

AFTER A WATER CROSSING:
Don't get lazy with the post-fun cleanup. Undiscovered damage, grit, and lubricant contamination will shorten your fun by shortening your vehicle's lifespan; depending on their nature and extent, these conditions can sometimes present a serious safety hazard. Check your axles for the telltale "mocha milkshake" signs of contaminated oil.

drive water out, and to check the diff oils for water contamination. Serious water contamination will result in gear oil that turns white, and this goo must be flushed ASAP. Small amounts of water will usually evaporate via the heat generated by driving. Units with closed-knuckle front axles (most early rigs and some later rigs like Land Rovers and Toyotas) will need further inspection to ensure that water has not entered these housings.

Crossing Logs

In wooded areas, deadfalls across your path are common. Sometimes these logs are small enough to cross; other times you have to get them out of the way by whatever means are practical. Crossing a log is done diagonally, similar to crossing a gully. The main requirements are that your rig have the ground clearance under the diffs, room under the belly, and a big enough approach and departure angle. It you have the clearance, simply put one tire at a time up and over the log until you are clear. This is done very slowly, both during the climb up the face of the log and stepping off. If the log is only slightly beyond your clearance, you can build up the approaches and step-offs for both sets of tires to gain the required clearance.

The important complications to crossing logs include the fact that the log may roll, move, or shift as you go over. Smaller timber may actually flip up and strike the vehicle or spectators. There also may be soft or slippery ground on either side of it that will reduce the traction available to climb over, or cause you to sink into the ground enough to reduce ground clearance to the point of hanging up.

Crossing a log is simply a tire-by-tire operation. One at a time, you carefully put one tire over the log. Stick-shift vehicles will require clutch, brake, and throttle finesse for this. Automatics will need left-foot braking. How big a log you can cross like this is determined by your overall clearance.

If the log is slightly taller than your clearance, use local building materials to build a ramp for both sets of tires. Often you need only a few inches of extra clearance.

Basic Rockcrawling

There are many types of rockcrawling, from boulder-strewn trails to vast expanses of sandstone commonly called slickrock. The key skills for successful rockcrawling of all types are a smooth driving style, good throttle and brake control, and the ability to pick lines.

One of the most common mistakes is to come off rocks too quickly. That's often because people do not use left-foot braking. Even if a rock is only a foot high, your rig will pick up speed on the downslope of the rock, and it may come down before you can get the right foot from the throttle to the brake. Coming down off the rock hard will compress the suspension, perhaps enough to use up that little bit of clearance and allow the undercarriage to hit somewhere.

One of the key insights in rockcrawling is learning that you are maneuvering both ends of the vehicle. If you need to put a front tire up on a rock so the diff will clear, you may have to maneuver the rear tire over the same rock or over a completely different one. Only some of the time will you be lucky enough to have a straight-through traverse. Many times, you'll be maneuvering around several rocks at the same time. Overall, many of the techniques you have learned in other terrain types apply here, but a few words are in order for each type of rockcrawling scenario.

Loose Rocks. These can range in size from gravel to basketball-sized rocks and from smooth to jagged. The smaller-sized rocks, especially weathered and rounded riverbed types, tend to slip and slide a good deal, so traction may be a problem. Climbing or descending a track covered in small rocks can be like driving on marbles. Throttle control is vital, as is the use of momentum. Keep moving and avoid large applications of throttle. On regularly driven tracks, you may find a "sweet spot" where the rocks have

SLICKROCK:
Slickrock appears all over southern Utah, western Colorado, and parts of northern New Mexico, as well as other isolated spots. Slickrock provides probably the most fun you can have rockcrawling in a stock or near-stock vehicle. Moab, Utah, is a place where ordinary 4×4s can do extraordinary things.

Smaller logs can spring up as you drive over them. In this case, no damage was done, but it's not uncommon for the flipped logs to strike the vehicle, or another vehicle, and cause damage. Potentially, a spectator could be in harm's way.

been compacted into a fairly stable surface. Outside of this area, you might find really loose stuff.

The larger rocks will move around as well. Many are anchored, but the loose ones have a bad habit of looking stable but moving at inopportune times. At best, it's a small jolt as the tire falls off the rock. At worst, you are thrown off onto another rock that's looking for a 4×4 part to nail. Loose rocks also tend to roll under the tire and get spit backward. These rocks can move with some force, so spectators should take care in some situations. Pick lines that will put your tires on the rocks you can't clear and you will be driving from one high spot to the next. This may involve a good deal of maneuvering, both to find the high points and avoid the things you can't go over.

Beware the tire-killing jagged rocks of all sizes. Always drive slowly through them, avoiding scuffing the sidewalls against sharp edges, and don't let the tires spin. In a sea of jagged edges, you'll have your eyes full watching out for potential hazards. Jagged rocks are particularly dangerous when wet, partly because the tendency to slip and spin is increased. Also, the edges that aren't sharp enough to slice when dry (they generally gouge) tend to cut when lubricated by water.

Large Boulders. Creative line picking becomes vital when you get into the big stuff. You'll literally be driving from one boulder face to the next, finding a path for all four wheels and fighting to keep the body and undercarriage clear of harm. How far you can go into this realm depends on the vehicle. Lots of clearance is important, as are low gearing, the added traction of a locker, and sticky tires. In all but the mildest "boulder bashing" environments, lifted tires are common, so a locker becomes a necessary part of the equipment package. This puts most boulder scenarios into the more advanced category covered in Chapter 7.

Slickrock. Slickrock: the term gives many people an image of ice-covered boulders or perhaps soapstone. It's just the opposite, actually. Driving on slickrock has been compared to driving on 100-grit sandpaper, and the analogy is a good one. Massive amounts of traction allow you to make climbs and descents that would otherwise be impossible. The question is, why

Picking your way uphill through a sea of rocks is slow, bouncy work. The key tip is to pick the line that keeps you clear of the taller rocks and your tire sidewalls from any sharp edges. On a very steep uphill, the increased need for traction can cause the tires to spit the rocks out behind.

TIRE-PRESSURE TUNING:
High tire pressure can provide a "fuse" for the drivetrain on grippy surfaces like slickrock. In theory, the tire will slip before something breaks. This lessens the capability of the vehicle to some degree, but it offers a way to reduce the odds of breakage.

A spotter/rock mover can be invaluable when boulder fields like this are encountered. Note the jagged, tire-killing edges of these rocks. This is a place to take care.

do they call it slickrock? The answer goes back more than a century, when pioneers were using horses shod with iron shoes and wagons with wooden wheels covered with iron hoops. Where a rubber tire grips slickrock with authority, an iron shoe slips as if it was on ice. The popularity of Moab, Utah, has made "slickrock" a common term among four-wheelers, mountain bikers, ATVers, and motorcyclists.

Not all slickrock is created equal, but all the usual techniques apply. Some slickrock has a crumbly surface that shears away and reduces traction somewhat. Also, slickrock with sand on it can be spooky. Ledges are common obstacles, and the bump technique will serve you well. The key to working a stock or near-stock vehicle over slickrock is to keep the tires on the ground and as evenly loaded as possible. Loss of traction due to articulation or weight transfer can stop an unlocked rig quickly.

Techniques for Preserving the Drivetrain. One of the problems of driving on many types of rock is that you can almost have too much traction. Many four-wheelers will respond to that by saying, "There's no such thing as too much traction!" True, of course, when you think just of getting over the obstacle. But if excess traction is combined with angles and maneuvers that can put all the engine torque on one wheel or put the drivetrain into a bind, things can go snap, crackle, or pop, and we're not talking about Rice Krispies.

If you've ever driven on pavement with your rig in four-wheel drive and the hubs locked in, you have an idea of what it feels like to put the drivetrain in a bind. As soon as you turn, tires start barking, and the steering wheel starts bucking in your hand. Your

One of the technological trends in four-wheel drive is hill descent control. When this Land Rover Freelander was new in 2002, it was still fairly new technology. It can be engaged by the driver in first gear; the system automatically engages the brakes to slow the vehicle without locking the wheels. It uses the existing computerized ABS system, but the driver keeps his foot off the brakes while the system is engaged. You could call it automatic cadence braking. This is a great stock SUV feature, especially with a 4×4 like the Freelander that has no low range.

Tire damage is one of the most common vehicle failures on the trail. Careful driving and being observant of the terrain features that can cause it can reduce the risk but will never completely eliminate it. That's why a matching, full-sized spare is a key item. This tire is a write-off.

Greasy mud, big rocks, and a downhill. Yeehaw! This descent was a semi-controlled slide. The rocks were useful as slowing-down devices, though the driver had to make sure to hit the tall ones with his tires and not his front diff. Climbing this would be nearly impossible for most rigs.

THE ROAD HOME:
Once you're off the trail and headed for home, be extra sensitive for the first few miles, listening for any unusual noises, vibrations, or odd characteristics in the way your vehicle drives. Keeping the radio(s) off will help you determine whether anything sounds suspect.

front and rear tires are turning at different speeds, and something has to slip or give. You hope it's the tire exceeding its traction and slipping and not a drivetrain part breaking. With less traction, such as in dirt, this slippage is less apparent.

Parts of the rockcrawling scene are angles and lifted tires. That means weight transfer may put most or all of the weight on one tire. If you combine that with a locker, that means all the torque is going to that one tire. If it happens to have more grip than some part of your drivetrain has strength, then *snap*, something lets loose! This is controllable by driving techniques that include knowing when to back off and having a

Double ledges are tricky. When the front and rear tires encounter ledges simultaneously, neither have traction. Most times, a "bump" is the answer, as long as the driver doesn't get carried away with momentum. This Grand Cherokee driver is hitting the double ledges at a slight angle, pulling the right side up the ledges first and letting the right tires use their available traction. It works well for him because he has a locking differential. With open diffs, it might be more problematic due to weight transfer.

feel for these severe angle situations and going easy, or picking other lines.

Some drivers of vehicles with weak links in the drivetrain will use tire pressure to prevent breakage. Reducing the tire footprint by maintaining a relatively high tire pressure will decrease traction.

The End of the Trail

Wise 4×4 skippers stop at the end of the trail to look the rig over for any damage. This check starts with the tires, since they are the most vulnerable part of your 4×4, and one of the most potentially dangerous failures. Look for cuts, blisters, and gouges, especially on the vulnerable sidewalls. Minor cuts and gouges are part and parcel of four-wheeling, but the important question is how you can tell if a slightly damaged tire is safe. The general rule of thumb is that if you can see cord material in the damaged area, the tire is probably not safe. Below that visible point, the tire may still be fatally damaged. Predicting exactly whether a damaged tire is safe or not is sometimes a mix of gambling and black magic. I have seen tires with little obvious damage fail in a short period and tires with a nasty-looking gouge that lasted for years. "If in doubt, swap it out," is always good advice, especially if you have a full-sized spare. You can then have it checked by a more knowledgeable party, such as a tire shop, when you get home. Bear in mind that tire shops and other outside sources will always err on the side of extreme caution in their judgments.

Beyond tires, have a quick look at wheel rims for obvious hits, at the suspension components for obvious damage, and make sure all the lug nuts are present. You will have noted any serious hits as they happened on the trail and probably had a look right then and there. It wouldn't hurt to take another look before you hit the pavement just to make sure there was no damage and that no problem has developed since you last checked.

CHAPTER 6
Basic Vehicle Tuning and Buildup: The Toolbox

Well-chosen modifications can turn the ordinary 4×4 into a trail hero. It took little more than a set of sticky tires and a rear locker for this otherwise stock Toyota pickup to climb this steep slab of rock.

Star Trek's Mr. Spock once constructed a computer from crude materials he described as "stone knives and bearskins." That was science fiction; in this real world, any tradesman will tell you that without the right tools and equipment, the job stops at some very basic level. While driving skill alone can carry you many miles into the outback, having the right equipment will take you farther and make it a better and safer experience. That equipment includes modifications to the vehicle itself and items carried within it.

Modification 101

The first lesson in modifying any vehicle is that you have to think beyond just one part. The whole vehicle must be balanced in strength and ability according to the uses you plan. When you get right down to the core of off-highway performance, there are only two things you need in a four-wheel drive: traction and clearance. Make improvements in those two areas and you're set.

Most of us don't have unlimited funds, so modifications must be chosen carefully to bring a good result for the money spent. The two most common mistakes are buying something on the basis of popularity instead of need, and buying based on bottom-line price. Popularity sometimes represents a commonality of need, but sometimes it represents merely what's "cool." What's cool may also serve a use or need, but maybe not for you.

As to price, remember the old apples and oranges adage. Unless you are looking at nearly identical products, don't shop on the basis of price alone. Look first at *what* you get, and *then* check the price and compare it to the other items that fit into the same general category. Remember, you get what you pay for! Some products are designed and built simply to be the lowest-priced item on the market and the prime candidate for those who shop by price alone. They are often far from being the best in terms of performance. Moderation of goals is a far better form of thrift than selecting the lowest-priced products in any category.

What's First? Recovery and safety items should obviously come first. Beyond that, some of your choices will be dictated by the type of terrain you generally traverse. Typically, tires and wheels follow recovery and safety items. A tire upgrade may necessitate some suspension modifications, a body lift, or both, in order to fit them. After that, lockers and drivetrain durability mods are of paramount importance. Depending on your rig, body and chassis armor fits in there at about the same point. These basic items can be supplemented, or complicated, by your personal needs and wants.

Do It Yourself? One of the big questions we all face is whether or not we should do the work ourselves. Labor prices being what they are today, you can save a lot of cash doing the work yourself, but only if you and your toolbox are up to it. In my opinion, a reasonably intelligent person armed with the necessary tools, including a manual, and a large dose of *patience* can accomplish a great deal. Note the emphasis on patience. Lack of experience is largely mitigated by patience and the ability to follow instructions. Roping in a knowledgeable friend for tricky parts doesn't hurt either.

A novice wrencher who wants to expand his mechanical horizons should start by buying a service manual and tackling some of the maintenance chores. Most towns have basic automotive repair courses, and there are books available on the subject as well. You should be able to track down a factory repair

What's first? That depends a great deal on the vehicle, but safety and recovery are first priorities in a buildup. After that, it's traction and clearance (or clearance and traction). The buildup usually starts with tires, which may or may not include a lift and gearing changes. A locker or limited-slip is often next. This T-100 was equipped with a factory locker.

manual for your vehicle, either through a dealer or on the Internet. At some point, you can even do some of the easier modifications. The biggest mistake I see is people setting their sights too high. That could be anything from choosing to overhaul and upgrade an automatic transmission as their second project to starting a locker installation Sunday at noon on a daily driver that needs to be used Monday morning. Both of these extremes are setups for angst and failure.

Bear in mind that there is an initial investment in tools that will reduce the bang-for-buck aspect. Still, most tools last forever. Aside from a few specialty tools with a narrow range of uses, whatever basic hand tools you buy can be amortized by the labor savings in the first few jobs and can be used until you pass them along to your kids. As always, you get what you pay for. Bargain-rate tools are no bargain when they fail at home or in the field.

Free Performance: Trail Tire Tuning

Correctly adjusting tire pressures for the trail is an important part of successful four-wheeling. The benefits of lower trail pressures can be dramatic. Your tires have three main tasks in the dirt. First, they provide a tractive grip on *terra firma* to move the vehicle, stop it, or turn it. Second, they are a part of your 4×4's suspension system and absorb a lot of the

COST-EFFECTIVE MODS:
If controlling costs is an issue, and it usually is, don't buy an item unless you need it. Once you conclude you do need it, look at it from the performance-for-dollar perspective as opposed to the bottom-line price.

To wrench or not to wrench? You can save a lot of moola doing the repair and buildup work yourself, and you don't necessarily have to be a certified technician. An old-timer like this Willys MB is about as easy as it gets in this regard. Some of the money saved from outside labor will be taken up by new tools, but generally you can come out ahead. If you are new at wrenching, the learning curve can be steep, but with patience, common sense, and a good manual, you can get to the top.

bumps. Third, they supply flotation to keep your rig *above* the ground and not *in* it.

From the traction standpoint, to recap what we talked about in Chapter 2, lower tire pressures allow the tire to spread out and put a larger footprint on the ground. More footprint equals more tire surface to grip the ground. Also, because the trail consists mostly of irregular surfaces, the tire conforms to it better at lower pressures, wrapping itself around rocks and other obstacles. A relatively small irregularity, such as a fist-sized rock, can lift a "pumped up" tire off the ground and reduce grip to nothing, perhaps at a moment when you really need it. Finally, the aired-down tire provides flotation due to the increased footprint. Your rig's total weight is supported by those four small patches of rubber on the ground.

Low Trail Pressure Caveats. Whether you should air down a significant amount for the trail, or at all, depends first of all on whether you have the means to air back up. All trails eventually lead back to the pavement, and driving home on low tires is dangerous and increases tire wear. If you can't air back up at the end of the trail, it's better not to drop your pressures much, if at all.

FLOTATION:
If the ground surface cannot support your vehicle's weight, the tires sink. A larger tire footprint spreads the weight over a larger area for better flotation. An added advantage is improved ride quality on rough surfaces.

DO IT YOURSELF:
Be patient and deliberate in your work and leave the time clock out of the garage. Eventually, your toolbox and experience level will grow to suit your own comfort level.

TIRE PRESSURE AND FOOTPRINT

A ProComp 12.50×35-15 Mud Terrain mounted on the front of the author's 4×4 at 30 psi. Approximately 1,500 pounds of weight are on the tire. The actual size of the footprint is 8.25×9 inches, for 74.25 square inches. That combination of pressure and weight yields a ground pressure of 20.2 pounds per square inch. Notice that the outer edges of the tread are indistinct. My normal front pressure is 28 psi.

The same ProComp tire at 23 psi. The footprint measures 8.50x10, for 85 square inches. With 1,500 pounds, that footprint yields 17.6 pounds per square inch. Notice that the edges of the tread are more distinct and that the footprint has grown longer.

Our ProComp at 10 psi. The actual size of the footprint is 14.25×10 inches, or 142.5 square inches. Ground pressure would be 10.5 pounds per square inch. Note that you can see the sharp edge of the outer tread block, indicating that the tire is flat on the ground. The footprint has grown 5.25 inches in length and 1.75 inches in width.

If you do choose to air down, there are some important factors to keep in mind while out there on the trail. The first is that handling will be adversely affected at any speed above a crawl. A low tire can be suddenly deflated in hard or overly quick turns by literally rolling the tire bead off the rim. An aired-down tire is more vulnerable to sidewall damage in terrain with lots of sharp-edged rocks. Also keep in mind that an aired-down tire reduces the rolling diameter, which decreases ground clearance by a small amount.

The Science of Low Trail Pressures. Assuming you have the ability to air back up, the question becomes how

An aired-down tire is vulnerable to all sorts of contortions. This wadded-up sidewall did not tear, but extreme flexing like this can result in damage to the carcass that might not immediately show. Airing down is a great boon to outback travel, but your tires carry the burden of it. You can minimize the impact by airing down according to conditions. Reserve those major air-downs for when they are needed, namely more extreme terrain.

LOWER PRESSURE, LESS CLEARANCE

The right front tire at 30 psi. Approximately 1,500 pounds on the tire. From the ground to the rim measures 8⅜ inches.

The same tire at 15 psi has dropped to 7½ inches from ground to rim. This action has decreased ground clearance under the diffs by ⅞ inch.

At 15 psi, the sidewall bulge is very pronounced. This bulge adds to flotation. As the tire sinks into soft ground, the bulge adds a few square inches of "tread" area to support weight.

low you should go at any given moment. It depends in part on the terrain. An easy day of 'wheeling might only require a small drop in pressure just to smooth out the ride a little. A more radical day might require a more radical drop in pressure. A drop of 10 psi (say from 35 down to 25) isn't going to be a huge problem for most rigs, but finding that low-as-you-can-go number may be a little trickier.

Just how low you can go on a non-beadlocked rim depends on two main factors: tire size and vehicle weight. Beadlocked rims are in a class by themselves, and we'll talk about them later. A third factor is the tire and rim combination. The volume of air in the tire is what keeps the bead seated, and a larger tire has more of that and can be aired down more. Look at the charts from Oasis on page 111 for some guidelines on trail pressures.

One item I would add to the Oasis chart is to equalize front and rear tire profiles. Using those charts, set the pressures and then measure the profile of the tires at the lighter end of the vehicle. The heavy end will be lower at the same pressure, so increase tire pressure at that end to equalize tire profiles front and rear.

The Mechanics of Lowering Trail Pressures. Airing down can be as simple as crouching down with a tire gauge and letting out the appropriate amount of air. This is the cheap and simple but time-consuming approach. My tests show it takes 2 minutes and 15 seconds to go from 30 to 15 psi on a 35×12.50-15 tire using an ordinary "pencil"-type gauge. Some owners with large tires will temporarily remove the valve core, and this is fast and cheap but a little risky if the core blows out of your fingers. My tests show this reduces air-down time by about 30 seconds per tire, including fussing with the valve core, but there is still a finite amount of time needed. In some informal tests where tires were timed on how long it took them to fully deflate from 30 to 0 psi with the valve core removed, it took a 30×9.50-15 tire about 3 minutes; a 33×12.50-15 about 5 minutes; and a 35×12.50 about 7 minutes.

OE AIRING DOWN:
Use more caution in airing down stock rigs with OE-size tires. In these cases, 15 psi is usually as low as you should dare go, and sometimes not even that far.

AIRING DOWN:
Lacking any other information, the old rule of thumb for airing down was to lower the pressure until the tire profile is reduced by 25 percent. That's still a useful guideline for all but the largest tires.

TIRE CONFORMATION AT LOW PRESSURE

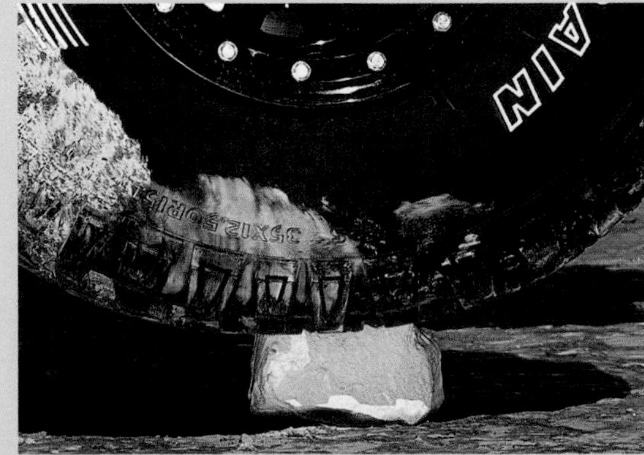

At 30 psi, there is little conformation of the tire to this small rock. Were this a small knob on a bigger rock, little traction would be offered here.

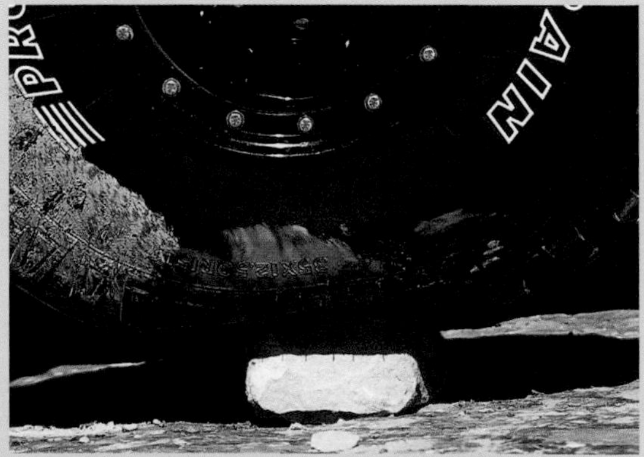

At 20 psi, the tire is doing a pretty good job of absorbing the rock. At this pressure, the tire could grip this knob like that hand in the old Uniroyal "Tiger Paw" commercial.

Airing down can be accomplished simply by working at it with a cheap pencil-type gauge or with a whiz-bang tool like this. This gauge screws onto the stem and removes the core for a more speedy pressure drop.

Methods of Re-Inflation: Compressors. Compressors come at assorted prices, with the price reflecting robustness and performance. The three most important performance specifications are airflow capacity in cubic feet per minute (cfm), duty cycle, and tire fill time for the particular size tire. The cfm rating is expressed two ways, at zero pressure or at "X" psi. The better performance spec is cfm at pressure, since it indicates the compressor's ability to pump against a "head" of pressure. This could be at 30 psi or 100 psi (or whatever). A compressor making 3 cfm at 100 psi is significantly more powerful than one that puts out 3 cfm at 30 psi.

Duty cycle is another important consideration. Some compressors can run continuously, but most cannot. They need time to cool, with that time increasing according to load and ambient temperature. The most user-friendly duty cycle specification is when it's expressed in time on versus time off; 10 minutes running versus 20 minutes off for cooling, for example. This time is calculated based on the maximum rated operating temperature of the unit reached while it's pumping against 100 psi pressure at 72 degrees Fahrenheit ambient temperature. When expressed as a percentage, duty cycle become a little more variable. A 100 percent duty cycle, of course, means the unit can run continuously. A typical unit with a 25 percent duty cycle can run 10 minutes with 30 minutes rest,

These adjustable devices from Oasis Manufacturing can be preset to the pressure you desire. Once that is done, when you get to the trailhead, you screw them on and continue. The tires air down to the preset pressure as you drive.

Some owners build hose setups whereby they can air down or air up two or more tires at a time. In some cases, an adjustable regulator is built onto the inlet/outlet to control pressure. There are a few similar kits appearing on the market as well.

but depending on how the manufacturer rates its unit in time on versus time off, the run/rest times could vary somewhat but stay at a 25 percent duty cycle.

How duty cycle relates to your choice is connected to fill time. If, for example, your compressor takes five minutes per tire to air them up to street pressure (that's 20 minutes for four), and if the duty cycle is 20 percent (8 minutes continuous), then you will have exceeded the unit's duty cycle midway into the second tire. By regularly exceeding the duty cycle, you will shorten the compressor's life, if you don't smoke the unit at an early stage.

Ultimately, the best way to select a compressor is based on tire size. A compressor that offers a reasonable fill time for your tire size and the duty cycle necessary to complete the job without undue strain is the "just right" choice. The sidebar on page 119 lists many current compressors and their performance, including tire fill times for many.

Airing-Up Tools. Beyond the compressor, the most important addition to any system is an air tank. A charged tank can reduce tire fill time significantly. The name of the game is volume; a charged tank may contain enough air essentially to inflate one tire without much help from the compressor. Tests have shown that a charged 2½-gallon tank added to an air system with a moderate-performance compressor can reduce the fill time of a 35-inch-tall tire by 1½ minutes when going from 12 to 30 psi.

Most compressors are electric. This ARB unit does double duty by supplying air pressure for the Air Lockers as well as for tire filling. It's a quality unit but a bit low on cfm, so it's best suited for airing tires no bigger than a 31×10.50, or preferably smaller. These small units can be mounted in a variety of locations.

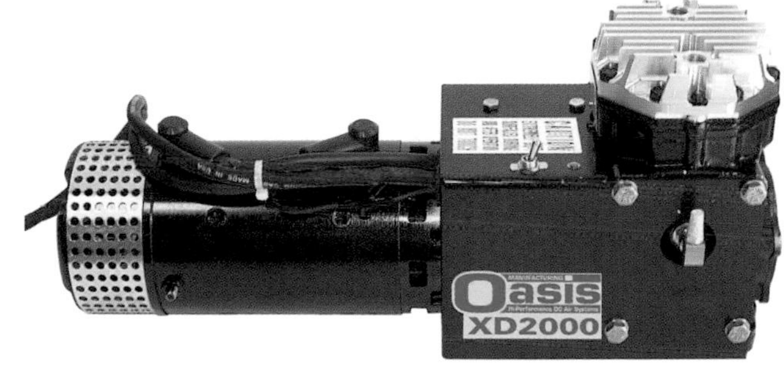

This Oasis compressor is currently the king of the electric units, with performance that matches some garage compressors. If you have big tires or air tools, here's the "Big Kahuna" huffer for you. The downsides are weight, amp draw, and cost. *Courtesy Oasis Manufacturing*

Another important element to any compressed-air system is the size of the air lines. Overall airflow capacity is limited by the smallest inside diameter in the system, wherever that might be (usually at the

AIR TANKS:
Air tanks are built in various sizes, usually from 2- to 5-gallon capacity. They can be mounted in any convenient spot, most often on the chassis or under the hood.

FOUR-WHEELER'S MATH

1) *Effective Gear Ratio*

The "effective" gear ratio illustrates the changes that occur when larger tires are installed with no changes to gearing. For example, by replacing 29-inch tires with 33-inch tires, your 3.54:1 axle ratio will perform, or "feel" like it has, a 3.11:1 ratio.

To obtain the effective gear ratio:

$$\frac{\text{old tire diameter}}{\text{new tire diameter}} \times \text{original ratio} = \text{effective ratio of new combination}$$

2) *Engine rpm at Speed*

This formula is useful for determining the changes in cruising rpm that might occur from axle ratio changes or larger tires.

$$\frac{\text{mph x total gear ratio} \times 336}{\text{tire diameter (inches)}} = \text{engine rpm}$$

3) *Equivalent Ratio*

This formula is used to find the axle ratio needed to bring the overall tire/axle ratio gearing back to an approximation of stock after you have installed larger tires. This will put your cruising rpm back to near-stock levels and improve acceleration. The number obtained must then be matched to the nearest available ring-and-pinion ratio available for your 4×4. It may be a lower or higher ratio. Most people go with the next lower ratio because rotating mass of the bigger tires will slow acceleration regardless of ratio changes. The slightly lower ratio will also help compensate for the worsened aerodynamics and increased rolling resistance that come with a lift and tire size increase. If your rig is particularly powerful, or you are willing to sacrifice some performance for economy, bias toward the higher available ratio. Finally, on rigs with extremely tall axle ratios (2.76, 3,07:1, etc.) better performance results are obtained with the formula by substituting 3.55:1 rather than using your existing ratio.

To obtain equivalent ratios:

$$\frac{\text{new tire diameter}}{\text{old tire diameter}} \times \text{old ratio} = \text{new ratio}$$

4) *Shotgun Ratios*

These are rules of thumb that seem to work more or less universally on rigs with average power to weight ratios. On underpowered rigs, bump to the next lowest ratio.

Tire Diameter	Gear Ratio
31	3.73–4.10
33	4.10–4.56
35	4.56–4.88
36–37	4.88–5.13
38+	5.13–7.00 (as needed)

valve stem of the tire). The largest and most important line should be from the compressor to the tank, and it should be at least ⅜ inch. Air tools will need ⅜-inch hose direct from the tank to operate efficiently, but the restrictions at the valve stem make only a ¼-inch I.D. line from the tank necessary for tire filling (though it won't hurt a bit to standardize to a ⅜-inch hose). Speaking of air tools, a sufficiently powerful compressor and air tank make air tools a very feasible option. Once you've used a good air wrench, turning nuts and bolts by hand feels like slow motion.

A final tidbit on airing up would include the anecdotal observations of industry people and four-wheelers that rubber valve stems seem to flow more air than do metal ones. Metal valve stems seem to slow both airing up and airing down. There are also high-flow valve stems available, such as Advanced Air Systems "Monster" valve stems. With these, you drill a second hole in the rim (aaakkk . . . measure twice, drill once!) and install a second high-flow stem on each wheel. These reduce air-down and fill-up time to a fraction of normal. Whether these are worth the effort and expense for your 'wheeling trips is a judgment call.

Methods of Re-Inflation: Filling with CO_2. One of the newer trends in four wheeling is the use of CO_2 tanks for tire filling. These are high-pressure tanks that contain liquid carbon dioxide. A certain amount of the CO_2 evaporates to fill the empty volume of the cylinder and maintains pressure at about 1,800 psi until the last of the

FOUR-WHEELER'S MATH

5) *Speedometer Correction*

Use these formulae to determine your correct speed after swapping tires or tires and gear ratios. Going to larger tires will make the vehicle go faster than the speedometer indicates. Don't forget to add in your overdrive ratio, expressed as a fraction (usually 0.7–0.8:1 on most rigs), so you need to multiply your axle ratio by your overdrive ratio to get the final drive ratio. Example: If you have a 4.10:1 axle ratio and a 0.70:1 overdrive ratio, 4.10x0.70 = 2.87:1, so 2.87:1 is your final drive ratio in overdrive.

Speedometer correction (tire swap only):

$$\frac{\text{new tire diameter}}{\text{old tire diameter}} \times \text{indicated mph} = \text{actual mph}$$

Speedometer correction (tire and gear swap):

$$\text{indicated speed in mph or KPH} \times \frac{\text{new tire diameter}}{\text{old tire diameter}} \times \frac{\text{old gear ratio}}{\text{new gear ratio}} = \text{actual speed}$$

Determining teeth needed on mechanical speedometer drive:

Use this if you have a mechanical speedometer and want to change the gear to correct the speedometer. You must know the original number of teeth on the gear and have accurately determined your actual versus indicated speeds. Bear in mind that the particular combination you need may not be available for your vehicle, so you'll have to select one that is close and live with a minor error.

$$\frac{\text{indicated speed}}{\text{actual speed}} \times \text{current number of teeth} = \text{new number of teeth}$$

To find final drive ratio (in OD): OD gear ratio x axle ratio = final drive ratio

liquid evaporates and pressure then gradually decreases. An adjustable regulator, with a high limit of 150 psi, controls output pressure. You can fill approximately 27 31×10.50 tires from 10 to 30 psi (in a quick 42 seconds each) from one 10-gallon tank. The 5-gallon units cut the tire number in half but retain the same fill time. Tanks that hold 15 and 20 gallons are also available from some manufacturers. The capacity refers to the amount of liquid CO_2 the tank will hold.

PAVEMENT ENDS

USING CO_2:
There is no serious downside to CO2 bottle use, except that if you run out of CO2 on the trail, you are without the means to fill your tires. While having a tank charged at 1,800 psi in your vehicle may sound a bit alarming, these tanks are quite safe. They are tested to 3,000 pounds and certified by the U.S. Department of Transportation.

A CO_2 tank like this is a very viable option. The smaller ones hold enough liquid CO_2 to fill a couple of dozen tires from 10 to 30 psi and come in a variety of capacities. They can also run air tools. The cost is about the same as a midlevel compressor without a tank, but the performance exceeds all electric or engine-driven compressors on the market. The downsides are the continued cost to refill (10–20 bucks) and the chance of running out when you need it most.

The bottles are made of aircraft-grade aluminum and can be filled at welding or fire extinguisher shops for $15–$25. Full, they weigh in at 40–70 pounds with the carrying handle and all the regulator pieces. A 5-gallon tank with mount, regulator, and hose is around $350, with the 15-gallon tanks passing $425 with a mounting bracket. A 20-gallon tank will set you back $500–$600. This puts them in the same realm as a mid-priced compressor alone, or a lower-end compressor and tank, but their performance is exceeded only by the most powerful and expensive compressors. You can also run air tools off these tanks.

Recovery Points

Recovery points are a basic necessity. Every 4×4 should have at least one up front and one in the rear. Recovery points can take many forms, including hooks, rings, shackle brackets, and others. The important part is that the individual pieces are rated for at least 1.5 times the gross weight of your vehicle and are solidly mounted to the chassis. The individual pieces of hardware can be purchased at four-wheel-drive shops, at a marine chandlery, and even at the better-equipped hardware stores. The better pieces will have a safe working load (SWL) listed on them indicating their continuous rated load capacity (see Chapter 8 for more details).

The front points may be the most difficult to fit. The more utilitarian rigs usually have bare chassis horns up front for attaching hooks, but later-model SUVs and trucks often have bumpers and plastic in the way. You or your favorite 4×4 shop will have to get creative in that case. A few late-model 4×4s still have recovery hooks.

In back, hooks can also be attached, but welded or bolted-on Class III or Class IV receiver hitches can

RECOVERY POINTS:
DO NOT use a receiver ball as a recovery point. Shock loads can break one off and turn it into a cannonball. If you must use a ball hitch for recovery, remove the ball and use the hole where it was mounted to attach a shackle or ring.

COMPRESSOR PERFORMANCE

Model	Type	CFM at 0 psi	CFM at Pressure (psi)	Tire Time	Max Pressure (psi)	Current Draw	Max Tire	Duty Cycle (amps)
ARB	E12, H, P	1.68	1.41 @ 20	160	105	20 max	31x10.50	20
Big Red	E12, H, P	1.38	0.95 @ 35	(1)	120	20 max	31x10.50	20
Chuffer (home)	(2)	5.50	-	48	-	NA	NR	NA
Chuffer (production)	(2)	0.75	-	480	-	NA	225/75	NA
"El Cheapo" (2)	E12, P	0.70	0.27 @ 35	1344	210	10 max	225/75	10
Extreme Aire	E12, H	4.00	-	(3)	150	40 max	35x12.50	100
Extreme Aire Jr	E12, H, P	1.50	-	(14)	150	22 max	31x12.50	50
Extreme Flow	B, H, L	-	8.0 @ 100	-	200	NA	UNL	100
EZ-Air	E12, H, P	-	1.36 @ 30	(4)	150	20 max	33x12.50	20
Oasis XD4000	E12, H, L	14.0	7.00 @ 50	(5)	125	180 max	UNL	100
Oasis XD3000	E12, H, L	14.0	8.0 @ 100	(5)	200	180 max	UNL	100
Oasis HP3000	E12, H, L	14.0	-	(5)	200	200 max	UNL	30
QuickAir1	E12, P, H	1.13	0.73 @ 40	(6)	115	11 max	31x10.50	65
QuickAir2	E12, P, H	2.18	1.45 @ 40	(7)	105	26 max	33x12.50	65
QuickAir3	E12, H	3.65	2.05 @ 40	80	70	46 max	UNL	65
Ready Air 12100, 12200	E12, H, P, L	-	1.05 @ 75	-	120	30 max	35x12.50	100
Ready Air 12500	E12, H, L	-	1.10 @ 175	-	175	42 max	UNL	100
Shop Compressor (8)	E220, H	14.0	10.2 @ 90	28	140	-	UNL	80
ViAir 100	E12, H, P	1.38	0.57 @ 100	(15)	130	14 max	31x10.50	15
ViAir 200	E12, H, P	1.94	0.81 @ 100	(16)	150	18 max	33x12.50	20
ViAir 450	E12, H, P	1.66	0.94 @ 100	(12)	150	19 max	35x12.50	100
ViAir 500	E12, H, P	2.93	1.40 @ 100	(13)	150	29 max	35x12.50	33
York Conversion	B, H, L	-	4.00 @ 90 (9)	45	(10)	NA	UNL	100

Notes on categories: **Model:** Make or model of compressor. **Type**: Key to codes: E12 = 12-volt electric; P = portable; H = hardmount; L = large and heavy, over 30 pounds; B = engine, belt-driven; E220 = electric 220-volt. **CFM at 0 psi:** Airflow (in cubic feet per minute) and 0 psi. This is the startup rate. As the compressor gets hot and has to pump against increasing pressure, the flow rate drops. These are manufacturers' specifications. **CFM at Pressure:** The most important specification. This rate is much less than the 0 psi rate because the unit is pumping against pressure. Compressors with high flow rates at higher pressures are the better choice. These are manufacturers' specifications. **Tire Time:** One of the more common standards is the time it takes to pump a 31x10.50-15 tire up from 10 to 30 psi. This is the default figure. If the available test information differs, it will be shown in the numbered notes below. This test info was compiled from my own tests as well as tests by manufacturers or from published sources. **Max Pressure:**This is the maximum pressure of the unit as given by the manufacturer. **Current Draw:** In the case of an electric unit, this is the maximum number of amps needed by the unit. The amp draw increases the harder the unit works. **Max Tire:** Because the volume of air needed to fill a tire is based on size, you need a larger compressor with a larger tire. This shows the largest tire suitable for a particular compressor, given reasonable wait times. These are my evaluations based on cfm flow rates. Use of an air tank could add enough capacity to bump this rating by one to two tire sizes. Key to abbreviations: UNL = unlimited, NR = not recommended. **Duty Cycle:** The manufacturer's recommended duty cycle indicating the percentage of an hour the unit should be run continuously. This does not necessarily mean, for example, that a compressor rated at 20 percent can only be run 12 minutes before having to cool for 48, it merely means it must have some cooling off time between 12-minute runs. ***Numbered Notes:*** **1:** 33x12.50 from 8 to 28 psi in 180 seconds. **2:** The homemade chuffer uses one cylinder of the engine as a compressor, so performance will vary according to the bore and stroke of the engine and engine speed. The tire filling data was taken from a Land Rover four-cylinder of 3.56x3.5-inch stroke with the engine running at about 550 rpm and filling a 30x9.50 tire. The downside was that a certain amount of the air-fuel mixture was pumped into the cylinder. The manufactured chuffers used the compression of the cylinder to drive a small piston, and their performance was considerably slower but safer. The production chuffer cfm is shown at 550 rpm. I have not seen a chuffer for sale in a number of years. **3:** 35x12.50 from 10 to 35 psi in 185 seconds. **4:** 35x12.50 from 15 to 35 psi in 408 seconds. **5:** Manufacturer's rating is 50 seconds to fill a 35x12.50 tire from 15 to 30 psi with HD3000. **6:** Manufacturer's rating is 180 seconds to fill a 31x10.50 tire from 15 to 30 psi. **7:** Manufacturer's rating is 150 seconds to fill a 33x12.50 tire from 15 to 30 psi. **8:** A typical medium-duty shop compressor of the type many dedicated home tinkerers may purchase. Shown for comparison purposes. **9:** These specifications are from York, who evidently tested their unit as a compressor at some point. The large-displacement York, 10.3 ci, is shown. 6.10 and 8.69 ci units are also available, as well as a new 12 ci unit. This number is variable according to compressor speed. This number simulates an "average" engine at idle. Since pulley sizes vary, the compressor can run faster or slower, and airflow will change. The GM R-4 and R-6 rotary compressors have a similar capacity. **10:** These units can generate upward of 200 psi but are usually regulated to 120–150 psi. **11:** While the installation kits (not available for every application) are not overly expensive, the cost also depends on whether you buy a new compressor or a used one. This is also a labor-intensive installation, though the performance is as close to a shop compressor as you can get. A dedicated junkyard scrounger and tinkerer could do this relatively inexpensively. **12:** Manufacturer's rating is 210 seconds fro a 35x12.50 tire from 15 to 30 psi. **13:** Manufacturer's rating is 125 seconds for a 35x12.50 tire from 15 to 30 psi. **14:** Manufacturer's rating is 120 seconds for a 30x9.50 tire from 10 to 25 psi. **15:** Manufacturer's rating is 225 seconds for a 31x10.50 tire from 15 to 30 psi. **16:** Manufacturer's rating is 185 seconds for a 31x10.50 tire from 15 to 30 psi.

Going from a 30×9.50 to a 35×12.59 tire is a big jump. In many cases it takes a 4- to 6-inch lift and a three-step gearing change (approximately 3.55:1 to 4.56:1) to correct the overall gearing. This is a fairly cost-effective upgrade on a full-sized pickup or SUV. It's more costly but still practical on the more off-highway-oriented 4×4s, such as the utility Jeeps. It becomes expensive and complex on small trucks and on SUVs. Tire size is your foundational choice. Pick your desired size and then follow that thread all the way through to find all the upgrades necessary. *Courtesy Jimmy Nylund*

count as a rear recovery point in most cases. These have a 2x2-inch receiver. Bolted-on ball hitches, called Class 1 hitches, are usually not stout enough, though some are, and the Class II hitches, with a 1.25x1.25-inch receiver, make marginal recovery points. Some pickup step bumpers are stout enough for recovery; many are not.

Tires and Wheels. A tire upgrade offers one of the biggest bangs for your upgrade buck. Bigger tires provide more of both of the primary four-wheeling elements: traction and clearance. A sticky tire can lessen the need for a limited-slip or locker. A rig with open diffs is essentially limited in traction to the amount of grip one tire on each axle can supply. As soon as one tire slips, the ball game is over. If the tire is sufficiently grippy and stays planted on the ground, that slipping point may never come, or will come less often.

TIRE FOOTPRINTS:
A taller tire will offer more clearance with only a slight increase in footprint. The wider tire offers a bigger footprint increase with no extra clearance.

TIRE FITMENT GUIDE

This is derived from a variety of aftermarket suspension and tire supplier sources. Use it as a rough guide for early planning. When you shop for a lift kit, the manufacturer offer lists a more focused snapshot of what tire and wheel combinations will work on your vehicle in combination with their lift kit. LT Flotation sizes (i.e., 31x10.50 versus 265/75R16) shown for ease of comparison. See conversion chart to metric sizes nearby. Positive offset rims usually necessary for all applications, as well as a tire that matches the rim width. Just because a particular amount of lift is listed does not mean such a lift exists.

TIRE FITMENT GUIDE

Vehicle	Setup 1	Setup 2
AM General/Hummer		
1983–2006 Humvee and H1	36x15.50	40x13.50 (4)
	37x13.30	42x15.50 (6)
		16.00-20 (10)
2003 and up H2	35x12.50	35x13.50 (4)
		37x13.50 (6)
		38x14.50(8)
		40x13.50 (10)
2005 and up H3	33x11.50	35x12.50 (4)
		36x15.50 (6)
		37x13.50 (6)
Chevrolet/GMC		
1982–1993 S/T SUV and pickup	30x9.50 !	31x10.50 (4)
		32x11.50 (4) !
		33x11.50 (6) !
1994–2006 S/T SUV and pickup	30x9.50	31x10.50 (4)
		32x11.50 (4) !
		33x12.50 (6)
1973–1987 pickups; '73–'91	31x10.50	33x9.50 (1.5)
Blazer and Suburban		33x12.50 (2.5)
		35x12.50 (4)
		36x15 (6)
		39x15 (6) !
		38.5x15 (8) !
		40x17 (8) !
		42x18 (10) !
1988–1998 pickups; 1992 and up	31x10.50	33x9.50 (4)

Key: **Setup 1** = Stock vehicle, maximum tire size that can be fitted. **Setup 2** = With a lift. Approximate suspension lift required is shown in parentheses. **"!"** denotes fender trimming and or body lift required.

TIRE FITMENT GUIDE

Vehicle	Setup 1	Setup 2
Blazer, Yukon, Tahoe,		33x12.50 (4)
Suburban		35x12.50 (6) !
		36x15 (8) !
		38.5x15 (10) !
1999–2007 Silverado/ Sierra	31x11.50	33x11.50 (2)
		33x11.50 (4) !
		35x12.50 (6) !
		36x15.50 (8)
		38x14.50 (9)
2000–2007 Tahoe, Yukon, XL,	32x11.50	33x11.50 (2)
Avalanche, Suburban		33x13.50 (4)
		35x12.50 (6)
		36x15.50 (7)
		38x14.50 (9)
2004–2008 Colorado/ Canyon	31x11.50	32x11.50 (2)
		33x11.50 (4)
Dodge		
1974–1993 Ramcharger,	31x10.50	32x11.50 (1.5)
Plymouth Trail Duster		33x12.50 (2.5–3)
		35x12.50 (4)
		36x15 (6)
		38.5x15 (8) !
1972–1993 W-250/350	31x10.50	32x11.50 (1.5)
		33x12.50 (2.5–3)
		35x12.50 (4)
		36x15 (6)
		38x15 (8) !
		40x17 (10)
1987–1993 Dakota	30x9.50	31x10.50 (4)
1994–2004 Dakota	31x10.50	32x11.50 (3)
		33x12.50 (6)
1994–2001 Ram 1500 pickup	31x10.50	33x12.50 (2.5)
		35x12.50 (4)
		37x13.50 (8)
1994–2001 Ram 2500/3500 pickup	33x12.50	35x12.50 (3)
		37x 15 (6)
		38x15.50 (8–10)

Key: **Setup 1** = Stock vehicle, maximum tire size that can be fitted. **Setup 2** = With a lift. Approximate suspension lift required is shown in parentheses. **"!"** denotes fender trimming and or body lift required.

TIRE FITMENT GUIDE

Vehicle	Setup 1	Setup 2
1998–2003 Durango	31x10.50!	33x11.50 (3)
		33x12.50 (6)
2002–2008 Ram 1500 pickup	33x12.50	35x12.50 (4)
		36x15.50 (8)
		37x13.50 (8)
2002–2008 Ram 2500/3500 pickup	33x12.50	35x12.50 (4)
		37x13.50 (6)
		38x15 (8)
2004–2008 Durango	31x10.50	33x12.50 (2)
2005–2008 Dakota	31x10.50	33x11.50 (4–6)
Ford		
1966–1977 Bronco	30x9.50	33x9.50 (2.5)
		33x12.50 (3–4) !
		35x12.50 (4–6) !
1978–1979 F-150, Bronco	32x11.50	33x12.50 (2.5)
		35x12.50 (4)
		36x15 (4) !
		38.5x15 (6) !
1973–1979 F-250	33x12.50	35x12.50 (4)
		36x15 (6)
		38x15 (8–10)
1980–1996 F-150, Bronco	32x11.50	33x12.50 (4)
		35x12.50 (4) !
		35x12.50 (6)
		37x13.50 (8–10)
1980–1997 F-250/350 (TTB)	33x11.50	33x12.50 !
		35x12.50 (2)
		36x15 (6)
		38.5x15 (6)
		40x17 (10)
1983–1992 Ranger/ Bronco II	225/75	30x9.50 (1.5)
		31x10.50 (4)
		32x11.50 (4) !
		33x12.50 (6)
		35x12.50 (8-10)
1993–1997 Ranger	31x10.50	32x11.50 (4)
		33x12.50 (4) !
		35x12.50 (8)

Key: **Setup 1** = Stock vehicle, maximum tire size that can be fitted. **Setup 2** = With a lift. Approximate suspension lift required is shown in parentheses. **"!"** denotes fender trimming and or body lift required.

TIRE FITMENT GUIDE

Vehicle	Setup 1	Setup 2
1991–1994 Explorer/ Navajo	235/75	30x9.50 (2.5)
		31x10.50 (4)
		33x12.50 (6) !
		35x12.50 (10) !
1995–1999 Explorer/ Mountaineer	235/75	31x10.50 (2)
	31x10.50 !	33x12.50 (4)
		35x12.50 (6-8)
1997–2008 Expedition,	31x10.50	33x12.50 (3)
Navigator, F-150		35x12.50 (6)
		37x13.50 (8)
1998–2007 F-250, F-350	32x11.50	33x12.50 (2)
		35x12.50 (4)
		37x13.50 (6)
		38x15 (8)
		40x13.50 (10)
1998–2008 Ranger	31x10.50	33x11.50 (4)
		33x12.50 (6)
2000–2008 Explorer/ Mountaineer	31x10.50	33x12.50 (4)
2000–2005 Excursion	32x11.50	33x12.50 (2)
		35x12.50 (4)
		37x13.50 (6)
		38x15.50 (8)
2001–2008 Explorer SportTrac	31x10.50	33x11.50 (4)
		33x12.50 (4)
		35x12.50 (6–8)
Honda		
1997–2002 Passport	31x10.50	32x11.50 (2)
I-H Scout II		
All	31x10.50	33x12.50 (4)
		35x12.50 (8) !
Isuzu		
1987–1998 Pickup	215/75-15	33x12.50 (3) !
	30x9.50 !	
1984–1991 Trooper	31x10.50	33x12.50 (4)
1990–2004 Amigo, Rodeo	31x10.50	33x12.50 (4)
1992–2002 Trooper/ Acura SLX	31x10.50	33x12.50 (4)

Key: **Setup 1** = Stock vehicle, maximum tire size that can be fitted. **Setup 2** = With a lift. Approximate suspension lift required is shown in parentheses. **"!"** denotes fender trimming and or body lift required.

TIRE FITMENT GUIDE

Vehicle	Setup 1	Setup 2
1999–2001 VehiCROSS	31x12.50	33x12.50 (4)
Jeep		
1942–1968 MB, CJ2A,		
CJ3A, CJ3B	30x9.50	7.50-16 (1)
		31x10.50 (1)
		32x11.50 (2.5)
1954–1986 CJ5,6,7,8	7.50-16	32x11.50 (2.5)
	31x10.50	33x12.50 (4)
		35x12.50 (6)
1987–1995 Wrangler YJ	31x10.50	32x11.50 (2.5)
		33x9.50 (3)
		33x12.50 (4)
		35x12.50 (4)
1996–2006 Wrangler TJ, Unlimited	31x10.50	32x11.50 (2)
		33x9.50 (1)
		33x12.50 (3)
		35x12.50 (6)
1984–2001 Cherokee XJ	30x9.50 !	30x9.50 (2)
		31x10.50 (2.5)
		32x11.50 (3) !
		33x12.50 (5) !
		35x12.50 (6+) !
1963–1991 Wagoneer SJ,	30x9.50	31x10.50 (4)
Cherokee SJ (narrow track only)		32x11.50 (4) !
		33x12.50 (4) !
		35x12.50 (6) !
1974–1986 J-Series PU,	32x11.50	33x9.50 (1.5)
Cherokee Chief (wide-track only)		33x12.50 (3)
		35x12.50 (4)
1993–1998 Grand Cherokee ZJ	30x9.50	31x10.50 (2–3)
		32x11.50 (4) !
		33x12.50 (6) !
2000–2004 Grand Cherokee WJ	30x9.50	31x10.50 (2)
		33x12.50 (4)
2002–2007 Liberty KJ	235/75	31x10.50 (2)
2005–2008 Grand Cherokee WK	31x10.50	32x11.50 (2)
		33x12.50 (4)

Key: **Setup 1** = Stock vehicle, maximum tire size that can be fitted. **Setup 2** = With a lift. Approximate suspension lift required is shown in parentheses. **"!"** denotes fender trimming and or body lift required.

TIRE FITMENT GUIDE

Vehicle	Setup 1	Setup 2
2005–2008 Commander XK	31x10.50	32x11.50 (2)
		33x12.50 (4)
2007 and up Wrangler JK, Unlimited	31x10.50	33x11.50 (2)
		33x12.50 (3)
		35x12.50 (4)
		37x13.50 (8)
Land Rover		
1958–1986 Series II, IIA, III	245/75	33x9.50 (2.5)
	30x9.50	33x12.50 (3)
	31x10.50	
1987–1994 Range Rover Classic	245/75	265/75 (2)
	30x9.50	31x10.50 (2)
		33x9.50 (3)
		33x10.50 (3) !
		33x12.50 (4) !
1986–1997 Defender 90/110	286/75	33x12.50 (2.5)
	32x11.50	35x12.50 (4)
		36x15.50 (6)
Mazda		
1987–1992 B2600	31x9.50	33x11.50 (2) !
1994–1997 B3000/4000	31x10.50	32x11.50 (4)
		33x12.50 (4) !
		35x12.50 (8)
1998–2008 B4000	31x10.50	33x11.50 (4)
		33x12.50 (6)
Mitsubishi		
1982–1986 Pickup	30x9.50	31x10.50 (3)
1984–1992 Montero	235/75	31x10.50 (3)
1987–1992 Pickup	30x9.50	31x10.50 (3)
1993–2004 Montero	31x10.50	32x11.50 (3)
2005–2008 Montero	32x11.50	-
2006–2007 Raider	31x10.50	33x11.50 (4–6)
Nissan		
1978–1986 Pickup	235/85	31x10.50 (3)
1987–1995 Pickup	31x10.50	32x11.50 (2)
		33x10.50 (4)
		33x12.50 (4) !
1987–1997 Pathfinder	31x10.50	33x12.50 (4)

Key: **Setup 1** = Stock vehicle, maximum tire size that can be fitted. **Setup 2** = With a lift. Approximate suspension lift required is shown in parentheses. **"!"** denotes fender trimming and or body lift required.

TIRE FITMENT GUIDE

Vehicle	Setup 1	Setup 2
1998–2004 Pathfinder	30x9.50 !	31x10.50 (3)
1998–2003 Frontier Pickup	235/75	31x10.50 (3)
		33x12.50 (5)
2000–2004 Xterra	31x10.50	33x12.50 (5)
2004–2008 Titan/ Armada	33x11.50	33x12.50 (3)
		35x12.50 (6)
2005–2008 Xterra	31x10.50	32x11.50 (3)
		33x12.50 (5)
Suzuki		
Samurai	235/75	30x9.50 (2)
		31x10.50 (3)
Sidekick, GeoTracker,	205/75	235/85 (1.5)
Vitara, XL7		31x10.50 (3)
Toyota		
1960–1983 Land Cruiser FJ-40	31x10.50	32x11.50 (1.5)
		33x12.50 (3)
1979–1985 Pickup/4Runner	32x11.50	33x12.50 (3)
		35x12.50 (6)
1981–1990 Land Cruiser FJ-60/62	31x10.50	33x11.50 (3)
1986 and up Pickup, 4Runner,	31x10.50	32x11.50 (2)
Tacoma		35x12.50 (6)
1991–1997 Land Cruiser FJ-80	31x10.50	33x11.50 (3)
1995–2006 T-100/ Tundra	31x10.50	32x11.50 (1.5)
		33x12.50 (4)
		35x12.50 (6)
2001–2008 Sequoia	31x10.50	-
2007–2008 FJ Cruiser	32x11.50	33x12.50 (3)

Key: **Setup 1** = Stock vehicle, maximum tire size that can be fitted. **Setup 2** = With a lift. Approximate suspension lift required is shown in parentheses. **"!"** denotes fender trimming and or body lift required.

FREE TIRE TEST RIDES:
Tire manufacturers often attend the large, national four-wheel-drive events and have mounted tires that you can test. If they have a size and type you want to try, this would be a free way to try some out.

Tire size increases come in two dimensions: height and width. Most times, a bigger tire comes with more of both. In some cases you can buy a wider tire of the same mounted diameter or a taller tire of the same width.

Unless a gear ratio change is planned, an increase in tire size would be limited by what your vehicle's existing gearing will accept. With a rig that has "high" gears (numerically low, such as 3.07, 3.31, 3.54), the effect on acceleration from a tire swap can be like starting in second gear. The effect of going from a 28-inch-tall tire to a 30-inch-tall tire is like trading 3.54 gears in for 3.31s (see the "Four Wheeler's Math" sidebar). If you have a low-powered rig for its weight, or a rig with exceptionally tall axle gearing, you may find that a 10 percent increase in diameter causes an unacceptable loss of performance. Powerful vehicles with a good torque/weight ratio may be able to accept more than a 10 percent change, if they have the room to fit the tires.

Irrespective of gearing, changes in tire diameter more than about 15 percent should come with an evaluation of drivetrain strength. Stress on the drivetrain, and on the axle shafts especially, increases with larger tires. Part of that is the increase in the weight of the rotating mass, and much is from the increase in the "lever arm" length of the tire radius. Draw an imaginary line from the center of the hub to the contact point on the ground. That is your radius, and the length of that line is the torque arm. A longer arm increases the load on the axle by multiplying the torque.

To help you understand the effect, 500 pounds applied to the end of a 1-foot arm on a rotating shaft equals 500 lbs-ft of torque on the shaft. Increase the arm to 2 feet and that 500 pounds is multiplied twice to 1,000 lbs-ft. The same thing happens, more or less, with tire radius. The axle is the "fuse" between engine torque, multiplied by trans and T-case gearing, and tire grip (a.k.a. traction torque). Fortunately, the tire is not glued to the ground. Or is it?

Modern tires are pretty good at delivering grip. Airing down or increasing weight from weight transfer on slopes will increase grip. While that's not the same thing as a tire glued to the ground, if you combine a taller tire with one that's more grippy and put it in a really good traction situation, those sticky new tires may generate *enough* grip to snap an axle part or two. In many cases, these pieces may prove to be adequate for a mild increase, but not always. Much depends on the intended use. Mild four-wheeling will increase the chances that a marginal combination of tire size and axle strength will survive.

When it comes to actually fitting the tires to the vehicle, the main thing to remember is that it's an inexact science. The first impediment is that tire manufacturers all build to a slightly different standard. Even among tires with the same rated size, one tire's mounted dimensions will not be the exact

Here's a very cost-effective tire upgrade that offers performance in between the stock tires and the monster meats. BF Goodrich makes a 33×9.50-15 tire (in both an All Terrain like this and a Mud Terrain) that will fit on a standard rim. It offers about an inch of increased tread width over the factory tire (a 215/75R-15). Aired down it will offer a sizable increase in footprint over the stock tire but is over 5 inches taller. The best part about this tire is that it will fit with a moderate lift. It appears that this Wrangler has been lifted via longer shackles alone, not the best choice in lift options, which indicates a lift of only about an inch. It appears to have plenty of clearance for the tires. A potential advantage of a moderate setup like this is that these tires are somewhat self-limiting in the traction area due to their moderate footprint. This could help prevent breakage of any weak links in the drivetrain.

same size as another's. This means you have to get the actual mounted dimensions of the tires from each manufacturer for comparison. Don't ask me to explain why, but one manufacturer's 31×10.50-15 tire may be 30.8 inches tall when mounted while another might be 30.3 inches. Also, as you will learn further on, the rim width will also dictate the ultimate section width. These simple facts can mean one tire rubs and another doesn't. Ultimately, lifts are required to fit most significant tire upgrades.

The tire-fitting guide nearby is a compilation of information gleaned from suspension manufacturers and four-wheel-drive shops. Remember that it's a *guide* and is not engraved in stone. It offers you a starting place, but the final test will be a trial fit. If you can make an arrangement with a tire shop to test-fit the tires you want, so much the better.

Tire Tread Designs. As far as tread designs go, you have to pick your poison and stick with it, or buy more than one set of tires. There are four basic tread types available, with a few subclasses. They are biased toward stellar performance in one area, but a careful choice will give you a tire that will be great for your particular environment and generally OK when you stray from it.

Highway Tread: This your ordinary passenger car tire and is designed with pavement in mind. A subclass would be *all-season* tires, which are tires specially designed to perform better in inclement weather. These are potentially more useful to the 4×4 owner who doesn't hit the trail much. Another subclass would be *performance tires*, dedicated to cornering and braking performance. Highway and all-season tires often lack the robust construction qualities needed for the trail.

All-Terrain Tread: Even though BF Goodrich makes a tire of this name, the term has come to represent a tire that is designed to perform well in a variety of off-highway conditions, as well as on the highway. The closed-tread design is usually quiet on the highway, though noisier than a street tire, but performs well in rocks and sand and on the highway. They are generally decent rain, snow, and ice tires also. As you would guess, they tend to load up in mud, but some of the AT designs are surprisingly good in the goo. An AT tire would be outstanding for a driver who mostly drives on the highway but wants acceptable trail performance.

MUDDERS AND ICE:
Some MTs can be positively dangerous on icy streets, so if this is a regular part of your scene, think long and hard before running an MT tire on your rig over winter.

SEVERE WEATHER TIRE RATING:
There is a new 50-state Severe Weather tire rating, which will get you past all but the most severe chain requirements. This rating is a relatively new addition to the tire grading regulations. It measures the tire's performance in snow and ice and is a better real-world evaluation than the old M & S rating.

The perennial favorite for the trail crowd is the so-called "mudder." There was a time when an aggressive tire like this Goodyear was only for the hard-core. Tread design has progressed to the point where they are good all-arounders for the trail. They are still less than ideal for certain street environments, namely ice and snow, but they are now decent day to day.

Like the mudder, the so-called all-terrain tire has advanced. Where it was once a distant second in the trail environment, the all-terrain tire has closed the gap. It remains a good choice for people who spend a lot of time on the street but still want a tire with some trail performance.

Super All-Terrain Tread: This is my appellation for a relatively new subset of the all-terrain category. I also call them the "missing-link" tire. These are tires that don't quite reach the level of the true mudder but are lots more aggressive than a typical AT. In many cases, they are superb rock tires and better in the goo than an all-terrain but better on the street than a mudder. These are much-needed midway-point tires that many are utilizing.

Mud Tread: Mud tires come in a variety of styles, from the old bias-ply mudders that give new meaning to the term road noise to modern radial mud designs that are surprisingly quiet and docile in other elements. As a rule, the radial MT designs are the weapon of choice for most four-wheelers. Their aggressive good looks play a part, but beyond their obvious attributes in soft stuff, they are generally outstanding in rocks of all types and good in deep snow. The MT is not good on the street in rain and is worst on ice.

Rock Tread: Again, this is my moniker for a recently popular adaptation of the mudder. Visually, the differences between a rock tire and a mudder are subtle. Combined with a tread designed for better grip in rocks, they may also use a soft-compound rubber that sticks to rocks like suction cups. Well, not really, but the difference is pretty dramatic. On the downside, these tires offer a much-reduced tread life because of the soft rubber compound.

The BF Goodrich Krawler T/A KX is a born and bred rockcrawling tire. You'd be forgiven for calling it a mudder, and truth be told, it's no slouch there. What makes it a rockcrawling tire? That starts with the rubber compound, which is soft and sticky. The tread blocks are soft and flexible, able to squirm and bite as needed. The sidewall lugs extend halfway down the sidewall to provide traction when using that part of the tire, as well as sidewall protection. The carcass uses two steel belts on the tread and four plies of nylon on the sidewall for impact resistance. Any purpose-built rockcrawling tires will have similar characteristics.

Snow Tires: Contrary to old myths, a good snow tire is not an open-lugged design like a mud tire. It is moderately open so that it can clean itself, but the tread design is close enough to compress the snow inside the tread and use its cohesion to supply traction. Snow tires also use sipes to aid in ice and wet-traction situations. Often, the rubber compound is changed in a snow tire to offer better ice traction. Some snow tires are studded, though studs are not legal in every state. The metals studs actually dig into the ice for traction. There are two common ratings for snow tires. First comes the old "Mud and Snow" rating ("M+S" on the sidewall), which allowed the manufacturer to rate the tire. That left a lot open to interpretation, so as of 1999 some tires use the new Winter Tire Traction rating. Tires so rated have to meet a winter performance standard and wear a "snowflake-on-the-mountain" symbol. Many all-season tires and some all-terrains carry this rating. Many MTs carry the M+S rating, but the "S" part doesn't mean much except in deep trail stuff.

The new trend in all-terrain is to go more aggressive. Modern computerized tread design allows a more gnarly tread without all the noise, wear, and handling pitfalls. The Mickey Thompson MTX is one of the milder of these more aggressive ATs, but in my own tests it proved itself superior on the trail to an "ordinary" AT with no serious penalty on the street. Snow and ice performance on the street was good.

Tire and Rim Matching. The advent of larger-diameter aftermarket rims and tires has made it possible to combine diameter for clearance with a lower-profile off-road tire for better street handling. We're not talking the "bling" look, characterized by huge rims and tires that look like three layers of electrical tape. A larger rim and a moderate-profile tire reduces the tire's flexibility on the trail, but many find it an acceptable loss. You can go too far in this direction, but for most people, maintaining a minimum of about 8–9 inches of tire profile, regardless of rim diameter, is a good compromise.

Forgotten Tire: The Spare. A major aspect of tire upgrades, and one that is often overlooked, is the spare. You can mount the new meats easily onto the vehicle only to find the spot designed for the spare won't carry the new size tire. The cure for this could entail relocating the spare to another location, such as an aftermarket swing-away tire carrier or a bed-mounted location. With some rigs, this can really be a can-o'-worms because of the lack of availability for such items or the physical impossibility of using them.

APPROXIMATE LT FLOTATION TO LT METRIC CONVERSION

Flotation	Diameter (in.)	Metric size
27x8.50R14	26.5	225/75R14
28x9.50R16	29.4	225/75R16
29x9.50R15	28.5	235/75R15
30x9.50R15	29.5	245/75R15
31x9.50R16	30.5	245/75R16
31x9.50R17	30.6	245/70R17
31x10.50R15	30.5	265/75R15
32x9.50R16	31.8	235/85R16
32x11.50R15	31.5	295/75R15
32x10.50R16	31.8	265/75R16
32x10.50R17	31.6	265/70R17
32x11.50R18	32.1	275/65R18
33x12.50R15	32.5	315/70R15
33x12.50R16	32.9	285/75R16
33x12.50R16	33.0	305/70R16
33x15.50R16	32.8	375/55R16
33x11.50R17	32.8	285/70R17
33x13.50R18	33.2	325/60R18
35x12.50R16	34.8	315/75R16
35x12.50R17	34.9	315/70R17
36x15.50R16	35.7	375/65R16
38x15.50R16	37.9	395/70R16

Some owners in the "where-the-spare" pickle will go the roof-rack route and mount a spare up there. That's a reasonable solution, but I don't like the idea of the raised center of gravity. Other folks just ignore the problem and run with the OE spare. That's a terrible solution if your rig has one of those tiny short-term spares and only a bad one for the OE full-sized spare. It depends on the difference in diameter between the spare and the rest of the tires. Having a radically shorter tire is hard on the axle and will work an open differential pretty hard. It will really fritz lockers, full-time four-wheel-drive systems, and traction-control systems because one wheel will be turning at a different speed than the other.

A spare to match the tires on the ground is important to getting home, too. A marginal tire reduces your traction by a significant amount. If you are stuck in a situation like this, make sure your primary traction axle, most likely the rear, has the best tires, even if you have to do a front-to-back tire rotation.

Speedometer Correction. Speedo correction will be necessary with a tire swap or a gearing change. You can do a quick-'n'-dirty odometer check using highway mile markers. Say the odo shows 1.1 miles over a measured mile. Divide the actual miles by the indicated miles to get your correction factor (1/1.1 = 0.9). Multiply the correction factor by the indicated miles driven to get the actual miles (e.g., 250 miles × 0.9 = 225 miles actually driven). If the number comes out the other way, say indicating 0.9 miles over an actual mile (1/0.9 = 1.11), then your 250 indicated miles are actually 277 miles (250 × 1.11 = 277).

The correction method for mechanical speedometers starts with determining the number of teeth on the speedometer drive gear. That's the one on the end of the cable. Before we get too far into describing that, bear in mind that sometimes you also have to replace the drive gear inside the transmission or transfer case to match the gear on the end of the cable. That involves major disassembly. The formula for determining the new gear needed from the old one is in the "Four-Wheeler's Math" sidebar. Speedometer shops also have a correction device available with assorted ratios that can be calibrated to your particular rig, but with the advent of electronic speedometers, the old-time speedo shop is a lot harder to find.

If you have an electronic speedo, there are electronic corrections available via reprogramming the ECU.

The back side of an alloy wheel will usually list its rated load capacity and maximum pressure. Obviously, you wouldn't want a set of wheels not rated for your rig's gross vehicle weight (GVW).

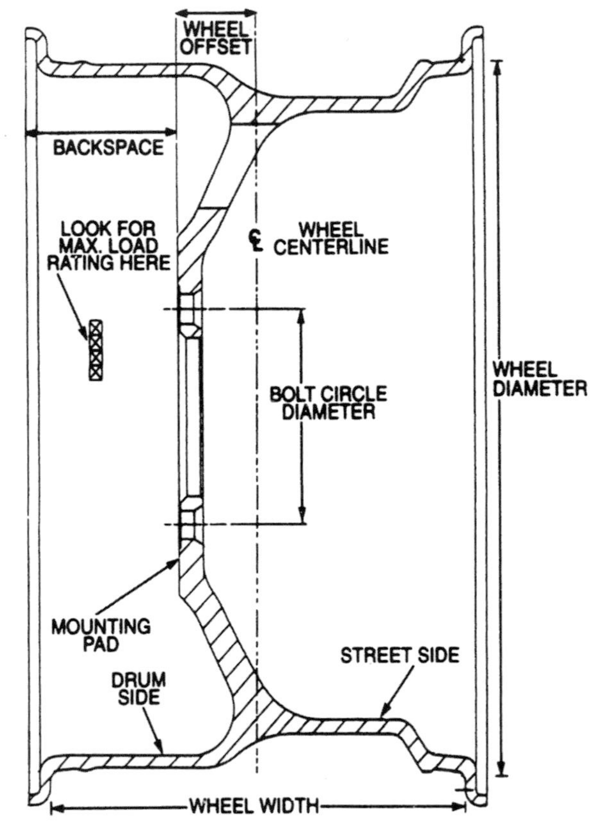

Anatomy of a wheel.

A steel wheel combines strength, low cost, and repairability. The single major downside is weight. With big tires that are also heavy, the combined weight of the rotating mass tends to slow acceleration and decrease braking efficiency. The heavy wheel can also be a factor in drivetrain durability. None of these become huge factors until the tires themselves become huge. This is not a beadlocked wheel, by the way. It's a wheel from ProComp called the "Street-Lock," which has the gnarly appearance of a beadlock without the harsh realities. The extra material on the outer rim actually seems to be good protection against rock damage.

Backspacing is a very important consideration. Measuring it is as simple as this.

WHEEL BACKSPACE:
Negative offset means that the wheel's centerline is farther away from the center of the vehicle than the mounting flange. Deep-dish wheels have negative offset.

The dealer can do that for you in many cases, though you will find some are unwilling to "mess" with a modified rig. Performance EFI programmers often have the capability to change the inputs for tire and gear ratios, but that is often subject to the particular vehicle manufacturer's original programming and hardware. There are also corrective electronic devices for popular applications that can be added, such as Super Lift's TruSpeed device. It can be calibrated to correct the speedo for nearly any tire and axle ratio combination. Ultimately, you can simply determine your error, post it on the dash somewhere, and hope you don't forget (or find yourself discussing the situation with an understanding policeman). In some cases, correcting the speedometer is vital to late-model engine management systems, and not doing so can cause no end of drivability problems.

Wheels. Choosing a wheel seems like a no-brainer and subject more to looks and taste than anything else. Not so! While looks are a part of the choice, function must be the first consideration. There are thousands of cosmetic choices but only a few functional ones. They boil down to size (dictated mostly by the tire size), offset, and material.

Original equipment applications often involve a steel wheel with a stamped-steel center welded to a rolled-steel outer rim. The advantage of steel wheels is that they are strong, easily repaired, and cheap. There's nothing wrong with using a stock wheel if it will fit your new tires. The disadvantages to steel wheels are mostly in the performance area. A vehicle equipped with light, alloy wheels will accelerate noticeably faster and stop shorter than a vehicle with ordinary steel wheels because there is less rotating mass to start in motion or stop. When upgrading to larger tires, lessening rotating mass can be an important factor.

One-piece alloy wheels are the most commonly seen alloy type on 4×4s. The two-piece, or modular, wheels are too delicate and shouldn't be used. Forged alloys are the brutes of the alloy wheel realm. A cast- or forged-aluminum alloy wheel can weigh 30 percent less than an OE-style steel wheel and 50 percent less than some heavy-duty steel wheels. Both the forged and cast wheels are tough and generally repairable, but they can be made unsightly by the rigors of the trail fairly quickly.

Choosing the Right Wheel. Whatever tire you have, it needs to be matched to the correct rim. That starts with rim diameter, but I think you know that a 16-inch tire must go on a 16-inch rim. Width is less clear; a tire will mount and hold air even if mounted on a rim with the incorrect width. The manufacturer of a typical 35×12.50-×15 might list a width range of 8 to 11 inches, meaning you will get the best performance from the tire if mounted on a rim in that width range. From there, look for a spec that lists "Measuring Rim Width" (MRW). That's the rim width the tire manufacturer used to calculate the section width of the tire. For our example tire, it measures 12.50 inches only when mounted on the MRW.

For every ½ inch wider or narrower than the MRW, the section width changes ¼ inch in the same direction. Say the MRW was 9 inches, the section width of the tire was 12.50 inches, and the rim width range was 8–11 inches. If you mounted the tire on an 8-inch rim, you'd reduce the section width by ½ inch. That might be just enough to clear that last little bit of rubbing. Bear in mind that when you go toward the narrow end of the range, it tends to pull the edges of the tread up. When you go wide, it tends to pull the center up.

Hutchinson's "Rock Monster" beadlock is one of the few DOT-legal beadlock systems on the market. The two-piece alloy wheel clamps the beads with a molded rubber sleeve. Hutchinson is the same company that builds the beadlocked wheels for military and civilian Hummers. *Courtesy Hutchinson Industries*

Staun's inflatable beadlocks come close to meeting the ideal "three bears" criteria . . . just right. They fit many rims but require a hole for a second valve stem. It's essentially a tire inside a tire. When inflated, it expands to force the beads against the rim and keep them there. Because it's light and located nearer the center of the rotating mass, it has minimal negative effects on balance. *Courtesy Staun US*

Those effects are minimal within the specified width range, but wear and performance can still be affected negatively. The MRW is usually the ideal.

Two wheel-related terms you need to understand are backspace and offset. Backspace is the distance from the inside wheel mounting flange to the inside bead. Offset is the distance the mounting pad is offset from the wheel centerline. Negative offset means the wheel rim is moved outboard on the wheel flange. If you keep the same wheel rim width, adding more negative offset will reduce backspace. You can determine offset by measuring backspace, subtracting it from the rim width and then dividing by two. An 8-inch rim with 5.5-inch backspacing has a 1.25-inch offset (8.0 - 5.5 = 2.5/2 = 1.25 inches). Remember that rim width is technically from bead to bead, not between the outer edges of the rim.

The extra width needed for a bigger tire is best added equally to the inside and outside to keep the offset roughly the same as stock and keep load on the wheel bearings where the factory intended. A stock 7-inch rim with 3.5-inch backspace might be replaced by an 8-inch rim with 4-inch backspace. One-half an inch is added to the inside and the other half-inch to the outside.

How much you can add to the inside may become a problem, especially on the front, so you may have to add more of the extra width to the outside edge. Using the example above, the 8-inch rim with a 3.75-inch backspace adds ¼ inch to the inside and ¾ inch to the outside. That changes the backspace minimally but adds more negative offset and loads the bearings a little more. Three-quarters of an inch isn't a biggie, but changing the offset a great deal in either direction can cause early wheel bearing failure and tire wear issues.

Your wheel should be rated for the load it will carry. This spec is available from the wheel manufacturer and should be cast into the wheel also. This usually works itself out, since an 8-lug wheel is usually rated for the load an 8-lug truck might carry. Trouble is more likely in the ½-ton truck, 5-lug realm, where the bolt pattern is shared with cars. You can lessen the chance of a problem by using high-quality cast or forged wheels, avoiding composite wheels that have a cast center with a spun-aluminum rim.

Beadlocks. These devices physically lock the outer tire bead to the rim so it can be run at extremely low pressures. Are they necessary? To the diehard gear grinder who runs hard-core trails in a specially prepped rig aired down to practically nothing, perhaps. The average 'wheeler in a dual-purpose machine would probably find them an unnecessary expense. Since the first edition of this book, the market for beadlocked wheels has exploded, with many choices available. The advantages are that you can run extremely low pressures and not worry about sudden deflation from rolling the bead off a rim. In extreme rockcrawling, these very low pressures can make the difference between making it and not.

SHOCKING CHANGES:
Situations that may change your shock needs include the mounting of larger tires, a change of spring rate, a major change in vehicle weight, or a change in driving conditions. In any of these cases, you may have to reevaluate your shock needs.

In general, there are two types of beadlocks: mechanical and pneumatic. The mechanical types come in several guises. In one type, the inner rim of the wheel is more or less of the normal type, perhaps with a more pronounced inner hump to better hold the bead. The outer bead is clamped between a flange on the rim and a bolted-on ring.

There are downsides to some of the beadlocks of this type on the market today. Some are very serious. This applies mainly to their use on the highway and explains why most are not DOT-certified for street use. First, they may be very difficult, or impossible in some cases, to get balanced properly. Correct assembly is vital to life and limb in the case of use on the highway. The bolts that hold the outer ring in place need frequent checking. Loose or broken bolts can allow the tire to deflate suddenly, so neglect them at your peril.

As with any product, there are better and worse beadlock wheels out there. The better factory-built beadlocked wheels equipped with only an outer clamp feature a centering ring for the wheel, some means to prevent the tire bead from spinning inside the clamped portion, and protection for the bolts from trail damage in the form of recessed bolt holes. The worst, in my opinion, are the do-it-yourself kits. It isn't that the kits are inherently bad; it's that you may be relying on unskilled welders, a poor or damaged wheel, and other unsafe or unreliable factors that could make the finished product an appointment to an accident.

The next type of beadlock is the two-piece, so-called "Humvee"-type of wheel. The wheel actually splits in the center. A hard rubber or metal spacer fits between the inner edges of the tire bead, and when the wheel is bolted together, both beads are clamped. The military Humvee wheel incorporates a solid wheel inside the tire as a run-flat device, but the aftermarket versions do not. Hutchinson Industries, maker of both military and civilian Hummer wheels, is now offering this type of beadlocked wheel for aftermarket use. It's expensive, and the applications are limited as yet.

WHEEL BACKSPACE:
Positive offset means that the wheel's centerline is closer to the center of the vehicle than the mounting flange. With positive offset, the deeper side of the wheel is the back side.

One beadlock product stands out as something completely different. The Staun beadlock is an inflatable device that fits between the beads of the tire. Once a hole is drilled in the rim, it can be used on almost any wheel. The carcass of the Staun is like a low-profile inner tube with a polyester fiber "tread" on the outer diameter and sidewall straps that push against the beads. When inflated to 48 psi, the Staun effectively forces the beads tightly against the rim, but it does not expand out into the major interior volume of the tire. A special channel allows you to inflate and deflate the tire normally via the existing valve stem hole. Though it's not advertised as a "run-flat" device, it serves as such . . . at least in a short-term, low-speed capacity. One minor downside noted by some is that inflation and deflation times are increased.

Suspension Mods, Lifts, and Body Lifts

A "mild" suspension lift would be no more than 2½ inches on SWB rigs and up to 4 inches on larger pickups and SUVs. Adverse effects would be few, but many rigs achieve a startling transformation. They can carry larger tires, get better articulation, and suffer only a minimal loss of street drivability. There are also modifications you can make to non-lifted rigs that can enhance trail performance.

Choosing Shocks. If you are buying a suspension kit, the shocks are usually included. Does this mean they are the best ones for your situation? Not always. Sometimes it pays to look at the upgrades available, or seek your own. If you are upgrading the shocks from a lift kit, be sure to match the required extended and compressed lengths needed for the lifted rig.

Sway bar disconnects allow for the best possible handling on the street when connected but the most articulation on the trail when disconnected. When used with a lift kit, the disconnects must be longer by the amount of the lift. This would hold true for the normal sway bar links as well. Disconnects sometimes come with lift kits.

As to the type of shock, the need can be divided into slow movers, fast movers, and rigs that are mostly stock and run on the street. Slow movers are the rockcrawler types. They may stay away from high-pressure gas shocks because they can cost some suspension flexibility. A good compromise can be had with shocks that use cellular gas or foam. Another good compromise is adjustable shocks. They offer the flexibility to dial-in the dampening for street or trail. A recent addition to the shock arsenal is remote reservoir shocks where the gas pressure (nitrogen gas) can be altered by the owner.

Fast movers could include those owners who primarily run desert tracks or milder trails where you can get up to speed for more than just a short stretch. For these folks, low- or medium-pressure gas shocks are a better choice to deal with the heat and foaming that comes from taking a bumpy road at speed. If you are a real fast mover, high-pressure gas or even remote-reservoir, adjustable-pressure shocks may be your ticket. If your truck is to remain fairly stock or spend most of its time on the highway, then some of the trick, self-adjusting units are a good choice. Low-pressure gas is always a good choice for stock or mildly built rigs.

As to quality, there are some hallmarks to watch for. Among the commonly touted shock specs are piston and piston rod size. In this case, bigger is better, with the larger piston running cooler and dampening better. A variety of seal materials are used, from simple neoprene to Teflon to more exotic materials like Nitrile. The durability of the seal is vital to shock life.

A larger shaft is stronger, though the material it is made from will play a part. They range from cast or sintered iron to induction-hardened steel to silicon bronze. The best shafts are made from forged steel and machined to a micro finish. The shaft is usually chrome plated, and the quality of this work will help

SWAY BAR:
A sway bar, or anti-roll bar, is a torsion bar that runs across the vehicle and connects one side of the suspension to the other.

determine how long the shock will last. Once the shock loses pressure and oil, it's history.

Some shocks have eyes on both ends or just one end. Either way, the quality of the welding will dictate how long that eye stays attached to the body in tough situations. On cheap shocks, it is attached by a couple of spot welds. Better shocks have continuous welds or are double-welded.

Sway Bar Disconnects. When weight transfer in cornering causes the vehicle to lean, the sway bar tries to keep the body level. You could look at it two ways—it either jacks the low side up or pulls the high side down. While the sway bar is great for pavement handling, it does restrict suspension articulation on the trail. The answer is a sway bar disconnect. With the pull of a pin, you can unhook the sway bar from the axle and gain an instant increase in articulation. That keeps the tires on the ground better for improved traction. When you get back to the pavement, a few minutes' work will have you hooked back up for good handling.

The latest iterations of the sway bar disconnect are the tunable types and the remote-controlled types. Neither of these has a very large list of applications (mostly Jeeps). In the case of the tunable types (the Skyjacker Rock Lock, Currie Anti-Rock, etc.), they are designed as much for off-highway uses as on-highway. Long travel, lifted coil-spring suspension rigs with a suspension soft enough to flex well can have stability problems. A sway bar that's tunable can offer some extra control. The aftermarket has been toying with remote-controlled sway bar disconnects. The OE market has had at least one such item for some time, in the Dodge Power Wagon, but such a product has yet to emerge from the aftermarket.

In the end, a sway bar disconnect is a very effective tool for many rigs and next to useless on others. How much articulation you can gain is partially limited by your vehicle's maximum suspension travel. Solid-axle rigs benefit most and have the fewest caveats. They can be useful to IFS rigs as well, but as you will learn below, they can be counterproductive if they allow so much downtravel that the CV joint binds.

If used only for a moderate amount of lift, coil spring spacers are viable choices for those rigs that can use them. This one is a 2-inch Skyjacker IFS spacer lift installed on one of Quadratec's fleet, a late-model Jeep Grand Cherokee IFS. The kit uses the original shock and coil spring. Polyurethane spacers mount above and below the spring.

Choosing a Lift Kit. Lifts are accomplished in various ways depending on suspension type. We will deal with the mild forms of lift in this chapter, but if you are interested in more radical methods, flip to Chapter 8. In recent years, some states have imposed lift laws that limit or regulate the amount of lift you are allowed to use. Research before you buy.

MORE LIFT, MORE BUCKS:
The more lift you buy, the more money you will spend. It isn't that 4-inch lift springs cost that much more than 2-½-inch springs; it's that you have to make so many other changes to make it all work. These include modifications to the steering and driveshaft and longer brake lines.

ADD-A-LEAF:
An add-a-leaf can be used to bolster sagging springs. Usually, it's a pretty hefty leaf, but the versions with a longer, thinner leaf provide a better ride than the short, very thick ones.

Leaf-Spring Lifts. For leaf-spring rigs, the front lift is always done with new springs that are longer and have more arch than the originals. With heavily arched leaf springs, uptravel must be restricted to prevent reverse-arching the spring, which could damage it, so a bump stop extension may be included. That's the downside to highly arched springs: They lose flexibility. A more mildly arched spring (less lift), however, may be able to use much of its newly gained uptravel, assuming the larger tires you also selected don't hit anywhere.

In the rear, leaf-spring lifts use new springs when the spring is mounted under the axle (a.k.a. spring under) but are often done via lift blocks on pickups and full-sized SUVs where the spring is mounted above the axle (a.k.a. spring over). The lift is equal to the thickness of the block. As the name implies, a lift block is a steel or aluminum block that's inserted between the spring and the axle perch. It requires longer U-bolts. Its main advantages are low cost and simplicity, but by retaining the OE spring, you are retaining stock ride and articulation. At low lifts this type works well, but at higher lifts spring wrap can be a problem.

Add-a-leaf products are offered by most aftermarket suspension manufacturers. This is another very inexpensive method to acquire lift, though the amount of lift available is less. With some small variations, they all involve adding a single, heavily arched leaf to your existing leaf pack. It can raise the suspension 1 to 1.5 inches with a corresponding increase in spring rate—which may not be desirable. Sometimes add-a-leafs are used to bolster sagging springs or to increase load capacity.

You will see some 4×4s lifted with longer spring shackles. This is a poor way of doing it. Shackle changes may be necessary with a lift, but they are best used for minor suspension geometry corrections than for true lift. If used only for lift, they can adversely affect geometry. Shackles will add lift but only to half of their actual length. If you put on a shackle that is 2 inches longer than stock, you only gain 1 inch of lift because you are lifting only one end of the spring. On occasion, a longer shackle can be used to level out the vehicle and change driveshaft geometry. In this context, it can be a viable option.

Coil-Spring Lifts. Coil-spring rigs with solid axles are lifted by either longer springs or by spacers placed on top of the springs. A longer shock or a shock extension is also used. With a mild lift, up to about 3 inches, a spacer is acceptable, but at the higher end, it may impart some undesirable suspension and steering geometry changes.

The suspension links are designed to offer specific steering and axle geometry. When a longer spring (or a spacer) is installed, the angle is increased, effectively shortening the eye-to-eye distance of the arm, relocating the axle, and changing caster and pinion

ROUGH ROAD

LIFT BLOCKS:
Some leaf-sprung pickups use spring-over front axles, but never, ever use blocks up front because of spring wrap and the dangerous possibility of the U-bolts working loose.

COIL-SPRING LIFTS:
Suspension geometry is not always an issue with mild, solid-axle, coil-spring lifts, but in some cases, new suspension links (i.e., radius arms, trailing arms) are necessary. This is what can make a coil-spring lift complicated or expensive.

A leaf-spring lift block can be used only on rigs that are in spring-over configuration, either factory or conversion, and only on the rear. The thickness of the block equals the thickness of the lift. The extra leverage of the block tends to increase axle wrap, especially on light-duty springs. Lift blocks seem to be the most trouble free on trucks with stiff springs, but a 4-inch block is about the limit. A block can be combined with lifted springs as well, such as a 4-inch lift spring with a 2-inch block for a 6-inch block.

angle. To correct this, longer and reshaped control arms, or corrective brackets, must be used to bring the suspension geometry back to normal. More detail on this will come in a later chapter.

IFS Lifts. The only real gain with most IFS (independent front suspension) kits is lift for bigger tires and usually a few performance improvements, such as the increased articulation you might gain from a solid-axle lift. IFS rigs are usually more limited in tire size, not so much by available lifts but by the strength of the front drivetrain components, which is often considerably less than most solid axles used on vehicles in the same category. Some kits involve cutting original bracketry from the chassis, leaving them more difficult to convert back to stock specs.

There are only a few ways to lift IFS vehicles, either by spacers (for coil-spring or coil-on-strut systems) that mount above or in the coil-spring pack, torsion bar re-indexing (for torsion bar systems), or suspension relocation (a.k.a. a "dropped" lift), which lowers the entire suspension/differential system and is used on all IFS rigs when large lifts are needed. Which system you can use is dictated by the type of suspension and the amount of lift you want.

IFS rigs have a plethora of pitfalls in the lift department, most of them revolving around geometry. The usual "safe" amount of lift for non-dropped IFS lifts is around 2–3 inches (variable among brands and models). The rear of IFS trucks is usually leaf-sprung, so all the tricks shown in the leaf-spring sections apply. A few 4×4s have IRS (independent rear suspension), and generally the same rules apply as to IFS.

Strut-Type. We'll define a "strut" as one that combines the coil spring and the shock. Some also call these systems "coil-overs," but that term usually applies more to aftermarket conversions than factory setups. Many of the latest IFS designs use struts. Strut spacers mount above and sandwich between the upper mount and the strut. Sometimes a spacer is fitted above or below the coil inside the strut, so the unit must be disassembled with a coil-spring compressor for installation. The third alternative is longer struts or struts that have relocated coil seats.

Torsion Bar Re-Indexing. Many IFS rigs with torsion bars have a leveling adjustment that some people use as a "free" lift. Without any other changes, this might be safe to ½ to 1 inch. Just like any other IFS lift, it will change the suspension geometry and CV joint angles. Ultimately, however, there isn't all that much adjustment available. A device that re-indexes the place where the end of the torsion bar is held in the chassis is used to gain extra lift.

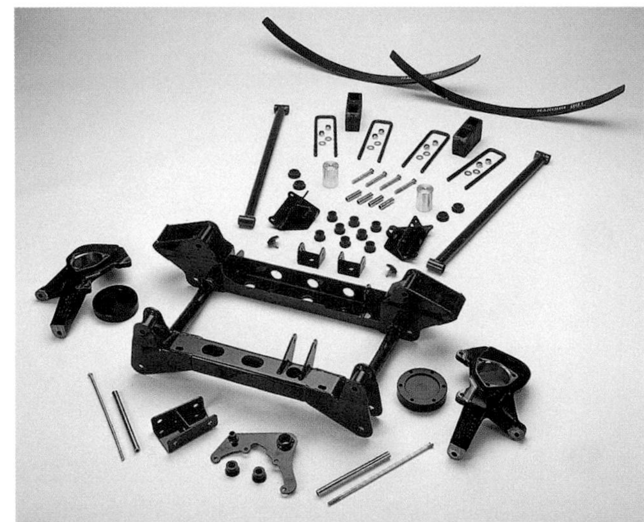

Some IFS lift kits use brackets to lower the entire suspension. This retains the original suspension geometry for the most part. Front driveshaft angles become an issue because the differential is lowered. This is a kit designed for a 1990s Chevy IFS truck. *Courtesy Rancho*

Drop-Bracket. The final IFS lift is the drop-bracket lift. In this case, the entire suspension, including the differential, is dropped via bracketry. This is the historic method for obtaining large lifts on IFS rigs. The advantages are that near-stock suspension geometry is retained and the CV joint angle is close to stock as well. The downsides are the cost and extensive installation effort of the kit. Because the strength of the kit depends largely on the quality of the new bracketry, you want high-quality, well-engineered pieces on these types of kits. Front driveshaft angularity usually requires some attention, but that's often addressed by the kit manufacturer.

IFS CV Axles. IFS CV (constant velocity) axles are worth a few words on their own. Typically, they are a combination of a six-ball "Rzeppa"-style CV joint at the outer end and a tripod-style joint on the inner end. A few have Rzeppas at both ends. The outer joint must transmit power with angularity from steering input and through the up and down of suspension travel. The inner tripod has to deal only with the up and down angularity, as well as plunge. Plunge is the in and out movement of the joint. Just as with a driveshaft, the CV axle changes length with angularity, so the plunge of the inner joint gives it a range of movement to do that. That same effect can be accomplished with special "cross-groove" Rzeppa joints, which are used on high-

Too much body lift. This is at least 3 inches, and look how the mount is tilted and tweaked. Not to mention, this is a plastic puck. A very rigid chassis is needed to make a 3-inch body lift practical for rigs used on the trail. It's best to keep body lifts no taller than 2 inches and used mainly for final correction of tire fit problems.

A Rancho IFS strut lift on a late-model F-150 pickup. It's shown in the fully drooped position. The original coil spring is used on a longer shock that has had the spring seat (1) moved to gain 2–3 inches of lift. When lifting this increasingly common suspension design, keep an eye on the upper ball joint (2). Is its range of movement maxed out? Also, will the upper arm contact the coil spring at any point in travel? Is the rack-and-pinion tie rod angle (3) excessive? If it is, the rack can be dropped, or (more commonly) the knuckle (4) can be replaced with one that has the steering arm (5) moved up to ease the angle on the tie rod.

PINION ANGLES:
Some builders will opt to set the pinion angle a degree lower in the rear and a degree higher in the front to help compensate for pinion angle changes under a torque load.

BODY LIFTS:
You see body lifts used often on IFS pickups, where a little extra space for already large wheelwells enables a sizable increase in tire size. Ultimately, the stiffer the chassis, the more body lift is OK.

end machines like Hummer H1s, or by splined shafts with a slip yoke (aftermarket).

Most kits increase the angle on the front CV axle shafts to some degree. Some less-well-designed kits run this angularity right to the ragged edge. Remember that the front outer CV joint has to deal with angularity from suspension movement *and* steering. If it binds due to excessive angularity, it breaks. Broken CV axles are one of the most common failures seen in lifted IFS rigs. Some of that is angularity, and some is due to the overload imparted by larger tires.

When you turn the wheels, or cycle the suspension, that puts the CV axle above or below a horizontal position. The CV axle shaft is pulled outboard (plunge). When the angularity of the CV axle is increased, it uses up some of that travel (moving the spider outboard). If downtravel or a hard turn pulls the spider to the end of its travel, it breaks. Better lift kits come with spacers that go between the axle flange and the CV joint flange and are designed to center the plunge depth on the inner CV joint according to the amount of lift. Some kits might include a new, longer CV axle that does the same thing. What could complicate the issue is if you cranked up the torsion bars or added another coil spacer for a little extra lift. You can check plunge depth by removing the inner CV boot and observing the position of the tripod spider inside. At normal ride height, it should be centered in travel. You can turn the wheels to full lock and cycle the suspension fully up and down to make sure the spider stays within its

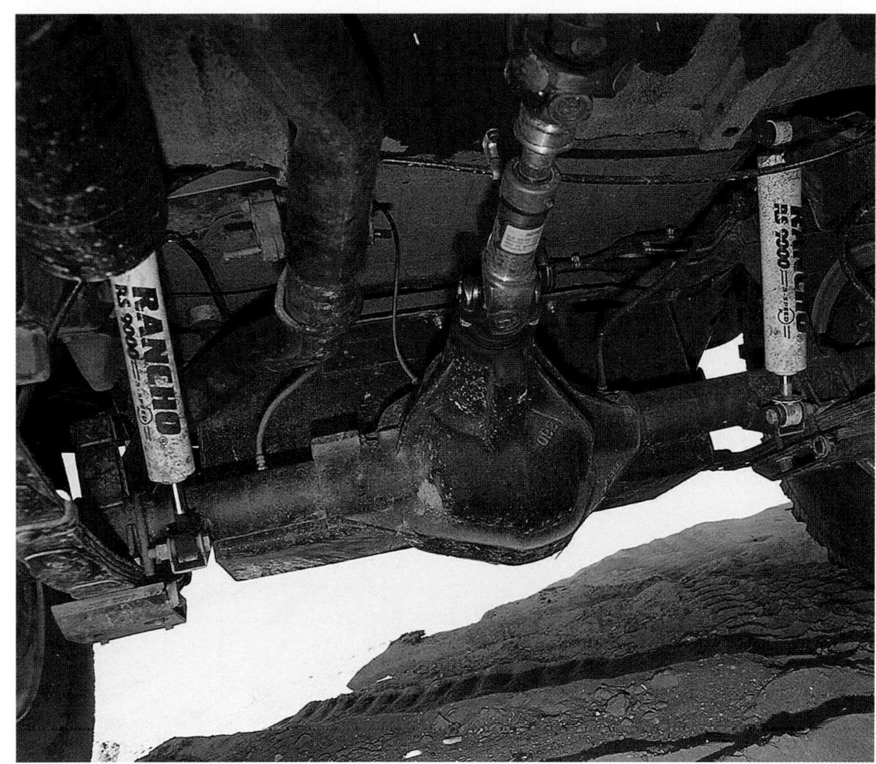

Driveshaft angles are critical at every lift level but especially for short-wheelbase rigs. Even a mild lift can be a problem if your rear driveshaft is less than 24 inches long. Level one of the fix would be a CV joint, though in some cases the shaft may not be long enough to use a CV. In that case, the answer is either relocating the T-case forward or shortening up the transfer case with a short-tailshaft conversion. In addition to a CV rear driveshaft, this rig uses a high-pinion Dana 60 differential (which is normally used up front) that raises the driveshaft several inches. It's an expensive answer. The upside is that you solve the driveshaft problem and end up with some beefy 35-spline rear axle shafts. The downside is the cost, the extra weight, and the loss of clearance. Running the differential at reverse its normal rotation costs some strength (20–30 percent), but a Jeep like this is probably OK with an axle of Dana 44 strength or so.

specified travel. If you run into problems, limit up or down travel as needed or change the thickness of the axle spacer to center the tripod.

IFS Lift Complications. Beyond the CV joint issues discussed above, some of the major complications of a non-dropped IFS lift are ball-joint angularity and/or the upper A-arm hitting the coil spring or shock. This later situation is usually accompanied by way-out-of-spec camber. Because the A-arm (or arms) is at more of an angle, it moves the front wheel position inboard and narrows the front wheel track. At an extreme angle, the upper or lower ball joint (usually the upper) may run out of travel (usually downtravel) and bind or break. Many better kits will include new A-arms with the design altered to correct the ball-joint angle. Often these new arms are also longer to bring the wheels back out to the factory position and to correct camber. Sometimes the steering knuckle is made longer to raise the upper A-arm and reduce ball-joint angularity.

Many newer IFS suspensions use rack-and-pinion steering. The rack is usually located so that the tie rods are close to being parallel with the ground at normal ride height. That minimizes bump steer and steering changes as the suspension cycles. With a lift, a certain amount (small or large) of angularity is imparted. This may be able to be compensated for at ride height by adjustments on the rod, but bump steer will be increased. The angularity also puts an added load on the steering unit that may hasten wear. There are two cures: the first is to relocate (drop) the rack; the second and most common is to install a new steering knuckle with the steering arm relocated to eliminate or reduce the angle.

Driveshaft Angularity. With almost any amount of lift, there are complications not directly related to the suspension. The first of these is with driveshafts. One major effect of lifting or lowering any vehicle is a change of driveshaft and pinion angles, as well as driveshaft length. Changing the operating angles of the driveshaft universal joints can have many negative effects, the mildest of which is vibration and shorter life.

The two universal joints, or U-joints, on each driveshaft should both operate at the same angle and at the same speed. That means the pinion end of the differential and the transmission/transfer case output must be parallel on two planes. If not, then one universal is operating at a slightly higher or lower speed than the other, and vibration is the result. The greater the difference, the greater the vibration. A difference of 3 degrees or less is usually regarded as "in the ballpark," though some rigs are very sensitive to any variation. The axle is the easiest place to make corrections. On leaf-sprung rigs, tapered shims are fitted between the spring perch and the spring to alter the angle. On coilers, the correction can sometimes be done via adjustable or offset control arm bushings, or adjustable control arms.

Driveshaft angle, or more specifically universal joint operating angle, becomes a problem with some lifts, especially with short-wheelbase rigs. The driveshaft angle increases more per inch of lift the shorter the driveshaft. The maximum angularity for most U-joints is about 30 degrees. This is a short-term maximum number. Continuous angularity is rated at 15 degrees for most universals, and service life will be cut by 75 percent when operating at this angle. One cure for rear driveshaft angularity problems is a CV joint. More accurately called a Double-Cardan, the CV takes two standard U-joints and couples them together with a housing that has a centering device. If you have a 20-degree angle, the CV essentially splits this between the two joints, giving them 10 degrees each, well within their operating range. If you want long U-joint life, start thinking about installing one when your operating angle reaches 8 degrees. Many front driveshafts are already equipped with a CV joint.

Up front, you run into more problems than just driveshaft angles. Any alterations made to the pinion angle on a solid axle to correct driveshaft angle or U-joint angles will change caster angles. Since caster affects straight-line tracking and braking performance, it's important to keep it within an acceptable range. Pinion angle and caster are inexorably tied together. If you change one then you will change the other, and the only way to alter this relationship is by rotating the axle tubes inside the diff case. In the case of IFS rigs, pinion angle is fixed, but if you use a dropped-style lift kit, you may have to address driveshaft angles to eliminate vibration.

Bear in mind that pinion angles change with suspension movement or by the torque effect of the axle (solid axles only). The rear pinion will climb under a torque load, and the front will drop. If this occurs at low driveshaft speeds, it isn't much of a problem because the U-joint can deal with the extra angularity going slow. If you happen to be spinning the wheels or are in a high gear with the drivetrain turning at a higher speed, it's a different deal, and U-joint failure is possible.

Some lift kits offer transfer case–lowering spacers to correct angularity issues. By lowering the T-case, you put the engine, trans, and T-case on a slope. Remember, you didn't drop the engine mounts. Seldom is this ideal. If you correct the rear, it often throws the front farther out, or vice versa. It also decreases ground clearance. On occasion, T-case lowering works adequately, and it's usually the least expensive option . . . hence its prevalence in some circles (mostly with short-wheelbase rigs).

Body Lifts. On vehicles that have a separate body and chassis, small pucks can be inserted between the chassis and the body to lift the body off the chassis. This allows for extra clearance in the fenderwells for larger tires. It's an acceptable and cost-effective means of fitting larger tires if not used to extremes. What's extreme? That's somewhat variable according to the vehicle and who you speak with about it. If you talk to me, I'll tell you that 3 inches is max and less is better. The part that spooks me is the extra leverage on the longer bolts. When the chassis flexes, it can tear out body mounts or snap mounting bolts. That is a possibility that increases with the body lift height. My opinion is based on actually using the truck on the trail. Some guys get away with tall body lifts because they don't hit the trail much.

Body lift pucks come in various materials, from a high-strength plastic to Delrin (a derivative of polyurethane) or metal. Within limits, they are all OK. I have seen the plastic pucks break, and I have seen dissimilar-metal corrosion problems with aluminum pucks on steel bolts. The former case is unusual, and the latter situation can be aided with a coating of anti-seize compound between the bolt and the puck.

Body lifts are best used for corrective purposes, i.e., to gain that last inch of clearance needed for the new tires in conjunction with other modifications. It's a good alternative for IFS vehicles needing a little extra room in the wheelwells. The downsides to all types are that it will sink your shifters by the amount of the lift, change the fan-to-radiator relationship, and change the

TRANNY OIL TEMPS:
The 250-degree mark is the hottest temperature your transmission should ever be allowed to attain for any length of time. At that temp, the oil begins to degrade seriously, and if ignored, it may result in shortened tranny life or immediate failure.

steering shaft angle. These issues are more troublesome in certain rigs than others.

Drivetrain

At the basic level, with stock or near-stock gearing and only a moderate increase in tire size, most of your concerns are with traction. OE drivetrains are generally (but not always) safe to about a 10 percent increase in tire size without strength or gearing upgrades, and that puts most of the harder-core upgrades into the advanced buildups chapter further on. Still, there are some durability aspects to consider apart from major upgrades.

Upgrade As You Break? As a precursor to all the other drivetrain stuff you will read in this chapter and in later ones, let's discuss the "upgrade as you break" option. Let's say that you snap a rear axle in your largely stock rig. Let's also say that there is an alloy replacement available that's 20 percent stronger than stock. Why not replace what you break with better parts? Of course, you'd need to replace both axles in that case, but by upgrading you've substantially increased the system's durability. In the case of an axle shaft, the alloy unit may only be a slight to moderate increase in cost over a bolt-in replacement. And if you're paying labor costs anyway, why not apply them to stronger parts?

Automatic Transmission Upgrades. Trail work can cause your 4×4's automatic transmission to generate massive amounts of heat. That tendency is increased with heavy loads, tall gears, and more difficult terrain. Overheated oil may go unnoticed in most OE rigs because they do not have trans fluid temp gauges. A few have a warning light. The risk of damage presented by overheating makes a tranny temp gauge one of your first trail upgrades if you have an automatic.

With the gauge installed, you can monitor trans temp during your heaviest-duty 'wheeling. Ideal temps are below 200 degrees at all times, but that's hard to achieve. More realistic is never to allow the temps to climb past 250 degrees for any length of time. Hot tranny oil can be cooled by stopping, putting the tranny into neutral, and fast-idling the engine at about 1,000 rpm for a while. If you find yourself in the red zone often, then an auxiliary cooler is in order.

> **COOL AUTOMATICS:**
> PAVEMENT ENDS
> Beyond an auxiliary transmission-oil cooler, an upgrade to synthetic transmission fluid can help your transmission survive longer at high temps because it does not break down as quickly as conventional oil, and it has a higher temperature rating.

Where to monitor temperature is the big question. Most gauge kits offer an inline sensor that mounts in one of the trans cooler oil lines. Mounting it in the "out" line tells you how hot the fluid is coming out of the converter (the hottest part). Installing it in the return line (oil going back to the trans from the cooler) tells you how effectively your coolers are working, and this return oil is most often used to lubricate the "hard" parts of the transmission, so cool oil is vital. The third spot is the transmission oil pan. This is the holding area for a major volume of oil used for all purposes. The two best places are either the "out" line, so you can monitor the extreme oil temp, or the pan temp, where the oil spends the most time at a specific temperature. Limiting how long the trans oil spends at high temperature is the key to long fluid life, so many people choose to monitor the pan temp. Installing a plug for a sensor in the transmission oil pan is more difficult and complicated than installing an inline sensor.

As for coolers, an oil-to-air cooler can knock off a good deal of heat. If you live in a warm climate, mount the new cooler so that the radiator (oil-to-water) cooler outlet feeds into the oil-to-air unit and then returns back to the transmission. If you live in a consistently cool or cold climate, reverse this so the outgoing oil from the trans enters the oil-to-air cooler first and then feeds back into the radiator cooler. This prevents overcooling in cold weather, which is also detrimental over the long term.

In tests I found that the factory radiator oil cooler on my old Blazer could knock at least 40 degrees off trans oil temp. With a medium-sized oil-to-air cooler, another 50 degrees of capacity was added. Bear in mind, though, that an oil-to-air cooler's efficiency is relative to ambient air temp and airflow. It is more efficient on cooler days and with more airflow.

Traction-Aiding Differentials. The most logical first step here is a rear limited-slip or locker. A "loose" limited-slip or an on-demand locker meets the demands of day-to-day driving. A limited-slip with really smooth characteristics on the street, however, would be easily overcome in rough terrain. In mild terrain, especially where traction is relatively even for both tires (i.e., no lifted tires, radical side-to-side weight transfer, or one tire on solid ground and the other in goo), a limited-slip would be an acceptable

FRONT AXLE WEAK LINKS:
Up front, the axle universal joints and sometimes the locking hubs are weak points on solid-axle rigs. For IFS-equipped vehicles, the CV joints may be the first item to go. Other weak links would include the CAD axle disconnect devices on both solid and IFS front axles, not so much from breakage as from engagement problems.

choice. Brake pedal modulation to encourage lockup would be a useful technique in this case. Also, a set of wider, stickier tires would be an asset, holding off tire slip as long as possible.

There is an option that fits below the on-demand locker in terms of cost and complexity but with better performance than a limited-slip. Eaton-Detroit Locker's nearly seamless gear-type Truetrac limited-slip is a viable option. Because it doesn't use clutches, it doesn't have to "break away" in a turn and is therefore better on slippery roads.

Not much can beat an on-demand (manually activated, driver-controlled) locker when it comes to a combination of street and trail performance. They are totally transparent on the street but give you a 100 percent lockup when you need it on the trail. This locker would be the more expensive option, and its complexity leaves it a bit more vulnerable to glitches, but its idealized abilities are attractive. By installing an ARB Air Locker, which uses a small electric air compressor, your tire airing-up needs might be addressed as well. Electric lockers like the Eaton E-Locker or the Auburn ECTED offer simplified, one-wire installation. The Auburn unit has a built-in, mild limited-slip capability when the unit is unlocked.

If cost is the bottom line for you, there are a number of relatively inexpensive options, such as PowerTrax's line of Lock-Right Lockers, the Eaton-Detroit Locker E-Z Locker, and the Aussie Locker. It all comes down to your wallet and your willingness to live with cranky manners.

CUSTOM ARMOR:
If there's no protective armor on the market to fit your rig, you can either "take yer chances" or find a shop that can fabricate something for you.

The fuel tank is a vulnerable spot that either isn't protected on OE rigs or is protected by just a thin piece of sheet metal. It doesn't help when it's hung way out the back. All Custom Fabrications built this major fuel tank guard that encloses the tank completely.

The rocker panels are one of the universal areas of vulnerability that should be addressed by anyone traveling where rocks can bite. The "rock sliders" on this Cherokee have prevented major damage in this case.

Every vehicle with an open top and older hardtop rigs built before roofs were reinforced (mid-1980s) should consider a roll bar or a cage. This TJ came equipped from the factory with a bar behind the seats. This kit from Rock Hard 4×4, available from Quadratec, augments the factory setup by adding protection up front and reinforcing the structure with braces. The beauty of this kit is that it all bolts together. Obviously, the application lists will dictate whether your particular rig can benefit from this type of system or not.

Axle Upgrades. The main weak points for many axles are the axle shafts and the differential parts (carrier, side gears, spider gears). This applies front or rear, but since the rear is the most heavily loaded of the two, a weak axle shaft will be at great stress in the rear.

In the case of vacuum-actuated CAD (Center Axle Disconnect) devices (many older Jeeps, GM S-10), it's mostly a case of keeping the hoses connected, leak free, and protected from damage. For the thermally or servo-motor activated units (IFS-equipped full-size GM products and others), the situation is more dire. They're unreliable, and it's very common to experience problems getting the unit to engage, or to remain engaged. Not having the front axle engaged can ruin your four-wheeling day.

The aftermarket has responded with two CAD devices. Vacuum-operated devices are available from Rancho and Warn. These are adequate, but when the vacuum bleeds off, the units will disengage. The beefiest solution is the 4×4 Posi-Lok. This is a cable-operated mechanical device that is fully-by-God-locked, and stays that way, when the driver actuates the control. These units are available for both the S-series rigs and the big trucks.

AFTERMARKET FUEL INJECTION: Bolt-on injection systems are available for many engines from Holley, Edelbrock, Electromotive, Howell, and others. They're the ultimate cure for the foibles of carburetion on the trail and usually offer a slight to moderate power increase as well. This is one engine modification I heartily recommend for all older engines used in rough terrain. They can be had in throttle-body or multi-port configurations.

For engines with distributors up front (Fords, many Chrysler V-8s, Land Rovers, and others), sprayback from the fan during water crossings can be a problem. This little cover is something I've seen on a number of Ford engines of the 1990s that I think could be adapted to many distributors. Even a simple step like this can help keep your engine running when water is splashing about.

Armor

With minimal ground clearance, some well-chosen armor is an investment in keeping your four-by looking good. What you actually need depends on the particular vehicle you drive. The most vulnerable areas typically are the rocker panels and the rear-mounted fuel tank, followed closely by the rear quarter panels, the transfer case, and the front diff housing. Remember that gnarly looking brush bars, nerf bars, and the like are popular visual enhancements but offer little real protection. They're good for one hit, and perhaps not even that. My advice is to opt for more substantial items designed as protection rather than for looks.

Engine

Unless you drive a heavy rig with a small engine, you are probably adequately powered for the trail. The engine is usually the last place to spend your four-wheeling dollars. More power is the American way, I know, but more than an adequate amount is of no real benefit on the trail in most cases. Most trail power problems are due to tall gearing anyway. There's a lot to say about engine performance, nevertheless. We'll hit some of the high spots here but leave the details to more specialized publications.

For most late-model fuel-injected engines, the first step would be a chip or a programmer. A programmer

Snorkels like this ARB unit are useful in more ways than preventing water ingestion. They deliver cool, clean air to the engine. After some tests for a story, I determined that the stock setup on a TJ like this essentially delivered warm radiator air to the engine, despite the intake duct being located to the front. Warm air lowers power output. Clean air is the other advantage. On the long, dusty, outback roads of Australia, plugged air filters are common. With a high-mounted snorkel, dust ingestion is reduced. Whether you like the looks or not is up to you. *Courtesy ARB*

is usually the better choice because it can give you a better performance bump than just about any other bolt-on item, plus they often allow you to change input parameters like tire size and gear ratio. Most also have diagnostic capabilities and will read and erase EFI trouble codes. Some are quite sophisticated, offering the ability to monitor fuel economy and check 0–60 and performance times.

Next up would be a performance exhaust. That can start with a replacement muffler. Replacing the OE muffler with a performance unit will often unleash about 60 percent of what a full cat-back system will, for one-third the cost. A cat-back system usually includes new, larger pipes. Bigger is not always better. Larger pipes tend to move the torque band of the engine into the higher rpm, while most of us want a boost in the middle-rpm range. Fortunately, most of the established exhaust suppliers know this, and the pipe choices are modest. In general, a pipe that's one quarter of an inch larger than stock offers a significant overall flow increase without any perceptible cost to low- and middle-rpm torque. Mandrel-bent pipes of any size offer significant flow increases over a standard crimp bend (often used by the OE and in muffler shops) because the inside diameter is not reduced at the bend. Tests show about a 30 percent reduction in backpressure from mandrel-bent versus crimped pipes with equal diameters.

Cold air intakes are all the rage, but they may not offer much to the average 'wheeler. Turbo diesels gain the most, especially those with modifications. Most factory systems duct in cooler air anyway, so the difference becomes airflow. Most intake systems flow enough for a stockish engine and normal rpm levels. If you see 5,000-plus rpm a lot, a high-flow intake system may be necessary. Airflow needs increase with other mods, even in the lower rpm.

If your trip will take you to an elevation above 3,500 feet for any length of time, I would recommend that you adjust the ignition timing for that altitude. To keep the engine running at some semblance of normal power at higher altitudes, the timing should usually be advanced 1 or 2 degrees for every 2,500 feet over 2,500 feet of elevation. The exact specs vary according to the manufacturer. It's important to reset the timing immediately after returning to sea level to avoid detonation (a. k. a. "pinging"). This is a moot point for the latest rigs without a distributor. They either largely adjust themselves or must be recalibrated for altitude electronically at the dealership with computerized equipment. In any case, these newer engines seem to self-compensate for altitude more accurately than any in the past.

Carbureted engines are most in need of tuning for the trail. Angles of any significance and severe motion are the bane of carburetors. Because they have an internal float bowl, the fuel within that bowl is subject to sloshing, resulting in fuel starvation or flooding that can make the engine die, sputter, or belch black smoke. Some carburetors are resistant to these problems, and some balk at the slightest climb, sidehill, or descent.

There are cures for these problems in some cases, but many times you must simply endure, or swap to an aftermarket fuel-injection system. These are usually bolt-on throttle-body injection systems that replace the carburetor with a throttle-body device that holds two or four injectors. There is also a smaller selection of bolt-on multiport injection systems. In many cases they are emissions legal.

Engine Waterproofing. "Waterproofing" is really a misnomer. About the best you can do is make your engine water-resistant. The overall goal is to make the engine safe from a moderate amount of splash. After that, coordinate any changes with a look at other vehicle systems so that everything is safe to one level of immersion.

The information that follows is by necessity somewhat vague. Because there are many different models and thousands of equipment variations, I can only offer general tips. I may not hit some of the more oddball situations at all. It falls upon you to capture the gist of the idea and translate it to your own rig.

Step one in the engine compartment is to address the air intake. Many newer rigs have the air intake ducted to the front, usually to one side of the radiator. In some cases this is in quite a low position. This is ideal for going down the road but detrimental if you go diving. With some rigs, you can temporarily disconnect this duct and direct it to another location for the duration of the crossing. Definitely direct it away from the fan. The ultimate cure may be a snorkel kit, but only a few applications are covered, most of them by ARB.

ENGINE WATERPROOFING:
Any place you see oil coming out, water can get in, so fix leaky seals and gaskets.

The next place to look is the ignition wires. Are they in good condition and do the boots at both the distributor and the spark plugs fit tightly? If additional sealing is needed, use only self-vulcanizing tape, such as the Pro Tape available from Accel. RTV silicone is not useful because it does not seal to the boots or cap. The distributor cap can be sealed to the distributor with RTV. The RTV will stick to the distributor body to form a sort of gasket. Some 'wheelers have found large O-rings that work, and, in fact, some caps and distributors have O-rings from the factory. Many distributors have small vent holes at the bottom, and most people advocate covering that hole. The distributor doesn't usually need venting to atmosphere. Electronic ignition control modules are usually sealed, but the connections can be affected, so some protection from splash might be in order, and the internal connection can be coated with dielectric silicone grease.

Most newer engines are completely sealed, but older engines can have filler caps, vent tubes, or dipstick tubes that may allow water to pass. Ancillary items should get a look, such as power steering pump cap vents, vents on brake boosters, EFI MAP sensors, vapor canister vents, and so on. Most of these are already splash resistant, though if any item is mounted particularly low, a vent extension might be in order.

Overkill? Maybe not. Certainly Anthony Hilbers, owner of this 1994 Jeep Grand Cherokee, doesn't think so. All of the unibody SUVs are susceptible to damage and tweaking from high-adrenaline four-wheeling. If damaged in a rollover, they are usually write-offs. The twisting forces and jolts, plus the forces of low gearing and big tires acting on chassis suspension mounts, all tend to tweak the basic structure. This exo-cage both protects the body from damage and beefs up the overall structure. This one is all custom-built, but there have been kits available for other rigs at various times.

CHAPTER 7
Advanced Skills and Buildups: Grizzled Gear Grinders

Extreme 'wheeling often involves steep angles and lifted tires. Sometimes, it all happens at the same time. One of the first skills is learning to be comfortable and calm in any position. Except upside down, of course!

Advanced four-wheeling is nothing more than an extension of the basics applied in more adrenaline-charged environments. For that reason, there's less to talk about and more to look at. The majority of the advanced techniques will be presented in photographic form.

Advanced terrain needs a vehicle up to the task: a built-up vehicle is absolutely necessary in the majority of cases. It's difficult to keep a stock or near-stock rig in one piece in the toughest environments, let alone get it through. It still comes down to traction and clearance, but getting more of those two elements requires more compromises and a greater level of commitment.

The Risk Factor

At the higher levels of four-wheeling, the vehicle damage risk factors are greatly increased. That includes mechanical problems and damage. The potential for injury is also higher in some cases, but because advanced machines have better safety systems, that potential is kept relatively low. The worst consequences of even the most difficult 'wheeling is often no more than a rollover. Adequate protection in the form of a roll cage and a safety harness usually results in nothing more than a good war story and shelling out some cash for repairs.

There are extreme risk-takers in our group—those high-flying four-wheelers who like to perform sidehill maneuvers at the edge of a 300-foot precipice. Some of this is done by highly skilled drivers in well-equipped rigs and sometimes by people with more raw courage than smarts. Obviously these folks are at much greater risk, regardless of how well-built their roll cage may be. This is where free will comes in. If you are willing to face those risks for braggin' rights, so be it.

The Advanced Driver

If the basic skills are the same, what puts the advanced driver ahead of the beginning or intermediate one? It's simply a matter of degree. With practice comes skill and eventually mastery. Four-wheeling is akin to mathematics. Basic addition and trigonometry are both mathematics but at vastly different levels of difficulty. Without having basic addition down pat, you can't learn the more advanced stuff.

Advanced driving is as much about outlook as anything—the ability to "see" the obstacle and the ways over it. It's an instinctive knowledge of the vehicle and its capabilities that comes from experience. I'm not sure it's possible to teach this in a book. That's why this chapter includes many photos with captions that

More extreme terrain results in more chances for this. Truth be told, these incidents are uncommon and don't often result in human injuries worse than hurt pride. Still, one of the reasons most hard-core rigs are Spartan in style is so that they are easily repairable. This Jeep was righted and driven the rest of the way. The sheet metal was repaired, probably with used bolt-on parts, and the rig is probably still four-wheeling somewhere. If this were a newer SUV, it would probably have been totaled. That's assuming you had coverage. Insurance may not cover you in a situation like this. Check your policy.

explain the situation and the solution. When it comes down to the nitty-gritty, it's confidence and practice that count. The learning will never stop until that day when you hang up your 'wheeling spurs for good.

The Advanced Machine

The advanced 4×4 is to the OE rig what the Six-Million-Dollar Man is to OE human . . . "better, stronger, faster," yada, yada! How a machine is built is somewhat variable according to the intended terrain. Most advanced rigs are built with all the basic performance enhancements and are designed to be useful in all types of terrain. There is also specialized equipment for specific terrain, such as a rockcrawler or a mud bogger. Either of these machines might be useful outside of its own element but perhaps less effective.

Side angles are one of the least comfortable positions that you can encounter. This driver seems supremely comfortable, with the flat ground below apparently disdained for the more tippy situation above.

The harsh environments are much harder on equipment. Prepare for more damage and breakage, but don't give in to the defeatist "ain't had fun unless sumthin' broke" philosophy. This is spoken by people unwilling or unable to improve their skills or equipment. Give up every dent or broken part like it was your last dollar. Be willing to analyze every broken part and take steps to correct the situation. Was it pilot error or does something mechanical need improvement?

It often comes down to money. Are you driving in terrain beyond your budget? If you can't afford the buildup beforehand, it stands to reason that you won't be able to afford the repairs afterward on a rig that's not prepared. There are two cures to this dilemma. Add more money for the buildup items or ratchet back your four-wheeling a few notches to limit breakage.

An advanced machine doesn't have to be a trailer queen. You can build in a lot of capability and retain a safe amount of street prowess (with a sane driver, at least). If you drive to and from the trail, however, you may be frustrated by breakage or damage that strands you in a town waiting for parts, or having to rent a truck and trailer to haul the carcass home. An advanced machine driving to and from the trail needs to be better built, better driven, and better prepared

Never get comfortable here! Extreme rigs get into extreme pickles. This rig and driver are well equipped for calamities like this and were on their way in a few minutes with nothing worse than a bit of scraped roll bar paint.

than one that only has to make it back to a trailer at the trailhead.

The advanced machine is usually an adaptation of one of a few commonly available rigs. It comes down to available buildup goodies and the general suitability of the platform. Sometimes the fickle nature of popularity comes into it as well. With unlimited funds and lots of time and skill, you can build a trail monster out of almost anything.

Sometimes obstacles are combined with tight clearance. Wooded areas in some states combine steep climbs and big trees. The key is to have a pretty good idea of what's going to happen. This climb tended to suck rigs toward the tree when the tires spun, so a light throttle was essential. Coming down steep wooded trails can be the yeehaw ride of your life, especially if the ground is slippery.

This is almost as steep as it looks. Drivers of very short rigs like this CJ-3B need to make sure that they won't nose over on the way down. The key here is to keep finely attuned and avoid any sudden brake application that would surely flip you "arse over tip," as the Brits would say. If the rear end does come up, a quick blip of the throttle will keep your wheels down. One other cure is to have a strap attached to another rig so it can lower you down.

Tight quarters and steep angles. This full-sized Bronco is only inches away from some custom bodywork. The key here is to plan the maneuvers and avoid slipping the tires. As soon as traction is lost, this rig's headed for the rock. Also, too much right rudder will run his tail into the big rock.

The only way to cross this famous Moab, Utah, crack without major tail dragging is to enter it diagonally and drop one wheel at a time. It's tough to do without a locker because many rigs pull a wheel or two, and the ones that don't can unload the low wheel enough to put that axle out of action. Even with a diagonal approach, rigs without really big tires and/or lots of rear overhang will scrape tail, if not hang up.

The drive out may be different than the drive in. A heavy rainstorm created a flash flood situation in an area that had been dry a few hours before. In some parts of the country, flash floods are a serious worry and can go from a trickle to a torrent in a matter of minutes. Fortunately this one didn't get much bigger, and everyone made it out OK.

Driving across deep snow requires the utmost care. This snow was several feet deep, and although the Range Rover was aired down for flotation, it broke through the crust in a spot where recovery was difficult. This vehicle was part of the 1994 Mount Washington expedition, where several vehicles from Rovers North were the first wheeled vehicles to reach the top of Mount Washington, New Hampshire, in winter. The entire trip was a balancing act atop snow as deep as 6 feet.

Tires. Most of what you need to know about tires was in Chapter 6. There are only some conceptual things to add here. "Big" is the key word. Tall for clearance, wide for traction. You'll do what it takes to put on the maximum practical amount of rubber, and that usually requires major upgrades in the drivetrain as well. The practicality aspect comes into play with drivability and a safe amount of lift to fit the tires. Short-wheelbase rigs require special care. Look at the nearby chart that lists approximate drivetrain/tire diameter relationships.

TIRES:
The tires are your main connection to *terra firma*, and that connection is the key to getting though any sort of advanced terrain.

Breaking trail in deep virgin snow is one of the most fun parts of winter 'wheeling. It's also tough on vehicles. Rotate the lead rigs so all can share the work and the fun. This Samurai poses on a fine winter morning in Utah's La Sal Mountains.

As Gordon Lightfoot sang, "When you're caught by the gale and you're full under sail, beware of the dangers below." Getting caught in a snowstorm on off-camber slickrock became a slippery experience one year at the Easter Jeep Safari. Some slipping and sliding earned more than a few excited comments. For some it came at a tricky moment. The big question here was to stop or to go ahead. With a better section ahead and more snow coming, it was thought best to continue before things got worse.

Drivetrain. A trail machine needs low gearing to compensate for the bigger tires and to improve performance. The combination of lots of torque multiplication and big, sticky tires will put major stress on drivetrain parts. Lockers are also a part of the game, and one axle shaft may have to handle *all* the torque when weight transfer and lifted tires leave you with essentially one tire to push your rig up and over. You need enough beef in all components to handle these stresses.

The torque multiplication goes downhill toward the axles. If the tires slip before some drivetrain part breaks, you're safe. If not, well, there you are with some shiny scrap metal. People who 'wheel a lot in rocks will need the strongest drivetrain because there lies the best traction combined with the steepest climbs and the most weight transfer.

The transmission's job is comparatively easy. All you have to be sure of is that its torque capacity matches engine output. Depending on the gearing in the

It's a wheelbase kinda thing! Experience, sticky tires, lockers, momentum, and wheelbase enabled this full-size Jimmy to walk to the top of Moab's notorious Pritchett Canyon's Rockpile in one shot. If you look closely, you can see the left front tire has bounded up a small ledge. This driver committed to a line and hit it, not backing off until the truck was at the top. The speed was not more than a fast walking pace and the engine barely above an idle.

tranny, the transfer case will probably also have an easy time, though if a splitter is used between the trans and T-case, the input torque can get high. Changes in the internal gearing of a transfer case can result in transfer case output shaft or drive chain failures due to torque multiplication. The load on the driveshaft and driveshaft universals is also increased by lower trans or transfer case gearing. The input load on the differential also increases in this case. In diffs that have weak pinion shafts, increased torque multiplication can result in a greater likelihood of pinion shaft breakage. For example, going from a 1.96:1 low-range ratio to a 4:1 ratio more than doubles the torque through the driveshafts and into the diff.

From the pinion, torque goes to the ring gear and is multiplied by the ring-and-pinion ratio. This multiplied torque will find its way through the carrier and differential, whether it's open or locked, and into the axle shafts. The strength of the side gear and spiders (or lockers or limited-slip) then comes into play. Even the carrier that holds all these pieces can be broken or distorted by too much torque. The differential housing

This 38.5×14.50-15 Super Swamper is a lot of tire for a CJ-7. Though this owner tried to keep the center of gravity low by minimizing lift and maximizing fender trimming, this is a relatively tippy Jeep. He did gain lots of clearance, however. In the terrain where this Jeep is used, mainly Arkansas and Oklahoma, these tires make sense.

Here's an argument for beadlocks on the trail. An aired-down tire is more likely to pop off the rim at low pressures, so in hard-core situations, a beadlock-type rim would have prevented this mess.

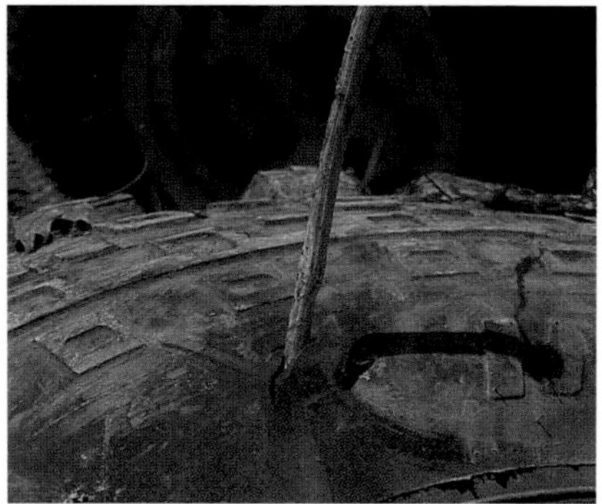

Another downside to airing down in a big way is the ease with which the sidewalls are damaged. There are times when the risk must be taken, but judge how much to air down by the terrain. An easier trip needs only a little airing down. Remember, you can always air down more later if you need it.

Siping is a trick that offers improved traction on rocks, as well as on the street in slippery conditions. Some tire shops can sipe your mud tires, but you will find the tire warranty voided if you do so. Some tires will "chunk," i.e., throw off small bits of tread around the new sipes. Siping is generally a good thing for the trail if done by a person who knows what he's doing, but it's not a universal benefit. Some tires gain more than others, and some tires actually go backward. Experiment at your own risk.

itself is also subject to distortion from torque. Finally, the torque goes through the axle shafts and to the wheels and tires to the ground. These shafts are the final link in the mechanical chain and take the most abuse.

Your task is to determine just how much beef you need the whole way down from the engine and choose components that are strong enough for the job. I'll show you how further on, though it's a somewhat inexact science. It will give you an idea, and based on the information available in the sidebars, you can see if your current or proposed setup is close to being up to the task.

Transfer Case Beefing/Improvements. Older OE transfer cases are cast iron and, overall, are much stronger

Continued on psge 158

No matter how big your tire—these are 38s—you will reach a rock you cannot "bump." This happens when the level of the top of the ledge is significantly higher than the level of the hub. If there were a bit of a slope, maybe the tire could bump up onto this obstacle. As it is, this appears to be a gigantic wheel block. With an aired-down tire, good traction at the rear, and a locked front axle, this situation can still be overcome. The rear needs to push enough to stick the front tire to that near-vertical wall so it can pull itself up. Obviously, the first requirement is sufficient approach-angle clearance.

BEADLOCKS:
Beadlocked rims are getting better and better, but they are still best left to trailered machines. If you have beadlocks on a daily driver, regular inspection is something you ignore at your peril. Hutchinson and Staun (both are in the source guide) offered the most daily-driver-friendly options as this book was written.

TRANSFER CASES:
Chains usually last longer on part-time transfer cases because the chain doesn't come into play until the vehicle is shifted into four-wheel drive. The chain is operational all the time in full-time cases.

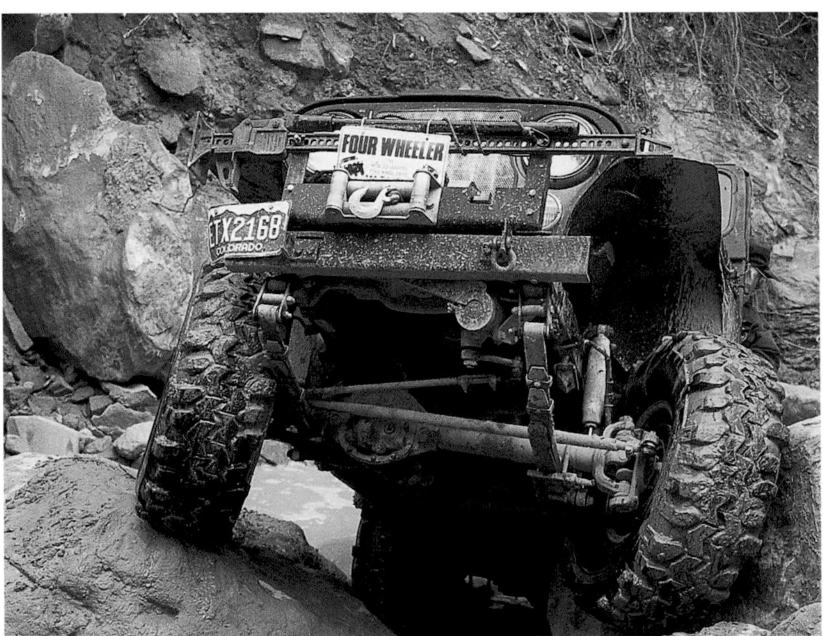

Wedgie! This driver is using the sidewall of his left front tire to help pull him up and over these boulders. He couldn't quite get the tires up the far side of the boulder on the right. His rear tire has just contacted the boulder and will walk him up and around. There was a bit of contact with the body sill, but it was armored with some plate. Serious rockcrawlers often think beyond the conventional approach. Taken slowly on smooth surfaces, sidewalls are fair to use.

There's nothing quite like a steep rock ledge with scree at the top and bottom. There isn't enough traction for a slow approach or to push the front up with the rear tires; once the front is up, the scree makes front traction almost nil. You can see the trenches dug by spinning tires of previous rigs. Momentum, but a light throttle, was what got this Jeeper up.

STEPPING OFF

Stepping off a high, steep ledge needs careful execution if your rig doesn't have major clearance.

Ease one tire down using the brakes and the traction from the three other tires. Manual-trans rigs will be in gear with the clutch in unless they have *really* deep gearing.

One down, three to go.

Two down, but see the pile of loose rocks ahead that may diminish braking capacity.

Three down, but some holes ahead. A rig with less articulation and less articulation balance would have been very tippy at this point.

Ease that tail down as slowly as you can, even if you have armor in back, as this Toyota does.

MAXIMUM RECOMMENDED TIRE SIZES FOR VARIOUS AXLES*

*For highway and moderate off-pavement use, with stock engine. Equipment in good condition is presumed. If you don't see it here, it's probably not a popular unit. This was compiled via conversations with assorted industry experts, not from scientific study, so use as a general guideline only.

Axle	Maximum tire size
AM General	
AMC-20 IS	38 inches
Chrysler Corporate	
AMC-20 (older Jeep), rear (stock two-piece axle/one-piece axle)	32/35 inches
7.9 IFS front	32 inches
8.0 IFS front	33 inches
8.25 rear, 27-spline	31 inches
8.25 rear, 28-spline	33 inches
8.75 rear	35 inches
9.25 rear	35 inches
Dana	
Dana 23 rear	31 inches
Dana 25 front	31 inches
Dana 27 rear	31 inches
Dana 28 IFS	31 inches
Dana 30 IFS	31 inches
Dana 30 front, low pinion	31 inches
Dana 30, front high pinion, small U-joint	31 inches
Dana 30 front, high pinion, big U-joint	35 inches
Dana 30 rear	31 inches
Dana 35 IFS	33 inches
Dana 35 rear	31 inches
Dana 44 IFS	35 inches
Dana 44 front, small U-joint	31 inches
Dana 44 front, big U-joint	35 inches
Dana 44 rear (tapered-axle 19-0spline/ flanged 30-spline)	31/35 inches
Dana 50 IFS	37 inches
Dana 50 front	37 inches
Dana 60 front	38 inches
Dana 60 rear, semi-float, 30-spline	35 inches
Dana 60 rear, full-float, 30-spline	36 inches
Dana 60 rear, semi-float, 35-spline	38 inches
Dana 60 rear, full-float, 35-spline	38 inches
Dana 70 front	38 inches
Dana 70 rear	44 inches
Dana 80 rear	44 inches+
Dana/Eaton S-110	44 inches+
Ford Corporate	
7.5-inch rear, 28-spline	33 inches
9-inch, 28-spline	33 inches
9-inch, 31-spline	35 inches
8.8-inch, 28-spline	33 inches
8.8-inch, 35-spline	35 inches
9.75-inch, 34-spline	37 inches
10.25-inch, semi-float	40 inches
10.25-inch, full-float	40 inches
10.50-inch, full-float	44 inches+
General Motors/AAM Corporate	
7.25-inch IFS	30 inches
8.25-inch IFS	33 inches
8.5-inch (10-bolt) front	35 inches
9.25-inch IFS	37 inches
7.5-inch rear	31 inches
7.63-inch rear	33 inches
8.0-inch rear	33 inches
8.5-inch (10-bolt) rear, 28-spline	33 inches
8.6-inch (10-bolt) rear, 30-spline	35 inches
8.875-inch (12-bolt) rear	35 inches
9.5-inch (metric 14-bolt) rear, semi-float	37 inches
9.5-inch AAM front	37 inches
10.50-inch (14-bolt) rear, full-float	44 inches
11.50-inch rear, full-float	44 inches
Isuzu	
8-inch rear, 17-spline (early Trooper)	31 inches
8-inch rear, 26-spline (late Trooper, Amigo)	33 inches
Land Rover Corporate	
8.5-inch, 10-spline, front or rear	31 inches
8.5-inch, 24-spline, front or rear	33 inches
9.25-inch, 24-spline (Salisbury)	33 inches
Mitsubishi	
Front IFS	30 inches
Rear (small ring gear)	31 inches
Rear (large ring gear)	33 inches
Nissan	
Front IFS (early)	30 inches
Front IFS (late)	31 inches
Rear, 27-spline	31 inches
Rear, 31-spline	33 inches
Suzuki	
6.9-inch front and rear (Samurai)	32 inches
Toyota	
7.5-inch IFS	31 inches
8-inch, front or rear	33 inches
8.25-inch rear	35 inches
9.5-inch rear (FJ-40, 30-spline)	35 inches
9.5-inch front (FJ-40, 30-spline)	33 inches

DOUBLE LEDGE

Though the tires look big on this Samurai, they're only 31×10.50s. The tall ledge is a bit high for tires this short, so this enterprising driver takes the oblique approach. One front tire at a time goes up the ledge. The Suzuki was in constant movement throughout this sequence.

With both the front tires up, the driver maintains the diagonal approach with his right rear, but notice that he has turned right a little. When the left rear hits the ledge and gets a good bite from momentum, he will goose the throttle a bit to hop up.

He's up and still moving. Note the deformed front tire on the second ledge. That's the momentum of the first hop pressing the aired-down tire (about 4 psi) against the rock. In that instant, the front axle will have a really good bite of traction. The 79-inch-wheelbase Samurai is short enough to fit on the first ledge.

Still moving at a steady pace. The front tires are up the second ledge, and the driver is watching the ledge. When his tire hits, he will goose the throttle yet again.

And he's up! This shot captures the moment the tires climb the ledge. This entire operation was done without slipping a tire and without slowing down. The Samurai was locked at both ends, fitted with low gears (about 120:1 crawl ratio) and a wide tire footprint, considering vehicle weight (well under 2,500 pounds). Bear in mind that this obstacle, nicknamed the Double Whammy, is notorious for defeating short-wheelbase vehicles.

On the left is a NV-231 transfer case with a slip-yoke-type rear output. On the right is a similar NP-241 transfer case with a short-tailshaft conversion. The conversion knocks quite a bit of length off the transfer case (variable according to the kit) so that longer driveshafts can be accommodated and driveshaft angles reduced with lifts. These conversions are available from several manufacturers for a small number of transfer cases built by New Process (NP), which later became New Venture (NV).

Continued from psge 153

than the later aluminum units but at twice the weight. The transition from iron to aluminum also marked the transition from gear- to chain-drive. Gear-drive, cast-iron T-cases are stronger overall, but aluminum T-cases have closed the strength gap, so don't automatically dismiss them. All the current transfer cases are aluminum, with the last all-iron units phased out in the 1980s.

Picking lines through a sea of boulders the size of medium dogs is a tricky situation. This is why this book has harped about big tires and clearance. Without clearance, it's a bash-fest. The key is to go from one boulder to the next and to put all four tires on lines that will keep the underside away from all the boulders. It's almost inevitable that a few boulders will have to be moved or repositioned. This would also be a good place for a spotter.

Gear-drive cases tend to be noisier than chain-drives but have a longer life. A set of T-case gears will usually outlast the truck, but a hard-worked chain-drive unit may need a chain replacement at 80,000 miles. Chain-drive units use planetary gear sets instead of standard gears, and because the dynamics of gear ratios can be built more compactly, it's easier to get lower ratios. While it's unusual to find a gear-drive transfer case with a ratio much under 2.0:1, chain-drive T-cases can be found at 2.61 or lower. With improved gear-cutting machinery, extra-low gear sets are now available for some of the older gear-drive units, specifically in the popular Jeep Dana 18, 20, and 300 line, as well as the ever-popular New Process 205.

TRANSFER CASES:
The aftermarket offers conversions for various transfer cases from 3.0:1 to a bit lower than 4:1. They are available for the popular units, such as the Dana 18, 20, and 300; the NP-205 gear drive T-cases; and certain New Process chain-drive units (NP-231, 241, etc.).

Talk about emptying the pool! This lifted Ranger driver is in a hurry and is making a bow wave the captain of the U.S.S. *Missouri* would be proud to see. The water is close to 3 feet deep, but tall tires and a lift keep the vitals out of the water. Note how the front and rear tires are pushing the water in two separate waves. You wouldn't be this aggressive with a stock vehicle.

This is a textbook water crossing. Doors-off water-wheeling can result in a bath, especially if you are in a hurry. An open rig like this Jeep TJ will fill quickly, but it will drain just as fast. Water may take quite a while to cover the floor of a closed rig with tight doors, and you might get across before a significant amount comes inside. This iron-laden water in the Iron Range OHV Park, near Gilbert, Minnesota, would stain any carpet.

Water, mud, and adverse camber all at once. Driving out of here would depend on tires and lockers. The lower tires are doing all the work. The upper tires are unloaded and not adding much to traction. The only thing to try here would be to back up and try to get the far tires on or against the bank for extra traction and maybe a little more level position. In the end, that winch ended up being the savior here.

CHOP SUEY MUD AND NO TURNING BACK

A steep drop into a bottomless pit of slime. The ramp will provide some free momentum, but it prevents backing out. Plus, the momentum isn't useful here because this is Chop Suey Mud, with sticks and old corduroy in it.

Splat! Here's the other problem. The steep entry noses the Pinzgauer deeply into the mud, creating a massive amount of drag.

The fully locked Pinzie does a bulldozer routine and manages to claw its way level.

With all four tires churning the mud into a chocolate milkshake, the Austrian-built rig claws along inch by inch. This is where the relative lack of power was a detriment. If the little four-banger had had a little more oomph, it could have gotten the tires spinning to sling off the cloying mud and let the tires bite. At 10,000 feet of elevation, that just wasn't possible. This driver did everything right, but he still had to take a strap to get all the way out.

In some cases, you can parts swap within certain families of transfer cases to produce a stronger unit—going to a wider "C" (Chevrolet type) chain in an NP-231J (Jeep) transfer case, for example, or swapping the early 10-spline NP-205 front output shaft with a later 30-spline piece. The New Process, later to become New Venture, transfer cases offer the most potential for parts swapping. Very little swapping is possible with the array of gear-drive T-cases out there, with the NP-205 having the most options because of its long production life.

In most cases, people who need a serious increase in strength make a swap—usually from one type of OE unit to another. Among trucks, for example, swapping out the chain-drive New Process or Borg Warner units for the beefy NP-205 cast-iron gear-drive is common. This older gear-type unit, available for older GM, Ford, and Dodge trucks, is remarkably strong, though with a marginal factory low range of just under 2:1. Among Jeepers, the Dana 300 cast-iron unit is a popular swap. For the ultimate beef in combination with a deep low range, the Advance Adapters Atlas transfer case is a popular, though expensive, option. Adapters are made for many popular trans/transfer case swaps, either from Advance Adapters or others.

Some strength improvements can come from modifications done for other reasons. Later short-wheelbase rigs (Jeep YJs and TJs) are prone to rear driveshaft angle problems when lifted. This problem is alleviated by a short tailshaft conversion, which reduces the length of the T-case by replacing the slip yoke output with a flanged output and allows for a longer driveshaft at a less steep angle. In some of the kits, that conversion comes with a much stronger rear output shaft.

Transfer case gearing changes are a useful way to get deep gearing for the trail and reasonable gearing for the street. Some people also use extra-low transfer case gears to give themselves extremely low gearing. Among factory T-cases for commonly seen light-duty rigs, the lowest I know of is the older gear-drive Land Rover LT-230, which is at 3.3:1. Most others in the "low" category are at around 2.7:1. JB Conversions, Tera Manufacturing, and others make 4:1 low-range conversion that fits many of the late-model New Process/New Venture chain-drive transfer cases. Though the primary market is for Jeeps, there are applications that fit some midsize and full-size rigs as well. Calmini offers deep transfer case gears for Suzuki and Nissan.

Splitters fit between the transmission and transfer case. This is Off-Road Design's (ORD) first-generation Doubler as installed in the author's rig. Up front is a GM 700R4 with the two-speed range box right behind. This cast-iron unit has a 2:1 reduction. Behind that mounts the legendary NP-205 transfer case. The NP-205 is one of the few transfer cases strong enough to handle the input of 2:1 reduction with a lot of torque to boot. The Doubler setup offers the standard 1:1 of high range, 2:1 low range, or a 4:1 low-low range. In addition the 2:1 reduction of the range box can be used in two-wheel drive. The Doubler is one of the heavy hitters in the splitter crowd, both in terms of its torque capacity and physical weight. In many years of production, ORD has managed to reduce the length of the Doubler considerably, as well as improving many internal conversion parts.

Versatility and beef! The Advance Adapters Atlas transfer case is the answer to the extra strength needed for hard-core four-wheeling. It comes as a two-speed or, as shown, a four-speed. The two are largely the same, but the four-speed unit has a planetary gear splitter with a 2.72:1 low gear attached on the input side. You have the choice of gearing in the Atlas itself of 2:1 or 3.8:1 (the two-speed has more choices). You do the math to get the potential ratios. The Atlas T-case is strong enough to take the extra torque input. The nice thing is that, aside from the ratio choice, you can also order what you want in terms of driveshaft yokes. The Atlas is pretty universal and found on everything from Jeeps to full-size trucks. The unit is very short as well, which makes it suitable for SWB rigs.

The Klune-V splitter is available with either a 2.72 or 4.0:1 low ratio. Those numbers would be multiplied by the transfer case gearing. A device like this would allow you to run highway-friendly gears but be able to drop into very low ratios for the trail. The caveat to this, or any other splitter, is the torque multiplication that feeds downstream from the splitter. An upgrade like this should come with an evaluation of the capacities of the downstream items, including the transfer case, driveshafts, and U-joints and axles. *Courtesy High Impact Gear*

Splitters and Underdrives. These are two names for the same type of device. In essence, they give you an additional gearing step-down, much like the transfer case. They are inserted between the transmission and the transfer case. There are some underdrives that bolt on behind the T-case, but obviously they are applicable only to towing and two-wheel drive. The Marlin Krawler was the first of these, with Toyota applications (still in business with good Toyota coverage). Then

SPLITTERS AND UNDERDRIVES: The splitter bridges the gearing gap between the mudrunner and the rockcrawler. On the downside, a splitter adds drivetrain length, weight, and complexity.

came the Off-Road Design Doubler and the Klune-V, all still available. There are others, and some have come and gone.

The Marlin Krawler and Doubler use gear-driven range boxes, while the Klune-V uses a planetary gear set. All add considerably to the drivetrain length, so a shorter rear driveshaft and a longer front driveshaft are necessary. This may restrict the applications to those above a certain wheelbase length. Recent Klune-V applications are short enough for Jeeps as short as Wranglers, but not CJ-5s, however.

Splitters have some advantages over the super-low-range transfer case conversions, namely gearing flexibility. They retain the original gearing for mild situations, but you can go lower when, or if, you need to. In some cases, the extralow T-cases are too low for the situation and you have no middle ground between that extralow gear and 1:1 high range.

Solid Front Axles. Solid front axles are inherently weaker than the rear for a couple of reasons. First, unless the unit has a reverse-cut (or high-pinion) ring gear, the front ring gear is driving on the reverse side of the teeth. This weakens it by as much as 30 percent. A reverse-cut ring gear in front is effectively as strong as one in the rear, though if a reverse cut is used in the rear, it becomes weaker by the same 30 percent.

The other weak link is the axle U-joint. These are the major weakness of most front axles. They are often weaker than the axle shafts and will break before anything else but the hub. Axle U-joints are generally what limit tire size. It boils down to this: the small Spicer 260–sized U-joints (older Dana 44 and recent Dana 30 axles) are conservatively limited to about a 31-inch tire; the Spicer 297 size (very late Jeep Dana 30, Dana 44 axles, and many GM corporate units) can handle a 35-inch tire; the Dana 178 (Ford Dana 50 TTB) and the Dana 332 (Dana 60 axles) can handle up to 38-inch tires. With the exception of a few late-model full-time rigs that use CV joints, and the import rigs, which either use CV joints or U-joints of unusual sizes, all solid front axles fit into these four U-joint sizes. In truth, my ratings are a bit conservative, especially

PAVEMENT ENDS

FRONT AXLES:
Another front-axle weak point is the outer axle shaft, which may actually snap before the U-joint. Some corporate axles and Dana axles have a necked-down section on the inner shaft that also reduces strength. (See "Axle Shaft Strength Chart" sidebar.)

AXLE SHAFT STRENGTH CHART

These yield torque ratings were generated via an engineering formula and should be considered approximations. They are useful to show the differences that size and material have on yield torque.

Size	Material	Yield Torque	Note
1.00-inch	1040 carbon steel	2,657.3 lbs-ft	1
1.10-inch	1040 carbon steel	3,639.8 lbs-ft	2
1.125-inch	1040 carbon steel	3,787.5 lbs-ft	3
1.16-inch	1040 carbon steel	4,160.8 lbs-ft	4
1.25-inch	1040 carbon steel	5,184.5 lbs-ft	5
1.28-inch	1040 carbon steel	5,571.4 lbs-ft	6
1.28-inch	4340 chrome-moly	9,147.4 lbs-ft	7
1.31-inch	1040 carbon steel	6,044.1 lbs-ft	8
1.31-inch	1340 manganese steel	6,473.1 lbs-ft	9
1.31-inch	4340 chrome-moly	9,923.5 lbs-ft	10
1.32-inch	1040 carbon steel	6121.6 lbs-ft	11
1.37-inch	1040 carbon steel	6,828.4 lbs-ft	12
1.37-inch	4340 chrome moly	11,211.2 lbs-ft	13
1.50-inch	1040 carbon steel	8,966.2 lbs-ft	14
1.50-inch	4340 chrome-moly	14,721.2 lbs-ft	15

Notes: **1)** Old Jeeps, Dana 23 and 41 10-spline, as well as old Land Rover Series rigs. **2)** The necked-down section on GM 28- and 30-spline front axle shafts and 30-spline Dana axles. Also a close approximation of the old Jeep Dana 25 and Dana 27. **3)** The OE stub axle of Dana 44 and GM 10-bolt front axles. **4)** Dana 30 and Dana 35 front and rear 27-spline axles used on Jeeps, Ford Rangers, and Bronco II. The 1.20-inch, 28-spline Ford 8.8 used on many small Fords is just slightly stronger. Mitsubishi trucks and SUVs are slightly stronger. **5)** Jeep AMC-20 rear (29-spline) and AMG Hummer IFS/IRS (not CVs). Newer Nissan SUVs and trucks are similar. **6)** The GM 10-bolt front or rear 28-spline axle. **7)** A 28-spline in 4340. **8)** An OE-type 30-spline axle, to include Dana 44 in many rigs, most Toyota axles, GM 10 and 12-bolt axles, and small-axle Dana 60 light-duty full floaters. **9)** A slight upgrade in material on a 30-spline axle. **10)** A 30-spline axle in 4340. **11)** The 31-spline Ford 8.8 OE axle. Old Nissan Patrol similar. **12)** An OE 33-spline axle like those used in the GM semi-float 14-bolt. **13)** A 33-spline axle in 4340. **14)** An OE 35-spline axle as found in a front or rear Dana 60 or a 30-spline, 1.5 inch, 14-bolt, full-float axle, a Ford 10.25 Sterling full-floater, or a Dana 70.**15)** As in number 14 above but in a 4340 alloy.

The axle U-joint, or CV joint, is the usual weak link on the front axle. As offered on OE rigs, the differential is always at least 50 percent stronger than the axle universals. This is a Dana 60 unit, generally acknowledged as the strongest front axle commonly available. As often as not, the big Dana 60 is swapped just to get these tough universal joints.

with Dana 60s. Some of the axles can be made to handle more tire with careful driving. The CV joints are generally weaker than standard U-joints, merely because of the pieces selected by the OE manufacturer, but they are more difficult to upgrade. In some cases the CV-type axles have standard U-joint replacements available, such as the various Birfield eliminator kits for Toyotas.

An important fact to remember about front axle U-joints is that there is a torque multiplication effect that occurs with steering angularity (see nearby sidebar). At maximum angularity, torque is multiplied at the inner axle yoke and U-joint trunnions by approximately 30 percent. If your U-joints are on the ragged edge of being strong enough, this will snap them. As you can see by the nearby chart, the effect is on a curve, so 15 degrees of angularity offers minimal multiplication.

There are a number of cures for weak front axles. The first is the obvious axle swap—e.g., a Dana 30 for a 44, or a Dana 44 or GM 10-bolt for a Dana 60. In some cases, the swap is a bolt-on; in others, specially built or narrowed assemblies must be used. This can get tricky, but there are now many alternatives that allow significant beefing-up of the factory axle.

Bearing in mind that you are mostly swapping for bigger U-joints, there are now super-strength U-joints available from CTM, Longfield, Ox, and Yukon.

This is a small sample of axles. On the bottom is a 27-spline Dana 35 unit. In the middle is a 30-spline Dana 44 C-clip-type, with C-clip. On top is a Dana 44 non-C-clip. The difference in strength between the 27- and 30-splines is approximately 30 percent.

Three wheeling! In some situations it's necessary, and this happens to be one of them. Because of the steep approach, a diagonal attack was needed. The dip just before the wall complicated the situation. If this truck wasn't locker-equipped, it would be stopped right here. The front doesn't have quite enough pull to get the rig up, and with one wheel in the air, an open diff in the rear would cancel out that axle.

FRONT-AXLE UNIVERSAL JOINT TORQUE LOADS BECAUSE OF INCREASED ANGLES

Torque at Tire	U-Joint Angle	Torque on Inner Axle Yoke/ Trunnions
2,500 lbs-ft	0 degrees	2,500 lbs-ft
	5 degrees	2,510 lbs-ft
	10 degrees	2,542 lbs-ft
	15 degrees	2,594 lbs-ft
	20 degrees	2,661 lbs-ft
	25 degrees	2,763 lbs-ft
	30 degrees	2,897 lbs-ft
	35 degrees	3,097 lbs-ft
	40 degrees	3,269 lbs-ft

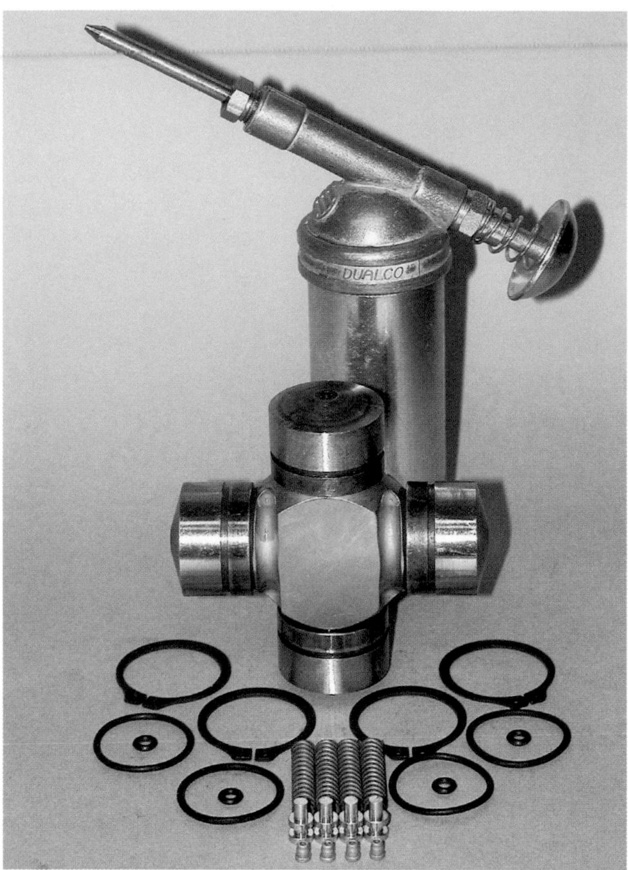

There are a number of super U-joints on the market, including this Yukon Super Joint. The common features are a stout alloy cross, usually 4340 or 300M. Some, like the Yukon, have a coating to increase wear resistance. The other common feature is that the needle bearings are eliminated. This allows the trunnions to be made larger and stronger. The caps then become bushings, and they are also made of a special alloy.

AVERAGE FRONT-AXLE UNIVERSAL JOINT ULTIMATE STRENGTH

Based on destructive testing of a small sampling of universal joints from various manufacturers. Interestingly, most brands, from high- to low-priced brand names, test within 15 percent of each other.

Spicer Number	Tensile Strength
260	2,949 lbs-ft
297	4,401 lbs-ft
760	5,200 lbs-ft
178	4,894 lbs-ft (estimated, only one test)
332	5,500 lbs-ft (estimated, only one test)

There comes a time when the size of the tires and the angles they need to reach will exceed the ability of a stock steering system, or even a modified system. That is where hydraulics comes in. A full hydraulic system, as you would see on a tractor, is sometimes used in rock buggies or trail-only machines but is not advisable for the street. Street systems usually combine the stock steering with an assist cylinder that's synched with the steering box. The steering box is modified to direct flow to the assist cylinder. You can buy preassembled kits or do as this hard-core 'wheeler/fabber did and build your own.

Direct strength comparisons are not available, but the weakest of these appears to be double the strength of the strongest Spicer joint for the same application. In some cases, the U-joint is actually stronger than the alloy axles. The upside is that they use a very high-strength alloy cross (see nearby U-joint anatomy shot) that's immensely strong. The downside is that they use bushings in the caps instead of needle bearings. As a result, they are the kings of brute strength but not longevity. To survive, they need very frequent lubrication and are not suited to full-time systems or applications where the vehicle will be used for long periods in four-wheel high. Some manufacturers have mentioned offering needle-bearing versions, but thus far none have appeared. Bear in mind that the newer Spicer cold-forged U-joints are about 20 percent stronger than the older styles and make a very cost-effective upgrade option.

The other factor to bear in mind when using the super-strength U-joint is that you *must* also use a super-strength axle. Putting an OE shaft with a super U-joint is like putting passenger car tires on a 1-ton

Big tires mean a reduction in braking effectiveness. This comes partly from the extra rotating mass and partly because the bigger tire has more leverage that the brakes have to work against. High-performance brake linings with a higher coefficient of friction are enough to compensate in most cases, but sometimes a greater cure is needed. Going to larger brakes or upgrading the rear brakes to discs is a good option. Off-Road Unlimited offers this rear disc brake conversion kit for the big GM 14-bolt full floater. Usually a new master cylinder is necessary for a rear disc conversion, as is the case for this kit. *Courtesy Off-Road Unlimited*

truck . . . the mismatch in strength is too great, and failure is imminent. Fortunately, alloy shafts are available for all the popular axles. The common 4340 alloy material is double the strength of the OE 1040.

In some cases, a larger shaft is available. The Dana 30 is an example. A special locker allows you to swap in a 30-spline 4340 shaft for the 27-spline size. Ditto for many Dana 44s, for which 33-spline shafts are available. A heavy pickup or SUV really should go with a Dana 60. A small-housing axle with a small ring gear can only handle so much stress.

Warn's hub fuses are becoming popular to protect vulnerable drivetrains. If you have Warn hubs, the locking ring can be replaced by one that's designed to shear cleanly at a predetermined torque load. This piece is easier and cheaper to replace than an axle or U-joint. The downside is that you are limited to the torque at which the hub fuse is designed to shear. You don't see them much in the advanced machines.

Finally, we get to the IFS category. When it comes to hard-core stuff, IFS rigs are not all that common. While there are some successfully campaigned IFS rigs in the advanced realm, they are almost always less successful than solid axles. It's just very difficult and expensive to make an IFS front end hold up with big tires and low gears. The performance issue is another matter. IFS rigs are more prone to lifting front tires, thus reducing the potential traction by one tire.

With the solid front axle fading fast with OE 4×4s, there is going to have to be a renaissance in IFS aftermarket products. We are beginning to see these things addressed in the import realm, but the IFS drivetrain issue has not been seriously addressed in the domestic realm. There are a growing number of swaps available that convert IFS to solid axles. Right now, that's the best option, and 'wheelers are converting many IFS GM trucks and SUVs. For the most part, these conversions are pretty tough and best done by a competent person with great welding skills. Even after paying for the labor, the job can come out at about the same cost as high-end IFS lift, and the performance is better.

Rear Axles. In many situations, the rear axle has to handle 30 to 50 percent more torque than the front. This is most often due to weight transfer in climbs or acceleration. Like the front, rear axle buildups follow some pretty general guidelines. It starts with axle shaft size, which is commonly expressed by diameter and spline count. A larger-diameter axle will have more splines (some of the big full-floaters are exceptions, such as big 1.5-inch shafts with 30 splines), and this equates to less reduction in diameter and more driving surfaces.

In a general way, you can rate axles for tire size by their axle-shaft size and spline counts. OE alloy 28-splines can handle 31-inch tires in heavy rigs and 33s in lighter ones. The 30- and 31-spline units are good for 33-inch tires in heavy rigs and 35s in lighter ones. The 32- and 33-spline units can handle 35s and sometimes bigger. The beefy 35-spline axles are easily good to 38-inch tires, more if they are full-floaters. There are some in-betweens also. Look at max tire recommendations in the nearby sidebar.

When you get into the stronger alloy steels, the equation changes. You will see three alloys in the aftermarket: 1541 (or 1540), 4340, and 300M. These numbers reflect the alloy "recipe," and you can find information on them in a nearby sidebar. These can easily jump the axle up to the next major tire size and sometimes two or three. Stronger alloys can also add an extra margin of beef within a tire size range. This latter tip is particularly useful for C-clip axles, where a snapped shaft strands you. Lockers can drastically increase the axle load because they will allow all the torque to run to a single shaft.

A few kits convert popular ½-ton semi-float axles to full-float. This eliminates the danger of a lost wheel from a broken shaft. It also offers the opportunity to

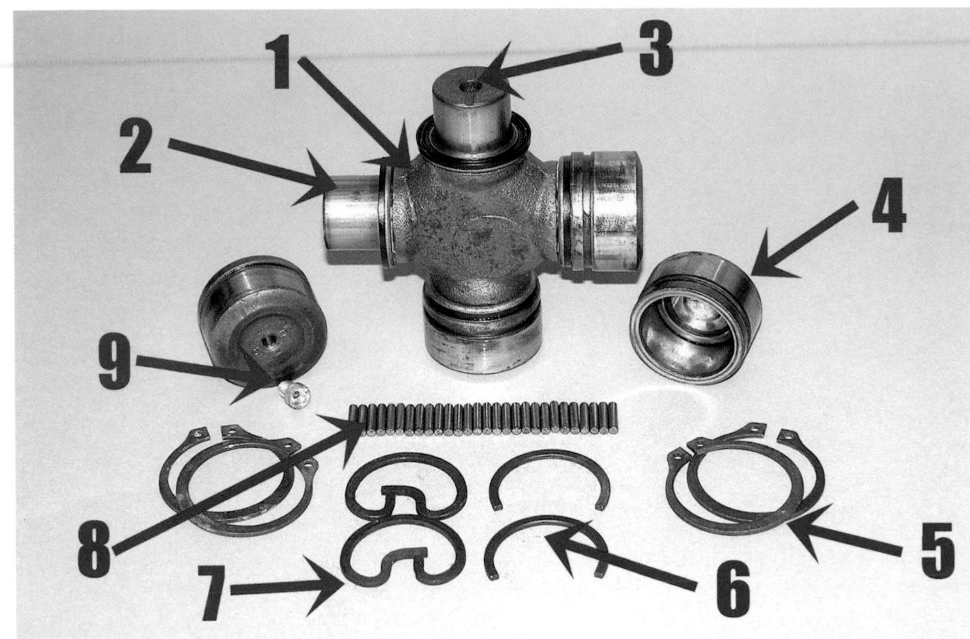

Anatomy of a Needle Bearing U-Joint. 1- Body (a.k.a. cross) 2- Trunnion 3- Grease passage (drilled through to opposite side and connected to passage on opposing trunnions) 4- Cap 5- Full circle external snap rings (replaces No. 6 on certain axles) 6- Half circle snap rings (retains cap) 7- Internal snap rings (used on certain U-joints) 8- Needle Bearings 9- Grease Fitting (screws into cap, sometimes into cross) .

upgrade to stronger 4340 shafts. The conversions do not offer a great increase in load-carrying capacity, just the separation of load-carrying and torque-delivery duties. The axle then only has to drive the wheel, not support the weight also.

Size upgrades are available for some rear axles. These can use the OE steel or an alloy. An upgrade from a 1.28-inch, 28-spline shaft to a 1.31-inch, 30-spline shaft, for example, adds 20 percent more strength. Many of the OE light truck axles (Dana 44, GM 10-bolt, Ford 8.8, among others) had both 28- and 30- or 31-spline versions. A change of carrier (or a 30/31-spline locker) is necessary. There are some custom builders who do similar things, such as Superior Gear's 30-spline conversion for the 27-spline Dana 35, or the 33-spline conversion for Dana 44s.

Housing strength is a consideration in some cases, especially with ½-ton trucks. Their light-duty housing is designed for their OE duties. Slap some big tires, low gears, and lots of torque to them, and they bend and twist like rubber. A hard-used ½-ton truck can really use a heavier ¾-ton axle. The fact that most ¾ tons use 8-lug hubs complicates the situation, though some 'wheelers will swap both front and rear axles (a Dana 60 front and 14-bolt rear in a GM truck or SUV, for example). There are 5- or 6-lug conversion hubs for front or rear Dana 60s available from DynaTrac, but depending on what axle you use, you may be forced to convert the front hubs to 8-lugs and switch wheels all around. That's actually a good thing because the connection between the hub and the wheel is often forgotten, and it's a definite factor in the drivetrain torque equation.

DRIVESHAFT UNIVERSAL JOINT DIMENSIONS AND TORQUE RATINGS

Note: This rating is for maximum continuous torque with no distortion or ill effects.

Series	Cap to Cap	Cap Diameter	Continuous	Short-Term Max	Deformation	Max Angularity
1310	3.22	1.08	130 lbs-ft	800 lbs-ft	1,600 lbs-ft	30 degrees
1330	3.63	1.08	150 lbs-ft	890 lbs-ft	1,850 lbs-ft	20 degrees
1350	3.63	1.19	210 lbs-ft	1,240 lbs-ft	2,260 lbs-ft	30 degrees
1410	4.19	1.19	250 lbs-ft	1,500 lbs-ft	2,700 lbs-ft	37 degrees

This cut-down Bronco rockcrawler could use a little more articulation to ease the "pucker factor" that comes from angles like this. A lot of bodywork and gear has been stripped off this old Bronco, so the first spot to look for improvements would probably be in the spring rates, both front and rear. If that left front spring were a bit softer, that side would compress more and ease the angle. In back, it looks like the rig has some pretty hefty leaf packs. Traction bars in the rear could also cause a lack of articulation. In any case, rockcrawlers need to learn to deal with lifted tires, no matter the cause.

DANCING IN THE ROCKS

The only school in which you can learn this is "the school of hard rocks." Lots of observation and seeing what works and what doesn't helps, but sooner or later you just have to do it. Be sure your rig is up to the job. Here Bill Tocholke walks his very built-up Jeep through one section of rocks in the Iron Range OHV Park. He's set up to put his left wheels (right to us) up onto that line of big boulders on the right and, as the arrows indicate, follow them off this little waterfall.

He's approaching the end of the relatively smooth track of boulders on the right and approaching a big step-down. Note how Bill uses the sidewalls on the left tire (arrow) against the rock.

The step-off to the right is a biggie, but the one on the left is not. He'll have plenty of braking control when easing down off the rock. While it looks like he's stepping into a sea of boulders, it's a relatively smooth sea.

DRIVETRAIN DEFENSE: A good defense strategy for drivers is to try to keep the tires as straight ahead as possible if a heavy torque load will be applied to the front axle. This reduces the chance of front axle failure, which often comes from a broken axle U-joint.

Gearing. We've discussed compensating for tire size by appropriate changes in gearing. Doing this puts you in the same relative performance place as the stock vehicle with OE tire size and gearing. What about gearing from a strict off-highway performance standpoint? There are four major considerations: terrain type, transmission type (automatic or manual), drivetrain strength, and torque to weight ratio.

What we are really talking about here is overall gearing. This is commonly called the "crawl ratio" and is the cumulative ratios of the transmission first gear, the low range in the transfer case, and the axle ratio. Crawl ratio has become a catchphrase, and like many trendy things, people can carry it too far in the quest to be cool. With the gearing choices available today, owners of some rigs can easily get crawl ratios down into the 200:1 area and even lower.

Automatics are a bit tricky to calculate because the torque converter amounts to a variable-ratio first gear. On average, they have a 2:1 ratio, which you would multiply by the "hard" ratio for the first gear planetary set. If you had a 2.41 mechanical ratio, you would multiply by 2 to get the approximate ratio. The problem is that this ratio changes with engine speed. Your converter may have a 2:1 ratio at 800 rpm, but by 1,200 rpm it's only 1.3:1, and by 1,500 rpm it's very near to 1:1.

What's the ideal crawl ratio? This takes us back to the four considerations discussed above. Starting with terrain, rockcrawlers need the lowest ratio and mudrunners need the highest. Rockcrawlers need to be able to drive at a slow, comfortable speed and to have the multiplication to climb very steep stuff at an engine rpm that leaves flexibility to slow down and speed up. When Stephen Watson at Off-Road Design conducted an informal poll, he learned that a 100:1 ratio (torque converter included on automatics) is the ratio of choice for the rockcrawlers in his large customer circle. This poll covered V-8–powered rigs with good torque to weight ratios, essentially rigs that would otherwise be no lower than about 60:1. The dedicated mudrunners he polled were exactly opposite at between 55 and 65:1, or higher. A dedicated mudrunner needs to get the tires spinning as fast as possible. Sand drivers are at the mudrunner side of the spectrum. The rest of us "all-arounders" fit somewhere in the middle, though biased toward the mudrunner ratios, with slight alterations to either side.

The torque multiplication of low gearing must be taken into consideration before going really deep, and I'll show you how below. Compensating for a poor torque to weight ratio can be more difficult. These rigs will need much lower gears to compensate.

Torque Loads. To plan modifications, it's useful to have an idea of the strength of the existing drivetrain. For many rigs, the area of most stress is at the axle assemblies. We first need to calculate how much torque

This is what happens when a driveshaft gets hit when under a torque load. Driveshaft diameter and all-around thickness are determined by the length and maximum rpm of the shaft. Diameters range from 2.5 to 4 inches, with the longer shafts tending toward the longer length. Wall thicknesses run from 0.065 to 0.083 inches. For low-speed, super HD applications, a 2-inch, 0.120 wall shaft is sometimes used.

Size plays a big part in determining where you can go. This Hummer is dancing around in a boulder-filled creek bed with only inches to spare. Careful spotting and good driving got him through the tough, tight places on this Dakota Badlands trail. Ultimately, the biggest rigs will be limited in some ways on a tight trail. Lots of armor "equalizes" the big rig somewhat, but a driver has to learn when the situation is just a "bash-fest" or even a no-go. You want to make that decision to abort early on, before things get so tight that you can't go ahead and can *barely* go back.

multiplication the drivetrain can generate. Next, we need to know how much torque it will take to break the tires loose. Then we need to know the breaking strength of the weakest part of the drivetrain.

The first two items are relatively easy calculations. The last one is more difficult. What is the weakest part? Certain information is readily available, but most of it is not commonly dispensed. Observation and logical deduction can point us to some of the more common failures for which there is some information. The yield strength of an axle shaft, for example, can be calculated based on its minimum diameter and material composition. The axle strength chart in the nearby drivetrain sidebar contains some common sizes and materials that you can plug into your own calculations. The calculation is fairly technical, and you need a materials handbook with steel formulas to make it, so I've done the brain twisting for you on some of the more common sizes and alloys. There is information on universal joints as well.

Step one is to find your engine's maximum net torque (manufacturers' figures from 1973 on are net torque; prior to that, they are gross torque: reduce gross torque by 20 percent to get a close approximation of net) and multiply that by your first gear ratio, T-case low range ratio, and axle ratio. Let's say you have a rig with the ubiquitous 350 Chevy engine with 290 lbs-ft of torque, an automatic TH-700R4 with a 3:1 first gear, a 2.61:1 low-range ratio, and 4.10:1 axle ratios. That does not include the torque converter ratio, which can multiply the ratio somewhat according to engine speed (lower rpm provide greater multiplication). I don't usually factor that ratio in because most of the experts say that it's a "soft" ratio and isn't much of an issue in calculating strength. The torque converter's lowest ratios occur at just above idle (800–1,200 rpm), and the engine isn't producing much torque at that speed. With manual trans, of course, you don't have a converter, and the above comments are moot.

By putting the numbers together we get 290×3.0×2.61×4.10 = 9,309.8 lbs-ft. That's 9,309.8 lbs-ft going to your carrier or locker, axle shafts, and tires! In truth, the engine will not be putting out max torque all the time, and the transfer of torque is not 100 percent efficient, so the final answer is multiplied by a "real-world" efficiency factor of 0.85, which drops it to a "mere" 7,913.3 lbs-ft.

CRAWL RATIO:
How do you calculate crawl ratio? Just multiply all the gear ratios together. A vehicle with a 4:1 transmission first gear, 2.72:1 low range, and 4.10 gears would have a crawl ratio of 44.6:1 (4.0×2.72×4.10 = 44.608). This final ratio offers the maximum torque multiplication for hard pulls or climbs.

The calculations above don't take into account one important factor—traction. Seldom, if ever, will your tires have the grip to handle that much torque. The tires usually break loose before the axle shaft (or something else) does. This is especially true with open diffs or loose limited-slips. The chances of something breaking are based on how much traction you have versus the strength of the drivetrain parts. Logically and in reality, that puts rockcrawlers at greatest risk.

There is a rough method of calculating traction, or more precisely, slip torque (the amount of torque required to break the tire loose from the ground). On level pavement, the calculation is fairly accurate. When you hit the trail, weight transfer, terrain angles, and such will be constantly variable, so we have to pick a high traction coefficient as the maximum possible number. Most times it will be less.

The first part of the slip torque formula involves knowing how much of the vehicle's weight will be on a particular axle, so you need to know front and rear weight. To get this, load your rig with a full tank of fuel, all your trail gear, and the extra bodies you commonly carry (or their equivalent weight), and go to the nearest scales. I go to the local landfill, where they charge for dumping by weight, but truck scales or scrap metal yards are good places also. First, drive the front tires onto the scale and record the weight. Then drive forward to get total weight with all four wheels on the scale. Finally, drive the front wheels off to get the rear wheel weight. I weighed one of my own rigs this way, so we will plug my numbers into the formula below.

My rig weighed 5,600 pounds with two people, 34 gallons of fuel, and my loaded-for-bear spares and tool kits. It has 35-inch tires with a rolling radius of 17 inches. Front weight was 3,100 pounds and 2,500 pounds rear.

The basic formula is:

$$\frac{\text{weight on axle} \times \text{coefficient of friction} \times \text{tire radius}}{12} = \text{slip torque (lbs-ft)}$$

or, plugging in my numbers:

$$\frac{3{,}100 \times 0.6 \times 17}{12} = 2{,}635 \text{ lbs-ft (for both tires)}$$

This formula only applies with equal traction on both tires and does not account for the type of differential. It really only applies if you have a true locker, which is capable of delivering 100 percent of the torque to one tire. With a limited-slip, you could reduce that amount by the bias ratio. A 60 percent bias ratio (4:1 locking factor), or 0.60, times the number you got in the above calculation reduces the potential single axle load to 1,581 lbs-ft. An open diff will always share the load between both axles because as soon as one tire slips, torque takes the path of least resistance and reduces the load.

Really good traction due to ground conditions could move the coefficient of friction up a bit. You can plug in any coefficient you want, up to perfect traction of 1.0, but it's unlikely you'll see it that high on the trail. Quizzing assorted engineers and experts helped to confirm this, though the sticky tires of today dictate working out worst-case scenarios if you are a dedicated

Here's an example of front-to-rear articulation disparity. The rear coil-spring suspension of most Land Rovers is capable of prodigious flex with some relatively minor modifications. It's more difficult and expensive to coax flex out of the front, and this holds true for nearly all rigs. To maintain maximum stability, it's best to keep the front and rear at about the same amount of articulation. It's acceptable to have as much as 10 percent more articulation in the rear.

rockcrawler with aired-down tires. Plug in a smaller-diameter tire, and you'll see the effect tire diameter has on the torque load. A 30-inch tire (14.5-inch radius), for example, drops final slip torque to 2,247 lbs-ft. Bear in mind that slip torque is not the end-all. There are also shock loads to consider as well as metal fatigue that has weakened the components over time.

Let's put it all together. We have the maximum potential torque. We have the torque required to break the tires loose. All we need now is the component strength of the various parts. My rig uses 1.31-inch, 4340 chrome-moly shafts that have a breaking strength of approximately 9,923 lbs-ft. Put that number between the 7,913 lbs-ft from the gearing and the 2,635 lbs-ft needed to break the tires loose (1,317 per tire), and they come up with a lot of strength in reserve. The engine/drivetrain doesn't have enough torque to break the shafts, and the tires don't have enough grip to exceed the breaking strength of the axle. The important part is that the axle strength exceeds the torque or the traction. The previous flanged semi-float axle shafts I used were rated for about 6,200 pounds, and I managed not to break them.

My own rig was geared a bit differently from the example. With the Off-Road Design Doubler, I had a choice of 2:1 or 4:1 low range ratios. In my lowest gears, I could generate 14,268 lbs-ft, which was enough to break a shaft, but I still didn't have the grip needed to break the axle. My modified diesel also generated considerably more torque than the example, even at 1,000 rpm.

With your front-end weight, you can take the same formula to find the weak link there, which may be the axle U-joints. You could use the level-ground figure or a reduced figure to account for weight transfer from the climb. In that case, don't forget to also figure in the multiplication factor of a U-joint at its maximum angularity just so you know. The 297 joints are similar in strength to the 1310 series listed in the driveshaft universal joint sidebar. The Dana 60 332 joints are similar to the 1410 series listed in the same place. Incidentally, I cannot precisely explain the disparity between the U-joint destructive tests done and shown in the sidebars and these Spicer ratings. Some of it is a safety factor that all manufacturers use. The rest is probably due to the manner of testing. If the equipment we used for destructive tests could test merely to the yield point, where the material just begins to permanently deform, the numbers would be lower.

Another use for this information is to determine whether the driveline U-joints are adequate. By calculating slip torque in a different way, you can discover the amount of torque on the driveshaft at the point where the tire breaks loose. If you compare the figures from this calculation to the max short-term driveshaft torque ratings in the nearby sidebar, you will find if you have any weaknesses there. Bear in mind that *usually* the driveshaft and yokes are rated for the same torque as the U-joints, but not always. Most smaller 4×4s have 1310-series joints, as do many ½-ton full-sized rigs. The 1330 series are found in some ½-tons and some ¾-tons. Some ¾-tons and many 1-tons use 1350-series joints.

The formula is:

$$\frac{\text{weight on axle} \times \text{coefficient of friction} \times \text{rolling radius of tire}}{12 \times \text{axle ratio}} = \text{driveshaft torque}$$

Or, using our numbers from above:

$$\frac{3000 \times 0.60 \times 17}{12 \times 4.10} = 621.9 \text{ lbs-ft}$$

That's inside the maximum short-term ratings given by Dana Spicer for all the U-joints listed in the sidebar.

Suspension

We talked about basic lift conditions in Chapter 6. Adding more lift for even bigger tires is just an extension of the same information. In an advanced rig, other factors come into play. Stability is important, so rigs with "nose-bleed-tall" lifts are at a decided disadvantage in uneven terrain. Articulation is another factor. The ideal is to have the suspension compliant enough to keep the tires on the ground as much as possible. Even a partially unloaded tire can deliver more traction than a lifted tire (assuming a locker is engaged).

The main goal with a modified suspension is balance: balance in articulation front to rear; balance between the lift height and a reasonable center of gravity; and, for rigs that are not trailered, balance between street performance and trail performance. Ride quality is another important factor.

Lifts and Center of Gravity. The quest to fit big rubber often forces many compromises. Some rigs can easily swallow big rubber, and others cannot without being lifted to the moon. It often comes down to how much fenderwell and sheet metal modification you are willing

Polyurethane is the bushing of choice for most suspension systems. It holds up better and usually allows more suspension movement. The greaseable type, as shown here, avoids the creaking for which unlubed poly bushings are notorious. Unlike rubber bushings, which consist of two metal sleeves with rubber bonding them together, the poly setup is made up of separate pieces. When the rubber bushing is flexed past its elasticity, the rubber tears away from the metal sleeves. The poly bushing is free to pivot as far as needed. On the downside, poly sometimes results in a harsher, noisier ride in the more cushy rigs where such things are important. Poly is not yet offered with the same softness as rubber, though the time is near when it will be. Most aftermarket suspensions come with poly bushings.

Longer leaf springs offer a combination of better flexibility and a better ride, though a conversion like this flatfender Jeep's is labor intensive and not for everyone. Note also that the springs have been attached outboard of the chassis via GM-style truck spring hangers. Combined with wider axles, this also offers an extra measure of stability to an otherwise narrow and tippy short-wheelbase rig.

to make. In my opinion, it's better to compromise a bit with a smaller tire than reduce stability to the point that it becomes a liability on and off the highway.

Articulation Balance. In most cases, it's easier to gain articulation in the rear. Many owners simply grab what they can get there and ignore the front end. This results in articulation imbalance and leads to instability. Instability translates into more severe roll angles in steep terrain. This means more tilt in certain situations and an increased propensity to roll.

Unfortunately, measuring articulation balance is not easy. You need an articulation ramp and lots of time for measurements. It's possible to do it in a shade-tree way if you have the ramp, but often you can observe it visually.

Articulation imbalance can be caused by more than a simple disparity in wheel travel front to rear. Mismatched spring rates may also cause it. If the rear springs are too light compared to the front, they will do all the flexing as the front resists articulation. The cure in this situation is either to go lighter on the front springs or heavier on the rear to force the front to flex more, or a combination of both. There are lots of compromises! The section below and the nearby sidebar will fill you in more on spring rates.

Spring Rates. Correct spring rates for the weight and ride height of your vehicle result in good ride and articulation. Spring rate is expressed in pounds per inch of movement, or lb./in. This is the amount of weight it takes to move the spring 1 inch. To move the spring 2 inches, it takes twice the weight, and 3 inches takes three times the weight, and so on. Obviously,

ARTICULATION BALANCE:
If it appears that your rig has lots more wheel travel in back than up front, you could be in danger. This is one of the problems with IFS trucks. The combination of lots of articulation in the rear with virtually none in the front makes the vehicle tilt more.

MODS FOR LIFT:
One way around the excessive lift situation is to fit wider-than-stock axles (full-sized Wagoneer axles on CJ-5s, for example), or take a Sawzall to the body to enlarge the fender wells. This can be done nicely by a body shop, but many hard-core 'wheelers would rather put money into other things

ARTICULATION BALANCE:
To avoid instability, your 4×4 ideally should have as much articulation in the front as the rear. In reality, a split of 40 percent front, 60 percent rear is close enough.

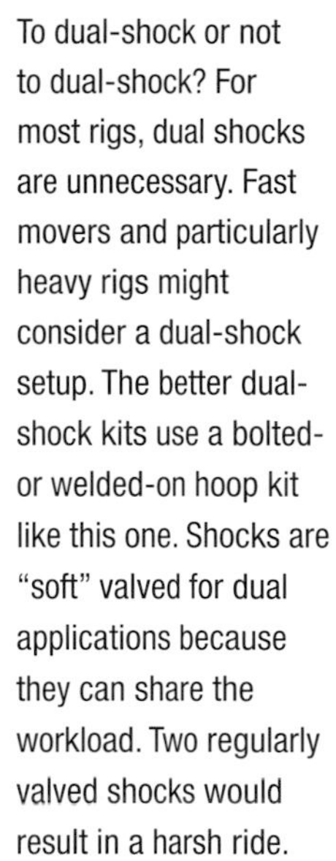
To dual-shock or not to dual-shock? For most rigs, dual shocks are unnecessary. Fast movers and particularly heavy rigs might consider a dual-shock setup. The better dual-shock kits use a bolted- or welded-on hoop kit like this one. Shocks are "soft" valved for dual applications because they can share the workload. Two regularly valved shocks would result in a harsh ride.

This is an extreme leaf-spring suspension for a Toyota. This is actually a conversion of an IFS truck. The late, great Advanced Off-Road Research offered this setup for conversions of IFS to the Toyota solid axle. The custom springs were long and supple, with not much arch, and were mounted above the axle. The Bilstein dual shocks are a high-end, remote-reservoir, gas-charged type. The nitrogen gas pressure in the shocks can be adjusted according to what is desired for the terrain. The suspension is shown at normal ride height. Note how the shackle is tilted back slightly. All in all, this is near perfection in a leaf-spring setup.

the higher the rate, the more the load capacity and the harsher the unloaded ride. The rates are chosen to balance these two elements. This is the same whether the vehicle uses leaf springs, coil springs, or torsion bars. In leaf springs, however, the friction of the leaves sliding past each other results in a little extra "perceived" rate, especially if they have gotten rusty.

Because springs often come with lift kits, can you assume they are correct for your vehicle? Not necessarily. Aftermarket springs are often a "one-size-fits-most" sort of deal. You can usually find a "standard duty" and "heavy duty" spring rate offered, the latter being stiffer. If you have the catalog, the spring rates may be listed in product specifications. If the rates are close to stock rates and you are satisfied with the ride and load capacity now, then you should be happy with the new springs. With leaf springs, a lift often requires more spring camber (arch), and this can require a higher spring rate to hold that arch. The procedure for selecting a spring rate is shown in a nearby sidebar.

Spring Rate Versus Spring Frequency. Though related, these are two separate issues. Rate describes

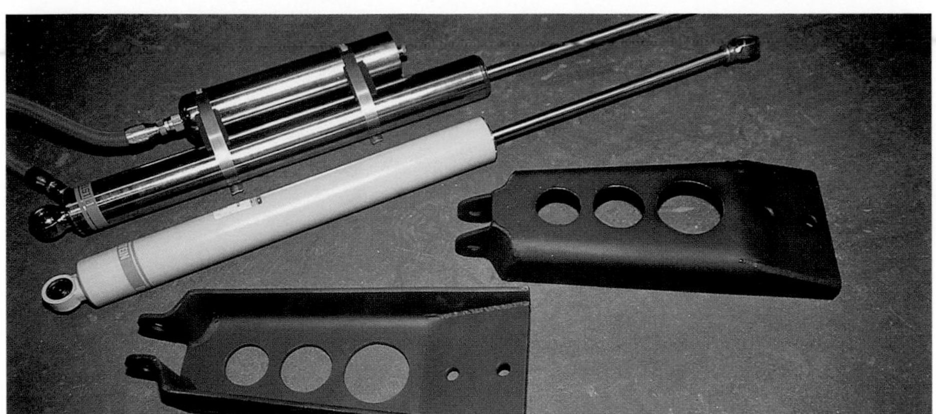

Mounting longer travel shocks usually entails relocating the shock brackets. This is a kit to raise the upper mount for a Toyota truck and allows for shocks with 14 inches of travel to be used.

CALCULATING SPRING RATE

Formulas Courtesy Skyjacker

These formulas work for leaf and coil springs. They can help you approximate ride height and your spring rate needs.

1) You will need to determine the weight on the front and rear axles. This can be done at a truck stop or any convenient truck scale.
   A. If your ultimate goal is to find a spring rate and ride height for a predetermined vehicle setup and load, weigh it in that configuration.
   B. If your goal is to determine a load capacity, you will need to weigh the vehicle once empty and once with the load.

Sample Problem. front weight: 2,400 lbs., rear weight: 1,800 lbs.

2) Divide the front and rear axle weights by two to determine the weight per spring. Deduct the weight of the axles, wheels, and tires, since it is weight not supported by the springs. Here are some educated guesses. Dana 30/35—250/200 lbs., front/rear; Dana 44—300/250 lbs., front/rear; Dana 60—375/300 lbs., front/year.

Sample Problem: Front 2,400 - 250 lbs. = 2150 ÷ 2 = 1,075 lbs. per spring

Rear 1,800 - 200 lbs. = 1,600 ÷ 2 = 800 lbs. per spring

3) Find the rate of the spring in pounds per inch.

Sample Problem: New spring rates front: 250 lbs./in., rear: 200 lbs./in.

4) Divide the load per spring by the rate per spring to get the deflection in inches.

Sample Problem: Front: 1,075 ÷ 250 = 4.3 inches of deflection

800 ÷ 200 = 4.0 inches of deflection

5) Now for some practical application. With coils, if you have the free length of the spring, you can calculate loaded ride height difference easily. By determining what the loaded height of the spring will be with the per-spring load, you can figure mounted spring-seat-to-spring-seat height.
   With leaf springs, you need free arch measurements and then you can deduct the loss of arch according to the spring rate and per-spring load.

Sample Solution for Coil Spring:

Front free length: 18 inches - 4.3 inches = 13.7 inches mounted height

Rear free length: 18.5 inches - 4.0 inches= 14.5 inches mounted height

If your original mounted heights were 11 and 12.1 inches, then you have gained 2.7 inches up front and 2.4 inches in back.

Sample Solution for Leaf Spring:

Front spring free arch: 7.6 inches - 4.3 inches = 3.3 inches free arch mounted at weight

Rear spring free arch: 7.25 inches - 4.0 inches = 3.25 inches free arch at weight

If your original free arch numbers were 0 .9 inches front and 0.8 inches rear, then you have gained 2.4 inches of lift in front and 2.45 inches in back.

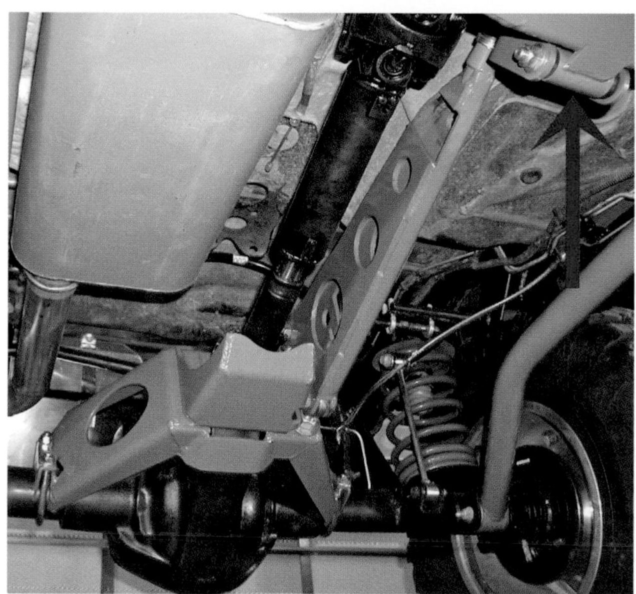
There are many ways to control axle wrap. The problem is doing it without impairing axle travel and articulation. AEV's Nth Degree Stinger is one product that delivers in all areas for Jeeps. It's shown here on a Dana 60–equipped Jeep coiler, but the version used for leaf-spring Jeeps is very much the same. The key is the shackle-like pivot where it attaches to the belly pan/crossmember. The geometry is carefully calculated to allow the axle to move in every direction except for the twist that comes from torque and axle wrap. It looks simple, but getting the geometry right took a highly skilled engineer. *Courtesy AEV*

only the load-carrying ability of the spring. Frequency is the natural rate at which a spring responds to an irregular road surface. It's a factor of spring rate and unsprung weight, the indicator of ride quality and, to an extent, handling. It's measured in cycles per second (a.k.a. Hertz, or Hz) or cycles per minute (CPM). A soft, cushy, "Caddy"-type ride would measure out as a low frequency 1–1.25 Hz, or 60–80 CPM. A firm ride would be 1.5–2.0 Hz, or 90–120 CPM. What most people would consider a brutal ride would start at a high 2.3 Hz or 140 CPM. At the same weight, a stiff spring has a higher frequency, and a soft spring has a lower one.

While rate remains the same with increased weight, frequency changes. A pickup rear spring has a very high frequency with the truck unloaded, but when you add the truck's rated load, the frequency drops. That accounts for the difference in ride between a loaded and an unloaded truck.

The most important aspect of ride tuning is how the frequencies of front and rear suspensions complement each other. In general, for the best ride, you want a lower frequency in the front than the rear. That way the front and rear springs finish their oscillations at close to the same time, making the car pitch less (i.e., "see-saw" motion). Generalities are difficult,

There comes a point at which the stock suspension can no longer be adapted. That's where the big-money suspension systems come in. It could replace a leaf-spring system with coils or, as shown here, go from a short-arm system to a long-arm system. Specific to a coil-spring, live-axle system, the more lift that is added, the greater the angle on the control arms. That reduces available travel, increases the shock loads on the chassis, and adds all sorts of handling quirks. The cure is to use longer arms, but this requires a great deal of reengineering. This is a good example from AEV. The long-arm Nth Degree system for Jeeps uses a replacement center crossmember as a pivot point for both the front and rear control arms. Yes, a system like this is expensive enough to make your vision swim, but the performance and durability are at the highest levels.

One of the growing aftermarket trends is the conversion of IFS trucks to a solid front axle. No rig needs it more than the older GM S-10 series trucks and SUVs. The S-10s are an otherwise great package that's hampered on the trail by an inadequate front drive system. Stage West Four-Wheel Drive Center, now defunct unfortunately, built this conversion that fits supple, long-travel springs and an ordinary Jeep Wrangler front axle to the rig. The result is radically improved articulation and trail performance, good street manners, and the durability to handle 35-inch tires reliably.

The Revolver shackle is an interesting design that can offer major articulation gains in leaf-spring vehicles. It drops in a knee-like fashion to allow several more inches of downtravel. It also pivots to allow the spring to twist a bit as it drops. Spring twist, or the lack thereof, is a factor in articulation. The weight of the vehicle seems to keep the Revolver in place on the highway.

but a short-wheelbase rig will have a rear frequency about 17 percent higher than the front. Given the same general specification, the difference will increase with wheelbase.

Other complications are that spring frequency is only part of the story . . . the straight-line part. There are also other handling elements to consider, such as roll resistance (the tendency of body lean) and the way body roll affects handling. Weight transfer in a turn lowers the frequency on the outside springs (more weight) and raises it on the inside (less weight). This increases load on the outside and decreases it on the inside. The least-loaded tire (usually the inside rear) loses grip first, and then the overloaded inner tire is overwhelmed and follows. That tends to make the vehicle oversteer (its nose rotates to the inside of the turn, requiring reduced steering input). To counter that, sway bars are installed, and they temporarily maintain desirable spring frequencies in turns. Now that you've been thoroughly tantalized with thoughts of spring frequencies, bear in mind that it's difficult to find an aftermarket spring that precisely matches every combination.

DUAL-RATE SPRINGS:
Dual-rate springs provide a softer rate for the first inch or so of travel, but then the rate increases. The spring rate of a dual-rate spring might be expressed as 155–230 lbs./in., for example.

Advanced Lifts. There's one type of lift we didn't discuss in Chapter 6: spring-over lifts. Some leaf-spring rigs, such as Jeep CJs and YJs, as well as Toyota Land Cruisers and IHC Scouts, are spring-under vehicles. One way to get lift with these rigs is to move the axle to the underside of the springs. This results in a lift equal to the thickness of the axle tubes plus the height of the new spring perch that must be welded to the top of the axle. The benefit is that you retain the supple OE springs and articulation. The downside is that you may experience problems with spring wrap and driveshaft angles.

This is a custom-built front suspension made to convert a GM IFS truck to a solid front axle. It uses a coil-over-type shock. This type of unit combines a coil spring and a shock. You may remember a version of this idea that your dad put on the old Ford station wagon to keep it from tail dragging when the family went on vacation. Other notable features of this setup include a downtravel-limit strap, Heim joints on the suspension arms and tie rods, and a very high level of workmanship. Custom work like this is not attainable from many shops. Self-trained engineers and welders may be OK, but let them apprentice on somebody else's vehicle first! *Courtesy Ben Stewart*

SPRING WRAP:
Spring wrap, or axle wrap, or just plain "wrap," is an effect of torque. As torque is applied through the axle to the tires, the axle twists, pushing the snout of the differential up toward the floor when the vehicle is moving forward. The spring resists according to its stiffness but may actually go S-shaped. This happens to all springs, but in a spring-over setup, the extra leverage increases the effect.

SHOCK LENGTHS:
Suspension travel is almost always limited by shock length. This holds true for both OE and aftermarket suspension systems.

The result of spring wrap is that the driveshaft and pinion angle changes—and if it changes enough, the U-joint binds and breaks. The other negative effect occurs if the tires lose traction. Suddenly released of torque, the springs snap back, and again the driveshaft takes the brunt. Spring rate, the length of the spring, gear ratios, and engine torque all contribute to this tendency.

Several cures exist for spring wrap, whether it comes from a spring-over or not. These include stiffer springs and torque rods of all types (a.k.a. traction bars). Some spring manufacturers, most notably Rancho, include a half leaf on the leading end of some of their springs that goes from the eye to just past the U-bolts. Often this is just enough to prevent wrap. Several companies build torque rods, but be sure any you consider buying will not restrict articulation. Some do.

Dual and Long-Travel Shocks. In nearly all stock suspensions, the shock length determines the limit of suspension travel. Ditto for many lift kits. One way to increase, or at least maximize, articulation is to install a longer shock. The first step is to disconnect or remove your existing shocks and see how much more travel or articulation you can get. Simply disconnect one end of the shocks and jack the vehicle up by the chassis until the wheels are off the ground. If you determine that the lower shock mounts are significantly lower than the extended shock, then you have some long-travel potential. From there you need to look at other factors to see if it's feasible to increase suspension travel.

Look first at your brake hose length. You may have to disconnect them temporarily even for the test. Solid-axle coil-spring rigs may drop to the point where the coil spring is released. With an independent front suspension rig, you may find that front-axle CV joint angles get to be excessive if travel increases significantly. Steering geometry may be affected adversely. Axle vent lines may be too short. Driveshafts may be too short or operate at too steep an angle. Some of these items can be corrected with effort and some cannot.

Next, uptravel needs to be considered. First, measure the distance between the shock mounts with the suspension extended all the way. Then compress the suspension all the way against the bump stop and measure again. You can simulate this measurement using the bump stop, or whatever else is your upward limiter, as a guide. Ideally you want a shock that has an extended length about ½ inch longer than your suspension's extended dimension and a compressed length about ½ to ¾ inch shorter than the compressed dimension. The extra downtravel adds a margin of shock and shock-mount safety. The collapsed distance is even more important, since the rubber bump stop has some give. If you accidentally bottom the suspension hard, you will still have some shock travel left. Bottoming the shock can damage it or break off the shock mounts. Taller bump stops or spacers can be used to fine-tune up-travel. Remember that tire/fenderwell clearance may be an issue with the suspension at the upper end.

The shock manufacturers often list the extended and collapsed length of their shocks. If you are lucky, you will find one that fits your dimensions. Most likely, you will have to relocate a shock mount to get the longer shock installed. There are various methods to relocating shock mounts, including kits, fabrication, and even a few bolt-on tricks.

Dual shocks are more necessary for fast movers because dual shocks tend to share the dampening load. Fast travel over bumpy ground generates heat in the shocks. In extreme cases, the shock can be cooked. The heat is reduced when there are two or more shocks on each side to share the load. Dual shocks are specially valved to be less stiff. In essence, the two shocks are valved to do the job of one. Various aftermarket shock kits are available for popular applications, but dual shocks are not necessary for most of us who move at a slower pace. If you fit in the slow category, your money is better spent elsewhere.

Steering Linkage. Two of the most common steering issues associated with modified rigs are the durability of the tie rod and drag link, and bump steer. Durability comes into play with the addition of large tires and tough trail conditions. Under the wrong circumstances, these factors can produce enough force to bend a factory tie rod like a pretzel.

From the replacement standpoint, several companies offer heavy-duty tie rods. These start with units that are designed to replace the OE setup. First on the list are units made of larger, stronger material. Some are adapted from truck tie rods that are more robust than the stock pieces but are still made of carbon steel. They vary in price but are usually under a hundred bucks.

Next up are replacement tie rods made of 4130 chrome-moly tubing that use the OE tie-rod ends. These vary in O.D. from ⅞ inch to 1 inch, with wall thickness from 0.188 inch to 0.250 inch. These are extremely robust pieces. The one disadvantage to 4130 is that if it does get bent, it will usually break when you try to bend it back. Ordinary carbon steel is softer and can usually be straightened.

HIGH-CLEARANCE STEERING: High-clearance steering kits are available for popular trail rigs. These keep steering components out of harm's way and also reduce bump steer on the trail.

High-clearance steering is necessary in some applications. This does two things: first, it allows the drag link to run more or less level, thus reducing bump-steer tendencies; second, it puts the tie rod and drag link higher, out of harm's way. There are complications to this conversion, including interference with the spring. In some applications, the tie rod mounts over the spring. Note that this Jeep has also had a spring-over conversion.

Big tires put more stress on the steering system. This can result in minor problems like bent steering rods or more major situations like broken steering boxes or a chassis cracked where the steering box mounts. It can even result in damaged steering boxes. Not all 4×4s are particularly vulnerable to this, but many of the popular trail rigs that are have the option of a brace. The brace typically mounts to the lowest part of the steering box and braces against the chassis rail on the other side. The PSC steering box offers a larger piston, which increases the "power" in your power steering. When combined with a high-output power steering pump, all but the biggest tires can be used.

Bump steer occurs when suspension movement tends to steer the vehicle. This occurs when the drag link is at an angle. When the axle moves up, the rod effectively gets longer and, in most cases, makes the vehicle steer itself. Ideally the drag link should be as level as possible, but lifts make the drag link reach down. This tends to increase bump steer.

The easy cure to bump steer is often a dropped Pitman arm. The extra leverage makes steering box damage more likely, however, so if a steering box brace exists for your rig, use it. This is a good idea for any advanced rig because big tires tend to put more stress on the steering box and the spot where it mounts to the chassis. Do not bend your Pitman arm by any means, including heat. It crystallizes the metal and makes it brittle. Better to stay alive and spend a few bucks on a made-from-scratch part.

SAMPLE POWER STEERING TEMPS

This will show the difference in power steering temps for various conditions. Test performed on a 1983 Blazer K-5.

Condition	Oil Temperature	Ambient Temperature
freeway, high speed	oil: 134 degrees	90 degrees
	pump: 139 degrees	
	box: 102 degrees	
city, stop and go	oil: 130 degrees	92 degrees
	pump: 150 degrees	
	box: 118 degrees	
trail, easy	oil: 153 degrees	95 degrees
	pump: 168 degrees	
	box: 172 degrees	
trail, hard	oil: 193 degrees	95 degrees
	pump: 227 degrees	
	box: 215 degrees	

Major lifts may require a complete redo of the steering linkage. In the factory steering setups on solid-axle rigs, the tie rod is mounted below the arms and is somewhat vulnerable to damage. Many four-wheelers mount their tie rods above the arms for clearance. This has the added advantage of lessening drag link angles and minimizing bump steer. Some machine shops can re-drill the tapered holes in the steering knuckles to accomplish this.

Steering Dampers. A steering damper is nothing more than a shock absorber for the steering system. It dampens the effect of tire vibration and feedback from road surface irregularities. These problems are inherent in all vehicles with large tires, 4×4s included. The effects are multiplied when you add even larger tires and lifts, so a steering damper upgrade is a vital ingredient to most buildups.

The OE damper may be inadequate, even in stock rigs, especially for fast movers. Tire size determines whether you need to upgrade your steering damper. Just as with shocks, a larger piston exerts more control, so the upgraded part will be larger in diameter. A damper will not control bump steer. As discussed, this is an issue of steering geometry. Nor will it control the vibrations that come from worn-out steering components.

Many newer vehicles are already fitted with a damper. In these cases all you need to do is add the beefier unit. In older rigs not so equipped, the aftermarket supplies bracket kits to mount the damper. The key is to have the damper centered in its travel so that it does not restrict steering movement. The unit should be mounted as high out of harm's way as possible, but even then steering dampers are often front-line casualties in hard-core 4×4 circles. The damper is best mounted to the drag link.

Occasionally you will see two or more dampers mounted. For most rigs, one is plenty. The dual setups come into play with really huge tires. If one good damper doesn't stop the vibration in your mild 4×4 with 33-inch tires, you probably have other problems. If you have a full-sized truck with 44s, then twin dampers are a legitimate mod.

Power Steering. Power steering systems use an oil that is nearly identical to automatic transmission fluid and is subject to the same temperature frailties. If you ever wondered how hot the power steering can get, look at the nearby sidebar. Overheated power steering oil can cause a loss of power assist at critical periods and result in early failure of the parts. Big tires and a hard trail can push temps up fast.

At about 212 degrees Fahrenheit, the oil in the power steering system starts to foam. The first symptoms of this will be a growling noise, which is an indication that the pump is cavitating, followed by intermittent loss of fluid pressure and power assist. Continual high temps will also degrade the internal seals and the hoses.

The answer is a power steering cooler, and this is considered a necessity in many rockcrawling circles. The cooler mounts on the low-pressure (return) line between the steering box and pump reservoir. Nearly any type of cooler can be used, including small trans coolers and engine oil coolers. If you rig something up yourself, make sure to use power steering–rated, high-temp hose.

The cooler is most needed at slow speeds, so placing it in the fan's airflow can reduce temps more than mounting it just anywhere. Even a spot on a fenderwell that gets some airflow from the fan is better than a dead area. Finding a good spot may be problematic under a tightly packed hood. As with any cooler, the number one consideration is placing it in a location that is safe from trail damage.

Even if you don't mount a cooler, at least change your power steering oil once in a while if you four-wheel hard. Just one hard trip can turn the fluid dark. Just like an automatic transmission, the fluid deteriorates, and it can degrade the performance of the system even before premature wear occurs.

The Dreaded Death Wobble. This is a condition that has become legendary for its ability to scare the pants off of four-wheelers . . . if not shake them off! Basically, it's a severe front-end vibration of a severity that makes you think the wheels are about to fall off. If it occurs at a high speed, you'll see your life flash before your eyes the first time, though the situation seldom has dire results. It occurs most often in built rigs with weak links.

Death wobble is essentially a severe vibration of the two front tires. One wheel begins to oscillate, and that starts the other one going. The vibration is transferred through the steering linkage, and because the wheels are out of sync with each other, the independent vibrations seem to feed each other and make the oscillations progressively worse.

There is no sure, single cure for death wobble and not always a single cause. It's usually several conditions arriving at a single moment in time that's ripe for the event. Let's go through the causes and cures, in order of importance, gleaned from several authorities in the field.

Tire Balance: The number one cause is out-of-balance tires. Yes, big tires are harder to balance, but how they are balanced is very important. The dynamic balance should place weights on *both* the inside and outside of the wheel for the best effect, regardless of appearance. Balance the tires to the proverbial gnat's posterior and have them rebalanced regularly as they wear.

Steering Damper: A good steering damper may stop death wobble before it starts. If one tire vibrates momentarily, no biggie, but if it can set the other wheel off, that's when the true meaning of death wobble may be found. A good damper can stop it in its tracks.

Loose Steering Parts: This just adds to the problem. Tight steering may prevent vibration from getting out of hand. Once the tire starts to wobble, if there is slop in the steering, it just gets worse.

Crossover Versus Inverted Y Steering: Oddly enough, a crossover steering system (or inverted T) will suffer from death wobble more often than the

BUMP STEER:
Bump steer describes directional changes in the front wheels that result from suspension movement rather than steering-wheel input.

inverted Y system. The inverted Y seems to absorb some of the vibration where the crossover sends the vibrations straight over.

Caster: More caster seems to make death wobble worse and vice versa. It has to do with an effect called *pneumatic trail*, which places the contact patch of the tire behind the steering axis. Imagine a shopping cart front wheel and how a tired cart wheel can get the wobble.

Scrub Radius: Positive scrub radius seems to act as a steering damper and can reduce the tendency to have a death wobble.

Tire Pressure: Tire pressure seems to play a part in the death wobble scenario, but nobody can agree on an ideal pressure because of too many variables. Experiment.

Engine

Just like in Chapter 6, we're not getting into major engine mods or swaps. The majority of 4×4s are adequately powered for the trail when properly geared. What we will discuss, however, are some durability modifications to make your engine hang together better.

The most common four-wheeling scenario is the slow-speed slog, grunting along at less than 10 miles per hour at just above idle speed. What if the outside

Aftermarket aluminum radiators are very efficient compared to the standard brass types. In critical cooling situations, they can mean the difference between hot and not hot. They are available in custom form or as direct replacements in a small range of applications. The electric fans on this 4×4 S-10 with a 350 V-8 conversion are a little more problematic. Obviously, these were installed because of the difficulties in the conversion. As for electric fans, there are electric fan kits available from Flex-a-Lite that are powerful enough to replace the engine-driven fan, and they are available for a small range of applications. Most of the cheap electric fan kits are incapable of stand-alone operation. Most engine-driven fans are capable of high airflow. The advantage of an electric is that it doesn't run or rob power when it's not needed.

What's wrong with this picture? Radical body surgery is a part of the game in the quest for ultimate clearance. In the case of this Toyota pickup, the prodigious rear overhang has been "bobbed" to a more reasonable amount. Along the way, some rear quarter-panel protection was added. The body projects only slightly past the amount of frame needed to support the aft end of the spring. Some 10 inches of body length was removed.

temperature is 100 degrees or more? You might answer that it's no worse than L.A. or Dallas traffic, and you wouldn't be too far from wrong, though a 'wheeling engine may be working harder. Often the OE cooling system is adequate. If it's not, and you have an automatic, realize that the automatic transmission has a cooler built into the radiator and that four-wheeling will drastically raise trans oil temp, adding to your cooling system's burden. An external tranny cooler will help. If you live in a perpetually warm climate, you might consider bypassing the radiator cooler altogether. Transmission coolers with thermostatically controlled electric fans are the ultimate in efficiency when airflow is in short supply.

Other ways to reduce operating temps in a hot running engine, beyond any repair or maintenance problems that should be eliminated first, start with a proper mix of coolant. Higher mixtures of coolant do not transfer heat as well. More water transfers heat better, but the boiling point is lowered. The ideal compromise is a 50/50 mix. High-flow thermostats that do not restrict water flow are another easy solution. Changing the opening point usually does little.

High-efficiency and larger-capacity radiators are also available. The best way of increasing radiator size is via frontal area, but that's not often possible, so we get by with another layer of cores. Larger fans with more airflow capacity may be available for your application. Along the same lines, a higher-flow water pump may be available. There are many water pump options for the common American V-8. I recently swapped from a 66 to a 100 gallon-per-minute pump in one of my rigs and noticed a huge difference when towing. Sometimes speeding up the pump by reducing the water pump pulley size may be enough to improve water flow at low speeds. In some cases, an engine oil cooler may reduce cooling system load.

Exhaust system mods, such as headers and free-flowing exhausts, can sometimes provide a small to moderate cooling advantage because much of the engine's

TRAIL COOLING SYSTEMS:
One thing you have on a slow-moving trail that's not in the big city summer commute scenario is engine load from climbs and uneven terrain. A good cooling system is vital.

GENERIC STEEL TENSILE STRENGTH

SAE Steel Grade	Yield Strength (psi)
1040	106,000
1050	146,000
1541H	164,000
4340	210,000
300M	240,000

heat goes out the exhaust and reducing backpressure allows more heat to escape. Most other engine mods increase engine temperatures, so if you are having heat problems, these mods may have taken away some of your reserve.

Small items seen on many hard-core rigs are the so-called "Moab" rollers. Placed on areas that are guaranteed to touch in a tight clearance situation, they allow the offending part to glide rather than drag. In most cases, these are fabricated items. In this case, they were built by AOR (Advanced Off-Road Research) as a kit for Toyota trucks.

COMMON STEEL GROUPS

The SAE (Society of Automotive Engineers) and the ASM (American Society for Metals) use a common, four-digit rating system for steel. The first two numbers indicate the steel group, and the second two indicate the amount of carbon in percent, with a XX30 grade having 3 percent carbon. Carbon adds hardness and changes the heat-treating characteristics.

10XX, 11XX, 12XX, 15XX

The carbon steel group. Most standard OEM axles are 1040 grade, a few are 1050. OEM axles are generally heat-treated to 40 Rockwell in the center with the outer layer at 55–60 Rockwell to a depth of about 0.180 inch. These grades all carry from 1.00–1.65 percent manganese.

13XX

The manganese steel group contains 1.45–2.05 percent manganese. If it contains 1.6–2.05 percent of manganese, it can be called an alloy steel. This grade is used by aftermarket axle builders because the high manganese content allows for more flexibility during the heat-treating process.

"H" Rated

These steels contain a measure of silicon but otherwise match the composition of a standard type, such as 1340. Silicon comes from quartz and sand, and when mixed into steel it adds a measure of hardness. 1340H, for example, has 0.15–0.30 percent silicon.

"M" Rated

These are modified steel recipes that have been given slight enhancements to alter or improve some characteristics. You will see two such steels in the axle world, 1541M and 4340M (also known as 300M).

43XX, 47XX

The nickel-chromium-molybdenum group. An alloy containing 0.65–0.95 percent chromium, 0.2–0.3 percent molybdenum, and 1.55–2.0 percent nickel. Chromium increases hardness and the elastic limits (when the material is quenched), as well as increasing corrosion resistance. Molybdenum and nickel also increase hardness.

CHAPTER 8
Recovery Techniques: Inertially Challenged

If you four-wheel long enough, you're virtually guaranteed to get stuck. You may get a little anxious or frustrated the first time, but with experience, it becomes another part of the game and an interesting puzzle. Most recovery situations are minor events that you can handle easily when prepared and equipped. It can get more serious and difficult at times, but with the correct safety procedures in place and a clear head, you can free your rig without injury to people or the vehicle. The recovery learning curve is usually not steep, and you can learn as much from watching and helping others as you can from doing it yourself, or *for* yourself. Since *somebody* always seems to get stuck on just about every group trek, you'll get plenty of chances to learn.

Basic Recovery Doctrine

Obviously, the first consideration is safety. Choose the least dangerous method of recovery. It's better to leave a rig stuck for eternity than to hurt or kill someone. With safety first in your mind, determine the best way out. Is it forward or back? That decision goes beyond just finding the nearest piece of solid ground and a way around the obstacle. What's the trail like ahead? If a miles-long recovery slog looms ahead and a relatively easy drive back lies behind, which is best in your circumstance? If your destination lies ahead, do you have the time and equipment needed for a Camel Trophy–esque, hours-per-mile grind?

If you are traveling in a group, let your recovery method suit the group—within the limits of safety and common sense, of course. If you are a die-hard hand-wincher, for example, and enjoy spending hours cranking on a mechanical winch handle, the rest of the gang will either be comatose by the time you're done or they will have left you behind. It's an etiquette thing not to delay your comrades unnecessarily.

Basic Recovery Equipment

There is always a risk of carrying too much gear and getting stuck from the sheer tonnage of it! Tailor your gear to the trip. No chain saws in the desert, for example. Still, there are a few items on the "A" list that should be considered vital, and we'll run though them here. Winches are covered in a separate section.

Shovel. A basic must-have. There are many uses for a shovel in the 4×4 world, from recovery to camping. First, some shovel basics. Shovels come with square, pointed, or round heads. They come with long or short

Safety, or the lack thereof, is perennial. Even in 1919, recovery incidents occurred, and a lucky Army cameraman caught this shot just as the tow rope parted and a hapless GI was hurled aside. The fully loaded World War I–era 4×2 "Liberty" Model B military truck was on a coast-to-coast crossing of the United States that pre-ran the proposed route of the first transcontinental highway. It also tested the transport arm of the U.S. Army. *National Archives*

SHOVELS:
A short, D-handle shovel provides the most utility in the most compact, easy-to-carry package. It's sturdy, versatile, and easily stowed.

This photo shows the difference between a digging shovel, right, and one meant to move dirt. Both are useful in the four-wheeling world, but if you have either, you can tailor what you carry to the conditions. For sand, snow, and mud, the shoveling blade is best. For piercing hard ground and making holes, the digging blade works best.

handles, and some are folding handles. The round or pointed heads pierce the ground better, but the square point cuts roots better. Some shovels have a rather large head, and some are small. Some shovel heads are tilted and counterbalanced for shoveling rather than digging. The small- or medium-sized ones are the easiest to carry and are easier to use for digging in close quarters, such as under a vehicle. From my own experience, I prefer the round or pointed tip, since it can deal with hard ground better, and a shallow lift for digging. All types have a potential place in the four-wheeling world, but what you carry will at least partially be dictated by what you *can* carry.

The bare minimum for any rig is the ubiquitous folding GI entrenching tool. The GI shovel is convenient, easy to pack, and useful for close-in work, such as making a flat spot for a jack. It's a great investment because it folds and locks, so it can be used as both a shovel and a pick. The problem is the small size, which necessitates getting up close and personal with your "work." Many four-wheelers carry them along with a larger shovel.

Here are a few of your shovel choices. From left to right, A: D-handle round-point blade; B: D-handled spade with square point; C: folding GI shovel; D: long-handled round-point. A and D are high-lift blades for shoveling. B is for digging. The old GI shovel can be used any way, but it's usually an on-your-knees job.

Next up are the short, D-handle shovels. These are very sturdy, and while they take you a little farther away from your work, they still involve some stooping. They're small enough to make stowage fairly easy, but they are not quite long enough to reach under the middle of a bigger rig.

Finally, the long-handled shovel is the best for frequent or serious use, but it is the most difficult to stow. Get one with a beefy handle, since the extra leverage makes the long handle easy to break in hard use. People living in mud country are fond of these shovels because they use them the most.

Axes, Picks, and Saws. People who regularly travel wooded areas usually have an axe or saw along. Fallen trees and hanging limbs make these items a necessity for the woods runner. Often a small hatchet or small saw is sufficient. There are folding saws available that can take care of small limbs. Some folks carry

If you are regularly in the woods, a saw is a very useful tool. Here is a selection of what I carry at different times. At the bottom is a small multi-blade saw that is always in the vehicle's basic kit. It's useful for limbs and wood up to about 6 inches in diameter. The other two are just varying sizes of bow saws that I carry according to how big the trees may be. Some people actually carry chainsaws. That may seem like overkill from some perspectives, but I've seen them earn their keep.

SAFE SAWS:
Keep your saw or axe stowed securely no matter how often a wooded stretch has you reaching for it. The same applies to your shovel. You never want tools—or any solid object—going airborne.

PICKS:
Some folks carry picks. They can be useful in rare circumstances, but most often they'll just be added weight. A particularly extended and remote trip might be one venue where a pick is justified.

Axes are very useful in wooded areas. With a good axe, you can cut through nearly any size timber given enough time and energy. From left to right, A: large hatchet; B: a "boy's" axe; C: a full-sized axe. The hatchet rides with me all the time. When I lived in more wooded areas and had less space in my old rig, I carried the boy's axe because it was more compact. I seldom carry the big axe, but you can see it's been used as well.

full-blown axes or saws that would make a lumberjack smile. Some even carry chainsaws. Choose your weapon according to need, but don't overload. If you have to pick one item, a hatchet is often more useful as a single tool than a saw.

The Max. If you carry all the stuff listed above, you'll use up a fair bit of space. What if there was a universal tool that did it all? There is, and it's called the Max Multipurpose Tool. Designed for remote firefighters, it's a tool that has interchangeable heads that include an axe, shovel, rake, and pick. It doesn't work as well in each of its guises as the single-purpose tool would, but you can have them all at your fingertips, and it's easy to stow. Along the same lines, the Hi-Lift Jack Company has a multipurpose tool setup in the form of its Handle-All. It features four tools. The same caveat applies as with the Max.

Recovery Straps and Ropes. A recovery strap or rope is another must-have that is part of trail etiquette. Recovery straps or ropes are used in most situations because they're faster and simpler than a winch. There are times when the slow, deliberate action of the winch

The Max from the Forrest Tool Company is a multipurpose tool. The new units have a polycarbonate handle that's much stronger. The kit includes the axe, a small pointed shovel, a rake, a mattock, a broad pick, and a hoe. A leather axe sheath and canvas carrying case are included. It does just about everything, though not as well as a purpose-built tool. The axe stands up pretty well against other axes. This kit is great for all but those with specialized equipment needs. It's a great "one-size-fits-all" tool kit.

Here are two ways of achieving the same thing. You can see the difference in design between the strap and the double-braided rope. Straps are more easily obtained, but in my experience, most people who have tried both like the ropes better for snatch recovery. I have both and use a strap mostly for towing because it's a little more tolerant of chafing, as well as being cheaper to replace when it gets worn from dragging on the ground.

is better and safer, but my own observations (by no means scientific) show that a recovery strap/rope is the best option 80 percent of the time when you are with a group. Of course, with a recovery strap, you do need another vehicle!

At the early points of four-wheeling history, manila, hemp, or nylon hawsers (a hawser is another word for "big rope") were used. The nylon strap came into favor in the late 1960s and is now standard fare here in the United States. Elsewhere, recovery ropes (a.k.a. "K.E.R.R."—kinetic energy recovery rope) are more common. Rope is making a comeback here in the United States, mostly through the efforts of a company called Master Pull.

The theory behind both types is stretch. The elasticity does two things. First, it cushions the shock, lessening the chance of shock loads breaking parts. The second is that it stores energy. The stored energy effectively multiplies the force applied. Recovery straps, or ropes, can be used for just a simple pull or for what is commonly known as a "snatch," or kinetic energy recovery. More on that a bit further on.

Recovery Straps. Typical recovery straps are made of woven nylon webbing, often used in cargo handling, that has eyes stitched in both ends. Strap widths vary from 2 to 4 inches, with capacity rated according to this size. A common 2-inch strap is rated for about 15,000 pounds and a common 3-inch at 22,000 pounds. Lengths run from 20 to 30 feet.

Most sources say that recovery straps will stretch by 15–25 percent. These ratings come mostly from the material (nylon) rating and occasionally from tests of an actual strap. The elasticity, of course, is directly

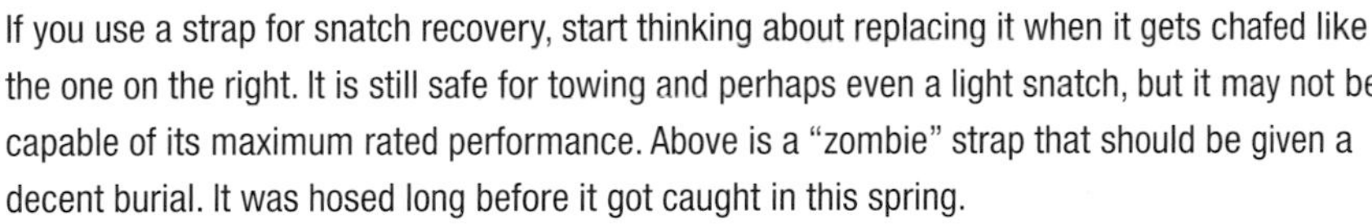

If you use a strap for snatch recovery, start thinking about replacing it when it gets chafed like the one on the right. It is still safe for towing and perhaps even a light snatch, but it may not be capable of its maximum rated performance. Above is a "zombie" strap that should be given a decent burial. It was hosed long before it got caught in this spring.

proportional to the amount of energy put into it and the strength rating of the strap. A strap with a lower load rating (e.g., a 2-inch strap versus a 3-inch) will stretch more than a higher-rated one when subjected to equal loads, but you need to make sure the strap is rated for 2–3 times the GVW of your rig to have a reserve of strength to account for wear.

Beyond the user tips you'll get further on, there are a few other less obviously common sense ones. A strap that's thoroughly wet is weaker by 10–15 percent than a dry one. If you must use it wet, factor the reduced strength into the pull. The material in a strap is weakened by long-term ultraviolet (UV) exposure, so keep it out of direct sunlight as much as possible. Higher-end straps have some UV protection built in, but why take the chance. Straps have a working life, even if they have no obvious damage. As the material ages, it becomes less flexible and more brittle. There's no easy way to test this at home, but reliable predictors are how much and how hard you work the strap. If you use it a bunch, consider replacing it every few years. One way to get the most mileage out of a strap is to "retire" a snatcher to lower-level tow strap duties when age makes it suspect.

There is a quality gap in strap manufacture. This is not so much with the strap material, which is largely generic, but with the stitching of the eye. To make the

RECOVERY STRAPS:
Better straps use nylon or another synthetic material for stitching. Anti-chafing material is usually sewn into the eye to reduce wear.

eye, the material is folded back, and the two pieces are stitched together. The quality of the stitching is vitally important, as is the material used for thread. In some cases, ordinary cotton is used, and it deteriorates with time and weakens when wet. Better straps use a synthetic material that does not deteriorate. There are no formal regulating agencies for the manufacture of recovery straps as there are for various industry lifting slings and straps, so the manufacturer or retailer is "on its honor" to supply a good product. That makes picking a strap somewhat a crapshoot. The odds move more in your favor with branded products from well-known and trustworthy manufacturers. The cheap "no-name" straps from those traveling tool shows are not always bad, but the odds that they will be are higher.

The care and feeding of recovery straps starts with cleanliness. Dirt is abrasive, and when it works into the material, it begins to "chew" the fibers of the material every time it's placed under load. The best way to clean a strap is to spray it with a hose nearly parallel to the surface so the dirt is washed off rather than into the material. Periodic inspection should also be a part of that care and feeding. Look at the stitched eyes in particular and for any damaged sections. Some straps have indicators built in that will show if the strap has been stretched past its safe limit. The indicator is typically a brightly colored thread woven into the material that will break and fray when the strap is stretched too far.

Recovery Ropes. Recovery ropes come in many forms, from the three-strand nylon ropes to double-braided rope. The double-braided material is what's on the market now, though three-strand is every bit its equal. Viking Offroad ropes, for example, run from ¾ to 1 inch in diameter and from 19,000 to 33,500 pound ratings. As with straps, common lengths run from 20–30 feet, but you can order longer. Just like straps, the ropes are rated to stretch, in this case from 15 percent to nearly 30 percent on average. The quality gap with ropes concerns the way the eyes are spliced, but splicing is inherently stronger than any other way of making an eye and is generally more reliable than a stitched eye in a strap. Recovery ropes should have some sort of chafing guard in the eye. Care and feeding of a recovery rope largely follows the doctrine above for straps. Keep it clean and inspect it regularly.

The correct method of connecting two straps or, in this example, two Master Pull Yanker ropes. Lay the ropes parallel to each other. Run the eye of line 2 through the eye of line 1 and pull it all the way to the other end of line 1. Now feed the eye of line 1 through the eye of line 2 and pull it through. When you are done pulling, the two eyes will meet like this. If you put the stick between the eyes as shown, it will prevent them from become semi-permanently knotted when put under a strain. Because there is no strain and the stick is carrying no load, you can use anything from a rolled up magazine to a stick. Best to keep the item light to avoid the potential of the missile effect. I like the stick because it can be used to pry if the ropes are really pulled tight. The lanyard on the stick allows you to attach the stick to one of the ropes so it won't be lost.

Recovery Ropes Versus Straps. Controversy is growing as to which type is better for recovery. At the moment, the people I know who have tested both prefer ropes. The consensus is that rope's increased elasticity absorbs shocks better. You can feel more of a jolt snatching with a strap than with a rope. Another advantage to rope is that the spliced eyes retain the strength of the rope, whereas the stitched eyes of the strap are not as strong as the strap itself. The stitching creates a weak spot on the strap material. A braided rope is often more than twice the price of a strap, but the performance is not three times better (maybe two times).

A Word on Chains and Wire Rope for Recovery. Some four-wheelers still rely on chains or wire rope for recovery. This is not good because they can add greatly to the danger aspect. There is zero give in chain and very little in wire rope. That means every shock and jerk is transmitted to the towing points, and this can break stuff. Many four-wheelers will not hook up to a chain to tow you out. The one good thing about chain is that when it breaks, or breaks an attachment, it's largely dead and drops immediately. Chains are useful for creating an attachment point in an area not equipped with one, as well as for making an attachment point on surfaces like rocks or (dead) logs that would damage a tree strap.

Tow Straps/Ropes. Tow straps or ropes are similar to the recovery straps and ropes, but they are usually of less capacity and have less elasticity. They are often shorter as well and are used primarily to tow a disabled vehicle from one point to another. They are preferable to a chain or cable in this role because their elasticity absorbs shock loads. Unfortunately, some people confuse snatch and tow straps and try to use the average tow strap for recovery, often with disastrous results. A quality tow strap may be up for some recovery work (a simple tow-out rather than a snatch) if it has a high enough weight rating, but it will be either too weak or not tensile enough for an all-out snatch. The worst possible solution is one of those cheap, packaged tow straps with hooks built into each end that are commonly available in department stores or discount auto parts stores. They break easily in the 4×4 realm, sometimes with dangerous results.

If you have a snatch strap or rope, you may be tempted to use it for a tow rope. It works fine that way, but along the way it may chafe on the ground, snag things, and otherwise suffer abuse that can weaken it. When you need it most in the snatching role, where 100 percent strength equals safely, you may not then be able to depend on it. Better to have a dedicated tow strap or "retire" an old snatch strap or rope to towing duties as noted above.

Jacks. The very least you'll need is an OE-style telescoping jack to change flat tires. The problem is that if you upgrade tire size, the OE jack may not have enough lift; an embarrassing situation if you didn't think of it beforehand. Also, OE jacks run from OK to utterly cheeseball. The old OE bumper jacks are usually dangerous, especially on a loaded rig. You can upgrade those old units with a telescoping jack as necessary, perhaps with a hydraulic unit. Many people opt for the legendary Hi-Lift jack.

The so-called "sheepherder's" or Hi-Lift jack is a useful upgrade. Hi-Lift is the name brand that has become a noun for any jack of this type made by a variety of manufacturers. The original Hi-Lift has been in production since 1905 and has spawned many copies. Hi-Lift jacks come in a variety of heights and weight ratings. The actual Hi-Lift brand lifts 7,000 pounds and comes in four sizes: 36-inch, 42-inch, 48-inch, and 60-inch. The slick part is that one can also be used as a manual 7,000-pound winch that will pull (or push) you 3–4 feet at a time. It isn't as easy as an electric winch, but it gets the job done. Storage and weight can be a problem in some rigs, but many rack and bumper manufacturers offer built-in storage brackets for them.

With any mechanical jack, you need to have a 1×1-foot piece of wood, or larger, for a base to prevent your jack from burying itself in soft ground. Marine plywood, at least ¾-inch thick, is best because it doesn't split. The Hi-Lift Jack Company makes a base especially for its jacks made out of molded, high-strength plastic. Hi-Lift also offers a variety of accessories that make your Hi-Lift more versatile.

There are also exhaust jacks, a.k.a. "bag jacks." They are large, very durable "balloons" that you fill with exhaust from your tailpipe. They work well and stow

PAVEMENT ENDS

CHAINS FOR RECOVERY:
If cable or chain is the only recovery option, make sure you (or the other driver) take up all the slack and apply a load before making the pull. Keep tension on the line at all times to avoid shock-loading the recovery point. Chains are most useful for fabricating an attachment point where hooking up a strap or winch cable directly would cause damage.

The Handle-All is a new multi-tool from Hi-Lift and includes a shovel, axe, sledgehammer, and pick, all contained in a soft case. Comparisons to the trusty Max will be inevitable. The selection of tools in the Handle-All is more 4×4 oriented, and the kit is more compact, albeit considerably heavier. I've never used the mattock, rake, or hoe in the Max kit. The Handle-All has a much better shovel than the Max, but the Max has a way better axe. The sledge is also very useful on the Handle-All. In use, the metal handle of the Handle-All tends to transmit a lot more shock when whaling on something than the wood or polycarbonate handle on the Max, so thick gloves are recommended. To answer the inevitable question, yes, the handle on the Handle-All will fit the Hi-Lift Jack, but the tool heads won't work on the Hi-Lift handle. When I add everything up, the Max and Handle-All are about even, but I give the Handle-All a slight edge because of its more useful selection of tools.

easily. They have a very broad footprint and could be very useful in soft ground of all types. They have long been in favor in places like Australia and Africa. ARB USA markets one in North America under the "X-Jack" name, and it will lift 8,800 pounds 31 inches.

Non-Winch Recovery Techniques

All of these involve recovery by "armstrong," that is, they take a certain amount of manual labor. In some cases they are alternatives to the use of mechanical devices. In others, these techniques are the best or the only solution to certain problems.

Sometimes all a rig needs is a tiny bit of momentary help, and this is the fast, time-tested, and simplest way. Just make sure the operation is coordinated with the driver.

The Manhandle. When the original jeep was designed in 1940, one of the design criteria was that it be light and small enough to be "manhandled" out of any situation by no more than four soldiers. In World War II, there were few purpose-built vehicle-recovery aids available, but even today, with all the great technology, it can still come down to human grunt. When a vehicle needs just a bit of help, the simplest solution may be for a couple of strong backs to give it a shove. In some cases, the manhandle is necessary only because some or all of those modern conveniences have been left behind. Ahem!

Simple and easy doesn't always mean safe. From the day the first stuck Jeep was manhandled out of a tricky spot, people have been getting injured doing it. It's important that the actions be coordinated and that the driver knows exactly what to do. Imagine a group running to push a rig up a slippery ledge, only to have an unaware driver decide to back out at that moment. Common sense also counsels people not to push or lift beyond their physical abilities. Don't expect four people to be able to lift the back end of a Suburban out of a hole. A Samurai, maybe.

Manhandling comes in several forms, starting with the ordinary push. A vehicle having traction problems and unable to move ahead can be given a shove by as few as one person, or by as many people as can find a spot to push. It takes very little time, and the rig is on its way quickly and easily.

The next common form of manhandling is the counterbalance. A rig on the edge of tipping over may

Here is the wrong way to counterbalance a rig, left, and the right way. The guys hanging on the old Rover are in danger of being bucked off by sudden movement or hurled some distance if the vehicle goes over and they can't get clear. The guys helping the Jeep are much safer. If the rig goes over, they can walk forward or let go of the strap.

A pullout recovery on a rutted muddy track is under way. The towing vehicle has straddled the ruts to get plenty of traction.

need only a little extra weight on the high side to be secure. You will occasionally see people hanging all over a tilted rig. You may also see them hurled off by the sudden movements of the vehicle as it tries to drive out. The safest way to counterbalance is not by hanging on directly but by attaching a strap to a high point on the vehicle and having the helpers hold the vehicle secure with it. You can get more people on a rope or strap than you can hang off a vehicle, or you can hook the strap to another vehicle or to a solid anchor point. If the rig ultimately goes over, all the people have to do is let go of the strap or walk forward. Never, ever, should anyone try to hold the vehicle up from the low side. Overall, it's better to let the rig go over than to get people injured in a vain attempt to save it.

A few burly souls can often roll a tipped rig back onto its wheels. Again, this is best done with bodies pulling on a strap or rope. When people are too close to a rolled rig being righted, they have a bad habit of getting hurt. The strap moves them away from the source of possible injury, and if something bad occurs, all they have to do is let go of the strap.

TOWING:
The towed vehicle should avoid running over the tow rope if possible. It won't hurt necessarily to have it under the vehicle, just not under the tires. Getting it under the tire often breaks the rope.

Pull-Out Recovery

A pull-out is often confused with a snatch. A simple pull-out, even if you are using a snatch strap, is not really a snatch. In that case, you are merely using the traction of another vehicle to aid one that is having difficulty. When the towing vehicle cannot generate the traction to pull the stranded rig out, that's when the snatch comes in. Read on.

Pull-outs are done slowly and gently by putting the towing vehicle on the best ground for traction and coordinating the pull with help from the vehicle in difficulty. All the stuff we talked about with regard to hookup points applies. The rope is attached, and the towing vehicle applies tension. At the command of a remotely sited spotter who will coordinate the recovery, both rigs will apply power.

The towed rig needs to go lightly on the throttle, just below the point of tire spin, or just very slowly turning the tires. Spinning wildly will cause the vehicle to leap ahead when it does find traction. The towing vehicle needs to apply a steady pull, using all the traction available but below the point of spinning the tires excessively. The vehicle may slip a tire here and there, but if you are making progress, stick with it. If you are sitting there merely spinning rubber, it's time for another idea before something breaks. Try to keep tension on the rope until it's clear that the stranded rig is out of trouble. This prevents the towed rig from running over the rope.

Snatch Recovery. The snatch, or kinetic-energy recovery is a tricky operation that should not be undertaken lightly. When a simple pull-out attempt

A bad place to break! The Hi-Lift can be used for vehicle repairs, in this case a broken front axle shaft. It's used to get the front wheels off the ground, and the Jeep is kept from rolling off the jack by the winch cable. Once the wheel was removed, it was strategically placed to act as a jack stand.

will not do the job, the possibility of a snatch can be considered. At that point, the smart first step is to look around for a winch. A winching operation is always preferable to a snatch. Why? Winching is a slower, more controlled operation and therefore safer. A snatch involves vehicles at speed and requires split-second timing and coordination. There's lots of energy at work, and if it goes awry, bad stuff happens. That said, the snatch is much faster, less complicated, and more appealing to people wanting to maximize fun time. In deciding on a snatch or a winch operation, ask the following:

- Do both rigs have very good towing points?
- Is the area clear? Tight quarters make the operation trickier.
- What are the ground conditions? Be less inclined to snatch in rocky terrain because of the danger of running the rig into rocks and the wheel blocking effect. Example: Don't try to snatch a rig up a ledge unless the height of the ledge is well below the height of the hub. If the ledge is higher than the hub, it becomes a *very* effective wheel block.

If, in light of these questions, you determine that a snatch is safe and practical, get the rigs properly attached (check the "Hookups" section in the winching area for some ideas on attachments) and clear the area of people. If possible, use an outside spotter, located in a safe spot that both drivers can see, to coordinate the operation. The two drivers can do it, but an outside person can do it better. The towing vehicle will back toward the stranded vehicle a few feet, and the strap or rope will be laid out on the ground so that it will pay out cleanly and not kink. On command, the stranded rig will apply a little power, and the towing rig will launch forward at a fast walking pace. The slack will come out, and the strap will rapidly come to attention and stretch like a rubber band. The energy of the towing vehicle in motion is multiplied by the elasticity of the strap, and, in theory, the stranded rig leaps from its predicament like a cat that falls into a bathtub.

What if it doesn't? The level of energy can be ratcheted up as much as the participants dare by applying more speed and distance. Backing up more and applying more speed will up the energy level considerably. The danger is that the energy will exceed the capacity of the strap or the towing points on either or both vehicles. That's where it gets dangerous.

How much speed or energy is enough? That point is variable according to the strap rating, the towing points of both vehicles, and the relative weights of the vehicles. It's so variable that it's hard to give a number. Most experts recommend speeds of no more than a fast walking pace and backing no more than one-quarter to one-third the length of the strap. You will see people use more energy than that, but within the speed and distance limits mentioned, assuming excellent towing points and a strap in good condition, you should be safe.

Especially with a strap, make sure it's not twisted when put under load. That puts additional strain on the material and can reduce its capacity. With either a strap or rope, lay it on the ground so it will pay out cleanly. For a serous snatch, avoid hooking two straps together if you can. If you need a longer strap or rope, do not connect two of them with a shackle or other heavy item. This just adds to the deadly missile effect if the strap or an attachment breaks. If you insist, against

HI-LIFT HI-JINX

The Hi-Lift can be used as a winch as well as a jack. Hi-Lift has a special Off Road Kit (see inset) that makes hookups easy, though you can use your own shackles and choker chain. First hook up to the dead man (in this case a tree; always use a tree strap) via a section of transport chain with hooks (1). Then connect the attachment bracket (3) with its section of chain over the lifting nose of the jack. Point the top end of the jack (4) to the vehicle that needs to be moved and connect the jack and vehicle with a strap, rope, or chain. The jack is lowered to the bottom of travel, and the chain on the attachment bracket is connected to the chain on the dead man side, taking up as much slack as possible. Now you can start winching. The short chain attached to the beam (2) is the winch tensioner. When you run out of travel on the beam, this allows you to maintain tension while repositioning the jack runner.

This is what happens when the bumper isn't up to supporting the weight of the vehicle.

If you don't have good bumper jacking spots or have a long-travel suspension, the Lift-Mate allows you lift via the wheel.

In soft ground, you need a base with a large footprint to keep the jack from sinking. You can use a section of 1-inch-thick plywood, but Hi-Lift also offers this high-strength plastic base.

This adapter from Hi-Lift allows it to be used on curved bumpers.

The Jack Mate slips onto the lower end of a Hi-Lift and provides a purchase on things like this knob on a boulder. It's lifting up the heavy front of the author's rig here during a test. It works! Note the eye for a shackle and the chain slot.

The long-arm suspension on this Jeep TJ was way too flexy to get the wheel off the ground when a repair was needed, so the suspension was chained up to limit downtravel, and that allowed the wheel to come off the ground.

KINETIC ENERGY DANGERS:
If a stretched rope or strap breaks, it will send its loose ends and any shackle or broken attachment point flying at speeds in excess of 100 miles per hour. Such projectiles can go through glass like air and punch through a body panel like an armor-piercing antitank shell. Keep yourself and other people well clear of towlines at all times and exercise equal care at the wheel.

all logic, to use a metallic connection, at least put a blanket or damper over it.

The best way to connect two straps, or ropes, (shown in a nearby photo) is to lay them side by side and feed the end of the first strap (strap 1) through the eye of the other (strap 2). Do the opposite on the other end, feeding the end of strap 2 through the eye of strap one. Pull them through each other until the eyes meet. The photos will make this clearer, but in the end you have a very strong connection. The problem is that, with a strong tug, the two eyes may be about impossible to separate afterward. If you place a 6- to 10-inch piece of hardwood between the two, you will likely be able to pry the two apart. Straps are usually harder to get apart than ropes. Some straps have eyes too small to feed the straps through easily.

Jacking Out of Trouble. This applies mostly to the sheepherder's jacks made by the Hi-Lift Jack Company and others. The techniques you'll see listed here are commonly used on the trail but are not always advocated by the jack manufacturer.

The first requirement for a sheepherder's jack is that your vehicle can safely use one without damage. Many modern rigs cannot because they don't have solid bumpers or jacking points. There are a few adapters available that can fill the gaps in some vehicle applications, but sometimes the only alternative is a replacement heavy-duty bumper or custom-built brackets. Check on your rig's suitability before shelling out for a Hi-Lift. In some cases, you can use a worm or hydraulic jack to lift a rig out of a hole or rut, but obviously, the degree of difficulty is higher, and the danger may be greater. Necessity is the mother of invention when you don't have the right tools, but think safe whatever you do.

Since Hi-Lifts come in various jacking heights, you need one that fits your rig. They all are rated for approximately the same weight capacity, but the amount of lift differs. A stock rig could use one of the shorter jacks, but a tall, big-tired rig will need the taller unit for obvious reasons. You need enough lift to reach the jacking point, account for suspension travel, and lift the rig clear of the problem.

Some rigs have so much suspension droop that the jack cannot go high enough to get a wheel off the ground. There are two solutions: One is to chain or strap the suspension at ride height so that it can't droop when you lift the vehicle; the other is to use Hi-Lift's Lift-Mate, which allows you to lift the vehicle by the wheel.

The most common scenarios for using a sheepherder's jack for recovery are for a vehicle sunk deeply into soft ground or hung up on an obstacle. The jack is placed to lift one end of the rig up out of the ruts or holes, which are then filled in. On soft ground, the jack will need a base to avoid sinking into the ground. Usually a 1-foot-square piece of flat material will work, but on extremely soft ground you might need something bigger.

The danger with a rig jacked up without the safety of stands is that the jack can release (not likely with a HD unit like a Hi-Lift, but possible), or the vehicle can roll off the jack. For that reason, the rig must be secured from rolling away from the jack or off to the side. Blocking the tires will keep it from rolling away, and a strap (or straps) from another rig or secured to a tree will keep it from rolling off to the side. Keep the jack handle in the up position, which locks the mechanism. Regardless of these precautions, *nobody* goes underneath the rig!

There is an unauthorized, but useful, technique called the "jack-n-drop." The vehicle is jacked up out of the holes or ruts and allowed (or encouraged) to roll off the jack to one side. In theory, the tires end up on solid ground. It works, most times at least, but it's hard on the jack. The manufacturers don't like to take responsibility for a jack broken this way, not to mention be liable for injuries. I've done it, but my opinion is that it's a lazy way to do the job. A responsible 'wheeler is going to fill the tire holes anyway, so why not start off that way?

Soft Ground Support. It's one thing to get stuck in a small hole, but it's another to face an endless sea of soft stuff. One method of support on soft ground is the use of sand ladders or planks. Sand ladder is the common name for PSP (perforated steel planking), or PAP (perforated aluminum planking), which is used by the military for building remote airfields. This is great and useful stuff in the right venue, but few four-wheelers have the need or the carrying space. It looks cool if you have a place to carry it.

The idea is to pave the soft stuff with material to spread the weight of the vehicle over a larger area. A short stretch may be needed, or a long one. Given a finite length of available material, it would be necessary to keep moving planks from behind to the front in a continual motion. In some parts of the world, four-wheelers have done this for miles at a stretch.

Alternatives? Use natural building materials. This could include logs and sticks. If you do, make them relatively short so they won't flip up and cause damage. Use only deadwood, please, and clean up the area up when finished.

Slippery Stuff. There are places where the ground surface will support a vehicle's weight but won't provide traction. Ice is the usual suspect, but greasy mud can play the same trick. On ice, some sand, dirt, or branches thrown on top can get you moving. The branches will work in mud, as can small rocks. For lack of anything else, your floor mats, tent, or clothing can work if you're prepared to write them off afterward.

Tire chains are probably the best bet. They bite into ice, and they work like paddles in greasy mud. There are mud chains and ice chains; the mud units use a chain with larger links. The ice chains will work OK in mud, but the mud chains aren't suited to icy highways.

Towing. This usually involves towing a disabled or partially disabled rig back to civilization. Bear in mind that many states do not allow rope tows on the highway, so you can expect some attention from the local constabulary if you drag a dead rig into town on the highway at the end of a rope. Bear in mind that vehicles with automatic transmissions should not be towed long distances unless they have a true neutral position on the transfer case or the driveshafts are removed to prevent the transmission from turning internally. Without the engine running, there is no internal lubrication for the parts that are in motion, so hard-parts failure occurs in fairly short order.

The strap needs to be long enough to leave time for the towed driver to react but short enough to keep both rigs on roughly the same section of the road. Fifteen to 20 feet seems a workable length, but longer can work as well. The shortening options are to tie a knot in the strap, which is not a good idea because they are almost impossible to undo, or to double the strap into a "Y," with the single leg at the towing vehicle and the double at the towed rig. Recovery ropes are a bit more tolerant of knots—simply tie a bowline to shorten the

JACKING:
If the vehicle is on an incline, jacking is very dangerous. Look for another way to solve the problem, such as one of the other recovery methods discussed in this chapter.

ROAD BUILDING:
To cross a stretch of soft ground, you could do what the old miners did in the Colorado mountains. They paved the roads with logs, and the practice was called corduroy. Some of that work is still there a hundred years later.

TIRE CHAINS:
Chains are truly remarkable in mud. You might even try them *before* you get stuck!

GOOD ATTACHMENTS, BAD ATTACHMENTS

So-So Attachment. The eye of the strap is inserted into the Class III receiver, and the receiver is pushed through the eye. This makes for a quick, economical attachment. This is a good attachment if the pin is a good one. A cheap pin may bend and be nearly impossible to remove. There is also some danger of chafing at extreme angles, but an advantage is that there is no heavy metal attached to the strap end to become a cannonball when something fails at this end.

Good Attachment. This receiver attachment from Warn is designed for use with a ¾-inch D-shackle rated for a safe working load of 13,000 pounds. Other manufacturers offer similar products. This is a stout setup, offset only by the remote possibility that an attachment failure at a high load could turn this hunk of metal into a cannonball.

So-So Attachment. In the absence of other proper hookups, this would be at the bottom end of acceptable. If the ball did shear off, it would be pulled forward.

Bad Attachment. When fed through a bow shackle for a double-leg pull, the main section of this 3-inch strap has a case of the "scrunchies" and would be weakened on a hard pull.

Bad Attachment. Double bad! A chain hooked to a trailer ball. How much worse can it get? The guy was thinking a little, though, and tried to loop the chain around the back of the drop hitch.

Bad Attachment. Not only is this a not-so-stout Class II receiver, the strap is hooked to a hitch ball. First off, the strap can slip off. Second, the 1⅞-inch ball can break off because of shock loads or overloading and become a cannonball.

Bad Attachment. Lots to talk about here! First is that the bumper probably isn't strong enough to handle a strong pull. Second, the sharp edges at the back of the bumper could cut the strap even if the bumper held on a hard pull. Third, where are this guy's tow hooks?!

Bad Attachment. The only bad part of this could be the inability to get the knot undone after a hard pull.

Good Attachment. This Crosby web shackle, available from Quadratec and other places, is ideal when you need to use the wide section of a strap, as in a towing bridle. This is a handy recovery item to have in the toolbox.

Bad Attachment. Factory tie-down points do not make suitable recovery points. They are designed to hold down one corner of the vehicle during transport. This one is already tweaked and is an accident waiting to happen.

strap. The tow strap should be moused (see "Hookups" in the winching section) to prevent it from falling off the towing attachment. Avoid dragging the rope or strap on the ground. Chafing will weaken it. The pace? Slow. Dead slow, as conditions warrant.

Towing requires a great deal of attention from both drivers. If the towed vehicle has an operable engine, it's best to have it running to supply power steering and brakes. Otherwise, both drivers should be aware that some extra arm and leg muscle will be required to steer or brake. The goal of both drivers is to keep tension on the tow rope. That means the towed rig will be using a lot of brakes and the towing rig will be gentle with speed changes and will clearly signal stops and turns. A CB is great for this, and you can and should also use mutually agreed-upon hand signals. Avoid running over the strap or putting abrupt tension on it. The towed rig driver will be busy enough to feel like the proverbial one-armed paperhanger!

Very rough ground, where the terrain must be covered extremely slowly, can be problematic. In steep terrain, the towing rig may not have the traction to pull the dead rig up a slope. In these cases, a winch or a second vehicle attached to the towing rig can supply the extra muscle needed. Turns can also be a problem; the towed and towing rigs must coordinate a line around tight corners. A long strap complicates turns.

Winches and Winching

This section encompasses all types of winching, both power and manual. We'll cover most types of power winches, though the manufacturer's instructions will take precedence when they differ from what you read here. We'll also show a few types of manual winches. While winching techniques are similar for all types, we'll give a few specifics on operating each kind.

Manual Winches. These run the gamut from the ordinary "come-along" that's available from the hardware store to some pretty fancy units that cost more than some power winches. Manual winches share one thing: The need for human strength. The mechanical advantage provided by some is such that they are not a huge strain to operate. Others will definitely get your sweat glands into operation.

There are still a number of four-wheelers who rely solely on a manual winch and their own strength for recovery. Stout-hearted souls, every one! There are other 'wheelers with power winches who use the manual winch as a backup. The manual winch can provide an additional source of power in complicated

The Superwinch EP Series planetary winches are well suited to synthetic winch ropes because they use an external brake located at the end of the planetary gear housing. No heat is generated in the drum like most planetary designs with drum brakes.

Worm-gear winches are a viable alternative for those who value brute strength and longevity over line speed. The Superwinch Husky 10 is one of the few surviving worm-gears still on the market. The Husky was used on most years of the Camel Trophy, and in many cases, the winches were transferred from one worn-out Camel Trophy Land Rover to the new replacement. Only a couple failed over the many years of Camel. Because the worm-gear drivetrain acts as a natural brake, these winches are ideally suited to synthetic rope.

recovery situations where pulls might be needed from more than one location. This is a rare event but is more likely in certain types of terrain. I see it used most in wooded hill and mountain country.

Manual Winch Advantages

1) Usually lower cost than a power winch.
2) Light weight.
3) Can be used anywhere; front, rear, or sides.
4) Can be left at home when not needed.
5) Good backup for power winch.

Manual Winch Disadvantages
1) They are, well, *manual!*
2) Usually they are lower capacity than power winches.
3) Require operator to be closer to cable.
4) They are slow.
5) They can be forgotten at home.
6) Those with built-in cable drums are short on cable.

Suggested Use
1) Primary recovery in low-cost situations.
2) Second source of pulling power for hard-core 'wheelers.

Power Winches. A power winch is operated by some type of motor, whether it be electric, hydraulic, or the vehicle engine via a PTO (power take-off). These are the three major divisions, but ultimately, the vehicle's engine powers all of them, directly or indirectly. If the engine is dead, the winch will be dead sooner or later.

Mechanical. Mechanical winches were once the standard. Some early winches were driven directly by the engine, but later ones use the transfer case or the transmission PTO drive points. They still have a place in commercial situations because of their nearly unlimited duty cycle. They are less popular with recreational users.

Because most PTO winches are powered through the transmission, they have as many speeds as the transmission has gears. The transfer case is not a factor, even if the PTO is driven from there, because it draws power from the transmission output shaft. In this case, the forward gears spool the winch in, and reverse spools it out. At any given engine speed, the winch is slower (and more powerful) in first gear than it is in high gear. PTOs may also be driven from certain heavy-duty manual transmissions via an access port in the side of the case.

The MileMarker hydraulic debuted in 1994 and offered recreational four-wheelers a shot at the utility and precision of a hydraulic winch. These units are powered by the vehicle's power steering pump.

Mechanical Winch Advantages
1) Longevity due to simple, robust construction.
2) Can be used for long periods at a stretch. Nearly unlimited duty cycle.
3) Flexible line speeds according to transmission gearing and engine speed. In high gear and at up to 2,000 rpm engine speed, they are the fastest winches.
4) Often have a large cable capacity.
5) Waterproof operation.
6) Very powerful.

Mechanical Winch Disadvantages
1) More difficult to use alone.
2) More difficult to use, period.
3) If the engine doesn't run, neither does the winch.
4) Increased maintenance, i.e., lubing driveshaft U-joints, oil in gearboxes.
5) Increased weight of unit.
6) Few choices available, few mounting kits available, and many newer rigs cannot be fitted because of lack of PTO driving points.
7) Complicated installation.
8) Relatively high cost.

Suggested Use
1) Owners who regularly work their winches for long periods.
2) Commercial applications.

Desirable or Necessary Improvements
(N = Necessary, D = Desirable)
1) Synthetic oil in gearboxes to reduce friction. (D)
2) Improved engine cooling system for heavy loads at prolonged low rpm. (D)

WINCHES:
The most recent feature added to the planetary gear winches is external brakes. These are totally safe for the use of synthetic winch rope.

The perennial favorite in recreational four-wheeling is the electric winch. It is inexpensive and light, and it comes in a huge variety of weight ratings up to about 15,000 pounds. Winches under a 6,000-pound rating should not really be considered, with the exception of extremely light vehicles. The "average" 4×4 should have an 8,000-pound winch, or more, depending on vehicle weight. This is a recent-vintage Warn 9.5ti mounted to one of Quadratec's fleet of built Jeeps. It is fitted with synthetic winch rope and an aluminum hawse fairlead. The Warn 9.5ti is a thermometric winch that has a motor temperature indicator on the control. Note the standard galvanized thimble spliced into the eye of the sling-style hook. A hook with the ability to close is an asset because it's not as likely to fall off at an inopportune time.

Hydraulic Winches. Hydraulic winches have been available for many years but were not generally used in the recreational market until the MileMarker unit appeared in 1995. The hydraulic power needed to run the winch can be supplied by an electrically driven pump, an engine-driven pump (either a belt-driven hydraulic pump or the power steering pump), or by a PTO-driven hydraulic pump.

Hydraulic winches are known for their ability to tolerate long duty cycles. They can have as long a duty cycle as a PTO winch, though there's some chance of overheating the hydraulic fluid. Commercial hydraulics are generally worm-gear units (essentially a PTO winch with a hydraulic motor), while the MileMarker (designed for the recreational market) is a planetary unit, essentially a planetary drive winch with a hydraulic motor.

Operation is similar to an electric winch with a few differences. MileMarker's two-speed has great pulling power in low, and the line speed at full load is good. When it comes to spooling in and rewinding cable or light pulls, using the high setting gives line speed that competes with the best of the recreational winches. The single-speed hydraulics aren't much faster with no load than with a full load, but while they may be slow spooling in empty, they are among the faster units with a load. Until another company comes out with a hydraulic winch for the recreational vehicle crowd, when we talk about hydraulics, we're essentially talking about the MileMarker.

Hydraulic Winch Advantages

1) Long duty cycle.
2) Waterproof operation.
3) Easy solo operation.
4) Simple installation.
5) Low weight.
6) Low maintenance.
7) Low electrical load.
8) Relatively low cost.
9) Precise control.
10) Fast line speed under load.

Hydraulic Winch Disadvantages

1) Slower line speed unloaded (single speed only).
2) When the engine doesn't run, neither does the winch.
3) Not suitable for all vehicles. Some do not have a sufficiently powerful power steering pump.

WINCH SAFETY:
Always wear gloves when working with wire rope. Broken strands can hook the skin and really tear up your hands.

WINCHING HALL OF FAME AND SHAME

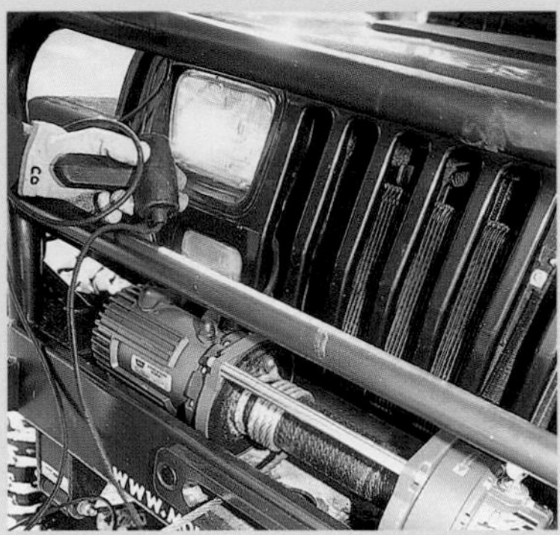

Fame. There are five wraps left on the drum, just enough to carry a full load. Poly rope needs two or three more wraps (seven or eight total) to hold adequately.

Shame. Unless you want your hands to look like raw hamburger, use gloves.

Fame. Checking the winch motor temp during a long, hard pull will preserve the equipment. If it's too hot to touch with a bare hand, it's too hot to use. Let it cool and let the battery charge.

Shame. This wire rope is history and shouldn't be used. It has lost a major portion of its strength at this point, and a full winch load may well break it.

Fame. Using a tree strap saves the tree for later enjoyment.

Shame. Hooking a wire rope back onto itself is a sure path to ruined rope and possibly a major failure.

Fame. Putting a damper on a highly stressed winch line is good insurance. If the cable or attachments break, the damper will help slow the cable down.

Shame. Routing a bare cable around a rock is asking for chafing damage or outright failure.

Fame. Route the winch control wire carefully to keep it clear of the winch drum and the tires.

Fame. Hook up to a rated shackle attached to a solid mounting point on a bumper that was designed for the purpose.

Fame. A piece of wood can be used as chafing protection.

Shame. When the spinning tires of this vintage Jeep flatfender hook up, it's going to leap far ahead of the Pierce Winch 9,000-pound unit, possibly overrunning the cable. All you need to do is give the winch a little assist. This worm-gear winch is so powerful that this driver could probably stand on the brakes and still be winched out.

Fame. It's best not to cross a loaded winch cable, but if you must, step on it as Bill Burke demonstrates, but only if the cable is stationary. This way, if something were to happen, you would simply be hurled aside rather than cut in half the hard way.

Fame. The proper way to butterfly a winch cable. It's much easier than respooling when winching situations are frequent. The key element is to make sure the cable will stay in place.

Shame. This brand-new wire rope was badly kinked against a sharp edge and broke under a strain. Luckily, nobody was hurt, and no other equipment was damaged.

Suggested Use
1) Vehicle recovery or work where long duty cycle, or precise control, is needed.

Desirable or Necessary Improvements (MileMarker)
(N = Necessary, D = Desirable)
1) Flush power steering fluid. (N)
2) Power steering cooler on return line. (D)
3) Improved engine cooling system for prolonged low-speed operation. (D)

Electric Winches. Electrics have all but taken over the recreational four-wheeling market and for good reason. They are lightweight, easy to operate, and easy to install. For the four-wheeler who needs occasional help out of sticky situations, they are a good choice. Currently, a wide variety of choices are available in terms of mounting systems, winch ratings, and winch performance.

There is a wide range of durability in the electric winch world. Most are best-suited for occasional recovery use and have a short duty cycle. The short duty cycle isn't a problem as long as you give the motor time to cool and the battery time to recharge. The upper-echelon electric winches have a longer duty cycle in terms of the motor's capacity to endure heat, but the electrical system drain can still be a problem without extra mods.

Electric Winch Advantages
1) Light weight.
2) Easy installation.
3) Easy operation.
4) Lowest cost.
5) Will run for a short while without the engine running (up to 5 minutes at a full load, depending on battery).
6) Widest range of applications.

WINCH SAFETY:
You must keep an absolute minimum of five wraps on the winch drum for wire rope and eight for synthetic. Any less may not be able to hold the load. The eyelet on the end of the cable or rope is not designed to hold much of a load. The correct number of wraps will bite into the drum and grip securely.

Electric Winch Disadvantages
1) Short duty cycle.
2) Severe loads on electrical system that can cause battery or alternator failure if duty cycle is exceeded.
3) Motors subject to overheating and failure if duty cycle exceeded.
4) Can be ruined by water.

Desirable or Necessary Improvements (MileMarker)
(N = Necessary, D = Desirable)
1) Increased-capacity battery. (N)
2) Deep-cycle battery. (D)
3) Dual batteries, one being an isolated deep-cycle. (D)
4) High output, continuous-duty alternator. (D)

Electric Winch Drivetrains. Three basic types of drivetrains have stood the test of time—spur gear, worm gear, and planetary. Each has some particular advantages and disadvantages. The only spur-gear unit to remain on the market is the venerable and legendary Warn 8274-50. Spur-gear winches are very fast but are usually at the high end of the full-load amp draw spectrum. On the downside, they are bulky (mostly tall) and will not fit on every vehicle.

Worm-gear winches go back as far as spur-gear types, but there have been few worm-only electric winches, and none in the recreational market. To remain compact, the worm-drive part of the unit is connected to the motor via two or more spur gears. The motor lies under or alongside the winch gear housing. The spur gears offer some extra gear reduction as well and reduce the size of the gear needed to drive the drum shaft. The advantages of a worm-gear setup are that they are very good at holding a load and need very little in the way of a braking mechanism. On the downside, they are bulkier, heavier, and slower.

Electrical Considerations. If you choose an electric winch, give some thought to your electrical system. If your winch is destined for occasional, relatively light-duty use, you can get by with your OE charging system and battery by taking care to keep winching duration short. Normal starting-type batteries do not like being deeply discharged, so winching at "five-on, five-off" intervals will allow the motor to cool and let your charging system pump some amps back into the battery. Bear in mind that permanent magnet motors, as fitted to many lower-priced winches, draw some 10–15 percent fewer amps than the heavier-duty series-wound motors, but they are less tolerant of abuse and heat.

Your first upgrade would be to install a more powerful battery. A deep-cycle or marine battery can withstand repeated discharges much better than a starting battery. You can make this change when you replace your current starting battery when it tires out. Also, buying the biggest, highest-rated battery that will fit your application will extend winching capacity.

Battery voltage and winch motor life are interrelated. The lower battery voltage goes, the hotter the motor gets. Ideally, keep battery voltage above 10 volts when winching and never run it below 7.5 volts. Unless you have a big battery or a big alternator, the only way to meet these conditions on a long pull is by stopping periodically to let your battery build up juice. The motor will then get a cooling-off period as well.

Some owners install a second battery just for the winch. A deep-cycle battery can supply more amps over a longer period of time than either a starting or a marine battery. If the second battery is isolated from the starting battery, you don't have to worry about being able to start the engine after a long winch pull.

Some owners also install a larger alternator to help with winch use. Industrial alternators rated at over 200 amps are available for many 4×4 engines. An example would be the Premier Power or the Wrangler Power Products line of HD alternators. Bear in mind that your OE alternator may handle extended use at full output. Most OE alternators have a short duty cycle at full output. Like a winch motor, they can overheat and go up in smoke when worked too hard.

Choosing Winch Capacity. The most important consideration is winch capacity. The manufacturers all come pretty close to each other in terms of recommended capacity. The minimum capacity to look for is your gross vehicle weight (not curb weight) plus about 15 percent. If your pickup's GVW is 8,600 pounds, add 15 percent and you get 9,890 pounds, rounded up to 10,000 pounds. The other rule of thumb is 1.5 to 2 times curb weight. If you anticipate harder-core situations, always opt for more capacity. As you will learn further on, rated power comes from the first (innermost) layer on the drum, so having the capacity to "pull your weight" from the outermost layer on the drum could come in handy someday.

Choosing Line Capacity. It stands to reason that more line will allow you to reach out farther. True, but more line is a mixed blessing. To start with, your winch's maximum rated pull is on the first layer of wire rope (see nearby chart). The rating decreases with each succeeding layer. The more line you have on the drum, the farther you are away from that maximum rating. The other consideration is that more line on a drum is easier to get snarled up, jammed, and kinked. Many winchers prefer less line on the winch but carry an extra 50-foot length as an extension. That's very easy to do with synthetic ropes, by the way.

A winch-mount bumper need not be ugly or clunky. This stylish ARB unit is sharp enough to work well even with a Grand Cherokee. This one has been painted to match. Look for a bumper that doesn't adversely affect approach angle.

Choosing Line Speed. Line speed is mostly an issue when spooling in after a recovery. It's handy, however, to have a winch that is not excessively slower or faster than your slowest crawl speed. A good match results

WINCH LINE SPEEDS

Line speed and rated pull are determined by the layers of cable. The principle is similar to how tire diameter affects axle ratios. The first layer, like the shortest tire, offers the lowest overall ratio, the slowest speed, and the most power. The last layer, like the tallest tire, provides the highest ratio and highest speed but is the least powerful.

Line Pull and Speed Versus Layer

MileMarker 10,500-pound unit, low gear

Layer	1	2	3	4
Line Speed	6.42 fpm	7.3 fpm	8.42 fpm	9.75 fpm
Rated Pull	10,500 lbs.	8,500 lbs.	7,400 lbs.	6,400 lbs.

in not overrunning your line and being able to use the wheels to easily assist the winch. Many winches are extremely fast unloaded, but all will slow down to between 1 and 8 feet per minute under a full load (most are 3–5 feet per minute), thus putting them all in the same general ballpark. A winch that's very slow when unloaded will take an eternity to respool, but then we can all benefit from learning to take the time to properly respool our winches each time. Zen winching!

Those who compete in rockcrawling competitions have a very legitimate issue with line speed. Because they are negotiating tough rockcrawling situations on the clock, they want a fast winch that will spool in fast. They will use the winch to get them over a bad spot, but they don't want to lose more time stopping to unhook, so the winch must come close to keeping up with the vehicle. The old standby was the Warn 8274, but now several companies are offering high-speed winches for competition, which combine a high-power motor with tall gears for blistering-fast line speed. Most of them have a small drum with a small amount of cable so they can spool fully out for the most pull and then have the least amount of line to deal with.

WINCH PULL:
Spooling out more cable is easier on the winch and generates more pull. It's the same situation as big versus small tires. The smaller "tires" (the wraps closest to the drum) offer a "lower" effective gear ratio, making it easier on the motor, lowering amp draw, and reducing heat.

WINCH SAFETY:
The operator of the winch vehicle is usually in the most danger if the cable breaks because it often snaps directly back. There are two things to do: first, lay a blanket, tarp, or coat over the winch cable to dampen the kinetic energy if the cable gets loose; second, raise the vehicle's hood—this will protect those inside more than safety glass alone.

Winch Features and Options. In the past few years, a number of big improvements have come to the electric winch world. First on that list are wireless controllers. Most of the manufacturers offer a wireless winch or a conversion kit. On the upside, they allow you to move farther away from the danger areas (within the range of the transmitter) or to a place where you can monitor the action better. That's also the downside because it moves you farther from the winch. A careless wincher could end up with a wadded-up winch cable, overheated winch, flat battery, or broken winch. Like any tool, it's all in how you use it. Remember to step back to the vehicle occasionally to check on the winch.

Electronics have made a foothold in the simple world of the winch. Solid-state MOSFET transistor packs can replace the traditional mechanical solenoids. MOSFET, which is an acronym for metal oxide semiconductor field effect transistor, is merely an electronic way of controlling the motor with no moving parts to fail. These devices have been around a long while but have only recently become affordable. The upside is that sticking, fried, and water-damaged solenoids are a thing of the past. The downside is in the extra initial cost, but in this case, they seem to be worth it. A few of the newer winches come standard with them, and many older winches can be retrofitted. Another upside seems to be slightly lower amp draw.

Some useful but rather gimmicky devices are appearing on winches. These include built-in lights, thermal indicators, and air compressors. Who knows what they'll think of next? In general, these devices are useful if you are willing to pay the price. In the future, perhaps they'll include a margarita mixer and a cappuccino machine. That's my facetious way of saying, "don't chase gimmicks if all you need is a winch."

Choosing a Mounting System. First off, I won't tell you anything about looks and style. Beyond that, obviously, the mount must be able to handle the pulling capacity of the winch. After that, the weight of the assembly (winch and mount) becomes an issue. Too much weight may cause your front suspension to sag and possibly bottom out on rough terrain taken at speed. Some rigs are more tolerant of this extra weight than others—pickups over SUVs for example. How far the unit hangs out will also dictate how much the unit is affected by weight. The further it hangs out, the more leverage it exerts. All this can be compensated for by stiffer front springs, but that adds to the overall cost.

Two other important considerations are how the winch mount affects your approach angle and the accessibility of the winch cable. A mount that seriously impairs your approach angle may be a net loss in the performance department, perhaps causing you to *need* your winch more.

Free access to the winch cable is both a cost and safety issue. If you can't properly respool your cable, it will get damaged. If it gets damaged, it may break and hurt you or someone else. Also, if the cable is difficult to access, you are more susceptible to hand injuries when trying to respool properly.

Portable winches are fairly popular and useful in many arenas. They have some inherent disabilities and a few great advantages. The main advantage is that they can be used front or rear. Most plug into a Class III–type receiver, but a few hook up via shackles, cables, and such. Most are electric, using special high-amp plug-in electrical connectors. One or two use a small gasoline engine. The main disadvantages are that they reduce approach and departure angles and do not tolerate side pulls well.

Wire Rope. Wire rope is the traditional heart of the winch. The three things that kill wire rope are abrasion, crushing, and fatigue. Wire ropes with more wires per strand, such as 6×37, are more resistant to fatigue because they bend more easily, but they are less resistant to abrasion because of the thin wires. On the other hand, 7×19 ropes are more resistant to abrasion but less so to fatigue, and they are less tolerant of small-diameter pulley sheaves on snatch blocks. The 7×19 is pretty universal, but some owners replace it with 7×37 WSC for more flexibility and a slightly higher breaking strength. The cost is nearly double per foot, however.

Wire rope can be made of various grades of steel, but most are grades of carbon or stainless steel. The steel type used is directly related to the rope's overall strength, flexibility, resistance to abrasion, and resistance to fatigue. Commonly, improved plow steel (IPS) and extra-improved plow steel (EIPS) are used. Most recreational winches use galvanized cable. The galvanizing reduces the strength of the wire rope by as much as 10 percent, but that's usually calculated into the nominal breaking strength listed for the particular rope.

Breaking strength, or nominal breaking strength, is the commonly shown specification for wire rope. Nominal is the key word. That spec does not presume any manufacturing defects from the factory or wear and tear from use. Though made of steel, typical wire rope is relatively fragile. It can be damaged by chafing, kinking, crushing, and normal wear and tear. Every tiny strand that breaks weakens it, and if enough of these tiny strands break, the entire rope will go. By the way, these broken strands (sailors call 'em "fishhooks") can rend flesh. Snip them off with wire cutters as they appear.

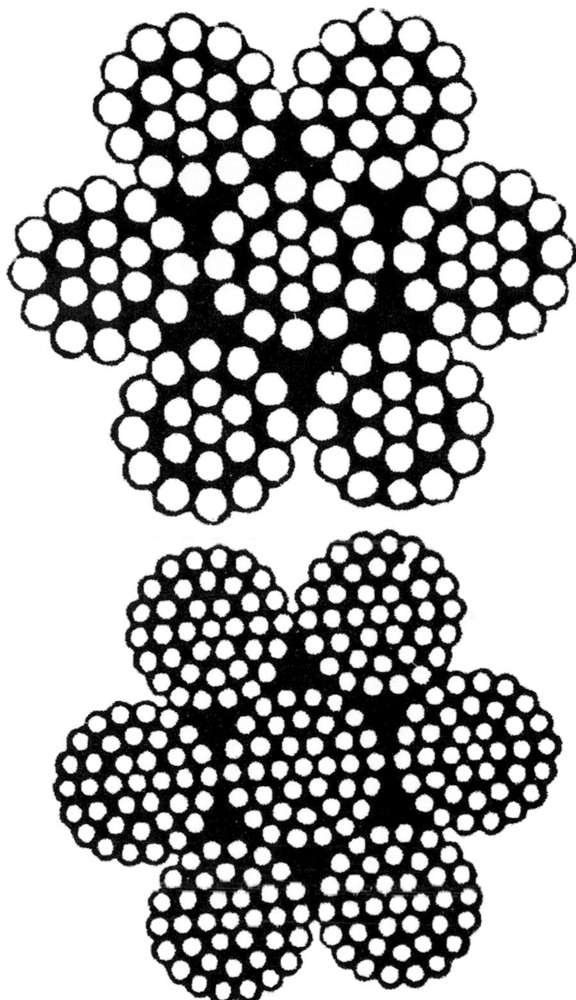

The two common types of wire rope used in 4×4 winches are 6×19 WSC (top) and 6×37 WSC. Most winches come standard with 6×19 WSC galvanized aircraft cable in assorted diameters. The 6×19 designation refers to the number and configuration of the strands that make up the wire rope, in this case seven strands (or bundles) of nineteen wires each. Seven-strand wire is made up of six strands around the seventh, hence the WSC (Wire Strand Core) designation. These wire ropes are also sometimes known as 7×19 or 7×37 SC (Strand Core).

The "cardinal sins" of wire rope use are to hook it back onto itself, allow it to kink, allow it to chafe against hard objects like rocks—especially sharp edges—or to allow it to get wadded onto your drum

This section of 5⁄16-inch AmSteel Blue synthetic winch line with a 9-ounce safety thimble weighs in the neighborhood of 3.5 pounds. A conventional hook would add 1–2 pounds. On top of that, this line is almost 30 percent stronger than an "average" 5⁄16-inch wire rope.

and crushed during a winching operation. All these situations shorten the working life of the rope and decrease your safety margin. Replace the rope when it gets damaged. There's no point hauling the winch around if it's not at full, safe pulling capacity.

Regular inspection is the key to wire rope safety. Periodically spool out all the rope. Start by inspecting the attachment point on the drum and making sure the bolt is tight. Walk the length of the rope and look for broken individual strands (which you can snip off with wire cutters), frayed areas (with lots of broken strands), crushed areas, and kinked areas. In the last three cases, it's usually an indicator that it's time to retire the rope. If the rope passes your inspection, carefully wind it back onto the drum.

Synthetic Winch Rope. Also known as "plasma" rope, synthetics are a relatively new form of winch rope. They have a long history in the fishing and marine venues and made their first appearance in four-wheeling in thc 1990s. Made of molecularly engineered materials with highly technical names, like *ultra high molecular weight polyethylene fiber*, it's stronger than wire rope of the same diameter (e.g., a 13,700-pound capacity versus 9,800 for 5⁄16 inch) and much lighter. A 120-foot roll of 5⁄16 wire rope, for example, weighs nearly 28 pounds with a hook attached. A 120-foot roll of synthetic weighs around 5 pounds with a hook. Synthetic rope is mostly "dead," i.e., it stretches very little (less than one percent) and, most importantly, does not store much kinetic energy. Unlike wire rope, if synthetic breaks, it does not snap back much, if at all. It also floats and can be spliced in the field, or, in an emergency, you can tie a knot in it. Gloves are not as necessary using synthetic rope but still advised.

There are a few caveats to synthetic rope. In a chafe-to-the-death competition, wire rope would win, though it would still be a write-off. Synthetic rope is also more vulnerable to being cut on a sharp edge. It is also less tolerant of heat. Winches that use a brake inside the drum—which includes most of the planetary winches out there—will generate a lot of heat when spooling out under power and with a load, i.e., lowering the vehicle. Winch manufacturers strongly caution against this lowering practice because it can overheat the brakes and ruin the winch. They advise doing it only in short spurts (20–30 feet at a time with a long cooling period), but as with many manufacturers' recommendations, they are ignored by some of us. Reports say that 800 degrees have been seen inside the brake drums by winch manufacturers who claim 500 degrees as a terminal condition for the winch.

Synthetic rope has a critical temperature of 150 degrees to about 450 degrees Fahrenheit, depending on type. Wire rope also has a critical temperature, but it's nearly double that of the best synthetic. You can see these critical specs in the nearby sidebar. The more common varieties of synthetic are around 150 degrees. Technora is around 450 degrees, with Vectran at around 300. Critical temperature is the point at which the rope's tensile strength begins to be affected. Some sources list about a 20 percent strength loss at critical temperature for some ropes, increasing with temperature until the rope reaches its melting point. The melting point is much higher (commonly around 285 degrees for most and up to 900 degrees for Technora). The rope largely returns to normal below its critical temperature, but repeated applications of critical, or near-critical temperatures can have a cumulative weakening effect called "heat aging."

BUTTERFLY CABLE:
There are two things to remember about butterflying. First, keep the cable tight at the drum end so that it doesn't get loose and turn into a rat's nest. Second, make sure the cable hook doesn't get loose. If it does, it can fall under your rig, wrap around a wheel, or hook something on the ground and bring you to a rapid stop.

In an emergency, two knots can be used with synthetic rope, the bowline (top, pronounced "bo-lynn") for attaching the line to an object, and the sheet bend for attaching two ropes to each other. In both cases, the capacity of the line is reduced, the bowline by 40 percent and the sheet bend by 50 percent.

There are several defenses against heat. The first, and easiest, is not to use the winch for lowering your rig, or to do so only in small increments with a long cool-off. Second, you could opt for the higher temp–rated rope, the catch being that these ropes come with either decreased capacity or decreased fatigue resistance. You can compensate for this by increasing the rope's diameter. Third, you can use a "combo"-style winch rope that uses the higher temp–rated rope for the first layer, such as Technora, with a long section of stronger rope for the rest. The weaker rope only comes into play when you are pulling on that last layer. You see some ropes fitted with nylon insulator sleeves on the first layer. Considering that nylon has a lower melting temp than the rope, they are largely useless. Finally, you can buy a winch with an external brake. These would include those with worm-gear drives from Pierce, Ramsey, or Superwinch. The Warn 8274 also has an external brake. Superwinch's EP series of planetary winches also have external brakes. There are rumors that other externally braked winches are on the drawing boards.

You will hear that only hawse-type fairleads should be used with synthetic rope. Experience has shown that's not an entirely accurate statement. In most cases, roller fairleads are better because they reduce friction and pressure at the point of contact. The problem is that all roller fairleads are not created equal. Some others will allow the rope to slip in between the rollers at the corners or have sharp edges for the rope to chafe upon. Many people prefer the Superwinch roller fairleads for synthetic ropes because they addresses these issues well.

Synthetic rope doesn't like to be bent at sharp angles, and when it has to be bent around a pulley, roller, or hawse, the radius of the bend should be at least three times the diameter of the rope (e.g., a ⅜-inch-diameter rope should have no more than a 1.13-inch radius). A roller fairlead usually meets, or comes closer to meeting, that criteria than a hawse (many of which are ¾-inch radius). If you use a hawse type, it should be polished steel or aluminum, or tubular steel with a radius as close to correct as possible.

Day-to-day operation using a synthetic winch rope is largely the same as for wire. The quickest way to kill it (and maybe you or another person) is to put it against a sharp edge under tension. You can avoid that by inspecting where the rope runs, your fairlead, bumper, winch bumper brackets, and so on, and make sure there is no chance for rope and edge to meet. Cut and grind away all such edges and grind a smooth radius on anything you can't remove.

As with wire rope, regular inspection is key to a long life. Military agencies often mandate replacement every three years regardless of use, but that may be excessive for the average 'wheeler. Spool out all the rope and start by inspecting where the rope attaches to the drum. Some abrasion and fuzziness on the exterior sheath is normal and goes to a dull color. Excessive "fuzzies" indicate the rope may be abraded enough to replace. Look carefully at areas where there are unusual changes in diameter or shape. Some crushing or flattening is normal and OK—the rope will pull back into shape—but if a section is unusually hard compared to the rest, or unusually shiny, it may be heat-damaged. The nice thing about synthetic rope is that if you find a bad section in an otherwise healthy rope, you can cut the section out and use a long splice to connect the pieces. Learning to splice has an uphill learning curve, but newbie sailors have been learning it for centuries, and so can you! Online resources and the rope manufacturers also may offer some training aids and tools.

Though most synthetic ropes are made with UV-resistant materials, the sun does age and weaken them. For that reason, a drum cover is a good investment in the long-term life of your rope. Most experts agree that a UV-resistant rope will fail for other reasons before it will fail from UV aging, but there may now be little-used 4×4 winches with synthetic ropes on them for 10 years, or more. You wouldn't trust your life to a rusty wire rope that's been on a winch drum since World War II; neither should you trust a frayed and faded synthetic rope that's been out in the sun for a decade.

In an emergency, you can tie knots into synthetic ropes, but those knots reduce the strength of the rope significantly. In their rope catalog, the Sampson Rope Company suggests two knots for emergency use, the bowline (which reduces the strength of the rope by approximately 40 percent) for most uses and the sheet bend (when you must connect two dissimilar-sized ropes), which reduces rope strength by approximately 50 percent.

Winch Techniques. Here we are near the end of the book, and I've got to warn you again about the double-edged nature of an aspect of four-wheeling, in this case the winch. It can be a convenience, a boon, and a lifesaver. It can also be a pain in the butt (or somewhere else) and a life-taker. The result is usually

Shackles are one of the universal items in winching and recovery. These are all screw-pin, or anchor, shackles. These are most often called "D" shackles, but the industry will call them "bow" shackles. Shackles are classified by the diameter of the bow. Only shackles with a working load rating on them should be used. This can be expressed several ways: WLL (Working Load Limit), WL (Working Load), or SWL (Safe Working Load). Each of these terms reflects the safe load limits for which the shackle is rated. The breaking strength is actually higher, depending on the steel alloy used, with design factors from two to five times SWL. Here are the sizes that come into play most often. From the lower right clockwise: the ⅞-inch has a 1-inch pin and a SWL of 17,000 pounds; the ¾-inch piece has a ⅞-inch pin and a WWL of 13,000 pounds; the ⅝-inch shackle has a ¾-inch pin and a WWL of 7,000 pounds; and the ⅞-inch red shackle has a 1-inch pin and a high SWL of 17,000 pounds. As you can see, two shackles of the same size can have different weight ratings. Buy the best!

Here are two common types of so-called snatch blocks, also known as pulley blocks. The upper unit is one from Superwinch and is a common and easily used two-piece type. It comes from various manufacturers in ratings from 6,000 to 16,000 pounds and with assorted sheave sizes. The orange one is a heavy-duty locking unit rated for 24,000 pounds with a 5-inch sheave. In general, the larger pulley is the better because wire rope is weakened at every bend. The larger the drum on the winch or the sheave on the pulley, the more strength is retained.

TOP FIVE WINCHING SAFETY TIPS

1. Replace damaged cable and hardware.
2. Hands off the winch controls while someone is working around the winch or winch cable.
3. Hook up only to solidly mounted anchor points. This doesn't include most bumpers, spring shackles, and so on.
4. Keep spectators well clear of the danger area.
5. Always wear gloves when working with winch cable.

up to the operator. Use it wisely, and you can have a four-wheeling career free of winching accidents.

Know Your Wraps. Keep at least five wraps of cable on the drum with wire rope and eight wraps for synthetic. No matter how a rope is attached to a drum, it's not enough to carry a full winch load. It's the wraps that carry the load. Wire grips the drum better and needs fewer wraps than synthetic.

Snatch Blocks: More Know Your Wraps. A snatch block is a pulley that allows you to double the line pull (and halve the line speed) or change the direction of a pull. It's a vital winch tool but not one that should be purchased without any consideration. With regard to using snatch blocks, there are ideal sheave diameters to use depending on type of rope. For synthetic, you want a sheave diameter a minimum of 8–10 times the rope diameter. For wire rope the minimum is 20 times, but the ideal is 51 times. With both types of rope, smaller sheave diameters result in reduced strength and increased fatigue. Fatigue is not often an issue in the 4×4 realm, but strength may be. This is especially true with wire rope. What it boils down to is that with a 5/16-inch wire rope, to have 100 percent of rated capacity you need a 15.81-inch-diameter sheave on the pulley. Generally, the biggest you will find is about 6 inches, and many are 4–5 inches. Those fall well into synthetic line territory, but for wire rope, a 6-inch pulley offers about 91 percent of the nominal tensile strength. The compromises in sheave diameter occur because the winch rope is usually rated stronger than the maximum winch pull, so the reduction in the rating still is inside a safety margin. Still, if you have an option, buy the largest-diameter sheave you can that is rated for your winch capacity.

The "Average" Winch Pull. A few years ago, I purchased a line dyno. This is essentially a very high-capacity scale with rings on each end that can be used to measure winch pull. I used it to measure winch pulls every chance I got and then compared my information with two other fellows with the same equipment. Based on that information, I have come to the conclusion that the average winch pull is between 2,500 and 3,500 pounds. I make no claims that this is scientific, but even situations that had the winch groaning in agony were only 3,500 pounds.

The basic winch kit is represented by this Warn accessory kit. It consists of a 10-foot length of 5⁄16-inch Grade 7 transport chain (SWL 4,700 pounds); an 8-foot, 2-inch tree strap; a snatch block (16,000 pounds, 4-inch sheave); a couple of 3⁄4-inch shackles; and a handy carrying bag.

Here's an example of a snatch block winching operation. The white Wrangler has slid off the road in relatively deep snow, and repeated attempts to drive it back onto the roadbed resulted in it going farther over the edge. The green Jeep cannot get past the white one because of the slippery conditions, so the cable was run to a tree and then back to the white Jeep. This pulled the Jeep back onto the road where it could continue in the 18-inch-deep snow. The driver of the white Jeep assisted the winch with the available traction.

My test illustrates a point. You will see a lot of damaged and abused winch cables out there, and, like me, you'll wonder what's been keeping those people alive. It's equipment overkill. Even a thrashed 5/16-inch cable, originally rated for 9,800 pounds, may be capable of supporting up to a third of its original capacity. But, it might not be. And you never know when your winch will be called upon for a full load. At that point, you would be holding a grenade with the pin out.

Respool Correctly. Take the time to respool correctly after each operation. If you make it a habit, you'll never forget and damage the cable by crushing it. During a winching operation, if the cable starts to collect on

THE BASIC WINCH OPERATION

You're stuck! Step one is to release the clutch on the motor so that the cable will freespool. How this is done varies from winch to winch. Once you've determined what you will use as a dead man, freespool the winch cable to that location. Gauge the difficulty of the pull, and if it will be a difficult pull, either spool out to the last layer on the drum for maximum power or use a snatch block to double the power.

Disengage the freespool on the winch and plug in the winch control. Route the wire so that it won't be caught in the drum, a tire, or anywhere else. Take up the slack in the cable and add a blanket, coat, or purpose-built kinetic energy damper to the cable.

Make a secure hookup to a solid object that won't move or be uprooted. If it's a living object, use a strap so it won't be harmed.

The safest place to winch from is the cockpit. If you are solo, you will have to stop periodically to make sure the cable spools correctly on the winch drum. If you use poly rope, this is less important because crushing cannot damage it.

one end of the drum, stop, secure the vehicle or load, unload the winch, unspool a few feet of cable, wind it onto the drum properly, and start winching again. In a real emergency, of course, do what you gotta do.

If the trail is a nightmare, and you are winching every hundred yards or so, it's acceptable practice to butterfly the cable around your front bumper or brush guard. This is nothing more than a tight figure-eight. It saves a good deal of time. Just make sure you keep the cable that is still on the drum tight so it doesn't "bird's-nest."

When you return from a trip after having used the winch, it can be worthwhile to respool at home in less intense circumstances. It's best to respool under a bit of a load—especially that foundational first layer. A slight driveway grade will offer that light load, or you can pull another vehicle with its emergency brake partially engaged. A tight spool prevents a line from an upper layer from worming its way down between loose coils below it and jamming, possibly damaging the cable. Spooling in under a load is even more important when installing a new rope, especially wire. Many people like to put a partial load on the cable to stretch it out and seat the lays.

Side Pulls. With a roller fairlead, you can safely pull about 15 degrees to either side, or up and down. Hawse fairleads are slightly less flexible, especially with wire rope. Beyond this, you put the winch and cable at risk. The most obvious problem for roller fairlead–equipped winches is that the cable will all wind onto one side of the drum. This can damage the cable by crushing it, and if enough cable gets built up on one side of the drum, it can break the winch. There may be times when an extreme side pull is necessary and worth the risk. If you stop and respool before the cable gets wadded too badly, the odds are much better that you can get away with it.

WINCH PULL:
A snatch block, or pulley, is a useful tool because it effectively doubles the pulling power of your winch while slowing line speed by 50 percent. In cases where a hard pull is needed and you can only run out a short length of cable, use a snatch block to run out more cable and double the line pull.

This is a simple single-line pull with the Jeep attached to a tree via a strap. The Jeep wasn't seriously mired and needed only a little help, so the single line was enough. He was on the second layer of cable on the drum, so his ultimate pull would have been reduced somewhat. Had the vehicle been more seriously mired, a double-line pull would have been necessary. Note that the tree strap is twisted, which reduces its strength.

With a hawse, chafing is the obvious problem. Wire tends to cut into a hawse with a heavy load. Synthetic does a little better if the edge is glass-smooth, but friction can create lots of heat, synthetic's Achilles heel.

Maximum Pulling Power. Maximum rated pulling power comes from the layer of cable closest to the drum. Every layer after that decreases the pulling power of the winch by about 10 percent per layer.

Electric Winch Tips. Keep all hands off the winch control when people are working around the cable or winch. That way you can't accidentally engage the winch when people are vulnerable. Route the winch control carefully wherever you are working so it doesn't get caught by the winch cable, a tire, or someone's foot.

When spooling in without a load, many electric planetary gear winches will continue rolling via inertia and spool in as much as two feet of cable. It's controllable when you know about it. When spooling in, especially that last foot or so, spool in with short spurts so as not to get fingers caught or strain any components.

An 8,000-pound electric winch will draw well over 400 amps at full load, and bigger winches draw even more. Even with the engine running, that kind of draw will pull a battery down in just a few minutes. If you have a voltmeter, watch it carefully, and when it stays below 10 volts while winching, wait a few minutes and let the battery build back up. To be on the safe side, if you have a single battery, don't shut your engine off after a long winching operation. There may not be enough amps left in the battery to crank the engine.

On a hard winch pull, the electric winch motor will get hot, and this heat can cook it to death. Periodically check the motor with your bare hand—keeping clear of the line—and when it gets too hot to hold your hand against it comfortably, stop and let it cool.

Mechanical Winch Tips. Using a mechanical winch is best and most safely done with two people—one to operate the PTO, transmission, clutch, and throttle from the cab, and the other to watch the drum and direct the situation. If you are outside watching the cable spool in, you can't easily stop the winch in an emergency. If you are inside, you can't make sure the winch is spooling properly or that there isn't some unseen problem occurring.

A mechanical winch won't stall like an electric winch when it reaches its load limit because you have what amounts to engine power behind it. Instead, something breaks. This could be the cable, the hook, or some part of the drivetrain. Fortunately, there's a shear pin built in somewhere between the gear drive and the drum. Make sure you have an extra or two. If you have an old winch that's out of production and parts are scarce, a machinist can make a shear pin. Don't be tempted to use an ultra-strong pin because that may allow some other, less easily replaced part to be overstressed.

Hydraulic Winch Tips. There's really only one hydraulic unit to talk about here, the MileMarker. It uses the power steering pump to supply hydraulic pressure. On installation, it's vital to thoroughly flush and replace the power steering fluid—doubly so if you have an older vehicle. Power steering fluid breaks down with age and heat. Old fluid will not permit maximum winch performance and may even harm the winch. On older rigs with lots of miles it might be advisable to have the pump pressure-tested at a competent shop. A small power steering cooler, which mounts on the return line, can help keep the fluid cool.

Using a hydraulic winch is very much like using an electric. Unlike the electric planetary winches, the hydraulic does not roll on from inertia while spooling in unloaded, but it might very slowly spool out while holding a heavy load. This occurs in high-time units

The choker chain in the winch kit is useful for things like moving logs. The chain is used where chafing might damage a strap and where there is no worry about the chain causing damage to living or valuable things. The chain can be useful for hookups on the chassis of rigs without proper recovery points. In older winches, such as the vintage Braden PTO winch on this old Power Wagon, a section of chain was attached to the end of the cable more or less permanently. This is the sign of a winch that was used for work rather than recovery. Note the fellow playing with the winch cable, sans gloves. Ahem!

Receiver winches can be handy, especially when you can put them in the rear. They can be left at home when not needed. On the downside, they are not tolerant of side pulls and may be difficult to install on a rig mired bumper deep. If left in place, they seriously degrade departure angle. They are the most viable option on rigs without good, or good-looking, bumper mounts available. On many rigs, the receivers can be installed behind those plastic valances so popular these days, with only the actual 2×2 receiver protruding.

where the control valves might leak slightly. A new unit shouldn't do this.

On MileMarker high-capacity winches that use ⅜-inch, 7×19 cable, the small diameter of the drum makes for a bit of a snarl on the last layer of cable because the cable isn't flexible enough to stay wrapped. Keeping tension on the cable prevents this, but swapping to a more flexible 6×37 wire rope or synthetic rope would solve this minor problem.

A SNATCH RECOVERY

A simple pull-out was attempted, but the Range Rover was stuck too deep. The recovery rope is attached and laid out so it can pay out with no interference.

At the "go" signal, the stuck driver powered up just a little, and Bill Burke, in the Defender 90, took off at a brisk walking pace.

The rope snaps to attention like a rubber band.

And the stuck Rover is on its way to the other side of the pit.

Getting out to wade for a recovery amounts to the worst of a bad situation. When there is ice in the water, double that assessment! This is a pull-out recovery to aid a Jeep with a drowned ignition system. Somebody has to get out to hook up in this situation. Usually, etiquette dictates the driver of the stranded rig do the unpleasant task, but in this case the rescuer in the Samurai does the dirty work.

This Blazer got off the road and nearly rolled down an embankment into a pond. There was no driving out and no snatching because of the imminent rollover danger. The answer was first to secure the vehicle front and rear with the straps seen in this shot. It took two winch vehicles, one each at the front and rear, to make the recovery. Snatch blocks were connected to trees up the hill to angle the pull and drag the truck sideways back onto the trail, as evidenced by the dirt piling up at the rear tire. The arrows show the locations of the cables. Two Jeeps with 8,000- and 9,000-pound winches had all they could do to drag it up. Bill Tocholke had to get up close and personal directing each winch independently. This was about as tricky a recovery as it gets.

Portable Winch Tips. Avoid hard pulls beyond a few degrees to either side on the Class III receiver-type portables or you risk bending the winch mount or tow hitch. If your rig has sunk into terra firma, you may have to dig to get the winch plugged in and hooked up. In the case of the rear mount, because the electrical cables are so long, expect some loss of power due to line loss. This can be compensated for by using larger-diameter, 00-gauge ("double-ought") cables.

Basic Hookups. There are two basic hookups, the single-line pull and the double-line pull. The single-line is just that. You run out enough line to hook up and start winching. As discussed earlier, if the pull is a hard one and you don't have enough cable out, it is the equivalent of trying to tow a heavy load by starting in fourth gear. If you can't spool out more cable, you would use

DEAD MEN THAT DON'T SMELL

Though not a huge rock, this sliver was ideally placed and wedged to provide a great dead man. The choice of a strap instead of a chain might result in some chafing, but some folks have an aversion to chain. It's acceptable as long as the strap is not allowed to deteriorate to an unsafe condition.

Neither the tree nor the boulder was quite solid enough on its own, but together, they were ideal. How convenient!

Though the dead juniper was more ideally placed for a straight pull, the live one was deemed stronger, and Bill Burke prepares the tree strap for use in the recovery.

Two lengths of transport chain were needed to make a secure dead man out of this boulder. A shackle can be used to attach the hook, or the hook can be attached directly.

With no ground anchor in sight, what can you do? If this is a common occurrence, consider the Pull Pal ground anchor. It folds up into the size of a Hi-Lift jack and comes in 6,000-, 11,000-, and 14,000-pound capacities. It holds well in most sorts of soft ground and sometimes will dig itself out of sight. A simple kick to the side and a pull to the rear will pull it out of the ground. After using the Pull Pal, fill in and tamp down the hole.

TREE STRAPS:
When a living tree is your dead man, always use a tree strap to protect it from damage. A winch cable or chain will cut through the bark of the tree and "girdle" it, which can kill the tree. Chains are useful in winching from rocks, dead logs, or rough surfaces that would damage a strap or cable.

WINCH MOTOR HEAT:
The winch motor will get hotter as the battery draws down, so taking a winch break periodically is good on two counts. It lets the winch cool and your battery recharge.

a double-line pull. With the double-line pull, a snatch block is attached to the vehicle being recovered, or the dead man you are winching from. The winch cable is then routed through the block and back to the winching vehicle and secured to a solid (preferably chassis-mounted) anchor point. Look to the nearby photos for "thousand-word" pictures and more info.

Advanced Hookups. The number of advanced hookups available is limited only by your imagination and equipment. Usually, advanced hookups are needed to change the direction of the pull. With enough snatch blocks, cable, and dead men, you can pull yourself out sideways or backward. You can also lift the vehicle to pull it out of a hole. Necessity is the mother of invention, and if you have enough equipment, you can perform some amazing feats. In the case of advanced hookups, look to the illustrations for a few ideas.

Winch Assist. Using your vehicle's motive power in self-recovery will ease the strain on the winch and reduce the chances of breaking something. You usually have a little traction. and it can be used to lessen the winch pull, but avoid getting overly helpful. This relates to our earlier talk about matching winch speed to crawl speed. If your rig suddenly grabs a bunch of traction while you are spinning tires, it could leap forward and overrun the winch cable. The other possibility is to gain some slack and then suddenly lose it, slipping back and jerking the cable. That puts a big strain on the winch, cable, and all the attachments. Assist the winch if and when you can, but maintain an even strain. If that isn't possible and you are jerking the winch, just go to neutral and let the winch do the work.

Sometimes you need to dig just to get to a recovery point. That's much easier with this folding shovel than it would be with hands.

Signals and Safety. Often someone outside the vehicle and in a position to see the big picture will direct a winching operation. This is a good practice. The best way for the driver/winch operator and the director to communicate is by hand signals. Spoken or shouted words can often be misinterpreted or drowned out by loud noise. See the nearby pics for a review of the hand signals. Before you start winching, review the hand signals the director will use to be sure you both have the same understanding of them.

A cable loaded with several tons of weight stores kinetic energy. If the load is suddenly released by the failure of a cable or a hookup point, the cable can snap back, up, or to the side with enough energy to cut a person in half. Kinetic energy dampers can be placed on the cable. This could be nothing more than a heavy coat, blanket, or tarp placed on the cable, usually nearer the hook-up end. There are also some purpose-built winch-cable dampers on the market. Keep spectators well clear of the operation for their safety.

Natural Dead Men. In the winching world, a dead man isn't the mortal remains of some poor four-wheeler. Rather, it's a solid anchor to winch from, or for securing the winch vehicle. You may be winching another vehicle that outweighs yours, or the ground conditions increase the pull to the point where your vehicle is dragged toward the stuck one. Sometimes, all you need to do is to block the wheels of the winching vehicle. Sometimes you need extra help. If the weight of your vehicle isn't enough to hold, a more solid anchor is needed. In these cases, you need a dead man.

A dead man can be another vehicle, a log, a rock, a tree, or whatever. It just needs to be something solid, heavy, and safe. You then back your rig up to the dead man, secure the vehicle with the appropriate chain or strap, and winch away.

Incidentally, when winching with an automatic-equipped vehicle, always use the parking brake in conjunction with park. Using park only may either break the park pawl (as mentioned in Chapter 4) or jam it. Sometimes a solid foot on the brake pedal, locking all four wheels, is needed. Some four-wheelers actually install brake-system line locks, which lock the brakes in the same manner. Other means of securing the vehicle could be as simple as rocks or wood blocks in front of the tires, or using terrain features like large rocks, logs, or gullies as natural wheel blocks.

Manmade Dead Men. Over the years, there has been a succession of devices built to provide a portable dead man. The Sand Spike, the Gopher, the Kro-Built, and others have come and gone. Some techniques, like burying the spare tire or adapting the Danforth boat anchor, are adaptations of equipment designed for other purposes. Others, like the Pull-Pal ground anchor, are purpose-built. Many of these ground anchor products have disappeared, but the Pull-Pal has stood the test of time. It is truly a remarkable tool that outperformed all the others and has survived.

WINCHING EFFORT

Because your vehicle is rolling on wheels, the effort required to move it is less than the same weight laying flat on the ground. That's why a single person can move a 5,000-pound truck by pushing but not a 5,000-pound crate. On a flat, hard surface, the person is only required to generate the grunt equal to about four percent of the truck's total weight (about 200 pounds). Ditto for the winch.

Ground conditions will increase the effort. A truck mired to the hubs in goo will require much more effort than a truck on pavement. Also the slope, if any, will increase the pull. Here is some information on how ground conditions and slope will affect winch pulls. These figures are averages taken from various winch manufacturers' information.

Ground Condition	Effort Required (as a percentage of total vehicle weight)
Pavement	2–4 percent
Grass	8–14 percent
Hard-packed sand	10–17 percent
Wet sand	15–20 percent
Gravel	10–20 percent
Soft, dry sand	25–30 percent
Shallow mud	30–35 percent
Deep mud	40–60 percent
Deep clay mud	50–70 percent

A slope will have its own factor, to which you will add the above ground condition factor. Calculating the effect of slope is simply done by approximating the slope in degrees and then multiplying it by the loaded weight of the vehicle and dividing that by 60. Whatever figure emerges, add this to your loaded weight to determine the approximate pull required. Then add the appropriate percentage of that weight for which the ground condition will account.

$$\frac{\text{slope (in degrees)} \times \text{loaded weight (lbs.)}}{60} = \text{winch pull}$$

winch pull × ground factor (in percent) = additional load

additional load + winch pull = total load on winch

Let's use an S-10 Blazer as an example. It weighs about 4,500 pounds, but with all the gear and supplies added, it's 4,800 pounds total. We're trying to winch it up a 50-degree slope consisting of shallow mud;

$$\frac{50 \times 4800}{60} = \text{4,000-pound pull}$$

4,000 x 35% = 1,400 pounds additional pull from mud

4,000 + 1,400 = 5,400-pound winch pull

So there you are, stuck and out of reach of any dead men, with no vehicles to provide a handy tow. Assuming you also don't have a Pull-Pal, what can you do? The age-old cure has been to bury the spare. It works, though only if the digger is dedicated. Dig a deep hole, at least as deep as the tire is tall. Also, dig a slit trench for the cable that gradually drops to the level of the center hole of the rim. Leave one side of the hole as perpendicular and solid as you can. Run the winch cable through the center hole and hook it to the stoutest, and I mean the *stoutest*, bar (or bars) you have. A spare axle shaft will do it, as will a Hi-Lift jack's beam (though they could be bent, so be prepared to sacrifice them), but a jack handle or a breaker bar alone probably will not be strong enough. Bury the whole thing again, with as many rocks and solid material as you can find. How well this will hold depends on the type of ground present and how well you did your work. Make the winch job easier by dig-

HELPING THE WINCH:
When helping the winch with your drive wheels, match the winch's speed. Overrunning the winch causes slack in the line and allows for a snarled cable. Lurching forward and sliding back against the cable can cause a jerk forceful enough to break the winch.

COMPARISON OF WINCH LINE CHARACTERISTICS

Here are most of the winch lines, by brand name, available for winches today, along with a generic wire rope. The synthetic lines may also be marketed under different names. Shown are the actual manufacturers' names. Wire rope characteristics vary considerably, but the types chosen represent what is normally supplied by the various winch manufacturers.

Brand	Diameter (inches)	MBS (lbs.)	Critical Temp (degrees F)	Melting Point (degrees F)
Wire Rope	7/16-7×19	17,600	-	-
Wire Rope	3/8-7×19	14,400	-	-
Wire Rope	5/16-7×19	9,800	-	-
AmSteel Blue	7/16	21,500	150	297
AmSteel Blue	3/8	17,600	150	297
AmSteel Blue	5/16	12,300	150	297
Plasma	7/16	21,000	150	284
Plasma	3/8	17,500	150	284
Plasma	5/16	11,700	150	285
Spectra	7/16	14,800	150	284
Spectra	3/8	13,900	150	284
Spectra	5/16	9,000	150	284
Superline	7/16	40,000	150	284
Superline	3/8	26,500	150	284
Superline	5/16	16,500	150	284
Technora	7/16	25,200	450	900
Technora	3/8	16,200	450	900
Technora	5/16	11,700	450	900
Vectran	7/16	21,200	300	625
Vectran	3/8	17,600	300	625
Vectran	5/16	12,600	300	625

Notes: MBS = Minimum Breaking Strength

ging the rig out as much as possible. Be sure to fill in your hole when done.

The easier solution is the Pull-Pal. It works like an old-fashioned plow and in most types of ground other than rock. It requires only soft enough ground to get a bite into and the right angle to work. The heavier the load, the deeper it will dig in. How much it will hold depends on the ground, but I've used it in snow, sand, and various types of dirt, and it has seldom failed to hold. Look at the nearby pics for some tips on how to use it.

Manual Winch Recovery. Many of the tips you read above apply to manual winches. Some of the differences include the fact that it's more difficult and potentially dangerous to assist the winch with the vehicle. The manual winch is simply too slow to keep up and because people are in close proximity to the cable and winch, you don't want sudden slack and re-tensioning. The manual equipment usually isn't as durable as the powered stuff, so it needs more care.

The great advantage to the manual portables is that they can be hooked up anywhere—front, rear, side, corner, bottom, or top. They can be used anywhere they are needed. For hard-core types, they make an ideal No. 2 winch. They are useful in case the main power winch gives out, but more importantly, they offer another option and dimension for complicated recoveries. If you have snatch blocks, you can perform the same kind of complicated "round-the-corner" hookups as with a power winch.

One of the worst winching glitches is when your rope or cable gets jammed on the drum. Won't spool in and won't spool out. Sometimes two strong men can get it undone. Sometimes you need to tug with a vehicle. Sometimes it's just about impossible to get it undone. The moral? Spool in properly, even during a winching operation.

I was once firmly dedicated to manual winching. This was mostly due to being semi-destitute, as opposed to being a tough guy. I *was* younger, stronger, and better able to endure in those days, but here are a few observations that might be useful. I learned that the fatigue of a long recovery led to stupid mistakes. I also learned that patience was required to avoid shortcuts. The slow pace of a manual recovery is an asset and a boon to clear thinking and a safe recovery. Use it!

A twisted, barber-poled strap loses some strength when maxed out. Given that this was a simple pull-out, the strap's limits were not tested. Taking a moment to stretch out and untwist the strap is a worthwhile habit, however.

"Better late than never, huh?" Probably not. This tree has been girdled twice. The odds are good it won't survive.

WINCH SAFETY:
If you are using a dead man to recover yourself, choose one that is solid enough to take the weight of your pull. Some four-wheelers have pulled logs, rocks, and trees down upon themselves.

The way the drum attachment is made on a synthetic line is important. Just as with wire rope, it's the wraps that take the strain, not the drum attachment. Various methods are used, but Viking Offroad's method may be the neatest. They utilize a specially made link, through which the line is looped, and then is fed through the line. Tension on the line clamps it pretty well.

Viking Offroad's safety thimble is a better alternative to the standard galvanized thimble and hook. It works with both synthetic and wire rope and is used in lieu of a standard hook. It allows for a wider variety of attachments, including a bow shackle as shown. It also prevents the winch line from being pulled through the fairlead and offers a solution to the "where to stash the winch line" question.

WINCHING HAND SIGNALS

1—Stop! One clenched fist could be regarded as a normal speaking voice. Double fists is a shout!

2—Winch in.

3—Winch Out.

4—A little bit. Could be combined with winch in or winch out.

5—I'm working on the cable at the drum. See the appropriate driver response in photo 6.

6—The appropriate driver response to number 5. The winch control laying in clear view on the dash. Showing a pair of empty hands is also commonly used.

COMMON WINCH SPECS, 6,000 LBS. AND UP

Manufacturer	Model	Max Capacity lbs., 1st layer	Rope Diameter/ Length	Motor Type/ HP	Amp Draw Max	Max Load Line Speed, FPM	Drive Type/ Ratio
MileMarker	H9000/HI9000	9,000	3⁄8-100	Hyd	2	6.2	P/6:1/1:1 (1)
MileMarker	H10500/ HI10500	10,500	3⁄8-100	Hyd	2	5.65	P/6:1/1:1 (1)
MileMarker	H12000/ HI12000	12,000	3⁄8-100	Hyd	2	5.65	P/6:1/1:1 (1)
MileMarker	PEC8	8,000	5⁄16-100	PM/4.1	300	5.0	P/210:1
MileMarker	SE9.5	9,500	3⁄8-100	SW/4.8	375	4.3	P/212:1
MileMarker	SEC12	12,000	3⁄8-100	SW/4.8	315	4.5	P/296:1
MileMarker	SI9500	9,500	3⁄8-100	SW/4.8	375	4.3	P/212:1
MileMarker	SI12000	12,000	3⁄8-100	SW/4.8	315	4.5	P/296:1
MileMarker	PE6000	6,000	5⁄16-85	PM/3.6	170	4.6	P/210:1
MileMarker	PE8000	8,000	5⁄16-100	PM/4.0	300	5	P/210:1
MileMarker	E9000	9,000	3⁄8-100	PM/4.4	305	5	P/210:1
MileMarker	SE12000	12,000	3⁄8-100	SW/4.8	NA	NA	P/294:1
MileMarker	EW9000	9,000	3⁄8-100	PM/4.5	300	4.3	P/NA
MileMarker	EW12000	12,000	3⁄8-100	SW/5.5	400	4.4	P/265:1
MileMarker	SI9500	9,500	3⁄8-100	SW/4.8	365	4.3	P/212:1
MileMarker	SI12000	12,000	3⁄8-100	SW/4.8	375	4.45	P/296:1
Pierce	PS654-8K	9,000	5⁄16-150	SW/1.5	400	3	W/470:1
Pierce	PS-654-8MK	12,500	5⁄16-150	SW/1.5	400	2	W/520:1
Ramsey	QM 8000	8,000	5⁄16-95	SW/5.5	420	8	P/126:1
Ramsey	QM 9000	9,000	5⁄16-105	SW/4.4	400	7	P/138:1
Ramsey	REP-8000	8,000	5⁄16-95	SW/3.8	405	5	P/126:1
Ramsey	REP 8500E	8,500	5⁄16-95	PM//NA	335	4.5	P/294:1
Ramsey	REP-9000	9,000	5⁄16-95	SW/4.8	420	2	P/138:1
Ramsey	REP 9500E	9,500	5⁄16-95	SW/3.8	420	3	P/138:1
Ramsey	Patriot 6000	6,000	1⁄4-100	SW/5.5	405	12	P/90:1
Ramsey	Patriot 8000	8,000	5⁄16-95	SW/5.5	420	8	P/126:1
Ramsey	Patriot 9500	9,500	5⁄16-105	SW/5.5	430	7.8	P/138:1
Ramsey	Patriot 9500UT	9,500	6⁄16-105	SW/5.5	430	7.8	P/138:1
Ramsey	Patriot 15000	15,000	7⁄16-90	SW/5.5	460	3.9	P/251:1
Ramsey	Triple-X 6000	6,000	3⁄8R-35	SW/5.5	405	12	P/90:1
Ramsey	RE 8000	8,000	5⁄16-150	SW/4.8 X	370	4.3	W/360:1
Ramsey	RE 12000	12,000	3⁄8-100	SW/4.8 X	380	3.3	W/470:1
Smittybilt	XRC-8	8,000	5⁄16-92	PM/4.1	-	-	P/265:1
Smittybilt	XRC-10	10,000	23/64-94	SW/5.5	425	7.2	P/218:1
Superwinch	S6000	6,000	5/16-100	SW/3.4	400	2.5	P/253:1
Superwinch	S9000	9,000	5/16-100	SW/4.2	420	2.5	P/253:1
Superwinch	EP6.0	6,000	21/64-100	SW/3.6 X	440	10	P/156:1
Superwinch	EP9.0	9,000	21/64-100	SW/4.6 X	350	6.4	P/156:1

1) A two-speed unit. **2)** With built-in air compressor. **P** = Planetary, **S** = Spur Gear, **SW** = Series Wound, **PM** = Permanent Magnet, **R** = Synthetic Winch Rope, **X** = External Brake

COMMON WINCH SPECS, 6,000 LBS. AND UP

Manufacturer	Model	Max Capacity lbs., 1st layer	Rope Diameter/ Length	Motor Type/ HP	Amp Draw Max	Max Load Line Speed, FPM	Drive Type/ Ratio
Superwinch	EPi6.0	6,000	21/64-125	SW/3.6 X	440	10	P/156:1
Superwinch	EPi9.0	9,000	21/64-125	SW/4.6 X	350	6.4	P/156:1
Superwinch	EP12.5	12,500	3/8-125	SW/5.6 X	350	2.6	P/261:1
Superwinch	EP16.5	16,500	7/16-90	SW/5.6 X	385	3.0	P/315:1
Superwinch	X6CD	6,000	5/16-100	SW/4.2	400	2.5	P/253:1
Superwinch	X9	9,000	5/16-100	SW/4.2	420	2.5	P/253:1
Superwinch	Husky 8	8,500	5/16-150	SW/4.2 X	405	1.5	W/229:1
Superwinch	Husky 10	10,000	3/8-90	SW/4.2 X	450	1.5	W/294:1
T-Max	EW-6500	6,500	9/32-94	SW/5.5	430	8.2	P/173:1
T-Max	EW-6500-WCP	6,500	5/16R-80	SW/6.6	410	6.5	P/173:1
T-Max	EW-9000	9,000	21/64-94	SW/6.6	425	7.56	P/173:1
T-Max	EW-9000-WCP	9,000	5/16R-80	SW/6.6	425	6.07	P/173:1
T-Max	EW-10000HD	10,000	23/64-94	SW/6.6	425	7.2	P/218:1
T-Max	EW-12500HD	12,500	3/8-94	SW/6.6	415	4.3	P/265:1
T-Max	EWI-10000	10,000	23/64-100	SW/6.6	410	6.4	P/218:1
T-Max	EWI-12000	12,000	3/8-100	SW/6.6	370	5.4	P/256:1
Warn	Tabor 9K	9,000	5/16-100	SW/4.3	559	5.9	P/216:1
Warn	Tabor 12K	12,000	5/16-80	SW/4.3	-	-	P-216:1
Warn	HS9500i	9,500	5/16-125	SW/4.6	425	6.67	P/156:1
Warn	HS9500	9,500	5/16-100	SW/4.6	425	6.67	P/156:1
Warn	M6000	6,000	5/16-80	SW/4.8	465	10	P/156:1
Warn	M8000	8,000	5/16-100	SW/2.1	423	3	P/216:1
Warn	M8274-50	8,000	5/16-150	SW/2.5 X	435	3	S/134:1
Warn	9.0RC	9,000	3/8R-50	SW/4.8	465	6.4	P/216:1
Warn	XD9000	9,000	5/16-100	SW/2.5	400	5	P/156:1
Warn	XD9000i	9,000	5/16-125	SW/2.5	400	5	P/156:1
Warn	9.5xp	9,500	5/16-100	SW/6.0	480	7.6	P/156:1
Warn	9.5ti	9,500	5/16-100	SW/6.0	480	7.6	P/156:1
Warn	9.5si	9,500	5/16-125	SW/NA	425	6.67	P/156:1
Warn	M10000	10,000	3/8-125	SW/2.5	475	3	P/199:1
Warn	M12000	12,000	3/8-125	SW/2.5	400	3	P/261:1
Warn	M15000	15,000	7/16-90	SW/4.6	460	2.48	P/315:1
Warn	16.5ti	16,500	7/16-90	SW/4.6	507	3.24	P/315:1
Warn	Dual Force HP(2)	9,500	5/16-125	SW/4.6	475	5.0	P/156:1
Warn	Dual Force HD(2)	12,000	3/8-80	SW/4.6	365	4.2	P/261:1

1) A two-speed unit. **2)** With built-in air compressor. **P** = Planetary, **S** = Spur Gear, **SW** = Series Wound, **PM** = Permanent Magnet, **R** = Synthetic Winch Rope, **X** = External Brake

CHAPTER 9
Navigation and Field Repairs: Bring 'Em Back Alive

Breakdowns are avoidable to some degree by good maintenance, but when they do occur, they may come at the most inopportune times. The middle of an off-camber, maximum-performance climb with a 50-foot dropoff is not the best place, but a broken U-joint doesn't give you much choice.

It isn't wise to venture out, especially alone, without knowing something about the area where you are going and how to get back. That requires a rudimentary knowledge of map reading and land navigation. In a similar vein, what you carry in the way of vehicle emergency and breakdown supplies, as well as the basics of how to repair a broken or ailing rig far from the nearest mechanic or shop, become more important the farther out in the boonies you go.

Navigation

The basics of navigation will enable you to read a map, use a compass and GPS (global positioning system) receiver, and generally have an idea of where you are in the outback. This section is not intended to turn you into another Frank Worsley (legendary navigator for arctic explorer, Ernest Shackleton) but to give you an overview of the procedures and equipment necessary for backcountry navigation. There are many good books on the topic, should you want more detail.

Since the first edition of the book, the whole navigation arena has been demystified by the advent of GPS units. Many newer 4×4s have them built in, and a soothing voice rises above your favorite tunes at appropriate times to direct you. Similar systems can be retrofitted to almost any vehicle, and handheld units have similar capability. GPS technology has progressed to the point of almost making the paper maps and compass navigation information that follows redundant. Almost.

The paper map and your ability to navigate the "old-fashioned way" is your backup, your Plan B. GPS batteries fail. There are areas in, and situations where, satellite reception may be poor because of cloud cover, trees, mountains, etc. A plethora of situations may come up when the old ways are the best ways, so don't give up on them just yet.

Paper Maps and Guides. It makes sense to have a map of the areas where you will travel. If you are going on an organized run, you could let that slide, but it's kinda fun to track the route anyway. No matter where you go in the United States, there's no good excuse not to have a map if you need it. Maps of every spot in the country are available. Between the USGS (U.S. Geological Survey), states, and even county governments, maps are available that cover almost every square inch of our proud country. There are private purveyors of traveling knowledge as well, offering road atlases, highway maps, and trail guides.

Available Maps. The USGS office has maps of virtually any location in various scales. Some are old, while some are quite new. You can order them from one of the branch offices of the USGS and can sometimes find them at state or federal park headquarters. The U.S. Forest Service and Bureau of Land Management each have their own maps, though they will only show lands under those jurisdictions. Most parks, whether federal, state, or county, will have their own maps available, and these may also serve to guide your way,

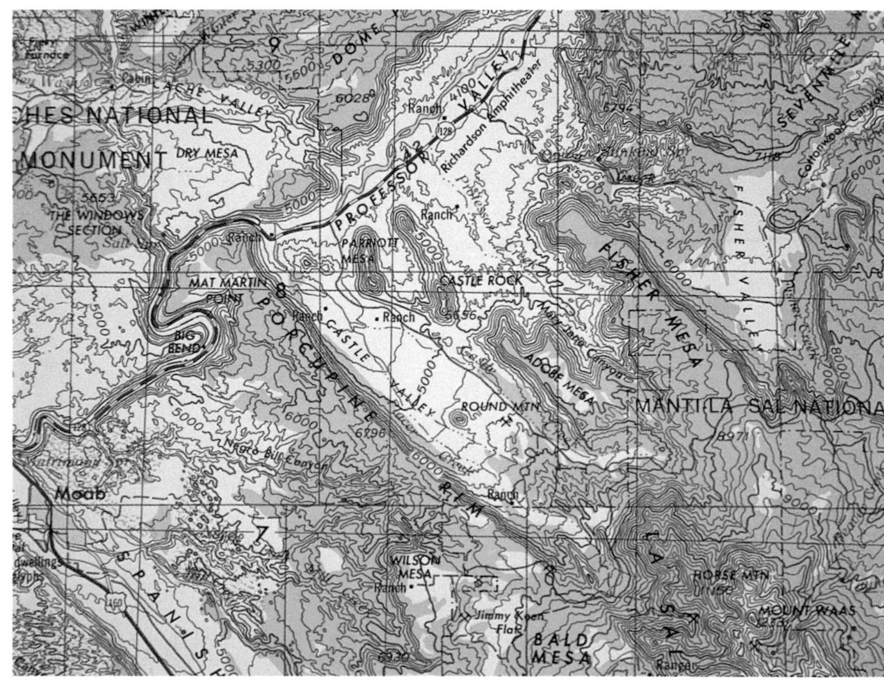

This is a typical USGS (U.S. Geological Survey) map. This is one of the more detailed maps in 1:24 scale that shows roads and even buildings. The entire map shows about 70 square miles of ground. Note the contour lines in this area that indicate lots of elevation changes. Close contour lines indicate steep grades, and as you can see, there's a lot of near-vertical around here. Contour interval on this map is 40 feet.

though sometimes with less detail than the USGS maps. They may be more current, however.

Another option is DeLorme's Gazetteer series. These are books that contain an entire state divided into grids. California, for example, is divided into two books (north and south) and 127 grids. This is detailed enough to see most roads and trails as well as terrain contours. DeLorme covers a good part of the United States state by state—certainly all the places where the best four-wheeling exists.

Electronic maps are available that can used in conjunction with a GPS or a laptop computer. Programs are available from DeLorme, and others, that contain very complete maps of the United States on CDs or disks. Many USGS maps have also been put onto CD-ROM.

Trail Guides. As the popularity of four-wheeling grew, so did a market for the creation of trail guides. These started out quite simple and crude but have developed into very accurate and sophisticated materials. They come in the form of individual maps of a trail or a popular four-wheeling spot, such as those available from Rick Russell, or books, such as those available from Charles Wells, Tony Huegel, and others, on four-wheeling in states or regions. These publications are usually incredibly detailed.

Map reading: Scales. Every map has a scale, whether paper or electronic (GPS), that indicates the area it covers and the details it provides. Think of the scale as the difference in view between the naked eye and binoculars when viewing the ground from high above. They are precisely scaled so you can measure distances accurately. You will commonly see three scales on

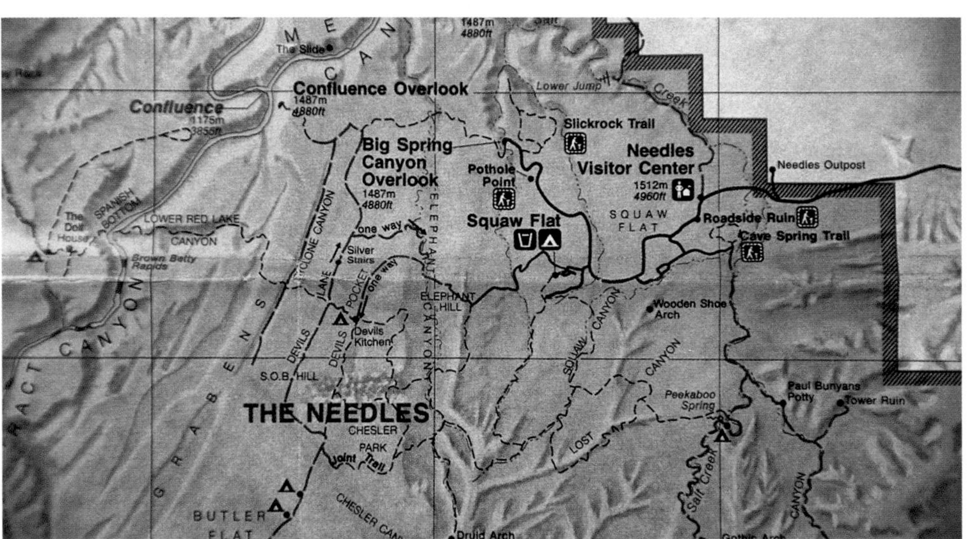

Here is a typical national park map. It's less detailed than the USGS topo maps, but it has most of what you need to find your way around. You may find some of the 4×4 roads missing from these maps.

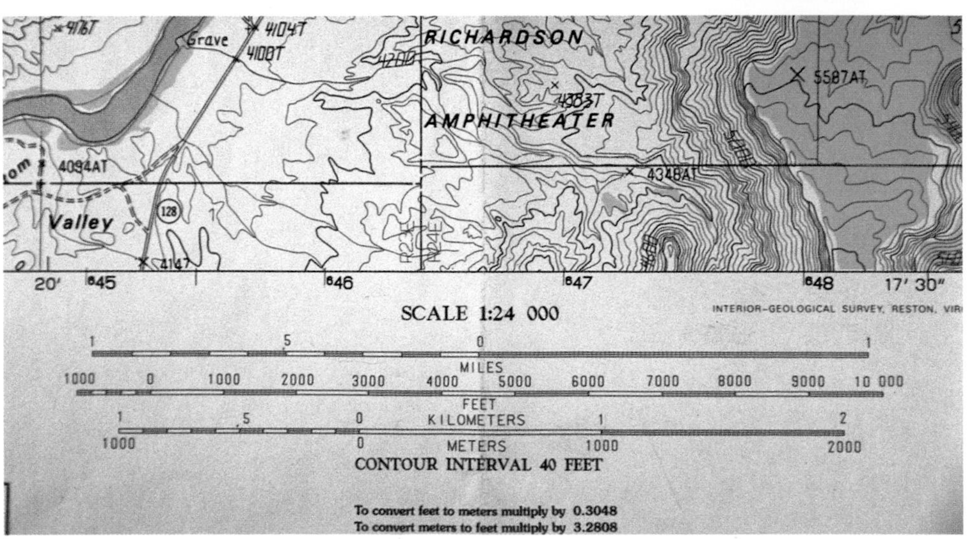

At the bottom of USGS topo maps are the important distance scales. This one shows miles, feet, meters, and kilometers. Contour interval is also shown.

USGS maps, with the 1:250,000 covering the widest area and having the least amount of detail. It represents an area 1 degree of latitude by 2 degrees of longitude, or about 4 miles per inch as measured on the map. Next up are the 1:62,500 maps that "zoom" in to about four times the magnification of the previous maps and cover an area of about ¼ degree each of latitude and longitude, or 1 inch to the mile. Finally, the 1:24,000 maps are the most detailed, covering about ⅛ of a degree of latitude and longitude, or about 2,000 feet per inch. The detailed maps cover about 70 square miles and are finely detailed. Other scales are seen on maps from various sources, so the first place to look on any map is the legend.

This shows a portion of the USGS maps available for the state of Nevada. The USGS has a map index for every corner of the United States. These same maps are now available on CD-ROM as well, so you can have the entire United States available on your laptop computer. The smaller maps shown here are 1:24,000 and the larger ones are 1:62,500. Four of the smaller ones will fit into one of the larger ones. Another section of this index shows 1:100,000 and 1:200,000 maps.

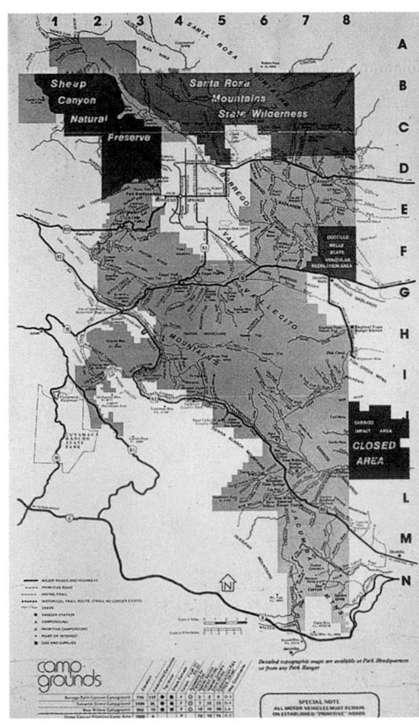

Here's a sample of a state park map, in this case an older map from the lovely Anza-Borrego Desert State Park in southeastern California. Most of the trails are listed with enough info to navigate around the park. Because the actual roads are clearly marked in most cases, there's little need for more detail.

Here are just a few of DeLorme's many state gazetteers. They give you a detailed view of an entire state, both the paved and unpaved roads. The scale is large enough that some details are left out, but I've navigated plenty of trails using only these and simple common sense. DeLorme offers the same items in more detail on a CD that can be integrated with a laptop and a GPS.

Here are three excellent representatives of trail guide books. These encompass much of Colorado and the hotspots of Moab. Author Charles Wells travels the country, running virtually every trail in his books, recording directions, obstacle locations, and GPS coordinates (which you don't need to use but are handy if so equipped). This is the highest standard for these types of books. There are many others by other authors for various places around the country. Some meet Wells' high standard and some do not. All can be useful if they are accurate. Wells debuted an Arizona guide in late 2001.

Map Reading: Topographical Features. Topographical, or "topo," maps show contours that will give you an indication of the terrain features. The topo maps on your GPS show basically the same features. The contour lines (see the nearby illustration) represent elevation above or below sea level and are marked with broad lines in evenly spaced intervals that give the elevation at that line, with dividing lines in between that can be either at 40- or 100-foot intervals. Peak elevations are also shown. The grade can be determined by how close the lines are to each other. Lines that are very far apart indicate a very shallow slope. Lines close together indicate a very steep slope. These contours can give you an almost three-dimensional look at where you are going

Compass. Every driver who ventures off-highway should have a compass. Not all of us are Daniel Boone, able to calculate accurate directions by looking at moss on trees (assuming there are trees or moss where you are!). There are two basic types: the magnetic compass and the electronic compass. One reads magnetic north, and the other true north. A GPS (more below) can be used for this purpose too, but it will eventually run out of battery power; the small handheld compass will work just as well today as 100 years from now.

The handheld compass must have a calibrated dial (showing 360 degrees) for taking bearings. It can be used in survival situations or for routine navigation. You may also want a vehicle-mounted compass *in addition* to the handheld (which stays in the survival

Maps are available from a great many sources, three of which are shown here. From left are a BLM map, a national forest map, and a privately produced map. All three are excellent examples with detail similar to USGS maps.

Special four-wheeling maps are available for select areas. These are a few of Rick Russell's Sidekick maps. The common element in these maps is that they are geared toward the needs of four-wheelers, so they show things like degree of difficulty for the trails, the locations of areas of interest, camping areas, and other useful stuff, not the least of which is how and where to get local help.

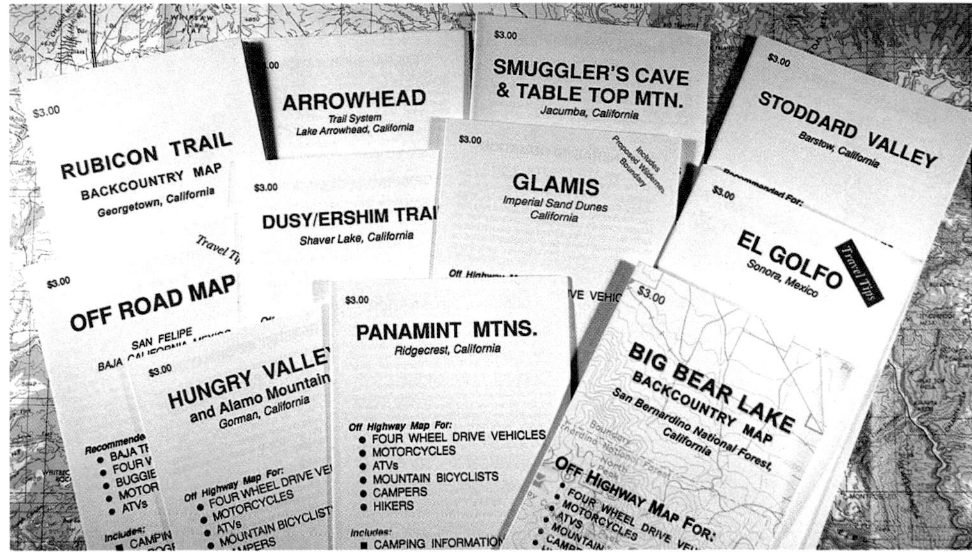

PAVEMENT ENDS

DECLINATION ERRORS:
The errors from declination changes over time are pretty minor over short distances. When you get into the hundreds of miles, the errors increase, but because we stick to established roads, we don't need pinpoint accuracy very often.

kit or is used for taking bearings). It's convenient and useful for "quick and dirty" navigation on the go. The GPS can replace a vehicle compass but not the emergency handheld.

Using the Handheld Compass. Two important factors that affect navigation by compass are *deviation* and *declination*. Deviation is the error imposed by outside sources, including ferrous materials (anything with iron), magnets, or electricity. Your 4×4, belt buckle, power lines, and electrical devices can all interfere with the magnetic compass and cause it to read inaccurately.

Declination is the difference between true north and magnetic north and changes according to whether you are east or west of the "zero" line where they briefly align. True north is located at the North Pole. Magnetic north is somewhere in Canada and still moving. Each topo map will have the declination from true north listed for that location, but older maps will be inaccurate because of the continual changes. There are isogonic charts available that can show you up-to-date declinations from any locale, but

This simple compass and a good map are all you need to find your way around. That doesn't mean you can't upgrade to a GPS. You can use the compass to determine a course from the map. Lay the compass on the map and use the body to mark an imaginary line from where you are to where you want to go, pointing the compass direction arrow toward where you want to go. You can draw a line from where you are to the destination, but the edge of the compass is usually good enough. Once the body is aligned, rotate the compass dial so that "N" points north, and align the orienting lines in the compass dials with the meridian lines on the map. If you pick the compass up and turn around until the red needle aligns with the red mark on the dial, you then have your course. Be sure not to rotate the compass dial.

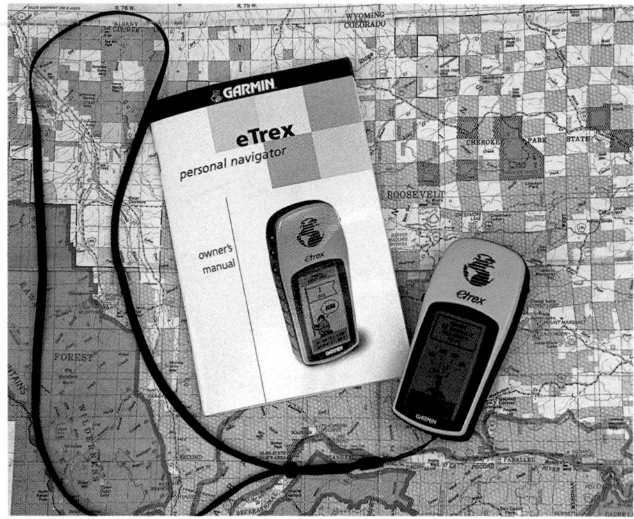

Until you've used a GPS and discovered the magic, you may be hesitant. A basic model like this E-Trex from Garmin is just above $100 and is worth the money for entertainment value alone. Given coordinates, you can find your way to or from anywhere. I find it most useful for mapping unknown areas so I can avoid getting lost. By marking waypoints at critical intersections, I can easily find my way back. They are useful even in non-four-wheeling situations. I recently located the long-lost corner marker for our farm, which was first settled in 1864!

Many GPS units can be integrated with a laptop for the ultimate mapping ability. You end up with a large, detailed screen, and you can upload digitized topo maps of virtually any area of the earth. An external antenna vastly improves GPS reception.

GPS:
The top-of-the-line mapping units can upload and download complete maps to and from map programs on laptops. They usually are equipped with higher-resolution screens and other features. They can record your route automatically as you drive and later allow you to print out a detailed map of your travels.

with a handheld compass, accuracy to that degree is impossible in most cases.

Take magnetic compass readings away from all sources of deviation, including your rig, belt buckle, pocketknife, and power lines. The main thing to remember is that the needle *always* points north. The part of the needle that always points north is usually tipped in red. The most common use of a compass is to determine the direction of travel or to determine your position by triangulating from two visible landmarks. The body of the compass is designed with an indicator arrow that you point in the direction you want to measure. Remembering that the needle always points north, the rotating dial has a red indicator that must be aligned with the red-tipped needle, and once done, the direction of travel will be shown in both degrees (0–359) and direction (N, E, S, W). If you want to navigate on that bearing, you just need to keep the needle and the indicator aligned.

The vehicle-mounted magnetic compass can only be used to indicate direction of travel. It's most useful at those moments when you face a fork in the road and aren't sure which way to turn but you know the general direction you need to go. The problem with a vehicle compass is that all the metal surrounding it creates a massive deviation. Even the magnetic effect of the ignition coil when the engine is running can throw the compass off. For that reason, the compass needs to be adjusted for the deviation. This is done by pointing the vehicle in known, accurate bearings, with the engine running, and adjusting the compass to match. The ideal is to use your handheld compass to find these bearings, but you can use streets that are known to run in a true direction.

GPS. The global positioning system is the high-tech new kid on the block. It's simple, easy to use, and deadly accurate. The military used it publicly for the first time to send cruise missiles into certain peoples' latrine windows during the first Gulf War, and today they are even more accurate.

GPS relies on 24 Navistar satellites in various orbits around the earth. They transmit on two frequencies, and the GPS units need to receive signals from at least four of them to determine a position accurately on both the horizontal and vertical plane. A GPS unit

GPS:
Many GPS units will make you a route map, whether it's a rudimentary squiggle on the screen or a detailed route superimposed on a real map that can be printed out.

also can measure speed and estimate time of arrival. Most GPS units locate your position within 60 to 100 feet on a horizontal plane, with vertical (altitude) readings to within 250–500 feet. *Selective availability* (SA) used to be an accuracy factor. It was a system that allowed the Department of Defense to make pinpoint accuracy available only to American or allied military units with the required decoders. With SA on, accuracy deteriorated to about 300 feet horizontally (or worse) and 1,000 feet vertically (or worse). As of 2007, it was reported that the SA system had been disabled permanently, so it should no longer be an issue.

All GPS devices now come as 12-channel parallel units, meaning they can continually track up to 12 satellites simultaneously. In a clear area, an average of 8 satellites are above the horizon and available for tracking. Older GPS units were serial (reading data from only 1 satellite at a time) and could track only 2 to 5 satellites.

A GPS can take a while to get its bearings. There are "warm" and "cold" starts. Each satellite is constantly broadcasting information on its location. This information is divided into a general "almanac" data, which is general information on the location of all the GPS satellites, and "ephemeris" data, which is precise and specific locational data on the satellite broadcasting it. On a cold start, the GPS knows only the general location of the satellites, so it has to search for each one. That can sometimes take a while.

On a warm start, the GPS has recently been on, and the ephemeris data, or some of it at least, is still close enough for the GPS to get a quick fix. The difference between a cold and a warm start comes down to the difference in time and distance since the last time the unit had a fix.

GPS reception is very much affected by mountains, trees, or buildings. Sometimes being in the inside of a vehicle is enough to disrupt the signal, though external antennas are available for many GPS models to cure that problem. That's why land vehicles still need to have paper maps and compasses in some situations. In the air or at sea, this is of lesser importance

This is navigation at its easiest, or so it would seem. People still manage to get turned around because signs go missing or are incorrectly placed. It behooves you to have a map of the area, even if you are in a closed OHV park like the late-great Paragon OHV park in Pennsylvania. In a more open area, such as a large state or federal park, signs may be few and far between, with authorized and unauthorized trails in between. The moral is that you cannot expect the same level of signage that you find on the street. Always get a map.

Most GPS receivers fit into one of three categories—basic units, point-of-interest units, or mapping units. They are further categorized by handheld versus mounted units, as well as by the size of their screens, computing, and storage power. They vary in price according to features. The basic units can find positions and store routes and waypoint informatio n but cannot download maps or point-of-interest databases. They can connect to a laptop computer and upload or download waypoints in conjunction with map software.

In addition to the basic capabilities listed above, point-of-interest (POI) units have more memory and can store the locations of parks, amusement parks, fishing locations, racetracks, or whatever interests you. Dads can look like real heroes, navigating the family right to the doorstep of whatever attraction is desired. These POI databases are available from various sources and can be updated. Specialized databases according to interest are also available, such as fly-fishing spots in Montana.

Using the GPS. Once you turn the unit on, it will immediately start searching for satellites. In a few minutes, it will have your location to within the error margin. This error has several names, including DOP (dilution of precision) or EPE (estimated precision error). Some units will give you an idea of the amount of error probable, and it depends on how many satellites the unit is able to track at any given time. The more satellites the unit has acquired, the more accurate the reading, and vice versa. Do not depend too heavily on altitude read-

TOOLS

The All-the-Time Kit

This is the crawling-on-the-ground minimum for any vehicle. Most of this kit will fit into one 19×9×9-inch plastic tool box. Beyond major overhauls, nearly every sort of repair could be performed with this kit.

1) Service manual.
2) A jack large enough to lift your *fully loaded* vehicle to change a tire. Make sure it has the reach to lift your rig if it has big tires. Include a 1-square-foot × ¾-inch plywood base for the jack to prevent it sinking into soft ground. Also include wheel blocks or identify something in your existing kit that will serve. If you have one of those short, wimpy lug wrenches, scrap it and buy one with some leverage (or use a breaker bar and socket).
3) Two flashlights. One small for the glove box and one larger for working. A 12-volt light with a long cord that connects to the battery is ideal as a work light.
4) Work gloves to avoid cut hands.
5) 3-pound sledgehammer for "persuasion."
6) 8- or 12-ounce ball peen hammer.
7) Combination wrenches ¼-inch to 1-inch (or metric 8mm–24mm). Add or delete as necessary to cover your vehicle's specific sizes.
8) Tubing wrench(es) (if applicable) to fit tricky fittings on your rig. Some rigs, like Fords, use a special tool to release fuel-line fittings. Get one—they aren't expensive.
9) Socket set in ⅜-inch drive with 6-point sockets as listed for wrenches, spark plug socket, 12- , 6-, and 3-inch extensions, swivel and long-handled ratchet. Optionally, a ½-inch drive socket set could be substituted, or a few of the larger sizes could be included with a breaker bar for those big, tight bolts. Why 6-point sockets? They hold better. But you may have some 12-point bolt heads on your rig, so you would need the appropriate sockets for them
10) Allen wrench set (if applicable).
11) Torx bit set (if applicable).
12) Test light for electrical circuits.
13) Wire cutters and/or combination wire cutter/stripper/crimper.
14) Pliers, both combination and needle-nose.
15) Large channel locks.
16) Locking pliers, small and large sizes.
17) Wire terminal crimping tool (see item 16).
18) Large adjustable wrench, 12 inches or better.
19) Small, medium, and large punches, center punch, and a cold chisel.
20) Screwdrivers, large, medium, and small in both standard and Phillips.
21) Hacksaw and extra blades.
22) Crowbar or pry bar.
23) A spindle nut wrench to fit your front axle and/or full-float rear axle (if applicable), with appropriate adapters to fit your ratchet or breaker bar.
24) Files, including a good-sized bastard file (coarse) and a couple of smaller, less coarse ones.
25) A siphon hose and funnel (suitable for ATF fill).
26) Jumper cables and/or "jumper" battery box.
27) Tire pressure gauge.
28) Valve core removing tool.
29) Scissors or utility razor blade/ X-Acto knife.
30) Air transfer hose.
31) Any specialty tools applicable to minor repairs on your particular rig.

For severe conditions, add:

32) 12-volt air compressor, portable or hard-mounted, suitable for your tires. (A good option: chassis-mounted air tank.)
33) Battery-powered or hand drill with a selection of bits.
34) One large and two small C-clamps.
35) Assorted wood blocks, 2×4, 4×4, etc.
36) Tire breakdown tools, including bead breaker and "spoon" bar.
37) Large pipe wrench.
38) Torque wrench.
39) Tire rod removing tool ("pickle fork").
40) Small grease gun with cartridges.
41) Under-hood welder, with welding mask, rod, etc. (very optional, but useful).
42) U-joint installation tool (easier for novice wrenchers, but not necessary for experienced).
43) Any specialty tools applicable for repairs on your particular rig.

ing in any case because GPS units have trouble reading it accurately. Many GPS units also feature a built-in electronic compass and altimeter.

You can have the unit display coordinates in several ways, but only standard altitude and longitude (in degrees and minutes) and UTM (Universal Transverse Mercator) are useful. UTM is a coordinate system that's a little easier to plot on a map than latitude and longitude. Most newer topo maps have both. Older ones only have lat/lon.

Before using the GPS in conjunction with a map, you must enter the map datum onto the GPS. Map datums are simple mathematical formulas that convert the earth's surface from round to flat. You must have the correct datum entered to get an accurate location on the map. All topo maps show this information, and GPS can match almost all the newer ones.

If you were starting off on a trip and wanted to find a particular spot, you could use the "Go-To" feature by entering the coordinates and selecting go-to, and the unit will direct you there. If the unit has mapping capability, it will show you the map, where you are on it, and perhaps even give you directions. Otherwise, you will just get the "that-a-way" arrow showing you the "as-the-crow-flies" direction to the destination and the approximate trip time. You have to correlate these directions with maps of the existing road systems to find your route.

If you set off on an unfamiliar trip, you can mark a waypoint at the start and waypoints along the way at critical turns, thus plotting your return trip. Waypoints are marked positions you can store on the unit. You can then use the go-to to find your way back to any of your en-route waypoints, or the first waypoint.

Many higher-end GPS units will map your route with as many waypoints as you elect to use. This is useful for mapping out a new trail in great detail and then later making your own map. Because GPS units are very power hungry, making lots of waypoints is practical only with those that have an outside power source, such as your vehicle.

Field Repairs and Spare Parts

Overall, current vehicles are much more reliable day to day than they once were, though perhaps more fragile and less tolerant of abuse. Because of the modern complications of sophisticated electronics, the days of bubble-gum and bailing-wire repairs are gone for many types of problems. Diagnosis is also more difficult. In the old days, when the engine quit, you checked for fuel and spark. No spark? Probably the points closed up or the condenser failed. No fuel? Probably the fuel filter was plugged or the fuel pump went bad. Today, if the engine quits, you can still look at the fuel pump or the filter, but it is likely an electronic problem. An ignition failure usually comes from a module or another electronic part. In some cases, you can do more harm than good by tinkering.

What about broken stuff? Drivetrains are still fairly simple, as are suspensions. You can still limp home on just the front or rear axle, or replace a broken axle shaft on the trail. Automatic trans repairs are no easier to fix than they ever were, and a grenaded transfer case strands you just as much as it did 30 years ago. At least a few things haven't changed.

Some of what you read below in the nuts and bolts sections may be beyond your current knowledge. It's up to you to bring that level of knowledge up to where those procedures are understandable—otherwise, they won't be much help when you break down.

Mechanical problems can occur anywhere, anytime, even halfway up a steep climb. In this case, the alternator belt failed just as a winching operation began. Without the alternator, the winch would have quickly drawn the battery down, so step one was to install a spare. The vehicle was carefully secured before work began.

Basic Field Repair Strategy

Think strategically about what you do and the likely emergencies for which you might need to prepare. There is such a thing as carrying too much. By overloading a rig with too much gear, you are inviting major breakage and decreasing performance. Tailor a breakdown kit according to your particular vehicle's weaknesses, how far in the boondocks you will be, the severity of the terrain, and how easily help is available. The nearby "Spares and Tools" sidebar outlines some ideas of what to carry and will answer many questions this section may generate.

To keep weight down, I vary the items in my own kit. A basic one is always with the vehicle, but when I'm going in harm's way on a very tough and remote trail, I load up with hard parts like spare axle shafts, universal joints, a spare driveshaft, and other heavy parts. I make it easy to add or remove items from the kit, tailoring it to the severity of the terrain and the likelihood of certain types of damage. If I pile in everything, which happens only rarely, I've got 500 pounds of extra equipment. Yes, I can feel the difference in performance!

The first defense against breakdowns is a well-maintained vehicle. Routine maintenance helps you find and address serious problems before they become an issue out on the trail. There is really no excuse for a maintenance-related problem stranding you in the wilderness. That said, fate is not always kind. Some breakdowns are largely unpredictable until they manifest themselves. Remember that the harder you work your vehicle, the more TLC it needs, and the more breakdown preparation you have to do.

The second line of defense is a well-prepared vehicle. That includes a common-sense breakdown kit but also common-sense modifications to suit the terrain. Taking a vehicle onto a tough terrain with a known weak link is almost as bad as a maintenance problem.

SPARE PARTS: The main trick is not to be stranded by a lack of little, easy-to-carry stuff. Think in terms of little things that will completely stop your rig. People have spent cold nights in the boondocks for the lack of a fuse, or the knowledge to work around that fuse failure.

ESSENTIAL SPARE PARTS

The Weekend Kit

This kit will cover your behind in most circumstances, especially if you are meticulous in keeping your vehicle in good repair. Many spare parts can be good used pieces that have been tested to work.

1) Inflated, serviceable spare tire; matches tires on ground.
2) Duct tape.
3) A selection of spare fuses, at least two of every size used in your vehicle.
4) At least one gallon of water over and above basic human needs.
5) Assortment of zip-ties, from tiny to huge.
6) Water pump, power steering, and alternator belts.
7) Radiator stop leak, heavy-duty.
8) WD-40 for frozen bolts and drying out wet electrical systems.
9) One quart motor oil, one quart auto trans fluid (can be used in power steering also), one pint brake fluid. Substitute one quart API G-4 90-weight gear oil for ATF on manual trans vehicles, in squirt-type bottle, but add one pint power steering oil. Motor oil can be used in place of 90-weight in an emergency.
10) One spare spark plug (if applicable), one spare plug wire long enough to work on any cylinder, points and condenser (if applicable), distributor cap and rotor (if applicable), one spare coil-on-plug (if applicable).
11) Fifteen feet of 10-gauge wire (this wire is large enough to work nearly any circuit) and a few shorter lengths of smaller wire. A selection of crimp-on electrical connectors, 18- to 10-gauge.
12) Roll of baling wire and small roll of plumber's tape.
13) Rags or heavy-duty paper towels.
14) Hand cleaner.
15) Tube of high-temp silicone sealer. Replace it annually.
16) Loctite thread restorer.
17) Small can of wheel-bearing grease.
18) Extra tire valve cores, caps, and at least one new valve stem.
19) Spare set of keys.
20) Small can of misc. hardware, including nuts and bolts, screws, washers, hose clamps, cotter keys, and so on.
21) Quick-set epoxy (JB Weld).
22) Fuel tank repair kit (suitable for your tank, either metal or polyethylene).

Heavy-duty kit, add:

This kit is in addition to what is listed above and should cover you for extended periods in primitive conditions or in areas with more breakdown potential. It is variable according to your past history and how well your rig is built up.

An example would be a generally acknowledged weak axle assembly that you have put in further peril by adding big tires and low gears. It's like rolling dice you know are loaded in favor of the house and then putting a big-money bet down.

When breakdowns occur, judge the safety of the jury-rig repair you have to make against the availability of help. Some field repairs make the later permanent repair more complicated and expensive. Don't double your repair bills with a questionable jury-rig if you are within easy reach of a tow or other help.

Overall, the most vulnerable parts of any 4×4 are the tires, so a few common-sense items in this area make a lot of sense. First off is a fully inflated, serviceable, full-sized spare tire. If your rig has a spacesaver or temporary spare, I would recommend upgrading to a full-sized spare to match the rubber on the ground. That may not be easy if there is no built-in storage for it. It could come down to installing an externally mounted carrier.

Tools and Spares Strategy. Regardless of your technical expertise, dealing with vehicle repairs in the field is a far cry from dealing with them in a shop or even your driveway. Imagination and ingenuity carry the day.

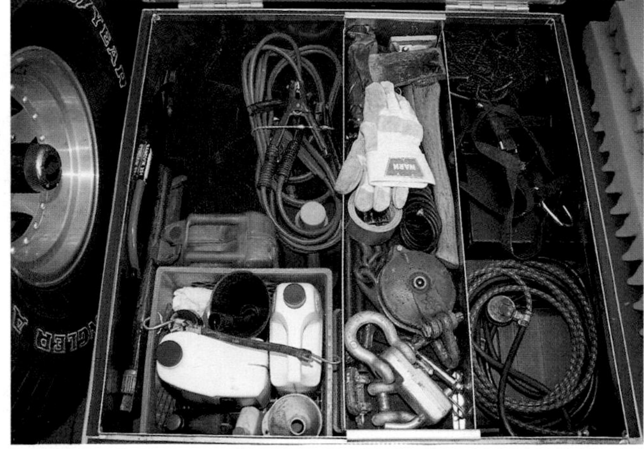

The Bum-V's storage box pretty much loaded for bear. The goal is to have the commonly needed items readily at hand. For me, that means the winch kit, strap kit, snatch rope, air hose, GI shovel, sledgehammer, and a selection of recovery hookup items. The foam rubber lays over the top of the load to keep it in place.

You can't carry *every* tool and *every* spare part with you wherever you go. The first tool you need is knowledge. A basic understanding of how vehicles work and a little wrench twisting experience is necessary if you expect

23) A tire plugging and/or patch kit and at least one inner tube suitable for your tire size so that a very damaged tire can still be made to hold air. Extra valve stems. Several extra lug nuts and wheel studs.
24) An extra fuel filter.
25) Brake cleaner spray.
26) Hose repair sleeves to fit your hoses, plus hose clamps.
27) Spare locking hub (used OK).
28) Spare front axle U-joint or CV joint.
29) Gasket-making paper.
30) Fuel line hose and clamps.

Super-heavy-duty it, add:
This is for hard-core 'wheelers in harm's way and is variable according to situation and level of buildup. It's simpler, more reliable, and lighter, for example, to upgrade to "unbreakable" status rather than carry a load of spares for a marginal unit, for example.

31) Three quarts SAE 90 (in squirt bottles), three quarts ATF, three quarts motor oil.
32a) For fuel-injected gasoline engines: spare control unit, spare fuel pump, and necessary installation pieces.
32b) For carbureted gasoline engines: carburetor gasket set, needle, and seat, and spare float. Spare mechanical fuel pump or repair kit (low-pressure electric in-line pump acceptable).
33) Electronic ignition module and/ or coil.
34) Wheel bearings. One each inner and outer, front and rear axles. Include one spindle bearing, axle seals, hub seals, and knuckle seals.
35) Starter or repair kit (mostly for manual trans rigs that regularly start in gear).
36) For manual trans vehicles: repair kits for hydraulic clutch, or spare clutch cable.
37) Spare rear-axle shaft. If offset axle, short shaft is most likely to break first. If C-clip axle, spare C-clip(s).
38) Spare spider and side gears, shims, cross-shaft, and lock-pin (if applicable).
39) Diff-cover gasket.
40) Complete spare front axles, both (delete spare U-joint). Alternate, one outer stub shaft and spare U-joint (usually the first to break and fits both sides).
41) ARB Air locker air hose fittings, solenoid valve, and air hose (if equipped with ARB).
42) Larger selection of nuts, bolts, and hardware. Include specialty items like extra spindle nuts, shock bolts, spring bolts, driveshaft U-joint bolts and straps, fill plugs, engine drain plug, tire rod nuts, and so on.
43) Spare tie rod, with ends.
44) Spare driveshaft (the most vulnerable one). Alternate or additional spare universal joints, one of each type. Include bolts, caps, or straps as needed.
45) Anything vulnerable or that has broken more than once. (Time for an upgrade?)

Storage trays similar to this are available from a variety of sources and make tools and spares stowage neat, clean, and safe. In the case of this Jeep CJ, it leaves useful stowage space on top.

This hard-core Grand Cherokee owner carries around spare front axles and CVs, as well as a spare tie rod in lieu of a beefed-up front axle. These parts were chosen based on previous failures, and the handsome carrying case is removable for easier trips.

to be of any use in a breakdown situation. You can gain this knowledge by taking night classes on auto repair in a local college or trade school. There are also numerous books written for beginners in bookstores and libraries to help you along. Once you gain a little confidence via knowledge, get some practical experience with maintenance chores on your own rig.

Once you have some basic skills, then a selection of tools becomes your next priority. First on that list would be a repair manual for your vehicle. Consider keeping a small paperback Haynes or Chilton manual, available in most auto parts stores and bookstores, in the vehicle at all times. While these manuals can't compete with a factory manual in terms of detail or scope, they are often easier to use and certainly less bulky to keep in the vehicle.

In terms of hand tools, the idea is to be able to do "the mostest with the leastest." The list in the sidebar and the photos show a sample kit, but each vehicle is a little different. By careful observation and checking, you might eliminate some items that aren't applicable and add a few that aren't covered. As far as quality goes, let your pocketbook be your main guide. Avoid the "X" brands. These tools are generally of very poor construction and often jam or break when put to the test. The best bets in cost-effectiveness are mid-priced made-in-the-USA brands, such as Sears Craftsman or SK Tools, which combine availability and quality.

How you carry your tools is another good topic. Avoid metal toolboxes because they are heavy and can damage items stored near them. Plastic boxes don't rust, won't scratch anything else, and are 80 percent lighter. You could also consider tool bags as an alternative for the same reasons. Another good idea is to have a small selection of very commonly used tools in a small roll placed where the driver can reach them easily. Who wants to dig for the toolbox through piles of gear to find a pair of pliers to pop the accelerator linkage back together?

Choosing spare parts to carry is an area that requires thought and judgment. Picking the right parts depends on how long you expect to be out of the normal maintenance and repair loops. Obviously, a weekend trip into the mountains requires less preparation than a Sahara expedition. You can base some of your decisions on the repair records of your particular type of vehicle. You can also get a feel based on your own experiences with the vehicle and have a talk with some local mechanics. Exclude major items like internal engine, transfer case, and transmission parts and evaluate the rest. Some weaknesses can be eliminated by upgrades or conversions to more reliable parts. Some faults are unimportant or easy to work around.

We've talked in general terms, but let's get to some specifics. What follows are some down-home fix-its for problems ranging from extremely minor to full-gonzo major. Many of these fix-its are avoidable by the means already discussed but are worth talking about because (a) parts can fail regardless of care and do so without warning, and (b) you're a human being and as such, brain flatulence is always a possibility.

Tire Repairs

Many people have been in the situation of having two flats on one run. The only option is a repair of the least damaged tire. There are a number of tire repair kits on the market, including the Safety Seal kit, which I have demonstrated for you in a nearby series of photos. These kits can safely and permanently repair certain types of damage and can also make temporary repairs adequate to get you out of the woods but not back on the highway.

In addition to a tire repair kit, a more extended trip may dictate carrying a tube and some tire patches and vulcanizing compound. A huge tear may not be repairable to a high-speed standard in the field, but you can stitch the sides together with fishing line or even baling wire, then put a big patch inside over the stitches and install a tube to hold air. A tire repaired in this manner is not safe for the highway or even safe for speeds much higher than 10 miles per hour, but it will get you to, or closer to, civilization.

Minor Electrical Repairs

Blown fuses are a fairly common failure. Step one is to determine if the failed circuit is vital or not. If it's not, and a simple fuse replacement isn't a cure, let it go and continue your trip. If a new fuse blows and no obvious short is found, try a fuse one or two sizes larger. For example, if a 10-amp fuse blows, a 15-amp may hold. Don't get carried away. Putting a 40-amp fuse in place of a 10-amp may fry wiring. Often, there is more than one electrical item on a single fuse. If one is vital and the other is not, you may be able to separate the two at the fusebox. If not, bypass the damaged circuit by running a wire directly to the important item from another power circuit. Make sure you use a fused circuit to power it and that the fuse is of sufficient capacity. If you have to eliminate some non-vital items to make the vehicle run, don't hesitate. Your mechanic and your pocketbook may suffer if you go wire-cutter-happy on a main wiring harness, but if it's a matter of survival or avoiding a long wait in the wilderness, you'll know what to do. You can also balance the cost of a tow against the cost of a repair if you are close enough to call for help.

If you suffer a blown fuse with no spare, use a non-vital fuse of the same or similar capacity to replace it. If there is no major short involved, a piece of wire or a bolt or anything conductive that will fit can be made to work. Just be aware that repairs like these are your last-ditch, crawling-on-the-ground solutions and

ELECTRICAL TRAIL REPAIRS:
An unfused circuit is a short waiting to happen. If there is an intermittent short and you eliminate the fuse, you'll find out where the short is rather quickly when the wiring harness goes up in smoke.

TRAIL ETIQUETTE:
Internal engine, transmission, and transfer case parts are outside the norm of reasonable spares for your trip. If you sense a problem in one of those areas, do yourself—and the others in your party—a favor and get it fixed beforehand.

TIRE REPAIRS IN THE FIELD

Tire damage is a relatively common occurrence, the likelihood increasing as the terrain difficulty increases. It makes sense to carry some tire insurance in the form of a good spare and a tire repair kit. This *Safety Seal* kit will repair the ordinary nail hole and can be used to temporarily repair worse damage. I used it to demonstrate the ordinary nail repair as well as something worse. The "worse" is not a good or safe repair for the street, but it will get you off the trail in the event of sidewall damage.

For your edification, I took a knife and made a 3-inch slash in the sidewall of a 31×10.50 tire. I used three Safety Seal self-vulcanizing plugs to fill the slit. As an experiment, I mounted the tire and drove five miles at up to 30 mph and then let the tire sit for a month. It did not lose a single pound of air from the 35 psi I originally installed. I would not drive at freeway speeds with this tire, but having been faced with more flats than I had spares, this option could have been a trip saver, if not a lifesaver. I must protect Safety Seal here by saying these sorts of repairs are not authorized or advocated by them, but I have seen them done countless times on the trail. The tire is obviously trash afterward, but it will have gotten you to a place where a new tire can be procured.

Oh no! A nail! Actually, you wouldn't believe how hard it is to get a nail into a steel-belted tire by hand.

Step one is to use the special lubricant and ream the hole with the probe tool.

The Safety Seal kit comes in a nice carrying box. These kits do not use a cement or vulcanizing compound, which is a plus. I have carried plugging kits previously and found that the compound had a short shelf life that always seemed to have expired by the time I really needed it. The self-vulcanizing plugs in this kit are ready for use and are good for at least six years.

After threading the plug through the slot in the insertion needle and applying the provided lubricant, push the plug into the hole until the sleeve touches the tire. Then push the sleeve against the tire to hold the plug in place as you withdraw the needle. The tire is repaired!

Only for you, dear readers, would I plunge a knife into the sidewall of a serviceable tire.

Three plugs filled the 3-inch slash nicely. I like to jam in as many as will fit. I put 35 psi into this tire immediately. As a test, I put about 5 miles on this tire at speeds up to about 30 miles per hour (faster than *you* should go!), and it held fine. I later let the tire sit in my garage, and it did not leak a single pound of air over a 30-day period.

result in what amounts to an unfused circuit.

Dead batteries are another fairly common failure. Obviously, jumper cables or a "jumper" battery pack are on the vital list and will get you moving again, but what if you are camping alone with your family without either of these and someone leaves the stereo on all night? If the battery is not stone-cold dead, putting it in a warm place for several hours (4–6) will help it regenerate. Depending on how far it was drained, it may come back enough to give you one more try.

A stone-dead battery would prevent any success at push-starting a manual-transmission vehicle. Alternators need a little bit of field voltage to energize them, and a battery with less than 2 volts won't do it. A 9-volt alkaline battery or a lantern battery applied to the "field" terminal of the alternator (positive terminal of the battery to the field, negative terminal to alternator case) could be enough to get the alternator energized for a push start, but be quick because the small battery will drain fast. Remember that all alternators are a little different, so consult your manual for specific information on the location of the field terminal. Old-style generators produce power regardless of battery condition.

In conclusion, when you get down to it, in a survival situation there are only a few priority electrical items on the vehicle—the engine electricals, perhaps the headlights, and maybe the heater. The rest is superfluous. If a major electrical meltdown occurs, rip wiring out of anywhere and get those vital pieces to work. You can do without the rest.

Suspension, Chassis, and Steering

Most suspension damage is a result of pilot error. Bent tie rods or any other steering or suspension link can be straightened enough to get by. Remove the offending part, find a rock, get the biggest hammer you have, and John Henry that part straight. Most steering rods are tubular steel and can be straightened without losing a great deal of strength. If they break, a rod can be inserted into both broken ends of the tube and welded, pinched, clamped, or bolted into place. Beware of solid or cast pieces. Cast parts may break as they straighten, and solid pieces may become fatigued and bend again very easily. Heating a cast part over a fire may prevent breakage when putting it straight, but the part will become brittle and may break under stress. By splinting the weakened part with steel rods and wire (or clamps), you can add a margin of strength.

Broken leaf springs can be splinted with a flat piece of metal and wire, hose clamps, or a C-clamp.

A broken locking hub is the most likely drivetrain failure four-wheelers at any level will experience. It's the weakest link in the system, and it makes sense to carry a spare. The aftermarket "premium" hubs are usually stronger than the OE hubs (by an average of about 15 percent according to industry sources). If you upgrade to better hubs, one of the old ones becomes your spare.

A regular bolt with the head filed to fit the receptacle on the axle can replace a broken anchor pin on a leaf spring. Broken coil springs can be overcome by using a piece of wood in its place to support the weight of the vehicle. A similar trick can work on leaf springs by jacking the vehicle up, putting a block between the axle and the chassis, and chaining the axle down. Either way the ride will be brutal, so take it slow.

Under-hood welding units, such as the Premier Power Welder system, are very useful for emergency repairs of all types, including suspensions. The system combines a high-output industrial alternator (useful for electric winch systems as well) with a welding box that uses high-frequency current instead of massive amounts of amps. You can actually get professional-quality welds with it, but perhaps more importantly, it's an easy system for amateurs to use.

SUSPENSION TRAIL REPAIRS: Suspension, chassis, and steering field repairs are designed to get you to the pavement where a tow truck can carry you the rest of the way for a proper repair. Your life is at risk with many temporary repairs, so don't count on them for high-speed driving, where a failure could be deadly.

Drivetrain

Drivetrains are another area where a controlled right foot makes for 98 percent fewer problems. Beyond that, wheel bearings can fail through lack of maintenance, or if water enters the hub. With water, the grease can fail rapidly, and bearing failure can come soon after that. The key is to stop before the bearing gets really bad and you lose the wheel and hub altogether. If the bearing completely disintegrates, you're hurting unless you have a spare. If the bearing remains in one piece, you can nurse it a long way by cleaning out all the metal and goop, repacking it in fresh grease, and taking it easy.

Manual transmissions can have failures but often will have at least one gear left with which to limp home. If something does fail but the trans still functions in some fashion, stop and drain out as much metal as you can and refill it with clean oil before you proceed. The metal floating around could kill it quickly and completely. The most common manual-transmission system failure is in the clutch area, specifically the release mechanism. Linkages can break and hydraulics can fail. If no repair is possible, the vehicle can be started in low gear and shifted carefully without disengaging the clutch by matching engine speed to gear speed. If the clutch assembly itself fails and the vehicle won't move, there's very little to do but lace up your boots.

Automatic transmissions usually give lots of warning before they fail. If the auto box starts to slip, stop ASAP and check the fluid level. The most common causes for auto trans failures are overheating, low fluid, or lack of maintenance. A leaking trans cooler line, for example, is not a problem in itself until the fluid gets low and the tranny starts to slip. It grinds itself up very quickly once slipping begins.

Broken rear axle shafts are possible and not uncommon. The only people who need to worry about safety are people with semi-float axles, which is most of us. Full-float axles, as seen on many ¾-ton rigs and all 1-tons, are safe to drive with a broken shaft. The obvious cure for a broken shaft in a semi-float unit is to replace it, and if you frequently venture into "axle-snappin' territory" you may (and probably should) carry a spare. Bear in mind that axles can break either at the outside or at the inner splined end. If they break on the inside, the broken stub will stay in the carrier, and the twisted splines may wedge it there. It may come down to disassembling the diff or removing the other axle, pounding the stub out from the opposite side with a long rod, and fishing it from the axle tube.

If you don't have a spare shaft, whether you can limp to civilization or not depends on whether you have a C-clip-retained axle or a pressed-bearing type. With a C-clip type, it's a definite no. With the shaft broken, the remaining parts of the axle and the hub, complete with wheel, will part ways with the vehicle. You can sometimes move a few feet before this starts to happen. One exception is C-clip axles that have rear disc brakes. The caliper will hold the axle in place to some degree. Many newer Dana and corporate axles are C-clip types.

A pressed-bearing axle can usually be driven a bit, though they will not always stay pressed in place. I wouldn't drive on the highway with a busted pressed-bearing shaft, but some people do. If the axle has been replaced, the mechanism holding the axle in the bearing may be damaged and won't hold as well as it should. The result would be losing a wheel and hub at highway speed.

Grenaded differentials, lockers, or ring gears are usually fairly hopeless situations without lots of spare parts. I have seen people with under-hood welders weld up broken spider gears to limp home on. Because you have another driving axle, you can usually get back to civilization on the remaining unit. If you have a C-clip-type axle, broken spiders and some types of carrier failures will release the axles. This often precludes the vehicle even being towed because the axles will not be

What's missing in this picture? A broken steering sector shaft (see arrow) is a trip-ending breakdown. There's no way to corn-cob it, and it will be a real bear to tow a rig in this condition. The most likely best answer here is to have a buddy make a parts run and bring back a used or rebuilt steering box.

The second-most common drivetrain problem is a broken front-axle U-joint. It's the first or second weakest component in a front axle, and it makes sense to carry a spare. The odds are less than 50/50 that the axle yokes will be too damaged to reuse. It depends upon how fast you get off the throttle at the first sign of trouble and the type of axle. Aftermarket alloy shafts survive more often than OE shafts.

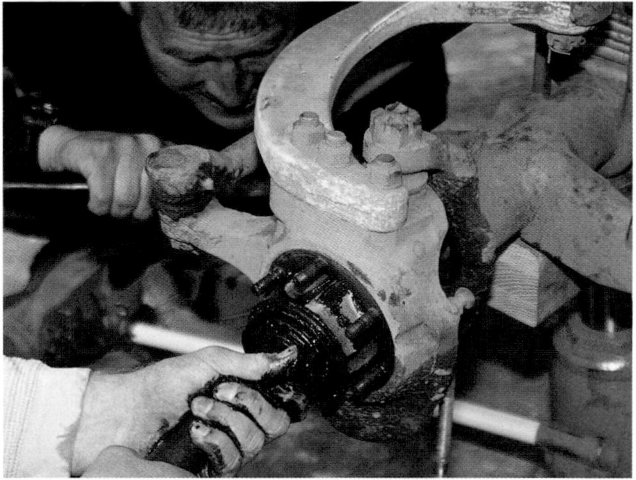

I have dozens of shots like this one, with industrious owners popping in a new joint or axle assembly. At least half the time, the ears of the axle yoke (either the outer stub or the inner axle) are damaged as well, so I like to carry a complete axle unit rather than just a spare joint. It's a faster exchange too. Good used pieces are OK. Note that this vehicle is not supported by jack stands, which are not practical to carry. The removed tire can be placed in a strategic location to prevent the vehicle from falling all the way if the jack lets go.

retained. Desperate 'wheelers with under-hood welders have welded the C-clips to the axle buttons to retain the rear axles long enough to limp to the highway.

If the vehicle will still roll safely, you will probably need lots of help from a towing rig or from your winch to get through on a tough trail. Don't overstress that remaining axle. The front, especially, is very weak compared to the rear. Once you discover that one of your diffs is "outta there," do what you can to isolate it. If it's the front, unlock the hubs and go into two-wheel drive. In the rear, it might be advisable to remove the driveshaft if you don't have a slip-yoke-type rear output on the transfer case. Slip-yoke T-cases will puke oil without the driveshaft in place.

Broken front-axle universal joints can be repaired sometimes if you carry a spare U-joint. If you get off the throttle quickly when you hear the ominous "snap," the yokes on the axle can sometimes be saved. I have seen a good number of front-axle U-joints replaced on the trail. A good portion of the time, however, the yokes are damaged too badly, and a new axle shaft, or shafts, will be needed. I have carried a spare pair of front shafts, inner and outer, with U-joints installed, for really rough terrain. That makes for a quicker change, albeit with some extra weight to lug around. Broken locking hubs are not uncommon. I carry a spare, as well as a solid drive flange (not available for all axles).

Driveshafts and driveshaft U-joint failures are uncommon except in the most extreme circumstances. In rocky terrain, the most likely failure is if one or the other gets hit and damaged. You get off easy if the unit is merely bent. Often, after a major impact, the tube will collapse and be twisted in half by torque. There's no cure here but a spare shaft, which is not on many spare parts lists—mine included.

Engines

Most engine failures stem from the engine's ancillary parts. Seldom does the actual engine fail, or fail to the point where it can't run. That depends on how you drive. If you're a high-revving throttle jock, of course, your odds for major engine problems increase.

Cooling System. Cooling system ills probably top the list of engine failures. Hoses are the main weak link, and that's why they should be replaced every few years regardless of how they look. If a failure occurs at the end of the hose near its fitting, it can often be shortened and reinstalled. Assuming you don't have a spare, hoses leaking near the middle can be repaired with duct or electrical tape, though this is often a so-so repair. A severely split hose can be sewn closed with fishing line and taped. The best hose repairs come from temporary sleeves that are manufactured in various sizes. You can cut out the damaged section and install the sleeve with a couple of clamps. This makes for an almost permanent repair, and the sleeves are easier to carry than spare hoses.

Bent tie rods or drag links are relatively common across the range of vehicles and terrain, but few are as spectacular as this one. As bad as this one is, it can be removed and straightened. The initial bend can be removed by prying against a large rock or in the receiver hole of a hitch. The final bit of straightening can be done on a hard, flat surface with a sledgehammer. Once bent and straightened, the rod will never be as strong as before, so it shouldn't be trusted beyond getting back to civilization. Solid tie rods or aftermarket tie rods made of alloy steel may be more difficult, or impossible, to straighten.

The chassis flex that results from difficult off-highway travel is a primary cause of broken engine mounts. It usually happens to vehicles with particularly flexy chassis, such as older Jeeps, most pickups, and long-wheelbase SUVs. A broken mount can allow the engine to slide forward a couple of inches and the fan to contact the radiator. In this shot, the damaged tubes are being pinched shut below the top and bottom tanks. It will effectively seal the leaks, but cooling capacity will be reduced. Heavy-duty engine mounts, often made of polyurethane, are available for many 4×4s.

The important step to remember with hose repairs, and many other cooling system repairs as well, is that most jury-rigs will not hold pressure. This means leaving the radiator cap loose. A pressurized system raises the boiling point of the cooling water by holding as much as 18 psi. This kind of pressure will blow a tape job all to heck. Another consideration is cooling system efficiency after emergency repairs. Combine an unpressurized system with a loss of coolant that further raises the boiling point (which you replaced with plain water, soda, beer, or even urine), and you have greatly diminished cooling capacity, perhaps up to 30 percent. This could be a problem in hot weather, making temp-gauge monitoring of vital importance.

Radiator damage is a possibility. Minor leaks can be stopped with the can of radiator stop-leak in your spare parts kit. I like the aluminum-based products like Alumaseal best, but the gloppy stuff like Bars-Leaks works also. There are some new ceramic-based products that reputedly work better than the aluminum ones. If you have time, epoxies like JB Weld can make a semi-permanent radiator tank repair. Major radiator repairs usually involve the core, which is composed of tubes connecting the upper and lower tanks (or left and right on a crossflow radiator) and a large number of cooling fins to radiate heat. When some of the tubes become damaged, the trick is to snip away the cooling fins around the damaged area of the tube, cut it, pinch off both ends of the tube, and roll the ends much like you would a tube of toothpaste.

Reducing cooling system pressure can slow water pump seal leakage. When a water pump shaft seal leaks, the fluid drains through a weep hole on the pump housing near the shaft area. As long as you have extra water, you can keep adding and driving.

As part of my set of cooling system emergency tools, I carry a 5-psi cap to fit my radiator. I have found this to be a good compromise between the original 18-psi unit and no pressure. This proved a very useful addition a couple of years ago when I nursed a blown head gasket home.

Belts. Drive belt failures are avoidable by regular changes, though I have seen some water and mud situations that destroyed otherwise good belts. Belts drive a number of engine ancillaries, many of which are not absolutely vital. You can do without air conditioning and even power steering if you must. The vital areas, in order of importance, are the water pump and alternator. Without the water pump, the engine will quickly overheat. Though the battery can run the engine several hours without the alternator, sooner or later it, too, will die. If one of the vital belts fails and you haven't a spare, one of the non-vital belts may fit. Even if it's a bit too loose, it may spin that vital pump or alternator enough to keep you going. Rope, leather belts, or even pantyhose can be used as a temporary belt to get you a few miles down the road.

Engines with serpentine belts use one belt to run everything. I've seen problems when the belt tensioner or the bearing on one driven item fails. There seems to be no way to corncob these setups back into operation in this case. It might be possible to figure a way to route the belt around such a failure, but in the ones I've studied, this did not appear to be possible. If I had a serpentine system, I might be tempted to carry a spare (new or used) tensioner assembly for some journeys. Whatever type of belt system you have, ask your mechanic to give you the old ones to use as spares when having them replaced in normal maintenance.

Fuel System. Plugged fuel filters are common. Bouncing around may cause the fuel pump to slurp up debris in your tank and restrict fuel flow when it reaches the filter. If the engine lacks power but runs more or less normally at low speeds, the fuel filter is a likely suspect. Carry a spare filter or two. Without a spare, plugged filters can be partially cleaned by blowing through them in reverse flow and tapping out the debris. Remember that with EFI, the system will be under high pressure, so don't just crack open the fuel filter lines without following the depressurizing procedure in the shop manual. Usually, pulling the fuel pump fuse and cranking the engine over for a minute will release most of the pressure, but your manual's instructions take precedence. Take appropriate fire precautions and put a rag over the lines as you remove them to reduce spraying.

Mechanical fuel pumps on carbureted engines usually fail because the neoprene diaphragm in them leaks or ruptures. If the pump can be disassembled (not common these days), a piece of rubber inner tube can be used as a temporary replacement. It won't last long in the fuel, but it might get you where you need to be. Another option for a failed fuel pump on a carbureted vehicle is to gravity-feed it. If you start a gravity feed from a fuel can held several feet above the carburetor through a hose leading down to the carb, the engine will run almost normally at slow speeds.

Fuel-injected engines are a class in themselves and a lot harder to nurse home. If the engine suddenly shuts off, look at the main EFI system fuses or for a major connection that has come adrift. This includes the fuel pump fuse. Most EFI fuel pumps are mounted inside the fuel tank. Have someone cycle the key on and off a few times while you press your ear to the fuel tank. You should hear the pump buzzing away. If not, check power to the pump (fuse, connections, or even the fuel pump relay, if so equipped). Without fuel pressure, you are stopped.

Found on road dead! Universal joints are not uncommon failures. The number one cause is lack of maintenance. The so-called "lifetime lubricated" U-joints are a major factor in this. If the grease breaks down (after 80,000 miles) or if water gets in, there's no way to know or to prevent failure except by periodically dismantling the joint and re-lubing it. Replace any failed or worn joints with a greaseable type and lube them regularly. There's old trail lore that says non-greaseable joints are stronger than greaseable, but some destructive tests done by Warn Industries a few years back that I included in a *Four Wheeler* magazine story showed them to be essentially equal in strength. Beyond the maintenance issue there are some rigs with extraordinarily small U-joints or weak straps and yokes. Jeep Wrangler YJs and many Cherokees are well-known offenders that need upgrades.

It may end up being the pump itself. Replacing an in-tank pump out on the trail could be a real bear. Some manufacturers put a cover in the rear floor so you can access the pump. Most just have you drop the tank. Dropping a full tank on the trail . . . yeah, right! It's possible, but . . . ? Fortunately, in-tank fuel pump failures are uncommon.

A minor problem may cause the engine to run poorly and give you an EFI warning light. In this case, the system goes into "limp-home" mode. It may run poorly, but it will run. Have a look under the hood for loose vacuum lines or wiring connectors. Sometimes letting the unit sit, key off, or disconnecting the battery for a few minutes (up to a half hour is necessary in some cases) will temporarily or permanently clear a fault. If the engine starts running rich (too much

This is what happens to a driveshaft that hits a rock while under a heavy torque load. Unless you have a spare, there's not much to do here. I have seen resourceful and skilled 'wheelers with underhood welders cut and section damaged driveshafts like this. That's beyond most of us normal folks. One cure for future failures is to have the new driveshaft built of heavier-wall tubing to resist damage.

This broken axle will make a nice stake! No fixing this puppy. Unless you have a spare, this is probably where you are stopped. This shaft was from a Dana 35 axle, which appeared on a large number of Jeep Wranglers and Cherokees. It's fine for street use but is well known for being one of the weakest axles ever to appear on a 4×4. It's not safe for more than medium-duty four-wheeling and/or a moderate tire size increase.

fuel) and blowing black smoke, there is some danger of overheating the catalytic converter. In some cases, it can overheat the floor of the vehicle, possibly even setting undercoating or carpeting on fire. Correct the problem if you can, but otherwise take regular cooling-off periods to reduce the danger.

In cases of poor engine performance or a rich condition, also check for a plugged air filter. If you've been driving in dusty conditions, there's a good clue for where to check. The air filter may be packed with dirt. Removing it (carefully so you don't let dirt fall behind it into the clean part of the intake) and gently tapping it against something will knock most of the dirt out. If you have compressed air, blowing it out (from the inside out) with low-pressure air is even better. Some filters will cease to flow air when wet, so if a running problem occurs right after a water crossing, that's another clue. Shaking the filter out to remove most of the water will usually do the trick, along with a little time in the sun. Airflow through the filter from a running engine, once you get it dry enough to flow *some* air, combined with engine heat, will dry it very quickly.

A leaking metal fuel tank can sometimes be repaired using an ordinary bar of soap. Seam leaks or small tears can be sealed by rubbing a bar of soap over the wound or cutting slices to push into it. Gasoline reacts with the soap, causing it to harden. Regular, old-fashioned soap is what works. Deodorant or scented bars may not do the job, but pure soaps like Ivory will. The only problem with the soap trick is that on modern rigs, the tank is partly pressurized, so the fuel cap may need to be left loose for the soap to hold. The best option is one of the commercial epoxy tank-repair preparations available in auto parts stores. It's a fuel-resistant epoxy. I've used it with great success and always carry two packages. It can also work on oil pans and transmission cases, as I have also found out personally.

If your rig has a polyethylene tank, ordinary epoxies will not stick to it. There are plastic tank repair kits; Permatex makes one that you can carry along for emergency repairs. There are even polyethylene welding kits you can buy for more permanent repairs, though any sort of heat or flame is not recommended around a tank with fuel or fumes inside.

Engine Internal. Internal engine failures aren't common. Catastrophic failures like thrown rods and sudden complete loss of oil pressure are fatal (to the engine). Knocks or noises can often be nursed quite a way. Again, gauge the ease of an outside rescue against the potential of increasing the repair costs. An engine with an internal problem may still run, but it most often is grinding itself up inside. The key elements are cooling and oil pressure. If the oiling system retains at least 10 psi pressure per thousand rpm, you have a chance.

Loud knocks with an accompanying loss of oil pressure usually indicate bearing problems in the lower end (crankshaft, connecting rods). A higher-pitched tapping could be the valvetrain and usually does not come with a loss of oil pressure. If accompanied by a miss, it could be a valve problem, a broken valve spring, a pushrod, or a rocker arm that has come loose or broken. The key to nursing an engine with sick innards is to run slow and easy. High speed or stress can put it the rest of the way out of its misery.

In Case of Vehicular Drowning

The usual scenario is that the vehicle was submerged deeply enough to kill the engine. That could happen from one errant splash in the engine compartment or complete or nearly complete submersion of the vehicle. Step one is to get the vehicle onto dry ground. Unless you are absolutely certain that it was only a splash onto the ignition that killed the engine, it's better not to crank it over until you make some checks. If you try, and the engine won't turn over, STOP! This is usually an indication that water has entered the engine cylinders and hydrolocked it. If water gets into the combustion chamber of the engine, it effectively stops it from turning because water does not compress as air does.

Once the vehicle is on dry land, remove the air cleaner. If the air filter is wet, or there is water in the filter housing, the odds are good that the engine has ingested water. In that case, remove the spark plugs (or the glow plugs or injectors from a diesel), ground each spark plug wire to the block, and crank the engine over with the key. This will pump the water from the cylinders, sometimes quite violently, so stand clear. Clear any water from the air intake system as needed, and if the air filter is wet, lay it out in the sun or on a hot engine to dry. Wet air filters do not flow air well, so get it as dry as possible before installing it and running the engine.

Before you reinstall the spark plugs, check the engine oil level. If there is obvious water in the crankcase, usually indicated by the oil level being over full, the best idea is to change the oil and filter on the spot. You may not have the oil and filter available for this, so if you let the oil and water separate (it may take a half an hour, but eventually the oil will be on top and the water below), you can loosen the drain plug and let the water out. When clear oil begins to flow, reinstall the plug. Drain this oil/water into a container and not onto the ground. Check the oil level and add whatever is needed. Run the engine a few minutes and let it sit again, checking for more water. Change the oil ASAP after reaching civilization.

The ignition system may also be wet, so remove the distributor cap (if your engine is so equipped). WD-40 sprayed in and around the distributor will help it dry. If your rig is a distributorless system, check all connections for water. If it has coil packs with short plug wires, remove the wires and clear out any water. If coil-on-plug, you may need to remove each coil individually for drying.

Fuel-injected engines may stop when the electronic pieces are soaked. First, check to see if the fuel-injection control unit (ECU) has been immersed. Some are quite water-resistant, while others are not. If the unit has been drowned, you are faced with removing it and emptying the water. If the unit has a removable cover, it can be opened for better draining and air-drying. Other fuel-injection components may also require drying out. You may be able to get these components operating in some fashion right away, but the majority are write-offs in the long term because of corrosion.

With the spark plugs reinstalled, the engine should restart normally. There will probably be a great spout of water from the tailpipe and some steam for some minutes afterward. Time and heat will dry out the rest of the under-hood components, though you may encounter electrical problems down the road because of wet connections or the resulting corrosion.

Other places to look for water are the transmission, transfer case, axles, and all the other stuff mentioned earlier. The cure is a complete change of all fluids. While you may be able to limp to civilization with water-contaminated oil in the diffs or transfer case, automatic transmissions are very vulnerable to water contamination. Running an automatic with more than a tiny bit of water contamination can result in total failure.

If the vehicle has been in deep water, there are a multitude of other potential problems. There's a good reason why flood-damaged vehicles are usually totaled! If yours goes in so deep that you get into these worst-case scenarios, unless you are stranded alone and have the expertise to solve all the problems, you are probably better off getting the rig hauled out and taken care of by pros. The general rule of thumb for modern vehicles is if water was high enough to reach into the dashboard in a significant way, you have a very hurting unit and a possible total.

IN CASE OF VEHICULAR DROWNING: Repeated attempts to start a waterlogged engine may cause serious damage. In fact, the engine may already be damaged from ingesting water if it was running when the water entered the combustion chamber.

APPENDIX 1
Glossary of Terms: Four-Wheeler's Dictionary

A-arm—A triangular suspension component used on independent suspensions. Also could be called a control arm, upper or lower. It pivots on the chassis at two points, at the wide end of the "A," and the pointy end attaches to the spindle.
ABS—The anti-lock braking system is an electronically controlled system that prevents skidding under hard braking by controlling and equalizing wheel speed. A two-channel system controls only the two wheels in the rear, while a four-channel system controls all four wheels.
Ackerman angle—A.k.a. toe-out on turns. Ackerman is an engineered value that describes the degree to which the inner wheel is designed to steer at a greater angle than the outer because the inner wheel covers a shorter path.
add-a-leaf—An inexpensive method of lift where an additional leaf is added to the leaf-spring pack to provide a small amount of lift at the cost of ride quality.
aftermarket—Vehicle parts or equipment not manufactured by the original equipment manufacturer (OEM, or OE).
amp draw—The number of ampere-hours (amp hours) needed to run an electrical device.
approach angle—The maximum angle of climb that a vehicle can surmount without hitting some part of the body, chassis, or mechanicals in the front.
arch—See *camber*.
articulated—When one tire is at its upper travel and the other at its lowest travel and the axle is at a severe angle in relation to the body. See also *cross-axled* and *articulation*.
articulation—The ability of a suspension to combine compression and droop on one axle. If a suspension articulates well, the body will stay relatively level, but the axles will operate at severe angles
aspect ratio—The ratio between the tire's width and sidewall height. Expressed as a percentage, it represents the tire's profile or the distance between the tread and the rim versus its section width.
axle wrap—Torque and traction combine to twist the axle (pushing the nose of the differential up when going forward and down going backward) into an "S" shape. The energy is stored in the spring until the tire slips, and at that point the spring snaps back violently. Sometimes this results in a hopping sensation, hence the other common term, "axle hop." It can be very hard on driveshafts and U-joints.
backspacing—Another term for wheel offset. It's the distance from the inside edge of the wheel to the mounting flange.
bead—The area that mates the tire to the wheel. This area is a critical part of the tire's construction and consists of a hoop of high-tensile steel wires to which the belts are attached. This anchors the belts as well as providing a firm grip on the rim.
bead filler—A solid rubber wedge built into the lower sidewall designed to stiffen the area near the bead.
beadlock—A type of wheel rim that prevents the tire from sudden deflation when used at low pressure.
bead seat—This is the smooth face on the bead area of the tire that seals against the rim to hold air.
beater—A 4×4 in rough condition. Usually one that looks bad but runs well.
beef—Strength. Also adding strength to a part: upgrading.
belts—The obvious engine accessory drive belts but also a tire-related term for the rubberized woven fabric that runs around the circumference of the tire under the tread. Polyester and steel in combination is the most common construction material.
binder—Short for "cornbinder." Slang for vehicles built by the International Harvester Company.
Birfield—Another name for a six-ball constant-velocity joint, usually used by Toyota or other Japanese 4×4 enthusiasts. The original design came from Hans Rzeppa in the 1920s, but one of the later manufacturers was Birfield Ltd. in England. The Birfield joint was introduced in the Toyota Land Cruiser in the 1960s. It isn't clear whether they were produced in Britain or under license in Japan, but the tooling to make these CV joints was elaborate and expensive. Many of these CV joints were stamped "Birfield."
blip—A quick stab of the throttle.
bogger—A vehicle built for running mud. Also another term for an aggressive mud tire.
bolt clips—A device used to keep the spring leaves lined up atop each other. This is the preferred method because it does not restrict the movement as the "cinch"-type clamps may do.
bottom—Compressing the suspension to the point where it reaches the bump stops.
boxing—Usually refers to chassis modifications, where the chassis is reinforced by closing the open part of a "C" or "U" section with additional material. It adds considerably to the strength.
built—Short for built-up, or heavily modified.
bump steer—Where a bump or movement of the suspension forces the steering system to steer to one side or the other.

Accompanied by movement of the steering wheel. Can occur at low speeds as the suspension moves up or down, or can occur at speed when bumps are encountered. It occurs to most 4×4s to a certain degree at low speeds, but at speed, it can be dangerous.

bump stop—A rubber or polyurethane bumper in the suspension that limits the upward travel of the wheel.

CAD—Center Axle Disconnect. A device that disconnects one front axle shaft (usually the long one) from the differential via a splined, sliding collar. It's commonly actuated by engine vacuum but can also be cable- or hydraulically operated. The idea is to reduce the parasitic drag of the front axle and prevent the driveshaft from turning in two-wheel drive, and it was conceived as an alternative to locking front hubs. This system only works with open diffs, and it still allows the differential side and spider gears in the differential to rotate. If a limited-slip or locker is installed, the left axle will then drive the ring and pinion and the driveshaft, usually causing a vibration at higher speeds.

camber—The built-in curve or arch in a leaf spring. Also a steering term indicating the inward or outward tilt of the tops of the front tires. Positive camber tilts them out (as viewed from the front), and negative camber tilts them in.

camber roll—The increase in camber that comes when the vehicle is steered hard to one side or another.

chafer—Rubber-coated fabric added to the bead area for strength.

Cardan joint—The original name for the common universal joint, named for the 16th-century Italian mathematician, Jerome Cardan, who established its basic principle of operation.

casing—The body of the tire, built up from cords and belts of material. Also known as the "carcass."

caster—The forward or backward tilt of the steering axis. Positive caster tilts the top pivot from the vertical toward the rear of the vehicle, and negative is the opposite.

center of gravity—The point of a vehicle where it balances on all planes. On most rigs, that point is somewhat forward of center and 1 to 2 feet off the ground, when viewed from the side, and slightly off to one side when viewed from the top. A lower center of gravity makes for a vehicle that is resistant to rolling over.

chunk—When a tire throws off small pieces of tread. Comes from heat and friction but can occur when a tire is siped.

compound—The mixture of material that is the "rubber" part of the tire. There are five basic ingredients: rubber, carbon black, plasticizers, a curing ingredient, and an ozone retardant.

compression travel—The amount of upward travel of a suspension above the static ride height.

contact patch—The part of the tire that makes contact with the ground and provides traction. The patch varies according to the tire size and the tire pressure used.

cord—The stranded material incorporated into the belts and plies that are made into the casing of the tires.

crawl ratio—Also known as final drive ratio. The maximum multiplied lowest gear ratio, to include first gear, transfer case low range, and axle ratio. If there is another gearing device, that ratio is also added.

cross-axled—When the front and rear axles are articulated opposite each other.

crossover steering—The steering system in which the two steering knuckles at the wheel ends are tied together directly with one rod called the tie rod. A drag link comes down from the steering box and attaches to one knuckle or the other to supply the steering input.

crossover SUV—Most commonly a car or minivan platform with, or adapted to, AWD.

crown—The center of the tire tread.

CV joint—Constant-velocity joint. Several types exist, including the six-ball Rzeppa (pronounced "Cheppa") joint, the similar Birfield type, the four-ball Bendix type, and the Herrington type consisting of two Cardan or U-joints. The result of all of these is the smooth transmission of power with no vibration. They are used on driveshafts and steering axles.

dead man—An anchor point to winch from. If can be just about any solid object capable of supporting the weight applied against it.

death wobble—An overly dramatic term describing a severe steering vibration.

declutching—Usually pressing in the clutch to uncouple the engine from the drivetrain. It can also refer to the neutral position of items like the transfer case, PTOs, winches, CADs, and other items that use a mechanical-type disconnect.

deep gearing—See *low gearing*.

deflection—Movement or compression of a spring. Also the amount the tire "gives" under load. Essentially, the difference between its free and unloaded radius and its fully loaded radius.

departure angle—An imaginary line or angle at the rear of a vehicle between the contact point of the tires and the lowest part of the rear overhang. This angle dictates the height and steepness of the obstacle that the vehicle can descend, as well as the angle of the climb the vehicle can make without dragging tail.

directional stability—The ability (or lack thereof) of a tire (or vehicle) to maintain a straight line rather than following irregularities in the road.

dragging tail—A.k.a. butt-dragging, tail-dragging. When the rear of the vehicle makes contact with the ground, especially on a climb or descent.

drag link—The steering rod that connects the steering box Pitman arm to the tie rod.

droop travel—The amount of downward suspension travel below the normal ride height of the vehicle, a.k.a. jounce.

drop Pitman arm—A special type of Pitman arm that is lower than stock. This reduces drag link angularity and bump steer.

duty cycle—The period over which a device can be operated before damage or undesirable effects occur. A cycle of on time versus off time.

eye—The loop in the end of the spring into which a bushing is installed and the spring is mounted. Also the eye in a rope or cable end.

eye-to-eye—The measurement of a leaf spring from the center of one eye to the other. Usually taken unloaded.
fairlead—A guide for the winch cable. Can be a hawse type, which is a simple opening with smooth, radiused edges. A roller fairlead has rollers on the top, bottom, and sides to guide the cable.
free arch—The distance between the top of the inside of a leaf spring to an imaginary line drawn between the center of the two eyes when the spring is unloaded.
free length—The unloaded length of a coil spring.
full-floater—A full-floating axle, which is one where the weight of the vehicle is borne by a separate stub axle and bearings rather than the axle itself.
GCVWR—Gross combined vehicle weight rating. The maximum weight for a vehicle, its cargo, and its towed load.
gnarly—Either some part that pegs the heavy-duty meter or a tough obstacle or section of trail.
granny—Low gears. First gear in low range, for example, is sometimes called "granny-granny."
green tire—This is the uncured tire, complete with all of its other components, waiting to be put into a mold and heated.
grenade—As applied to four-wheeling, to destroy a mechanical part in a spectacular way.
grip—A term used to describe the traction, or friction coefficient, of a tire on the ground surface.
gusset—A reinforcing component used to strengthen a connection of two structural members.
GVWR—Gross vehicle weight rating. The maximum weight for a vehicle and its cargo.
hammered—Beaten, abused, trashed.
high-centered—Hung up at the center of the vehicle. Can also be used when hung up on the axle.
high pinion—A hypoid axle with a reverse-cut ring gear. The pinion is above the axle centerline.
hook up—To gain traction.
high gearing—Numerically low gear ratios. Generally speaking, ratios from 2.50:1 to 3.54:1 are considered "high." See also *tall gearing*.
hydrolocked—An engine that is prevented from turning by water in the cylinder. Water does not compress. Sometimes also called "hydro'ed" or "hydraulic'ed."
IFS—Independent front suspension.
inverted-T steering—A type of steering linkage in which the drag link attaches to a place on the tie rod inboard of the knuckles, rather than at the knuckles.
inverted-Y steering—A.k.a. the "Haltenberger" system. A type of system in which the drag link attaches to the opposite axle knuckle and a short tie rod connects the other knuckle to a point near the center of the drag link.
lift—The raising of a vehicle to gain trail clearance and clearance for tires.
limited-slip—A traction-aiding differential that will supply a preset amount of torque to the tire with the most traction.
line—A path through or over an obstacle that provides traction and clearance.
line pull—How much pull the winch can generate. This is variable because there are several ways to measure it. Most winch ratings are taken from the first layer of cable. Winch ratings assume an adequate battery.
line speed—How fast the cable spools onto the drum. Line speed varies according to load, gearing, motor power, and which layer of cable is in use.
locked up—A vehicle with a locker or lockers.
locker—A traction-aiding differential that will provide 100 percent of the torque to either axle or both.
low gearing—Numerically high gear ratios, a.k.a. "deep" gearing. Generally speaking, from 4.10:1 to about 6.13 (pretty near as low a ratio as you can find for light-duty truck and SUV axles) are considered low gears. Lower than 4.88:1 is considered "super" low. Ratios from 3.54 to 4.10 are regarded as moderately low.
low-lock—Low range.
main leaf—The first or primary leaf of a leaf spring. Often this is the only leaf with an eye, though the second leaf may also have one that wraps around the outside of the main leaf.
meats—Tires, especially big ones. A.k.a. "zapatos," or "skins."
military wrap—This is where the second leaf of a leaf spring loops loosely around the main eye. As the name implies, this was originally mandated by the army so that the vehicle was operable with a broken main leaf.
mogate—An old army term for being able to move under power.
multi-link—A coil-spring suspension with multiple locating links.
nail—To fully depress the accelerator pedal. To "punch" it.
nerf bar—A rocker guard.
NOS—New old stock. Old parts but never used and still in their original boxes.
NVH—Noise, vibration, harshness.
OEM—Original equipment manufacturer. Also "OE." A term sometimes used to describe a stock vehicle.
off-camber—Tilted sideways on a slope. Sidehill.
overwound cable—Where the cable spools off the top of the winch drum.
Panhard rod—The transverse link that locates the axle laterally on a coil spring and some leaf-spring suspensions. A.k.a. "track rod."
part—To break; referring to the cable.
permanent-magnet motor—A simple motor that uses two magnets instead of energized field coils. The advantages are compact size and a lower amp draw than *series-wound* motors. Power and performance characteristics are similar to the series-wound. The disadvantages are that they generate more heat at high loads and have an increasingly shorter duty cycle as the load increases. Permanent-magnet motors may also produce less power at below-zero temperatures. These motors are most often used in the lower-capacity or lower-priced winches.
pinion—The input drive for the differential, or a shaft with a small gear attached. The "spider" gears in an open differential are also called pinions.

pinion angle—The angle of the differential input pinion in relation to the horizontal position.
pin offset—Describes a situation when the anchor pin that locates the axle onto a leaf spring is not centered on a spring. Specifically, it is the distance the pin is off-center.
Pitman arm—An arm that attaches to the output shaft of the steering box. It converts the rotating motion of the steering box into lateral motion for steering.
pitch—Also called ramp. Refers to how tightly a spring has been wound. Close-together coils have less pitch than coils that are farther apart.
planetary gear—A multi-piece gearset that consists of the sun gear in the center, the planet gears(two, three, or four of them) that rotate around the sun, and a ring gear around them all.
posi—Slang for a limited-slip differential. Named after GM's "Posi-Traction" unit, which was built by Eaton.
prerunner—In reality, a truck designed to prerun a desert race course. Also a style of truck devoted to going fast in the dirt. Can be 4×4 or 4×2 but has a very compliant, long-travel suspension that's built for frequent flying.
progressive rate—Springs with rates that increase as they are compressed.
proportioning valve—A device in the braking system that apportions brake pressure front and rear.
PTO (power take-off)—A mechanical device that uses engine power, either directly or through the drivetrain, to power the winch or some other device. Many winch PTOs drive off the transfer case, and some drive off the transmission.
pumpkin—Slang for the removed part of a removable carrier differential, a.k.a. Hotchkiss design, such as a Ford 9-inch or a Toyota.
rack-and-pinion steering—This system eliminates the conventional steering linkage and steering box. A long rod, with tie rods on the ends, connects the two wheels. The rod is in a housing that lies parallel to the ground and has teeth on one side. A spur-type gear is in mesh and connected to the steering wheel through the steering column. Steering wheel input moves that rod left or right, steering both wheels directly.
radius arms—Fore and aft locating arms for multilink suspensions. A.k.a. trailing arms.
ramp breakover angle—An angle formed from the contact area of the tires and the lowest part of the vehicle's midsection. A measurement of clearance.
rate—The amount of weight it takes to deflect a spring. Expressed in pounds per inch. It takes 200 lbs. to deflect a 200 lb./in. spring 1 inch, 400 lbs. for 2 inches, and so on.
rebound—The action of a spring returning to its natural ride height or preset "memory" position.
ride steer—An undesirable symptom most often a problem in lifted 4×4s with track bars. As ride height changes, the transverse track bar changes the position of the axle in relation to the other and imparts a slight amount of steering input, which the driver must correct. This happens most often on lifted rigs with a great deal of angularity on the track rod.
ring gear—A circular gear in the axle housing that provides the axle gear ratio in combination with the pinion gear, a.k.a. "crown" gear.
road—Any path over the ground designed for motor vehicle travel.
roll angle—The amount of body angle, or lean, the vehicle experiences on rough terrain.
roll steer—An undesirable symptom, most often seen in long-travel coil-spring rigs, whereby body roll changes the position of the axle and tends to steer the vehicle in a turn, requiring constant driver corrections.
RTI—Ramp travel index. A measurement of articulation and suspension travel calculated by driving one wheel up a ramp until one rear wheel lifts, measuring the distance up the ramp level with the hub center, and dividing that measurement by the vehicle's wheelbase.
scrag—A.k.a. "presetting." A method of setting the position "memory," or the permanent height or camber of a spring. After assembly, the spring is placed in a press and deflected a predetermined amount. This is usually past the normal deflection the spring will encounter in use.
section width—The sidewall-to-sidewall width of the tire. Not to be confused with tread width.
semi-float—An axle that supports the weight on the axle shaft as well as driving the wheel with it.
series-wound motor—This motor has field windings that consist of copper wire wound over an iron core. A series-wound motor is larger than a *permanent-magnet* motor and has a much longer duty cycle (more resistant to heat). It draws more power than the permanent-magnet type with nearly the same performance characteristics. These motors are most often used in the higher-capacity, higher-priced winches, or winches designed for commercial applications.
shackle—Either a D-shaped connector used for winching or recovery, or the pivoting link at one end of a leaf spring that allows the spring to "grow" longer or shorter as it flexes.
shear pin—A carefully designed pin in a PTO winch that is designed to break before something else does. Because PTO winches are driven by engines with 100 times the power of an electric motor, the shear pin is calibrated to break before the winch or winch cable does. If you have a PTO winch, you should have a couple of extra shear pins just in case.
shotpeening—Referring mainly to leaf springs. Steel shot is sprayed at high pressure on the surfaces of the leaves to compress the surface of the steel and surface-harden it. The technique is also used to surface-harden other metal parts, such as connecting rods.
siping—Slits or cuts in the tread blocks that allow the blocks to move and grip. Sipes can be built into the tire by the manufacturer or added later. Siping usually enhances the wet and icy performance of the tire.
slushbox—Slang for automatic transmission.
snatch block—A high-capacity pulley used for winching.
snatch strap—A kinetic-energy recovery strap.

spool—The careful laying of the cable onto the drum, with the wraps wound tightly on the drum: tightly beside each other and tightly atop each other in succeeding layers. Also a solid carrier that connects the axle to the ring gear directly, with no differential.
spool in—To bring cable in on the winch.
spool out—To let cable out on the winch.
spotter—A person outside the vehicle who guides the driver over tricky obstacles.
stall point—The point at which the winch stops under a load. This is often shortly past the unit's maximum line pull.
stall speed—The amount of slippage built into an automatic-transmission torque converter rated by rpm. It's basically a measure of the torque multiplication of the converter. It can also be seen as "flash stall," which is the engine rpm attained at a full-throttle start from a dead stop.
static ride height—The normal ride height of the vehicle at rest, with no dynamic forces working on it, such as cornering.
stock—As delivered from the manufacturer; unmodified.
suspension travel—The total amount of up-and-down movement of the suspension with the axle on a level plane.
T-case—Short for transfer case. Some parts of the world use the term *transfer box.*
taco'ed—Bending some component into a "U" shape, or nearly so.
tail gunner—The captain of the last vehicle in a group on a trail ride whose primary job is to make sure nobody gets left behind.
tall gearing—Numerically low gear ratios. Generally speaking, ratios from 2.50:1 to 3.54:1 are considered "high." See also *high gearing.*
taper—Some manufacturers taper the ends of each leaf of a leaf spring. This allows for a softer-rate spring, as compared to a dimensionally similar untapered leaf, and reduced friction.
TBI—Throttle-body injection. A fuel-injection system that injects fuel into the airflow at the throttle butterflies atop the intake manifold.
threshold braking—A technique of applying the maximum braking pressure short of the tire lockup point.
tie rod—The steering rod that connects the two wheels together.
toe-in/out—A steering geometry adjustment. Toe-in is where the front edges of the tires point in toward each other. Toe-out is the opposite.
torque—Measured in pounds-feet (lbs-ft). Force times distance. One pound of weight applied to the end of a 1-foot bar produces 1 lbs-ft of force.
torque converter—A fluid coupling/clutch used in automatic transmissions. It consists of three main parts: the impeller, which is driven by the engine; the turbine, which is connected directly to the transmission; and the stator, which lies between the two. The spinning impeller pushes the transmission fluid against the blades of the turbine, which forces it to spin in the same direction. The stator directs the flow of the oil.
torque jacking—An undesirable symptom of lifted coil-spring suspensions where the application of torque from tire grip is translated into a height increase.
torsion bar—A type of spring. One end is solidly attached to a chassis member, and the other end is attached to one of the control arms. This converts the up-and-down movement of the suspension into twist on the torsion bar.
Toylet—A Toyota powered by a Chevy engine, a.k.a. "Chevota."
TPI—Tuned-port injection. A GM high-performance multiport fuel-injection system.
traction—The conversion of engine torque into motion.
trail—Four-wheeler slang for an unimproved road.
trailer queen—Usually a show rig that travels by trailer. Can also be used for rigs that are trailered to and from four-wheeling spots. For some, this is a derisive term.
TTB—Twin Traction Beam. A Ford semi-independent front suspension for 4×4s used from 1980 to 1997.
U-bolt—The U-shaped bolt used to attach the axle to a leaf spring.
U-joint—Universal joint, a.k.a. Cardan joint.
underwound cable—Where the cable spools off the bottom of the winch drum.
viscous coupling—A device used either to lock a center differential or to transmit power. It consists of a number of plates in a sealed case full of silicone gel and input and output shafts. Half the plates are attached to one shaft, and the other half are connected to another, but they are alternating. When there is a difference in speed from one side, the silicone gel thickens and couples the unit together.
void ratio—The ratio of open areas in a tire tread versus the parts that actually contact the ground.
wheel travel—The total amount of up-and-down movement of the suspension as measured at the hub.
wire rope—The most correct term for the winch cable on your winch.
wire size—The coils of a coil spring are made from a bar of metal that is wound and tempered. Wire size refers to the diameter of this material.
yield point—The point where a material permanently deforms. It may not actually break, but it's severely weakened.

APPENDIX 2
Sources

Bibliography

Auto Math Handbook
1992 John Lawler
HP Books
1-55788-020-4

Automotive Electrical Handbook
1986 Jim Horner
HP Books
0-89586-238-7

Bosch Automotive Handbook
1993 Ulrich Adler, Editor
Robert Bosch GmbH
3-1-419115-X

Brake Handbook
1985 Fred Puhn
HP Books
0-89586-232-8

CB Radio
1976 Leo G. Sands
A. S. Barnes
0-498-01969-1

Chevy & GMC Pickup Performance Handbook
2000 Jim Allen
MBI Publishing Company
0-7603-0798-9

Differentials: Identification, Restoration and Repair
2006 Jim Allen and Randy Lyman
Ring & Pinion Service, Inc.
978-1-4243-2661-7

4-Wheel Freedom
1996 Brad DeLong
Paladin Press
0-87364-891-9

Handbook of Off-Road Driving
1990 Julian Cremona/Keith Hart
Ashford, Buchan & Enright
1-85253-211-4

How to Make Your Car Handle
1981 Fred Puhn
HP Books
0-912656-46-8

How to Tune and Modify Engine Management Systems
2003 Jeff Hartman
MBI Publishing Company
0-7603-1582-5

Jeep 4×4 Performance Handbook, 2nd Edition
2007 Jim Allen
MBI Publishing Company
978-0-7603-2687-9

Land Rover Experience
1994 Tom Sheppard
Land Rover Ltd.
0-9514493-4-6

Machinery's Handbook
1978 Oberg/Jones/Horton
Industrial Press
75-1962

Mark A. Smith's Guide to Safe, Common Sense Off-Road Driving
1991 Mark A. Smith
Mark A. Smith's Off-Roading Inc.
Pamphlet

Performance With Economy
1981 David Vizard
S-A Design
0-931472-09-1

Power Secrets
1989 Smokey Yunick
S-A Design
0-931472-06-7

Shifting Into 4WD
2001 Harry Lewellyn
Glovebox Publications
0-944781-02-2

Why Skid
1995 Bridgestone Winter Driving School
Rally-Art
Booklet

Winching In Safety
1989 Peter Hobson
Land Rover Ltd.
0-9512235-1-8

Wired for Success
1995 Randy Rundle
Krause Publications
0-87341-402-0

Clubs & Enthusiast Organizations

Most of these are associations or clubs from which you can find or choose a local group.

Arizona State Association of Four Wheel Drive Clubs
(602) 258-4BY4
www.asa4wdc.org

Blue Ribbon Coalition
(208) 237-1008
www.sharetrails.org

California Association of Four Wheel Drive Clubs
(916) 381-8300
www.cal4wheel.com

Colorado Off Highway Vehicle Coalition
(303) 539-5010
www.cohvco.org

East Coast 4-Wheel Drive Association
(800) ECST4WD
www.ec4wda.org

Great Lakes Four Wheel Drive Association
(313) 477-8165
www.glfwda.org

Mile-Hi Jeep Club
www.mhjc.org

Minnesota 4 Wheel Drive Association
mn4wda.com

Red Rock 4-Wheelers
www.rr4w.com

Southern Four Wheel Drive Association
www.sfwda.com

Southwest Four Wheel Drive Association
www.swfwda.org

Tread Lightly!
(800) 966-9900
www.treadlightly.org

United Four Wheel Drive Associations
(757) 410-5636
www.ufwda.org

Driving Instruction and Guided Trips

Badlands Off Road Adventures
(310) 374-8047
www.4×4training.com

Bill Burke's 4-Wheeling America
www.bb4wa.com

Bridgestone Winter Driving School
(800) 949-7543

The Driving Company
(408) 370-9321
www.thedrivingcompany.com

Esprit de Four
www.espritdefour.com

4×4 ABC
Harald Pietschmann
www.4×4abc.com

The 4×4 Center
(802) 864-8565
www.the4×4center.com

The Hummer Driving Academy
(866) 258-831-9547
www.amgeneral.com/vehicles_hummer_academy.php

International 4-Wheel Drive Trainer's Association
See Website For List of Certified Instructors
www.i4wdta.org

Iron Range Off-Road
(651) 335-7878
www.ironrangeoffroad.com

Jeep Jamboree USA
(530) 333-4777
www.jeepjamboreeusa.com

Jeep 101/Camp Jeep
(800) 825-JEEP
www.jeep.com

Land Rover Adventures
www.landrover.com

Nemacolin Off Road Driving Academy
(866) 344-6957
www.nemacolin.com

Offroad Academy
British Columbia: (778) 338-4440
Yukon Territory: (867) 334-7401
www.offroadacademy.com

Off-Road Experience
(925) 606-8301
www.offroadexperience.com

Overland Experts
(860) 873-9250
www.overlandexperts.com

Porsche Driving School
(888) 204-7474
www.porschedriving.com

Sedona Jeep School
(928) 274-570
www.sedonajeepschool.com

Western Adventures 4×4 Driving School
(760) 789-1563
www.4westernadventures.com

GPS, Guidebooks, Maps, and Navigation

DeLorme
(800) 561-5105
www.delorme.com

4×4 Books
(308) 381-4410
www.4×4books.com

Fun Treks Inc
(877) 222-7623
www.funtreks.com

Garmin
www.garmin.com

Magellan
www.magellangps.com

Sidekick Off-Road
(877) 628-7227
www.sidekickoffroad.com

Trimble
www.trimble.com

USGS
www.usgs.gov

Parts and Services

Accel
www.accel-ignition.com
(216) 688-8300 (tech)

Advance Adapters
www.advanceadapters.com
(800) 350-2223

Advanced Air Systems
www.powertank.com
(209) 366-2163

AEM
www.aempower.com
(310) 484-2322

AEV (American Expedition Vehicles)
www.aev-conversions.com
(406) 251-2100

AFE (Advanced Flow Engineering)
www.afefilters.com
(866) 503-9911

AGR
www.agrperformance.com
(817) 626-9006

Alcan Spring
www.alcanspring.com
(970) 241-2655

Alcoa Wheels
www.alcoa.com/alcoawheels

All J Products
www.boulderbars.com
(909) 370-4800

Alloy USA
www.alloyusa.com
(866) 352-5569

American Racing Equipment
www.americanracing.com

Amsoil
www.amsoil.com
(715) 392-7101

Ansul Inc.
www.ansul.com

ARB
www.arbusa.com
(425) 264-1391

ARP
www.arp-bolts.com
(800) 826-3045

Art Carr Performance
www.artcarr.com
(325) 698-6667

ATS
www.atsdiesel.com
(800) 949-6002

Auburn Gear
www.auburngear.com
(260) 925-3200

Aussie Locker
www.aussielocker.com
(585) 723-1489

AutoFab
www.autofab.com
(619) 562-1740

Auto Meter
www.autometer.com

B & M Racing & Performance Products
www.bmracing.com
(818) 882-6422

Banks Power
www.bankspower.com
(800) 6018072

Baumann Engineering
www.baumannengineering.com
(864) 646-8920

Bed Bolts
www.bedbolts.net
(503) 348-3692

Bestop
www.bestop.com
(800) 845-3567

BF Goodrich Tires
www.bfgoodrichtires.com

Big O Tires
www.bigotires.com

Bilstein
www.bilstein.com
(858) 386-5900 (west)
(704) 663-7563 (east)

Borla
www.borla.com
(877) 462-6752

Bridgestone/Firestone
www.bridgestone-usa.com

Bushwacker
www.bushwacker.com
(800) 234-8920

Carburetor Shop
www.customcarbs.com
(909) 947-3575

Centerforce
www.centerforce.com
(928) 771-8422

Center Line Performance Wheels
www.centerlinewheels.com
(800) 345-8671

Classic Tube
www.classictube.com
(800) 882-3711

Clifford Performance
www.cliffordperformance.net
(888) 471-1161

Code 4×4
www.code4×4.com
(970) 625-8998

Collins Brothers Jeep Parts
www.collinsbrosjeep.com
(800) 699-5337

Comp Cams
www.compcams.com
(800) 999-0853

Cooper Tire
www.coopertire.com

Cragar Industries
www.cragar.com
(877) 827-2427

Crane Cams
www.cranecams.com
(386) 252-1151

Crower Cams & Equipment
www.crower.com
(619) 661-6477

CTM
www.ctmracing.com
(760) 450-0006

Currie Enterprises
(714) 982-5300
www.currieenterprises.com

Dana Spicer
www.dana.com

Daystar Products
www.daystarweb.com
(800) 595-7659

Denny's Driveshaft Service
www.dennysdriveshaft.com
(716) 875-6640

Doetsch Tech
www.doetsch-shocks.com
(619) 442-7300

Drivetrain Specialists of Las Vegas
www.drivetrain.com
(800) 216-1632

Dutchman Motorsports
www.dutchmanms.com
(503) 257-6604

Dynatrac
www.dynatrac.com
(714) 596-4461

Dynomax
www.dynomax.com

Eastwood
www.eastwoodco.com
(800) 343-9353

Eaton Detroit Locker
www.eatonperformance.com

Eaton Detroit Springs
www.eatonsprings.com
(313) 963-3839

Edelbrock
www.edelbrock.com
(310) 781-2222

Edge Products
www.edgeproducts.com
(888) 360-3343

Electromotive Inc.
www.electromotive-inc.com
(703) 331-0100

Energy Suspension
www.energysuspension.com
(949) 361-3935

Explorer ProComp
www.explorerprocomp.com
(800) 776-0767

Extreme Outback Products
www.extremeoutback.com
(866) 447-7711

Flex-a-Form
www.flex-a-form.com
(864) 261-7006

Flex-a-Lite
www.flex-a-lite.com
(800) 851-1510

FlowKooler
www.flowkooler.com
(805) 544-8841

Flowmaster
www.flowmastermufflers.com
(800) 544-4761

Four X Doctor
www.fourxdoctor.com
(818) 845-2194

4xHeaven
www.4xheaven.com
(800) 800-1679

4Wheel Drive Hardware
www.4wd.com
(800) 333-5535

4Wheel Parts
www.4WheelParts.com
(866) 912-7906

Fox Racing Shox
www.foxracingshox.com
(619) 768-1800

Gale Banks Engineering
www.bankspower.com
(800) 601-8072

Gear Vendors
www.gearvendors.com
(800) 999-9555

Genuine Gear
www.4wheelparts.com
(877) 474-4821

Gibson
www.gibsonperformance.com

GM Powertrain
www.gm.com/automotive/gmpowertrain/

Golen Engine Service
www.golenengineservice.com
(800) 591-9171

Goodyear Tire and Rubber
www.goodyear.com

Go Rhino!
www.gorhino.com
(888) 427-4466

Griffin Racing Radiators
www.griffinrad.com
(864) 845-5000

Hayden Inc.
www.haydenauto.com
(951) 736-2608

Hawk Performance
www.hawkperformance.com
(800) 542-0972

Hays Clutches
www.haysclutches.coms

Hedman Headers
www.hedman.com
(562) 921-0404

Hella North America
www.hella.com

Hesco
www.hescosc/com
(205) 251-1472

High Impact Gear & Transmission
high-impact.net
(888) 898-4331

High Performance Coatings
www.hpcoatings.com
(801) 501-8303

Hi-Lift Jack Company
www.hi-lift.com

Holley
www.holley.com
(270) 781-9741 (tech)

Howell Engine Developments
www.howellefi.com
(810) 765-5100

Hutchinson Wheel
www.hutchinsoninc.com
(609) 394-1010

Hypermax
www.gohypermax.com
(847) 428-5655

Hypertech
www.hypertech.com
(901) 382-8888

Interco Tires
www.intercotire.com

Jacobs Electronics
wwwjacobselectronics.com
(216) 688-8300

JB Conversions
www.jbconversions.com
(337) 625-2379

J.E. Reel
www.reeldriveline.com
(909) 629-9002

Jet Performance
www.jetchip.com
(800) 535-1161

JKS Manufacturing
www.jksmfg.com
(308) 762-6949

K&N
K&Nfilters.com
(800) 858-3333

KB-Silvolite Performance Pistons
www.kb-silvolite.com
(800) 648-7790

KC Hilite
www.kchilites.com

Kelly Springfield Tire Company
www.kelley-springfield.com

Kenne-Bell
www.kennebell.net
(909) 941-0985

Kidde Safety
www.kiddeus.com
(800) 880-6788

Kilby Enterprises
www.kilbyenterprises.com
(888) 465-4529

Klune-V
www.klunev.com
(888) 898-4331

Longfield
www.longfieldsuperaxles.com
(360) 893-0235

LuK Clutches
(800) 274-5001
www.lukclutch.com

Mag-Hytec
www.mag-hytec.com
(818) 786-8325

Magnaflow
www.magnaflow.com

Marlin Krawler
www.marlincrawler.com
(559) 252-7295

Master Pull
www.masterpull.com
(877) 797-0202

Matkins Extreme
www.matkinsextreme.com
(406) 248-3797

MAX
www.maxax.com
(707) 937-2141

Mean Green
www.mean-green.com
(724) 694-8290

Michelin
www.michelin.com

Mickey Thompson Tires
www.mickeythompsontires.com

MileMarker
(800) 886-8647
www.milemarker.com

Modine Manufacturing
www3.modine.com

Mopar Performance
www.mopar.com

More Power Puller
Wyeth-Scott Company
www.wyeth-scott.com
(800) 743-4521

Moser Engineering
(260) 726-6689
www.moserengineering.com

Motive Gear
www.motivegear.com
(800) 934-2727

Mountain Off-Road Enterprises
www.mountainoffroad.com
(970) 625-0500

National Spring
www.nationalsprings.com
(800) 399-3852

National Tire and Wheel
www.ntwonline.com

Northern High Performance
www.northernfactory.com

Novak Conversions
www.novak-adapt.com
(877) 602-1500

Oasis Manufacturing
www.oasismfg.com
(949) 768-4311

O'Brien's 4-Wheel West
(916) 773-3278

Off-Road Design
www.offroaddesign.com
(970) 945-7777

Off-Road Unlimited
www.offroadunlimited.com
(888) 365-0244

Old Man Emu Suspension
www.arbusa.com
(425) 264-1391

Optima Batteries
www.optimabatteries.com
(888) 867-8462

Ox Locker
www.ox-usa.com

Painless Wiring
www.painlessperformance.com
(817) 244-6212

Paul's High Performance
www.paulshp.com
(517) 764-7661

Pertronix
http://pertronix.com/
(909) 599-5955

PIAA
www.piaa.com
(800) 525-7422

Pierce Sales
www.piercewrecker.com
(800) 658-6301

Posi-Lok
www.4×4posi-lok.com
(517) 279-7177

Powermaster
www.powermastermotorsports.com
(865) 688-5953

Power Slot
www.powerslot.com
(818) 709-4800

PowerTrax
www.powertrax.com
(864) 843-9275

Precision Gear
www.precisiongear.com
(734) 946-0524

ProComp Tires
www.procomptires.com

Progress Manufacturing
www.equalizerhitch.com
(800) 478-5578

PSC Motorsports
www.pscmotorsports.com
(817) 270-0102

Pull Pal/Premier Power Welder
www.pullpal.com
(800) 541-1817

Putnam Hitch Products
www.putnamhitch.com
(800) 336-4271

Quadratec
www.quadratec.com
(800) 745-2348

Ramsey Winch
www.ramsey.com
(918) 438-2760

Rancho
www.gorancho.com
(734) 384-7804

R&P 4wd Parts
www.r-p4wd.com
(503) 557-8911

Randy's Ring and Pinion
(866) 631-0196
www.ring-pinion.com

Ready Air
www.readyair.com
(800) 982-0409

Reese Products
www.reeseprod.com

Reider Racing
www.reiderracing.com
(800) 522-2707

Richmond Gear
www.richmondgear.com
(864) 843-9231

Rock Hard 4×4
www.rockhard4×4parts.com
(308) 750-4690

Rock-It
www.rock-it.com
(714) 639-4933

Rock Krawler
www.rockkrawler.com
(518) 270-9822

Royal Purple
www.royalpurple.com

Rubicon Express
www.rubiconexpress.com
(877) 367-7824

Safety Seal
www.safetyseal.com
(800) 888-9021

Sam's Off-Road Equipment
www.samsoffroad.com
(800) 446-5503

Scan Gauge
www.scangauge.com
(888) 433-5664

Sealed Power
www.federal-mogul.com

Skyjacker
www.skyjacker.com
(318) 388-0816

Stainless Steel Brakes
www.stainlesssteelbrakes.com
(800) 448-7722

Staun USA
www.staunproducts.com/staunusa.php
(949) 645-7733

Stillen
www.stillen.com
(866) 250-5542

Stockton Wheel
www.stocktonwheel.com
(800) 395-9433

Strange Engineering
www.strangeengineering.net
(847) 663-1701

Summers Brothers
www.summersbrothersracing.com
(909) 399-5121

Sun Performance
www.sunperformance.com
(714) 708-7730

Superchips
www.superchips.com
(888) 227-2447

Superior Axle & Gear
www.superioraxle.com
(888) 522-2953

Superlift
www.superrlift.com
(888) 299-4692

Superwinch Inc.
www.superwinch.com
(860) 928-7787

T and J Performance Center
www.tandjperformance.com
(714) 633-0991

TA Performance
www.taperformance.com
(480) 922-6807

TCI Automotive
www.tciauto.com
(888) 776-9824

Tera Manufacturing
www.teraflx.biz
(801) 288-2585

Throttle Down Kustoms
www.throttledownkustoms.com
(406) 374-2285

T-Max Winches
(877) 862-8629
www.t-maxwinches.com

Tom Wood's Custom Driveshafts
www.4xshaft.com
(800) 496-4238

Trailmaster Suspension
www.trailmastersuspension.com
(928) 636-7080

Tri-County Gear
www.tricountygear.com
(909) 623-3373

TSM
www.tsmmfg.com
(303) 688-6882

Tuff Country Suspension
www.tuffcountry.com
(800) 288-2190

Tuffy Security Products
www.tuffyproducts.com
(800) 348-8339

Turbo City/Rock-It
www.turbocity.com
(714) 639-4933

University of Northwestern Ohio
www.unoh.edu
(419) 998-3120

U.S. Gear
www.usgear.com
(888) 874-3275

U.S. Radiator Corp.
www.usradiator.com
(323) 826-0965

Valley Industries
www.valley.us.com

Viair
www.viaircorp.com
(949) 582-6868

Viking Offroad
www.winchline.com
(818) 506-9789

Volant
www.volantperformance.com
(909) 476-7225

Warn
www.warn.com
(800) 543-9276

Weld Racing
(800) 669-9353
www.weldracing.com

Wet Okole
http://wetokole.net
(888) 246-5653

Wilwood Engineering
www.wilwood.com
(805) 388-1188

Wrangler NW Power Products
www.wranglernw.com
(800) 962-2616

Yokohama Tire Corp
www.yokohama.com

Xenon
www.teamxenon.com
(800) 999-8753

4×4 Vehicle Manufacturer Websites

Chevrolet—www.chevrolet.com

Dodge—www.4dodge.com

Cadillac—www.cadillac.com

Ford—www.ford.com

GMC—www.gmc.com

Honda—www.honda.com

Hummer—www.hummer.com

Infiniti—www.infiniti.com

Jeep—www.jeep.com

Kia—www.kia.com

Land Rover—www.landrover.com

Lexus—www.lexus.com

Lincoln—www.lincoln.com

Mitsubishi—www.mitsubishicars.com

Nissan—www.nissan-usa.com

Toyota—www.toyota.com

Index